# CONFESSIONS OF
# "The Old Wizard"

*

# CONFESSIONS OF

# "The Old Wizard"

## THE AUTOBIOGRAPHY OF
## HJALMAR HORACE GREELEY SCHACHT

Translated by Diana Pyke

ILLUSTRATED

HOUGHTON MIFFLIN COMPANY BOSTON

The Riverside Press Cambridge

1956

The Riverside Press
CAMBRIDGE · MASSACHUSETTS
PRINTED IN THE U.S.A.

Neither violence nor power of the purse
　　Fashion the universe
Ethical action, spiritual force
　　May reshape the world's course.

*Hjalmar Schacht*

# INTRODUCTION

THE SECOND OF SEPTEMBER, 1948, was a particularly sultry day. Somewhat ill at ease in my fur coat I stood at the exit of Ludwigsburg Internment Camp waiting for the turnkey to come and open the door for me. My wife was waiting outside with my lawyer. Plucky Manci, who for years had been fighting a desperate battle against every kind of obstruction, in order to have me released. Now, at last it had happened. She had come to fetch me in Dr. Schwamberger's car. Now and again she would raise her hand and signal unobtrusively, which meant: Only a few minutes more, and you'll be free!

Seconds passed. Two young press photographers had taken up their stand beside the gateway ready to record on their film my first step into freedom. I waited. The photographers grinned. They were obviously already looking forward to the caption: "Wearing a fur coat in a temperature of 77° F., the former president of the Reichsbank is released from Ludwigsburg." There would be no point in trying to explain to them about the coat. What did they know of four years' imprisonment under the Gestapo, of American and German Denazification tribunals? How could they tell the condition of the clothes I wore under that coat?

A couple of workmen came by and, attracted by the interesting drama, stopped to light cigarettes. I could hear their conversation.

"There's Schacht," said one. "They acquitted 'im yesterday."

"Think they'll let 'im go?" the other asked. He wore a pair of blue dungarees, and from the waist up was clad only in his own sunburned skin.

"Nope," said the first man slowly. "I don't b'lieve they will. They'll find some reason or other to pop 'im back in the jug!"

They spat into their hands, picked up their tools and departed. Their talk could not be described as encouraging. Vox *populi*, I thought.

The turnkey arrived, rattled his keys and solemnly opened the great gate. The cameras clicked; someone asked me a question. Manci cut him short and led me to the car. I sank into the back seat next to the man who for months past had conducted my defense.

"Let's get away," said Manci, "away from here . . ."

I don't know if it was that same evening or on one of those that followed that I decided to write my memoirs. For the first time in four years, one month and ten days I was a free man. Ever since seven o'clock on the morning of July 23, 1944, when the Secret State Police had arrested me, I had been pushed around like a postal package. Other people had assumed responsibility for my person, had transferred me from one prison to another by car, plane and truck; they had conducted me from my cell to the courts and back again to my cell; had threatened me, shouted at me, spoken me fair. Prison air is the same the world over. I had been imprisoned for conspiring against Hitler. After Hitler was dead, I was imprisoned for aiding him. Men who knew nothing of my country or of my personal circumstances had confronted me with ready-made judgments on my person and my country and had flung these judgments in my face.

I was seventy-one years old and suddenly once more a free man. My wife and children were living in a kind of log hut on Lüneburg Heath. I had lost everything I possessed — money, house, land, even the wood I had once planted.

Such a situation makes a man think. He begins to reflect on his future as well as his past life. I was not greatly concerned about the future. As a young man I had worked my way to the top; I could do so a second time. In my family we mature late and remain active well into the biblical years. Such had been the case with my grandfather, a parish doctor in a small North German town. The same had been true of my father, who as a young man had emigrated to America, returned to Germany six years later and for a second time built his life anew. I could not do otherwise. No — I had no fear of the future. I would work, I would not fail the three people who depended on me.

The past was a somewhat different matter. It may of course be argued that four years of prison, concentration camps, international tribunals and denazification courts were ample for a man to come to terms with his past. That is a mistaken assumption. There is no time during an enquiry for a man to come to terms with himself. One is handed over, defenceless, to those authorities who — from the prison warder to the foremost public prosecutor — never for an instant relax their grip. Unswervingly, unremittingly, they endeavor to catch you out, to pin you down, to prove something against you. You need to have presence of mind, to be constantly on the qui vive if you are not to weaken. Exposed to every kind of trick and brow-beating, granted concessions one day only to have them withdrawn on the next, you are no longer a free subject but a target for the law. This was the case, whether in the National Socialist concentration camps, as "war criminal" in an American prison or in the camps of the denazification tribunals. In our world political tribunals aim at taking their victims by surprise. Serious thought is possible only for a free man.

A few days after my release I went for a walk beside a stream in a wood. I love woods and water. On my former estate (now in Russian hands) there were woods, and lakes with waterfowl — herons, sawbills, divers, wild duck . . .

The sun had set in a mighty turmoil of color: tattered clouds of red, orange and yellow mirrored in the water. For some time I stood gazing at the scene, then sat down on a bench.

"Are you not Dr. Schacht?" said a voice at my elbow.

I looked up, startled. A man — a complete stranger — had approached noiselessly and now sat down beside me.

"Yes," I said.

He held out his hand. "I'm so very glad to meet you, Dr. Schacht," he said. "I have always wanted to shake hands with you."

We shook hands. "What can I do for you?" I asked.

"Nothing," he said. "I just wanted the chance to talk with you. You're a free man now, aren't you?"

"It looks like it," I answered. He shifted to a more comfortable position, took out a cigar case and handed it to me.

"Won't it be robbing you?"

"Not a bit of it!" was his grandiose reply. "Cigars are my business — been in the trade thirty-five years. Don't you remember me?"

"I haven't the faintest . . . "

"I came to see you once . . . at that time I was traveling for a cigar factory. I'm on my own now, thank goodness. Business is good, people are buying again since the introduction of the D-mark . . . "

" You came to see me?"

"I was going to tell you about that." He handed me a match. "I called on you at the Reichsbank. My firm wanted to name a new brand of cigars after you. The Hjalmar Schacht Cigar, President brand, ha-ha-ha!"

His laughter stirred my memory. "I remember," I said, "but I couldn't recall your face. You called on me and wanted to pay for the use of my name?"

"Right," he said. "And it would have been a good stroke of business for you too. A box of cigars on the house every week as long as you lived."

"Is the firm still in business?"

"And how! It's going full steam ahead!" cried the cheery cigar merchant.

"Pity I turned the offer down," I ventured, for the sake of saying something.

"Yes, isn't it?" he retorted.

We smoked side by side for another quarter of an hour, then he rose, shook me long and warmly by the hand, and departed. Poor devil, his expression said — what have you got now? The Reichsbank is kaput, the Reich is kaput, the President deposed. They've no further use for a president of the Reichsbank these days. Look at me — I'm only a cigar merchant, but I'm the owner of a business and that's better than a Reichsbank. If you had only agreed to let those cigars be named after you, you would now be receiving a free box every week.

That is what he would have said. I threw away the remainder of his cigar and closed my eyes. The encounter had jolted me out of the present — way back into a past which I found difficult to think about again.

True, my past had been referred to often enough in Nuremberg, Stuttgart and Ludwigsburg; they had endeavored to furnish documentary proof, so to speak, of every step in my life. But was it the past that had been conjured up there — was it really the actual living past? In Nuremberg and in the denazification courts my accusers had submitted documents which they believed covered my past history down to the remotest detail. The defense and witnesses had for their part submitted other documents containing entirely contradictory information. Men with whom, in the course of my public life, I had engaged in sharp but objective controversy now appeared and testified on my behalf. Friends such as, for instance, Bishop Wurm came forward; he was concerned in an action that had been brought against me and ostentatiously shook hands with a witness who had spoken in my defense. Nevertheless the evidence of witnesses was just so much dead stuff, so much legal material set down on Four-Folio Form No.DIN. A. Not one of those sheets of paper — whether used for or against me — was the real past but merely a bit of it, torn from its context, and therefore dead.

I thought of the nearly seventy years during which I had consciously lived. How much had happened during those seventy years! At the time of my birth the new German Empire was seven years old. Bismarck was Chancellor; the Hanseatic city of Hamburg was still outside the German Customs Union. When I was eleven, Germany had three emperors in one year: Wilhelm I, the Emperor Frederick, and Wilhelm II. Germany was a country of aspirations; year by year her power increased. As a student in Kiel I had witnessed the building up of our fleet and the terrifying iron shapes of the new armored cruisers and battleships. When I married, three years after the turn of the century, Germany seemed at the height of her power. The old Bismarckian system of alliances still held. No one dreamed that behind Germany's steady, continued ascent as a new Colonial Power there lurked the hideous menace of a world war. Surely it would be presumptuous to think of attacking this new Germany? Were not we — the latecomers among the peoples of Europe — in a fair way to catch up with the rest?

It seemed so at that time. No one bothered about the future. Yet the peaceful dream of my married life lasted only eleven years; then came the war, and four years later the first collapse. I was forty-one years old and manager of a bank when the Germans came pouring back to the Reich, embittered, starving, ripe for revolution. But the revolution did not materialize, or did so merely in disconnected fashion. The Emperor departed, the troops were disarmed. In place of the Emperor, Germany had a President of the Reich and a cabinet of party ministers. But the political change could not blind us to the fact that we were ruined. The impoverishment of our people, the drop in the value of the mark continued their irresistible course. The path we trod after the First World War was marked by such milestones as the Hunger Blockade, Dictated Peace, Inflation. Almost exactly five years after the collapse of Germany I was drawn into politics, from which I have never since been able to escape.

I was forty-six years old when in 1923 the Government offered me the post of Commissioner for National Currency, followed shortly by that of President of the Reichsbank, an appointment bestowed upon me by President Ebert. I accepted the appointment, and stabilized the mark.

My first wife, Luise, had presented me with two children, a

daughter, aged twenty at the time of my appointment as President of the Reichsbank, and a son seven years younger. Three years after my nomination I spent Christmas with my family in Lausanne. As usual we had decorated a Christmas tree and lighted the candles; the children had been called into the room and stood side by side while Luise read the Christmas Story from the New Testament. My thoughts traveled to Germany. There, for the first time in years, thousands of families were experiencing a like peace and security. People who worked received money with which they were able to buy goods; money which would be worth the same tomorrow as it was today. In my pocket was a letter written in bad German from a steward on a sleeping car. "Dear Dr. Schacht, for the first time in years we have been able to put some presents under the Christmas tree and we have you alone to thank for that. When my daughter Mieke came home yesterday she was humming 'Who was it stabilized the mark, why no one else but Doctor Schacht,' * and I thought I would let you know and hope it will give you pleasure. Yours truly . . ." I had received many such letters. People had often spoken to me on the street and shaken me by the hand — people personally unknown to me who were thankful and full of hope for a future with stable currency . . .

All this I saw again in my mind's eye as I sat on the seat that evening. I tried to conjure up the real past. Did anyone mention these things during my questionings by the Gestapo? Or remember them at Nuremberg and Ludwigsburg? Yes, they had done so. But I had the impression that none of my accusers had any conception of what had happened in Germany at that time. They had already made up their minds — determined to think the worst of me.

In my ears there re-echoed the prison noises, the questions fired at me by judges, defenders, prosecutors: "What did you . . . ? Why did you . . . ? How did it happen that at such and such a time you . . . ?" Incessant, unending!

Life had not stood still when the German mark was stabilized. Only a few years later I was, in the eyes of many of my former friends, the best-hated man in the country, who deserved to be shot out of hand. "The destroyer of German economy. The black-coated capitalist. The abhorred friend of the Jews. The corrupt National Socialist" — frequently all together and in a hopeless jumble.

I rose from the seat and went back to my wife in our temporary abode. Manci (whom I married in 1941) looked at me enquiringly.

* Wer hat die Mark stabil gemacht, das war allein der Doktor Schacht.

"What have you been doing?" she asked.

"I've been sitting on a bench — thinking."

"What about?"

"About the past. Memories cropped up of their own accord."

"What sort of memories?"

"Memories of the past. The collapse of the Weimar Republic — Hitler — my second term as president of the Reichsbank — my work as Minister of Economic Affairs."

"What started you thinking about all that?"

"Because I'm dissatisfied; because I have the feeling that the entire judicial procedure to which I was subjected during the past four years only served to conceal the true facts. Isn't that queer? For four years it has been nothing but talk, and going through documents, taking down evidence, hearing witnesses, contesting judgments, taking Counsel's opinion — and what is the result?"

"You have been acquitted," she said.

"That's one aspect of it," I conceded. "I have been acquitted. I have never doubted that one day I would have to be acquitted. But when I think back over all the things that were brought up for and against me during those years, then — "

"Then what?" she asked.

"Then I would like to sit down and put on paper the true history of that epoch. The history of my epoch as I experienced it — not as an American or Russian accuser sees it — nor as one of the defense sees it. They have only one object in view — they want to see a prisoner condemned or acquitted. I don't want to be one or the other. I want to speak freely of those things about which people still keep silence — even today."

"Well — why don't you?" she asked.

All this happened at the beginning of September 1948, immediately after my release by the Denazification Tribunal, which, in the beginning, had sentenced me to eight years' penal servitude. Since that evening my thoughts had been busy with past events — in so far as time permitted. My first task, of course, was to find some means of supporting my family — my wife and the two little daughters who were slowly growing accustomed to the sight of their father. My daughter by my first marriage is independent; but my son Jens, at the age of thirty-five, had been killed by the Russians because (so one of his comrades told me) he had collapsed during the death march on the way to prison.

In the meantime I have written two books, *Settlement with*

*Hitler* and *Gold for Europe*.* Both take a definite stand in regard to definite problems, or deal with certain chapters of my life.

The present book is something different. It contains the thoughts of an old man of seventy-six on the subject of his own epoch. I myself have played my part and have endeavored to influence this epoch. I have often been called a wizard — let this then be the memoirs of a wizard. There is nothing in my past of which I need be ashamed. Every human being brings to his life certain inborn characteristics. He can — as the Scriptures tell us — put his talent to profit, or he can bury it. I was at pains to place my gifts at the disposal of the nation to which I belong.

In addition, I am constrained by an urge which for as long as I can remember has been an integral part of all my actions. I would like to join my voice to those who seek to dispel the poisonous miasma that clouds our era. Terrible things have happened during my lifetime — even more terrible things can happen tomorrow if we refuse to learn from the past.

But to be able to learn, we must acquaint ourselves with the past, we must know how these things originated, how they ripened in secret. Since November 1923 I have repeatedly raised my voice in protest against excessive luxury, against the defaming of an entire nation, against arbitrary party influence, against the madness of war. My writings and speeches have made me enemies; my life has been threatened; I have been attacked from many angles. But results have proved that I was right in my prophecies and warnings, and that those who attacked me were wrong.

For this reason I once again turn the pages of my life from the beginning.

---

* *Abrechnung mit Hitler. Mehr Geld, mehr, Kapital, mehr Arbeit!*

*

# CONTENTS

\*

# ILLUSTRATIONS

Frontispiece: The Man with the Cigar

Following page 378:

# CONFESSIONS OF
# "The Old Wizard"

# I

## THE SCHACHT AND THE EGGERS FAMILIES

A BANKER, according to popular opinion, has an easy time of it. He sits in a bank and waits for people to come in and bring him money. Then he puts the money into profitable undertakings, pockets the profits at the end of the year and pays his customers some measly dividend. It is the simplest calling in the world. Simple, and therefore unsocial. A doctor, they argue, a locksmith or a roadmender, *they* do real work. Bankers don't *work*.

I have known many bankers in my time. Some of them were lazy; the majority however were very busy, highly intelligent men, indefatigably intent on extending their field of action. They had to, otherwise their banks would have paid no dividend at the end of the year.

What the malcontents forget, however, is something quite different. No one thinks of asking where bankers come from! Do they grow on trees — or study in schools of banking — or do they belong to mysterious banking dynasties? Yes — and no. Undoubtedly there were, and are, dynasties of banking families — the Mendelssohns, for instance, who, in addition to financiers, produced poets, musicians, artists and scientists. Others again come from the small, hard-working classes of our society — like that director of the German Reichsbank whose father had been a messenger in the same institution.

In a word, it is stupid to speak of "the bankers." Anyone doing so puts himself on a level with those who think one can pass judgment on "the Jews," "the Negroes," "the railroadmen." In every calling there are black sheep and white, and I shall have something to say of both.

My own family was by no means well-to-do. When I was born my parents were poor, and many decades were to pass before my father felt he was standing on firm ground. For as long as I can remember, my parents had to struggle with heavy financial problems that overshadowed my entire youth.

For a long time I did not know what I wanted to be. I began by studying medicine, switched over to Germanistics and finished up with political economy. I obtained my doctorate in the faculty of philosophy. No fairies placed in my cradle the prophecy that I should one day become president of the Reichsbank.

That would not have been possible in any case, for there was no such thing as a cradle in the Schacht home. On the contrary, when the midwife had taken possession of me, smacked my behind, bathed me and wrapped me in the linen set out for the purpose, I was popped into a "donkey" standing ready in my parents' bedroom. A "donkey" is a wooden frame on trestles with a piece of sailcloth stretched between the two lengthwise staves. It was in this rickety contraption that I was laid by the midwife of Tingleff in North Schleswig on January 22, 1877. It had snowed in the night and my father had to get up at crack of dawn to clear a path for her and the doctor.

He had married five years previously — in the Episcopal Church in New York, corner of Madison Street and Fifth Avenue. It had been a true love match. My parents had first met in the little town of Tondern. At that time he was a student — not a very hopeful candidate for a middle-class marriage. But when he had passed his examination he took the bull by the horns and did what many Germans were doing in those days: he emigrated to America and was granted American citizenship on December 11, 1872.

But he did not forget the girl in Tondern. When he had found a job in a German brewery in New York he wrote to her and suggested she should join him.

My mother was twenty-one, my father twenty-six when they married. It was a perfectly ordinary, middle-class marriage, though admittedly achieved under somewhat dramatic circumstances.

My mother made the crossing to New York in one of those old-fashioned steamships still to be seen on old engravings. In the center is a towering funnel; masts fore and aft; the top deck piled high with bales of goods; below, a vast expanse of steerage deck which housed those unfortunate travelers not possessed of sufficent funds for a cabin.

At the age of seventy-four my mother compiled an account of her adventurous journey. Nothing illustrates more clearly the tremendous changes that have taken place in our world than a comparison between trips to America then and now.

My mother, the youngest daughter of my grandparents, had just passed her twenty-first birthday when she received the summons from America. Her mother gave her consent to her joining her fiancé, but only on condition that an elder brother should accompany her. Fortunately she had a whole crowd of older brothers; and a loyal maidservant from Schleswig-Holstein was also allotted to her. The trunk containing her trousseau and linen also held the wedding dress of muslin trimmed with real lace. In addition, she took with her a small myrtle tree from which she intended to gather her bridal wreath.

Thus equipped, the three adventurers boarded the steamer *Franklin* at Copenhagen. The vessel belonged to a young shipping firm in Stettin whose ambition it was to establish an American Line. But while still in Copenhagen the steamer was delayed for a fortnight owing to storms in the Baltic. And when the loading of provisions and coal was being hurriedly completed, a trimmer fell overboard between the ship and the pier, and it was impossible to rescue him. On top of everything they put to sea on Friday, October 13. (This is the first of several "thirteenths" that were destined later to play a part in my life.)

A storm in the Channel compelled the captain to go round by North Scotland, where the steamer ran into fog and lay for days in the Atlantic, scarcely moving, and with her foghorn hooting mournfully. My mother and her brother shared the only first-class cabin with nine other passengers, including a teacher and the wife of a merchant with whom she made friends. The ship carried no second- or third-class accommodation; on the other hand there were three hundred passengers on the steerage deck.

During the entire journey the little myrtle tree remained safe and sound under a skylight, and blossomed and flourished in the sea air — a good omen for the end of this frightful voyage.

Those on board very soon noticed that the cargo had been badly stowed. The ship listed in the mighty North Atlantic breakers and rolled intolerably. In the second week it was found that not enough drinking water had been taken aboard. By the captain's orders the steerage passengers were supplied with distilled sea water instead of any of the available fresh water. Possibly because of the inadequate sanitary conditions, cholera broke out on board; it spread with alarming rapidity and claimed in all thirty-five victims among the steerage passengers. Night after night those in the first class shuddered as they heard bodies being lowered into the sea, wrapped only in sailcloth. My mother suffered tortures of anxiety during this time, as her maid was one of the steerage passengers.

When the tragedy was at its height the first officer came to the

cabin and begged for help for a six-year-old boy, son of a family of
Jutland emigrants. His father, mother and three brothers and sisters
had died of cholera and the boy's clothes had been burned to prevent
infection. My mother gave linen and wool from her dower chest;
the women cabin passengers made new clothes for the lad and took
him into the cabin, where his friendly personality did much to cheer
the little company.

But their tribulations were not yet ended. The *Franklin* had
"economized" not only in drinking water — fuel too was running
short. It became necessary to chop up the bunks in the steerage in
order to heat the boilers. During the last weeks before their arrival
in the New World all passengers were restricted to one wineglassful
of water a day. When, finally, the machinery became faulty and
the compass went wrong, the proud vessel *Franklin* of Stettin proceeded at random westward, as did Columbus of old, on the way to
discover the new continent.

They actually did so on December 2, 1871; but the name of the
port was not New York, U.S.A., but Halifax. The passengers' hopes
were dashed by the Harbor Authorities who had no wish to introduce cholera into Canada. Whereupon rebellion broke out. When
a boat made for land to collect fuel and provisions, one of the passengers leaped overboard, swam after the boat and succeeded in
reaching land, where he regaled reporters with all the details of
their nightmare voyage; with the result that my father first learned
of his fiancee's ordeal through the press.

But even when the *Franklin* at last approached New York from
Halifax he was not able to welcome my mother. On the contrary,
the New Yorkers were so terrified of the cholera ship that they
threatened to fire on her if she did not remain as far as possible out
in the roadstead. An old warship, the *Hartford*, took over the
*Franklin's* passengers and kept them in quarantine for three weeks.
It was only through the good offices of a kindly harbor physician
who had compassion on them that they were able to correspond
with one another.

My mother had to climb through a cabin window on board the
*Hartford*. During the uncomfortable transfer from one vessel to
another she clung fast to the little myrtle tree which had suffered
least of anyone or anything during the voyage. With her brother
and the Schleswig maidservant she spent a lonely Christmas in
the roadsteads of New York. The day before they were finally released from their otherwise very pleasant confinement in the *Hart-*

*ford,* someone accidentally left the porthole open and the myrtle tree was frozen. So my mother, like all American brides, had to wear orange blossom instead of a myrtle wreath when she was married on January 14, 1872.

My parents remained another five years in the States. Then the pull of Germany proved too strong and my father decided to go back. His return to the old home was influenced probably by a variety of reasons. He had left Germany shortly before the Franco-Prussian War. By the time my mother joined him a change had already come over the German scene. An empire had arisen, and with it a rapid economic advance went hand in hand in the period that followed. Why should he remain in America when the old country suddenly offered so many possibilities?

The matter left him no peace. It pursued him when he sat at the desk costing up accounts; when he foregathered with other German emigrants at the Club; when he went to the German Church on Sundays. Five long years. In the autumn of 1876 it got the better of him. He threw down his pen, gave his notice, bought the tickets and traveled back to Germany with his family — now three in number: himself, my mother and my eldest brother Eddy.

Not that he had failed in America. It was sheer homesickness that drove him back.

During the voyage my mother drew his attention to the fact that his family would shortly consist of four persons. To which he remarked — as all husbands probably do in such cases: "We'll manage! Three or four — what's it matter? We'll find room somewhere . . . "

So I can truthfully say of myself that I am the offspring of two continents, separated by three thousand miles of ocean.

My full name — the Mayor of Tingleff in North Schleswig shook his head as he entered it in his register — is Hjalmar Horace Greeley Schacht.

The Hjalmar I owe to my Grandmother Eggers, who urged my father at the last minute to tack it onto Horace Greeley so that I might have at least *one* decent Christian name!

Because of these three names I have been taken alternately for an American and a Swede. In Germany I am better known as Hjalmar; my English friends usually called me Horace. During the period of the Resistance in Berlin my intimate friends, when they spoke of me, used the name "Horaz." * A popular newspaper in

* Pronounced Horahtz.

the 1920's purported to know better: it declared that my real name was not Hjalmar Schacht but Chajim Schachtel, that I was a Jew from Moravia and — but I needn't say more. In spite of my foreign Christian names I am and remain a German.

How my father hit upon these three curious names is soon told. During his seven years in the States he was not only a managing clerk, bookkeeper and businessman, but he also took a keen interest in the public life of the U.S.A. which at that time was experiencing the results of the Civil War. He was a particularly enthusiastic admirer of an American of sterling character, a candidate for the Presidency and friend of Carl Schurz — Horace Greeley. This liberal-minded North American politician, whose memorial stands in New York, had founded the New York newspaper *Tribune*, later to become the well-known New York *Herald Tribune*. My father, who regarded Horace Greeley as a model, resolved that his next son should be named after his idol. The fact that he was no longer living in America at the time of that son's baptism did not worry him in the least.

Recently, at the age of seventy-five, I acted as adviser in financial matters to four countries of the Near and Far East in succession (Indonesia, Iran, Syria and Egypt). In this connection the American weekly *Time* published an article comparing me with an old country doctor prescribing for his patients the well-tried remedies of hard work, thrift and careful planning. Underneath the picture of myself standing between General Naguib and my wife, *Time* had written: "Go East, old man."

Many readers may not have completely understood the double meaning of this caption, which is a play on words. Seventy years previously an American politician had urged the young people who were frittering away their time in the eastern seaports of New York and Boston to go out to western America, to the broad open spaces that offered scope and big opportunities for courageous pioneers. His slogan, which became world-famous, ran: "Go West, young man." The name of that politician was Horace Greeley.

I do not know how many times my father met this great politician. Nor do I know why he did not follow that advice and go out to the American West instead of returning home. It certainly would not have been due to lack of courage. More probably it was the feeling that he was a German — that the reconditioned Germany offered great opportunities — that he wanted his children to grow up in Germany.

So — we came back. Perhaps my mother also exerted some pressure. When, later, she spoke of those five years she always added that the American climate had never suited her. The temperature of New York in summer does not agree with Northerners.

Children seldom learn the motives that lead their parents to decide on this or that course of action.

When I read that caption in *Time* I wondered suddenly what would have become of me if — during that winter before I was born — my father had hit the western instead of the eastern trail? Should I have taken up banking in America? Or should I have grown up on a farm in the Middle West and followed in the footsteps of those countless German colonists who had settled as tillers of the soil in the New World?

Perhaps a reader will laugh out loud at the idea of the president of the Reichsbank as a farmer in Michigan! The idea is not so farfetched as all that. All my forebears on my father's side, down to the most recent generations, were peasants. I come from a Dithmarschen peasant family.

Dithmarschen peasants are not real peasants. As an old chronicle has it: "A Dithmarschen thinks he's a peasant! He's much more like a country squire!"

The Schacht family came originally from the old province opposite the Hanseatic city of Hamburg. In the beginning therefore we belonged to the left bank of the Elbe. Then we crossed the river and went north to Friesland.

One of my ancestors had twenty-four children by four wives and died at the age of a hundred and twenty. The family was vigorous, tough and attached to the soil. There is not a Marschen peasant but clings to his bit of ground . . .

Now and again I take down an old volume from my library containing a description of the life of these peasants, a chronicle full of references to the endless duel between man and ocean. The inhabitants of the Lower Marshes were nicknamed "spade peasants," who continued unremittingly to throw up dykes with their long spades (especially fashioned for use in heavy clay) in order to preserve their fields from Father Neptune's greedy encroachments. Theirs was not always a placid existence. Now and then there might be a generation that was able to harvest peacefully what it had sown — but the next generation was sure to experience a spring flood or a breach in the dyke; mice gnawed through the walls; change of moon and storms from the west would drive the North Sea right over the high-water mark. The volume briefly chronicles: "The farmer and his family remained on the roof for a week: two women, three children, and seventeen head of livestock were drowned." It was an endless battle, which produced a taciturn, wary, tough people who — if they were not prematurely drowned — attained a ripe old age.

What do you want? I sometimes asked myself in former years; Do you imagine your ancestors had an easier time of it? How often must it have happened that a seventy-year-old countryman had to stand and see children and grandchildren drown, and his fields turned into mud-covered, silted-up, useless land. He never would own himself beaten, but picked himself up and began again.

Yet another trait strikes me as typical of this heritage: you will find no outward signs of sentimentality in a North Friesian farmhouse. The constant battle with the Marsh demands from the inhabitants the utmost self-control. Expressions of affection are rare; feelings are hidden rather than revealed. But to hide one's feelings does not mean that one has no feelings to hide.

I have been described in public as hard and callous, invariably by those who knew me only superficially. They simply could not conceive that a man outwardly as "buttoned up" as I am can possess such a thing as a heart. I regret this impression, but am unable to change it. A man is not only what he makes of himself — he carries with him the invisible heritage of a long line of forebears.

The first to break with the tradition of agricultural work and large families was my great-grandfather. I don't know why he left home: anyway, he went to Büsum and opened a general store. He became a *Koopmann* (a small shopkeeper), as they say in our part of the world.

The countryside around Büsum is flat; fogs envelop the coast, gulls scold and scream above the sandbanks. The inhabitants are wheat farmers, charcoal burners, cattle farmers. These Dithmarschen peasants may be slow, but they're sharp-witted, sarcastic and full of sound common sense, and they don't let anyone outsmart them.

My great-grandfather did so well with his business that he was able to send his only son, my grandfather, to college. My grandfather was the oldest Schacht known to me personally; he ended up as parish doctor in Friedrichstadt. He was a real dyed-in-the-wool offspring of the Dithmarschen peasantry, with blue eyes, bushy eyebrows and a rounded full beard; tall, broad-shouldered, self-confident. There were many good tales about him all over the countryside.

Anyone who has studied the history of the English Revolution under Cromwell knows what is meant by the term Nonconformist.

Conformists are people who are content to go with the contemporary stream. Nonconformists are the exact opposite. Such people are intolerant of any authority imposed from without; they look on politics as a question, not of expediency but of character.

The stories about Grandfather Schacht are all concerned with his nonconformist nature. He studied medicine, first of all in Copenhagen, later in Kiel. That was during the stormy thirties, and what was more natural than that my grandfather should be mixed up in the students' political activities. He had to get out of Kiel head over heels, and took his M.D. degree at Rostock.

In 1850, when he was already an established doctor in Süderstapel, the town became involved in the military discussions between Schleswig-Holstein and Denmark. Süderstapel changed hands more than once, and each time all the municipal officials had to present themselves at the Town Hall and swear allegiance to the new ruler. My grandfather did this twice. Then he lost patience. On the third occasion, when the beadle arrived to conduct him to the Town Hall, he found my grandfather standing at his front door with a loaded pistol.

The beadle rattled off his summons in the local dialect. "Now, Doctor, you'll have to come to Town Hall and take the oath." My grandfather gazed lovingly at the loaded pistol and answered in his deep bass:

"I'm fed up with all this coming and going. The next one who sets foot inside the door gets shot!"

The beadle noted this pronouncement, went back to the Town Hall and repeated what he had heard. The mayor scratched his head — and exempted the Doctor from further oaths of loyalty.

To the end of his days my grandfather never altered. Less of a businessman than his father, he nevertheless succeeded in winning the respect and affection of his fellow men, but he was always hard up, for which he had only himself to thank. If a patient did not actually insist on paying more my grandfather would send him a bill in which each prescription carried a uniform charge of ten cents. I myself witnessed this astounding accountancy in 1892 when I visited him during the Hamburg cholera epidemic. We went to the house of a well-to-do tradesman suffering from rheumatism. Grandfather examined him, recommended a liniment, warm compresses, and wrote a prescription for pain-relieving pills.

"What's the fee, Doctor?" asked the patient, before we left.

"A dime," said my grandfather.

"But the man's rolling in money," I said to him later; "you

could have made a proper charge." He walked beside me, erect, pipe in mouth. "You don't understand," he said. "Doctoring isn't just a business."

The "dime policy" however was the more questionable because he treated poor patients without charging them even this small sum. So he never achieved wealth and could make only scant provision for his family. And that family was by no means a small one — two children by his first marriage and nine by his second. But the doctor held to the parable of the lilies of the field — They'll grow up somehow, he must have thought — and grow up somehow they did. No one knows what became of the children by the first marriage. Of the eight sons by his second marriage with a minister's daughter, five emigrated to America and made good there.

My grandfather's main gift to his sons was the sonorous and numerous Christian names with which he endowed them without consulting his wife beforehand. My father's christening gives a good idea of the procedure:

"What is this child to be called, Doctor?" the minister of Süderstapel asked my grandfather as they stood at the font while my grandmother hovered near, all agog. Grandfather cleared his throat and began: "William — Ludwig — Leonhard — Maximilian ..."

"Have you finished?" interrupted my grandmother.

Grandfather, startled out of his recitation, took refuge in offended silence, and my father escaped with four names.

Not for the life of her would it have occurred to Grandmother to use her husband's Christian name. She called him Schacht; that was how women usually addressed their husbands. She was a kind-hearted, unassuming woman with a general education such as, in those days, was to be found almost exclusively among daughters of the manse.

I have already mentioned that I owe my name Hjalmar to the intervention of my Grandmother Eggers. Her choice of name was not fortuitous — one of her sons was Hjalmar, Baron von Eggers.

My mother's maiden name was Constanze Justine Sophie, Freiin * von Eggers. She was born on June 6, 1851, at Dyrhavegaard near Kolding, and her marriage with my father brought entirely new blood into the Schacht family.

* The nearest English equivalent to *Freiin* when applied to the unmarried daughter of a Baron, would be "the Honourable."

The Eggerses came of old Hamburg stock. Four weighty tomes have been written about them, but I have little desire to copy out the interminable family trees.

> *Hans Eggerdes is my name,*
> *A Councilor in Hamburg known to fame.*
> *White are the roses on my shield,*
> *No stain my coat-of-arms doth yield.*

So runs the legend, in old German, under the portrait of my mother's oldest known ancestor. The picture shows him in chain and mail and helmet, tunic and jeweled belt, with two-handed sword, lance with pennant, and pointed shield bearing a device of three white roses.

The descendants of this Hans Eggerdes turn up repeatedly in the history of this Hanseatic town. Among them are councilors, chief elders, justiciaries, merchants. One died of the plague in 1695, others emigrated eastward. In the ninth generation Henning, minister at Süderau, founded the Schleswig-Holstein branch of the family from which my mother came.

These Schleswig-Holstein Eggerses were the most successful, inasmuch as they were raised first to the ordinary nobility, later to the hereditary peerage. Nevertheless the other branches have not remained idle. There is hardly one of the learned professions or services, from ecclesiastical councilor to painter and major general that is not graced by one or more of the Eggers kinsfolk. The family is also connected by marriage with the physical sciences through Oerstedt, with the fine arts through Charlotte Buff (Goethe's immortal Lotte in *The Sorrows of Werther*), who is known to have married a Kestner. Her granddaughter married an Eggers in the middle of the last century.

In my mother's time the Eggers family had already passed their zenith, exemplified in the person of Christian Ulrich Detlev, Hereditary Baron von Eggers, Doctor of Law, Councilor to the King of Denmark, Lord Lieutenant of Kiel, Commander of the Order of Dannebrog, and so on. But signs of physical decline were already apparent. He was unable to use his legs before he was five years old, when he learned to walk. He was an infant prodigy, silent, thoughtful, with a thirst for knowledge and an absolute passion for learning — with, at the same time, an irresistible leaning toward the military profession. Who can fail to draw a parallel between this lad and

such historical examples as the young Blaise Pascal, or Prince
Eugene, for whom the French had no use as a soldier because he
was too delicate for them, and who, thereupon, went over to the
Austrians.

Christian von Eggers was a shining light in his day, a universal
genius who foregathered with all the celebrated men of the time.
He traveled untiringly all over Germany, represented his country
at foreign courts and — here's a nice story for those who believe in
historical connections — carried out a finance and currency reform
in his native Denmark. Currency stabilization is obviously in the
blood, so to speak.

Together with Count Andreas Bernstorff he worked for the libera-
tion of the peasants from serfdom. In spite of being a martyr to
asthma, headaches and insomnia, he evolved a working schedule
and kept to it unflinchingly. Every other night he would work the
whole night through, standing at his desk. He fought his headaches
with blood-letting. A man of iron will, he made up for his lack of
physical strength by relentless energy. He died at his desk, while
engaged on a written work, in 1813. Denmark owes him much.

He was my great-grandfather, the same relationship as that of
the Büsum shopkeeper on my father's side. Sometimes I wonder
what would have happened if the two old gentlemen had ever run
across each other. It is quite possible to picture my great-grandfather, the hereditary baron, driving through Büsum in the course
of his travels, and his carriage losing a wheel just in front of the
local store. Being thirsty, he would call on Storekeeper Schacht
who would be standing in the doorway, in his shirtsleeves, an apron
tied round his middle.

"Good day, my good man," would be Great-grandfather Christian
von Eggers' greeting to Great-grandfather Schacht. "You've a fine
store here."

Great-grandfather Schacht would doff his little black cap and
reply: "Well, d'you want to buy something?"

"What have you?" von Eggers would ask.

"A whole box of cigars — Virginia," Schacht would answer.

"I don't smoke," would be the Baron's comment.

"Well, that's a pity," the tradesman would counter.

And then they would stand and look at each other. The hereditary baron and the small shopkeeper of Büsum. One with his hand
on the wheels of Europe, the reformer of laws, justice, peasant
conditions, currency — the other seeing to it that the Dithmarschen

country folk didn't go short of salt and tobacco. Actually, the two are not so unlike. The difference lies in their mode of life — the one restless, driven hither and thither by his manifold duties, his ambition and his thirst for knowledge; the other with no worries — his only anxiety that his son shall turn out a first-rate doctor. The one stands on the heights, where the air bites and saps the strength; the other lives in the valley, content with his own lot, ambitious only for his son. Descent and ascent rubbing elbows . . . no — such an encounter would have been most unlikely.

How my great-grandfather in Büsum would have laughed if any-one had told him: "Well, this grandson'll be courting that man's granddaughter one day!"

"Ho-ho-ho!" he would have roared. "That's not bad! Say that again."

Christian von Eggers' son, my grandfather, Chief of Police in Schleswig, left nine children unprovided for. Gone was the mighty urge which for a century had governed the family. All the hered-itary barons von Eggers found their niches — but they no longer had their hands on the wheels of Europe. And the youngest daughter, Constanze, followed a young teacher to America and married him over there.

# II

## THREE TOWNS BEGINNING WITH "H"

TINGLEFF, where I was born, is a biggish country village east of
Tondern in the mixed German-Danish district. When I was there
in 1920 for the plebiscite it was proved that Tingleff was the most
northerly village with a German majority. After we lost the First
War the Allies assigned the land beyond the so-called Clausen Line
to Denmark: thus it happens that today my native village belongs
to Denmark.

My father taught in a private school in Tingleff. The house in
which we lived still stands — a little, inconspicuous house among
many others exactly like it.

The following year we left the little place and moved south to
Heide in Dithmarschen, thereby coming full circle — for the
Schachts were Dithmarschers and during the whole of the Middle
Ages Heide had been the focal point of this debatable Peasants'
Republic. Father said goodbye to the teaching profession and
became editor of the *Heide News*. In addition — since a journalist's
career did not carry a sufficient income — he was bookkeeper to Herr
Viehdal, a wealthy cloth merchant who also owned the *Heide News*.
And finally, very reluctantly, he set my mother up in a small
haberdashery business where she sold miscellaneous goods, lace
ribbons and thread. True, she did no sensational business, but it all
helped, and she did it for my father's sake.

Those were the lean years. Unlike their Biblical counterparts
there were more than seven of them and they led us in time to
three towns beginning with "H" — Heide, Husum and Hamburg.

The *Heide News* was liberal-minded and very original. It may be
difficult to picture the activities of such a newspaper in the 1880's;
modern provincial newspapers obtain almost all of their material,
with the exception of local news, ready for press and often actually
in matrix from agencies and leading-article syndicates. They no
longer represent independent opinion. Even in the *Heide News*

there was plenty of space for local news — church services and markets, the water level and reports of accidents, festivities and obituaries — but alongside these items there was plenty of thoroughly independent political discussion — politics in general, cultural items, literary criticism — all written by the editor. Ready-made whole-sale ideas had not yet succeeded in stifling individual thought.

At no other period of his life did my father have the same chance of exploiting his ready wit, his gift of repartee and his knowledge of the world. He was a many-sided man whose only fault was that he disliked going into society. Of a retiring disposition, perhaps also a little awkward, he did not seem to fit into the social milieu to which my mother had been accustomed. Here in Heide on the other hand, in his own surroundings, among people who spoke his language, he felt entirely at home.

The dull-wittedness of the local inhabitants must frequently have got on my father's nerves. His comments on meetings of the town officials were often pungent and sarcastic. The *Heide News* there-fore had decided views of its own (that is, my father's) and the public expected this. After all, we lived in Schleswig-Holstein, a German province which was in a state of continual ferment owing to Danish nationalism. In addition, the "Liberals" were in the majority: in a land where the people depend for a living on cattle feed, cattle-rearing and cattle-dealing the individual is all against bureaucracy and in favor of free economy.

Repercussions from my father's journalistic activities were not lacking. District councilors, clergy, and men of letters wrote to him; a voluminous correspondence followed.

As I was only five years old when we left Heide my recollections of this period are naturally somewhat hazy. I have dim memories of the house in which we lived — the dark passage leading to the back door. Once through that door we were in Mother's garden where there were always a few flowers as well as vegetables and herbs. Here I used to play with Herr Viehdal's curly-headed sons until I was tired and would trot back to Mother's haberdashery store. Then she would show me some of her treasures, let me mess around in a piece box or "help" her in the kitchen.

One small incident from the Heide days remained for a long time in my memory. I was nearly five. At the end of our long kitchen garden was a tiny wooden hut which might once have been a stable. Now, however, an old, childless widow lived there, eking out a miserable existence as a charwoman, and even worse off than we were. I was rather scared of the old woman, for outwardly she was just like the picture of the witch in the fairy tales. But occasionally curiosity proved too much for me. So it happened that I saw her one day eating her supper, which consisted of a thick slice of black rye bread. I noticed that there was no butter on it, except a tiny scrap in one corner.

"You haven't any butter on your bread," I said.

"Well, my child," the old woman replied, "I haven't enough money to buy butter for a whole slice. But look, I have put a wee dab of butter in the very last corner, and now I eat from the other end and look forward with each dry mouthful to the last bit, when I shall have the butter too. That last bit will taste just as good."

A few evenings later my father told a story which fits in well with this little occurrence. In order to appreciate the circumstances you must know that Heide was a celebrated cattle market — the largest in the whole province. Indeed the little church, situated to one side of the marketplace, must have felt quite lost.

In the spring the Dithmarschen peasants would buy up the young lean stock from the poorer pasture lands. The cattle grew fat of their own accord on the rich meadows of the marsh, and in the autumn were ready for killing and driven to market. Marketdays in Heide were one huge hustle and bustle of men and cows. Dealers and wholesale slaughterers from Hamburg and large neighboring towns crowded into the inns, inspected the cattle in the pens and concluded their deals with the farmers. There was much haggling and reckoning at which the farmers showed themselves no less adept than they were at husbandry.

Business over, everybody flocked to the public house in the evening and had a rare old time celebrating the experiences and events of the day. Of course my father had to report all the goings on for his paper. One evening he came home and described the gay doings of the farmers and cattle dealers.

"Their pockets were bulging with money and they kept jingling their coins while they drank and talked big. But do you know, wife, what they drank?"

"Beer — or grog," said my mother.

"Not a bit of it. Champagne was just good enough for these gentlemen."

But is was not merely the champagne that aroused his indignation. One of the cattle dealers — or maybe farmers — a bumptious, self-satisfied fellow, evidently found that he couldn't spend his money fast enough on drink alone. As he was already as drunk as could be, but still wanted to get rid of his cash, he had sent for a hamperful of champagne, raised his heavy stick and with one stroke had knocked off the heads of every single bottle.

My mother shook her head in disapproval. Then she put us to bed, took a small tumblerful of water into which she poured a few drops of oil, placed a cork with a wick on top and lit the wick. That was our nightlight which burned till morning. Whenever we awoke during the night the tiny flame was always burning and shed a queer bluish light on the whitewashed walls of our bedroom.

That evening it was a long while before I could get to sleep for thinking again and again of the old woman with the wee dab of butter on her bread and the broken necks of the champagne bottles.

My father had undoubtedly bettered himself when he accepted Viehdal's offer to take over the editorship of the *Heide News*. Unfortunately the improvement began and ended there. He worked hard on his paper, infusing into it wit, humor and intelligence and sarcasm; but neither the number of advertisements nor the number of copies showed any sign of increase. When, after four years, he realized that things would never be different he packed up and started looking around for another job. He found one in Husum with a Jew named Gold who was looking for a manager for his soap factory.

So we moved to Husum — "the gray town by the sea" as the poet Theodor Storm has it. Storm had lived there in his capacity as County Court Judge for several decades and had retired on pension a few years previously; a splendid old man with snow-white side whiskers, beloved and admired throughout Germany for his exquisite poems and delicate sensitive stories. For more than one reason Husum and Storm are indissolubly associated in my mind. Both are melancholy, mysterious, somewhat old-fashioned.

Holding on to my mother's hand I would walk along the cobbled streets, mostly polished smooth by the drizzling rain, and gaze admiringly up at the gabled houses rising like steps on either side. I was especially charmed with the little carved turret on the Town Hall.

One day my mother took me to the dame school in Husum, where I remained for a year. I was a healthy five-year-old; there was no reason why I should not begin to learn my A.B.C's. So every day I trotted through Husum wearing my cap and carrying my satchel; with my schoolfellows I played by the harbor and stared entranced at the vessels arriving from strange parts of the world.

In the meantime my father had donned the soap boiler's blue apron and taken over the management. Each time Mother took us children to see him at the soap factory she returned home rather depressed. The working premises reeked of rancid fat, they were cold and slimy with remains of soap. The fat in the barrels was revolting, the great vessels full of corrosive solutions, the bursting sacks of caustic alkali, the vats in which the masses of soap were boiled with glycerin — everything was strange, weird, dangerous and somewhat oppressive. Even the vials of perfume which were added to the mass of stuff when the process was completed were not able to reconcile Mother to the soap factory. She disliked our father's job because she saw that he disliked it.

My father was anything but a cheerful soap boiler. For a long time he would not realize that a man who was capable of turning out a first-rate political article may be a wretchedly bad soap boiler, and that one job is by no means as good as another; that the post was not too much for him but quite simply not his line.

There are different versions of the happenings of that year 1882–83; but somehow or other the soap factory went bankrupt. Had Herr Gold engaged my father solely in order to have a scapegoat ready to hand? Had my father anything to do with the non-success of the soap made in Husum? Did the firm go smash entirely on its own without his having had anything to do with it? I don't know. All I do know is that one day the doors of that unsavory concern closed for good, and once again we had to uproot. This time our goal was the Hanseatic city of Hamburg.

We entered Hamburg — the town in which my ancestors (not my father's) had held the highest positions — through the back door, so to speak. At that time I was just six years old.

Hamburg has always been a hard nut to crack. Her inhabitants know the value of money; millionaires and starving folk are to be found within her walls. Social distinctions were greater in Hamburg than in other German cities. The shipowners, retail traders, heads of the big old-fashioned counting houses — they were the rich. The dockers, stevedores, ropemakers, day laborers, auxiliary workers, casual laborers — they were the poor.

We arrived in Hamburg without a penny, having left behind us in Husum a bankrupt soap business. For my father the outlook was not encouraging. He had knocked about the world for thirteen years and for ten years had been a married man. My brother Oluf was on the way, Eddy was going to secondary school. It was an anxious time for our little household when we came to Hamburg in 1883.

My mother had need of all her courage and all her faith to enable her to weather the setbacks and vexations of those early years in Hamburg, and, in addition, to keep up her husband's spirits.

My father's own nature had a lot to do with it. In his younger days he had been a restless wanderer, unable to remain for long in one place. His great-grandfather had still belonged to the farming community; his grandfather had invested the portion made over to him by his brothers in a general store, where it had multiplied. To a certain extent my father's grandfather had been a fixture; in this way he had been able to put his talent to good account and, since he had but one son, had sent him well equipped into the world. My grandfather went to college, built up a practice, and spent the money left by his father, the Büsum shopkeeper, without troubling to ask where it came from. Nor did he bother much about making provision for his sons. They had to start from scratch — but this time without farming relations and a steady business.

My father's position and that of his seven brothers was therefore a thousand times more difficult, especially when one realizes that they came from an entirely intellectual home. Their father was a doctor, their mother a minister's daughter. They had outgrown the peasant class. But they had no intellectual relations who could help them. All this explains much of the restlessness that led to my father's roving habits.

I have inherited a little of that restlessness. I too have a fair amount of quicksilver in my blood, exactly like Eddy, who traveled over half the world and for many years practiced as a doctor in Assuan in upper Egypt. But we owe it also to our father that this same restlessness, far from proving a handicap, actually contributed to our advancement. He laid the foundations of the new Schacht family. His was a hard road with many setbacks, and he had no one to advise or help him — except our mother.

In our early Hamburg days we lived in the back of some premises on a suburban street. Our windows looked out onto a square, paved back yard where we used to play when we were not in school. The neighborhood children eyed us somewhat askance the first time we encountered each other. We gave as good as we got — sneers, challenges, finally blows. In the end it was one glorious rough-and-tumble. When eventually we formed part of the gang belonging to this block of houses we used to play on the streets, in the *Heiligengeistfeld*, or in the yard.

Streets in those days had not been turned into death traps by motors. Only now and then did the cobbles echo when a brewer's dray drove down the road drawn by huge horses with docked tails and little earcaps. Or else it would be an omnibus — forerunner of the electric tram which at that time was unknown. This was a horse-drawn bus with five wheels, four of which were connected with the driving while the fifth ran on a rail and kept the clumsy vehicle on its course. Sometimes we children would place a heavy stone on the track. Then the bus would have to stop, the driver would jack up the wheel high above the ground, drive over the stone and let down the wheel again.

Such was the easygoing machinery of those days. It must be admitted that the driver was not so easygoing — he hurled abuse at the brats who played him such a dirty trick.

One day my father returned from town looking very cheerful. After many unsuccessful attempts he had at last found another bookkeeping job with the big coffee importers Schmidt-Pauli & Company.

Eddy, meanwhile, had passed his entrance examination and was in the first form at the Johanneum, Hamburg's famous classical grammar school. It must have given my father profound satisfaction that his eldest son was able to attend this excellent institution. How he managed to meet the school fees month by month is a mystery. But manage it he did, and every morning Eddy would leave the house three quarters of an hour before school was due to begin, and walk across half Hamburg in order to fill his head with knowledge.

In the evening Father would devote himself entirely to us; he would talk about technical inventions, great scientists, history, commerce and world economics. He would remark, for instance: "There are trains now with a little cogwheel underneath. The cogwheel runs on a third rail between the two other rails. Can you imagine, Mother, why they do that?"

Mother would shrug her shoulders. "Maybe so that they can brake better," she would answer. "The trains do go so fearfully fast!"

"Nonsense!" said Father. "It's so that they can travel up mountains."

"Why do they want to go up mountains by train?" enquired Eddy.

"They want to go everywhere," my father explained. "Technical invention stops at nothing — it wants to spread everywhere. That's a part of human nature. One day we shall even be able to fly."

"To fly!" we children exclaimed.

"People already fly in air balloons," he went on. "They make a huge bladder which is filled with hydrogen, which is lighter than air. In this way man can ascend right up into the clouds. If they can incorporate a motor and steering gear they will be able to fly wherever they please . . . "

But my father's streaks of bad luck were not yet over. True, his salary with Schmidt-Pauli & Company was adequate, but it depended on the efficient running of the business. Unfortunately this efficiency was lacking.

It was in 1885 or 1886 that a large-scale gamble in coffee ended in sensational failure in Hamburg. The consumption of this favorite beverage had steadily increased since the War of 1870 and the firm of Schmidt-Pauli & Company had gambled on an upward tendency in the market. But the upward tendency did not materialize and Schmidt-Pauli found themselves unable to meet their obligations. They were compelled to dismiss nearly all their employees, including my father.

Once again we struck a bad patch. For months my father called on one firm after another in his search for a suitable position. He found casual work here and there; but his earnings amounted to mere drops in the ocean; our total income was nowhere near sufficient. We lived literally from hand to mouth.

I well remember my eighth birthday during that period. In our home it was customary to give each birthday child as many oranges as he was years old. That year, however, must have been an especially bad one for us — anyhow, on my birthday morning I received only two oranges and a fifty-pfennig piece.

"Run and get five cents' worth of coal," my mother said, and laid the money on the table. Silently I picked up the bucket and the coins and trudged along to the coal merchant's, who had set up business in a cellar. One or two women were gossiping in the gloomy place, a candle burned on an upturned packing case, bundles of firewood were stacked against the wall and at the back was the coal depot.

"Hullo — come for some more coal?" the coal merchant asked, interrupting his conversation. Perspiration had left wide streaks on his black face. On his head he wore a sack, hood fashion.

"Five cents' worth," I said. He pocketed the cash — the price of two drinks — and filled my bucket with scraps of coal.

"Who's that?" a woman asked as I went out.

"One of Schacht's kids. His father was with Schmidt-Pauli and they bought so much coffee they couldn't get rid of it."

Yes — it was a bad stretch.


One evening my father returned in high spirits from a lengthy trek through Hamburg. He burst into the living room, tossed his overcoat onto a chair, grabbed hold of my mother and gave her a kiss. That in itself was a rare enough occurrence in our somewhat reserved household, where hardly anybody ever kissed.

"Mother," he said, somewhat excitedly, "I've found something!"

My mother clasped her hands over her heart and exclaimed: "What have you found?"

"A post where I can make use of my American experience. A post — not highly paid, but there are prospects."

"What is the name of the firm?"

"I'm a bookkeeper in the American Equitable Life Insurance Company," my father said.

Equitable Life Insurance — the reasonable, just, fair Life Insurance Company — however one cares to describe it. Ever since that evening the name has a pleasant sound for me. For it was here that my father found that for which he had been seeking and longing throughout his hopeless, endless tramps all over Hamburg, knocking and being turned away from one door after another — it was here that he found a position in life — a niche.

He entered the service of the Equitable Life Insurance and they treated him fairly according to the promise implied in their title. He remained there thirty years, advancing step by step up the ladder, earning more money, until in his old age he was General Secretary of the Berlin Office . . . About this time he built a small house in Schlachtensee — and what could be more natural than that it should be called Villa Equitable?

No world-shattering event. But I was just sufficiently sensible to understand what this news meant.

Eddy would be able to continue at the Johanneum, and there would certainly be a place there for me too. The family was now secure; we could count on regular money every month; it would even be possible to save a little. Splendid news!

On August 19, 1887, Grandmother Eggers died in my parents'

house in Hamburg. I still distinctly remember the funeral rites; the bier in the best parlor, the dark coffin, the relations who had come to pay final tribute to their mother.

Grandmother came from Itzehoe, north of Hamburg. Her father was a well-to-do unassuming middle-class merchant, Evers by name. She had met Friedrich von Eggers in her parents' house. The only son of the famous Christian Ulrich Detlev, he was a good match. In the course of years she had nine living children, among them six sons. But when my grandmother was in her seventies it was not to her wealthy sons that she went, but to her youngest daughter Constanze, although the latter had perhaps less money and also less comfort to offer the old lady than any of her brothers and sisters. I assume that she was her mother's pet. Perhaps too my grandmother longed for a return to the middle-class surroundings from which she came. Whatever her reasons, she turned up one day in Hamburg when I was nine years old, and remained with us till her death.

By this time Father's dream had come true: we were living in the front part of the house and were looked upon as belonging to the better-class tenants. The days of back premises were over. That, however, did not mean that we were able to indulge in unbounded luxury; Father's income was still too small. The Equitable Life Insurance was a safe job, but it was certainly no gold mine.

In my mind's eye I can conjure up a clear picture of our home in those days. It was very simply furnished; plain carpets on the stained floors, one or two color prints on the walls; a glass-fronted bookcase held Father's favorite books (classics, of course) in stamped, gold-decorated cloth bindings. I particularly remember Shakespeare's Works next to volumes of poetry — Goethe, Schiller, Heine — a couple of novels by Dickens, who at that time was not yet reckoned as a classic but was uncommonly popular; and several books in the Tauchnitz edition. In the evening Father would take a volume from the bookcase and read aloud to us — a poem, a bit out of a play — and discuss it with us. Throughout his life good books were a real need of his. Music did not interest him as much: that was more in the Eggers line.

Gone were the days when we bought five cents' worth of coal. At least the living room, where Eddy and I sat and did our homework, was always warm. Oluf, "the baby," took his nap in a corner of the room.

We still had no maid. Mother had to do all the work — cooking, mending, washing, scrubbing. Even now I can't imagine how she did it and managed to keep cheerful and good-tempered. At the time we took it for granted. She was up before anyone else of a morning, and made coffee for Father and the two schoolboys. When we arrived home the house was tidy, the beds made, the fire burning brightly in the living room, the dinner ready. What did we have for dinner? Well, in those days our meals were very simple; buckwheat cakes, a large dumpling and *Swartsuer*, a kind of Spartan black broth, not unlike the broth that the Lacedemonian warriors had in their youth. The plain food was wholesome and nourishing and there was plenty of it.

We didn't even know what fancy food looked like, until a certain occasion which made a great impression on us children: the Eggers Family Gathering, which took place in the spring of 1887, about six months before Grandmother's death. Our family would probably not have been so interested in this festivity had Grandmother Eggers not been living with us. The fact, however, that she was the doyenne of the baronial line was a potent reason for holding the festivity in Hamburg in her honor.

Between forty and fifty people sat down to dinner in the dining room of a Hamburg hotel, where they feasted, drank and listened to speeches. At intervals the children were brought in; old memories were revived and — so far as the men were concerned — a great many cigars were consumed.

At the time, this family gathering attracted quite a lot of attention. My impression is that the Hamburgers considered it rather absurd. After all, we lived in a Hanseatic city which from the thirteenth century onward had been tremendously conscious of its sturdy middle-class citizenry and whose aristocracy had kept clear of titles. Malicious tongues could not refrain from jeering at this baronial display, and later there was a popular saying in Hamburg about "those Eggerses and their high-and-mighty ideas."

At any rate there remained the recollection of a splendid feast, smartly dressed people and, in my case, the picture of my mother among her relations. At that time she was thirty-seven years old and certainly the loveliest of all the women present. She had a finely chiseled face, dark hair in which a few silver threads were already visible, and great dark expressive eyes. She was there among the others, beautiful, kindly, joining in the lively conversation at intervals, but for the most part listening. Everyone liked her, and I was immensely proud of her.

Mother had a small but very pretty singing voice. When the daily tasks threatened to be too much for her, her favorite song was "Wait on the Lord, my soul, be not dismayed; commit all to Him, He will come to thine aid . . ." But she did not sing religious songs only.

"Sing to us, Mother," we would beg when darkness had fallen and we had finished our homework.

She needed no urging. In those days anyone wanting music had to provide his own. My mother was musical by nature. Singing to us was at the same time a recreation — German songs, dialect songs, Danish songs. When Mother sang we sat silent, listening. And many hours later when we lay in bed we would sometimes hum "Little Ole with his umbrella . . ." (one of her Danish tunes).

Mother was equally at home in two languages. She had learned Danish almost before she had learned German — not surprising, seeing that she was the granddaughter of a Danish councilor. But it was not until half a century later that I learned how deep-rooted was the Danish element in her nature. On her deathbed in 1935 in Berlin-Schlachtensee she began to mutter to herself. The doctor and the hospital nurse stared at one another in astonishment. She was saying the Lord's Prayer in Danish.

At that time I myself was nearly sixty. All my life I had spoken German with my mother. But the memory of her Danish home proved stronger than the habit of a lifetime. Her last words revealed that she was back once more in the land of her birth.

# III

## THREE EMPERORS IN ONE YEAR

BETWEEN the ages of six and nine I attended the preparatory school of the Teachers' Training College. I had to cover quite a tidy distance to school which did not grow any less when, at nine years of age, I passed the entrance examination for the Johanneum, the grammar school, famous throughout Germany, founded in 1529 when German classical education was at its zenith.

The entrance examination at the Johanneum took place at Easter in 1886, just after my ninth birthday. My parents, of course, took me to the venerable building, escorted by brother Eddy proudly sporting his school cap and overflowing with good advice. In the big entrance hall we met other parents with their children, all looking very serious and whispering softly as if they were at a funeral or an execution.

At last a master appeared and conducted us — without our parents — into a large room where we were examined on every possible subject for four long hours. Admittance to the Johanneum was no trifling matter.

My biographer, Dr. Franz Reuter, describes my method of passing the entrance examination: "In the Arithmetic test for the Sixth [lowest] Form Schacht distinguished himself by arriving at a different result from all his fellow candidates . . ." And Norbert Mühlen (of whom more later) in his book *Schacht the Magician* says: "In arithmetic he achieved a wrong total. A strange omen for a future master of financial calculation . . ."

Luckily I did better than the average in other subjects, so I passed just the same.

If later on I had taken up law or theology nobody would ever have breathed another word about that examination of 1886. As it is, people to this day tackle me on the subject. "A banker who is bad at figures," they say. "How on earth is that possible?" Then I tell them the story of the famous mathematician who was obliged to resort to a slide rule. "Nine divided by three, gentlemen," he would say, "is — one moment, please — is two, decimal nine, nine, nine . . . let us say approximately three!" And for all that he really was an exceptionally good mathematician.

In spite of my low marks in arithmetic I have not been entirely unsuccessful in my career as banker and president of the Reichsbank. A bank inspector or manager is not a bookkeeper. His work entails expert knowledge of quite different subjects; for example, psychology, economics, common sense, ability to make decisions, but above all, insight into the intricacies and the nature of credit.

When, on my arrival at school, my address was noted, I very soon learned that the wealthier Hamburgers did not live in St. Pauli.

"Eimsbüteler-Chaussee? — What sort of neighborhood is that?" my better-off schoolfellows would ask.

I didn't know how to answer and the fact that our address was not up to standard made me very uncomfortable. Although I was among the brighter pupils it did not prevent my being cold-shouldered, and only when I reached the higher forms did I manage to make some impression.

My father had to strain every nerve to send both Eddy and me to the Johanneum. We knew that, because of us, he never went to the theater, or drank wine, and that he allowed himself only one cigar a day — and that one of the cheaper brands. Our life at home was one of Spartan simplicity; we received no pocket money for non-essentials, and as for our clothes they were certainly not in the latest fashion.

"Anyone who wants to get on in the world must learn not to depend on externals," Father would sometimes say. I don't know whether at that time we children understood just how bitterly this consistency affected him. After all, he could easily have followed his own father's example and not bothered so much about his sons' future.

It is possible that this perpetual denial of the outward pleasures and enjoyments of life influenced his character and made him hard. If that was the case he suffered under it more than we did. Anyhow, he never lost his zest for stimulating discussions on literature, international politics, trade and technics, for he would talk with us of an evening, as he had always done, and he followed our progress at school with close attention.

There comes a time in every boy's life when his ambition is to wear long trousers. His voice breaks, he begins to shoot up, and his long thin legs embarrass him. Somewhere too there exists the object of his hero worship — a young master, a top-former — and this hero naturally wears smartly cut, well-fitting long trousers and in other ways behaves like a grownup.

So I began to worry my parents, telling them that I was one of the more advanced pupils in a form where the other boys had been going about for ages with tubular leg coverings! High time that Schacht Junior also donned long trousers!

My first pair was a severe shock to my self-esteem for some time to come. My father took me to an outfitter's and after a long search picked out a pair made of good, strong hard-wearing shoddy. Do you know what shoddy is? True, it is an English product, but it certainly is not a good example of what is understood by English cloth. A rough, hairy, feltlike, shapeless affair without "polish," unless it be at the knees and the seat.

I put on the trousers and went off to school. The collective result was not what I had hoped. My classmates looked at me and burst out laughing: "Schacht's wearing shoddy trousers!"

All my pleasure in the trousers was spoiled. I struggled all the more savagely with irregular verbs, spherical trigonometry and the adventures of Odysseus.

Perhaps my masters sensed something of this struggle. They were excellent instructors; no windbags, but warmhearted human beings.

At that time there was a man whose name was held in high honor by masters and pupils alike. He was Professor Hermann Schubert, the mathematician of the Johanneum; about forty years old, a native of Potsdam who, at the age of twenty-seven, had been awarded the large gold medal by the Danish Academy of Science for a work on *Characteristics of Spatial Curves of the Third Dimension*. Later he edited the "Schubert Collection" which published textbooks for students of mathematics and mathematical physics.

Schubert was one of the last of the humanistic mathematicians: the next generation already included names like Planck and Einstein, after which the universal conception of the humanists was superseded by mathematicians, technicians and natural scientists.

But we of course could foresee none of that. School was a self-contained unit; the subjects forming the hub around which other activities revolved were languages, history, religion, literature. Mathematics, physics, chemistry, natural science were, so to speak, the outer circle. I was chiefly interested in the intellectual sciences, less so in other subjects. In this way I managed to maintain my place in the Upper Third just as Eddy had done.

But I did not push myself forward. Remarks in my school report such as "A wide-awake pupil, but not above the average, even among his schoolfellows" may have been connected with such experiences as the one with the shoddy trousers. I think I took refuge in solitude by way of reaction to the social differences.

The sons of the "better class" households were members of the exclusive rowing and sailing clubs which met on the Alster. They had their own boats, attended dancing classes, sported frock coats at an early age and in summer went with their parents to Switzerland, Italy or Norway.

The other boys had no part in these wonderful doings. If we found the heat too much for us in summer we took a five-cent steamer ticket and for another dime we hired a cabin at the free public baths. It was all great fun and very healthy — but still — it was not the same thing!

The contrast was never more apparent than on the occasion of my final examination. It was customary in those days for examinees to present themselves in frock coat and dress shirt, so I had to find some way of procuring these necessary items. The problem was solved by the fact that the examination was divided into two parts held on two successive days. I was due to attend on the second day; a schoolfellow of about my build had been assigned to the first. When his ordeal was over I slipped into his outfit and took my turn.

I can never sufficiently stress all that I owe to the classical humanistic education of the Johanneum. Not only did it enable me to become acquainted with the outward sequence of ancient history, renaissance, classicism and romanticism, but above all it afforded me an insight into the spirit and character of these eras. It imbued my life with a sense of harmony, an objective tolerance, and opened my mind concerning the development of my own time; and it equipped me to face success and failure with common sense, stoic courage and unshakable confidence.

On the occasion of the Johanneum's fourth centenary celebrations in 1929 I was able to express my gratitude by the establishment of a foundation, the income from which would enable two graduating students to spend some time abroad. Unfortunately this foundation was one of the victims of currency depreciation.

The decisive years of my life occurred between 1888 and 1892, between my eleventh and fifteenth years.

In 1888 Germany had three emperors in succession. In October of the same year Hamburg was included in the German Customs Union.

In 1892 there was the great cholera epidemic in Hamburg — the last of its kind within the Empire. A few months previously my parents had moved to Berlin.

Until then I had no real conception of the power and importance of a German emperor. Wilhelm I, a white-haired patriarch, lived in Berlin. I knew vaguely that he had been severely wounded in 1876 when someone had attempted to assassinate him, and for six months his son Friedrich had taken over the reins of government. This same Friedrich represented the hope of the free middle classes. Wilhelm I and his Chancellor, Bismarck, might be outstanding, wise and at the same time moderately inclined foreign politicians. But what, said many people, was the good of foreign policy when internal questions still remained to be dealt with?

The nation looked to Wilhelm I's successor to give the middle classes a larger share in the government, to ensure a more liberal development in German internal politics, and replacement of inherited aristocratic privileges by middle-class institutions.

That none of this was based on any fundamental difference of outlook or "philosophy of life" between people and government is certain. Perhaps there would never have been such a thing as a "philosophy of life" in Germany had things developed along somewhat different lines. But the unhappy events of the "Year of the Three Emperors" involved what amounted practically to the passing over of an entire generation. Germany stepped from the era of conservative thought straight into the Socialist era. Liberalism, which Bismarck once described as "the early crop of socialism," never came into the picture at all. A Liberal period would have entailed the achievement of the necessary compromises such as had been achieved in England. New political tendencies would have developed gradually; the connecting link between the aristocratic reigning house and the Marxist masses would have been found.

The Liberals hoped that all this might come to pass during the eventual reign of the Crown Prince Friedrich, who had more than once indicated that he was a progressive thinker, quite prepared to make a change from the hidebound methods of the old emperor. Thirty years of a Liberal middle-class era would have relieved Germany's internal political tensions (the result of a too rapid industrial development), and attracted a stratum of political leaders from the ranks of the middle classes.

It was in 1888 that I heard the word "cancer" (*Krebs* \*) for the first time. The Emperor Friedrich, it was said, suffered from cancer of the larynx, but we had no idea what that implied.

Nowadays every child knows the meaning of the word "cancer." I remember that the dread, ominous word stuck in my mind for a long time. I would have liked to know what the "crab" in the Emperor's throat looked like.

The year began with the publication in the newspapers of daily bulletins concerning the bad state of health of His Majesty the Emperor Wilhelm. The grownups looked very grave when they read these bulletins. Wilhelm was nearly ninety-one when he died. When, ten years previously, the attempted assassination by the anarchist Schilling failed, the love of an entire nation went out to the eighty-year-old ruler. His military past (a thorn in the flesh to many a democrat) was forgotten, as was his action against the German Revolutionaries of 1848. People saw him for what indeed he was — no genius, but a patriarch on the imperial throne, a moderate, wise old man who knew very well how to follow the counsel of men whom he trusted. When he died in March 1888, and our school flag was lowered to half-mast, the whole nation mourned him. The Emperor Friedrich III succeeded his father on the throne; my father had great hopes of him.

At that time I understood nothing of politics. Everything seemed to me wonderfully arranged: when one emperor died, another succeeded him. Obviously emperors never died out. But I remembered a talk I had with Father one summer evening in that year. As usual we were all sitting around the table; outside, the sky was aglow with the colors of the sunset; in the kitchen we could hear Mother busying herself with the dishes she had just cleared away.

"Bad news from Berlin," said Father suddenly to Eddy and me. "The Emperor's cancer of the larynx is worse — they say it's incurable . . ."

"Who will come to the throne then?" I asked.

Father took the opportunity to read us a little lecture on the Hohenzollern laws of succession, with excursions into the laws of succession of European dynasties. Suddenly he broke off short and stared out of the window; obviously he had forgotten what he had been talking about.

\* *Krebs,* a crab; also cancer.

"Too late," he said suddenly, "much too late."

"What's too late?" we asked.

"The Emperor Friedrich came to the throne too late," said Father. "The old emperor was ninety years old. Couldn't he have retired fifteen years ago? Even then the Emperor Friedrich would have been over forty — just the right age for an emperor."

A few days later flags were once again at half-mast: the Emperor Friedrich too was dead. He had reigned for ninety-one days. Within a year a third emperor sat on the throne — Wilhelm II.

The event aroused much comment. "Three emperors," said the optimists. "Just see what we can do; if need be, we can produce three emperors in one year . . ." The pessimists did not regard this fateful year as a confirmation of Germany's strength. Their remarks were, in the main, very similar to my father's.

This time there was no need for anxiety about the new sovereign's health. True, some of my schoolfellows hinted that the Emperor had one arm shorter than the other, but the pictures that now appeared in all the bookshops showed him as an exceedingly well set up, personable young man, a knight "without fear and without reproach" with shining eyes and a fine dark mustache. He had the typical Hohenzollern high, somewhat sloping forehead and round his neck he wore a gold chain with cross and crown. I looked at him with the mercilessly sharp eyes of youth and decided that I liked him better than his father and grandfather. I said as much to my father one day at dinner. He raised his head and looked at me a little mockingly. "So — you like him!" he repeated. "Well, well, he might almost be your elder brother!"

That was an exaggeration. Wilhelm II was twenty-nine when he ascended the throne. Only much later did I realize that twenty-nine is very young for a responsible position such as that assumed overnight by the man with the smart military mustache.

One of the young emperor's first official acts after his accession was the laying of the foundation stone of the extension to the Free Port of Hamburg, by which Hamburg was included in the North German Customs Union.

Up to the year 1888 Hamburg was foreign territory from the customs point of view. For her inhabitants this was most advantageous, for all food from overseas came into the city at cheap international competitive prices. But it was bad for trade, for the vast purchasing power of the German Empire was difficult to tap owing to high tariff walls. The great mass of the population engaged in commerce and industry or in transit trade could not profit by the low food prices if they were unable to earn the necessary money by adequate production and sales.

Of course everyone, including the Prussian neighbors, exploited the exemption from duty to the full. Small quantities of goods were allowed to be brought in duty-free from the free zone to the customs district in the course of so-called small-scale frontier traffic; and the adjoining Prussian towns Altona and Ottensen took advantage of this. Whenever we children visited an aunt in Ottensen we had to join a shopping queue of neighborhood children who were going to buy things at the nearest grocer's shop in Hamburg. Then after we had done our shopping we would march back proudly in single file through the dividing line of posts to the customs officials, each one showing the quarter pound of coffee, sugar, tea and so forth which we were allowed to take in free of duty. We saw nothing queer in this procedure, nor had we any idea of the economic pros and cons of the much discussed customs problem.

Uncle Wieding, however, had a very clear idea. (He was an old family friend whom we had "adopted" as an uncle.) Uncle Wieding had once wanted to marry a member of the Eggers family — my mother's sister Antoinette. But she turned him down and married instead the Danish Councilor of State Oersted, a nephew of the famous Professor of Physics. Uncle Wieding never quite got over the disappointment. Being of an entirely guileless and kindly disposition he took on the part of a favorite uncle to the children of his idol's sister. He often came to see us, took a great interest in the children's progress and presented us with apples and cookies which he invariably extracted from his coat pocket directly he entered the house; he addressed Mother as "little woman" and carried on lengthy discussions with my father. Their pet subjects were literature and "Stadtsbestes," a homely expression used by the Hamburgers of those days to describe what we, somewhat more sophisticated, now speak of as "city politics."

Uncle Wieding was an independent shopkeeper and dealt with English stockings and knitwear. He was a model of probity, well educated and kindhearted, but he was also one of those strictly logical sensible folk who find it hard to understand that people do not always act according to the dictates of reason. As a result he belonged to the Liberal political party; that is, to those people who are sound enough in theory but in practice seldom have a large following. For the masses do not look on things as they should be in theory but as they strike them in reality. The theoretically correct, however, is seldom striking. The striking thing is the extreme, the extravagant, whatever lies outside the domain of logic, reason and convention.

The inclusion of Hamburg in the German Customs Union was the first important political event of my life. For Uncle Wieding, however, it was a financial blow. His English stockings were more expensive owing to the duty; they had to stand up to competition from Saxony. Nevertheless Wieding swore by his English hosiery. He found fault with the inferior imitations from Chemnitz but could not prevent their growing better every year and finally surpassing the English goods in quality and appearance. Uncle Wieding's business steadily declined. Eventually he made up his mind, and notified his customers that Julius Wieding's was closing down for good; he didn't want to strike out on any new lines. Henceforth he lived on his income and his principles — a modest but contented existence.

By a stroke of luck I managed to get a good place for the ceremonial of laying the foundation stone of the Free Port. The father of one of my playfellows was a wholesale butcher living in a road known as "Bei den Mühren" between the inner harbor and the customs canal. We had a fine view of the scene of action from a platform erected above the front steps of the house. The shop was much patronized by the dockers. Every afternoon between four and five the butcher would tie a clean blue-and-white apron around his middle, pick up a big dish of sausages and carry them through to his customers in the shop. From the living room we could see and hear him selling his hot sausages and joking in dialect with the workmen.

Bei den Mühren is a romantic corner of old Hamburg. From the Old Wall the Burstah runs down to the wooden bridge over the Nicolaifleet, and continues as the Mattentwiete to what was then the bridge over the Sandtorkai, which lies further behind the harbor. Sea and land dovetail into each other at this point; everywhere are quays, moles, bollards, barges, boats, old hulks and little pleasure steamers.

On October 15, 1888, the Emperor Wilhelm II was to lay the famous foundation stone in the corner tower of the Sandtorkai Bridge. One can picture the excitement of a fourth-form schoolboy over all the preparations. I wasn't in the least interested in the continual arguments of the grownups over the harbor. The chief thing was that a real Emperor was coming and I should see him quite close!

Hours before the actual ceremony people were crowding in the direction of the Mattentwiete and the inner streets of the Old Town so that they might at any rate see the Emperor of Germany drive past: middle-class citizens in dark suits, leading their children by the hand; their wives, with umbrellas, walking beside them.

At last we caught sight of the guests of honor in frock coats and top hats. Distant cheers; the clatter of hoofs over the Mattentweite; then a carriage drawn by four horses, in which sat the twenty-nine-year-old Emperor, in full-dress uniform. He bowed gravely and waved to right and left.

I can't remember any of the speeches of that afternoon; I was completely taken up with gazing at the Emperor, standing erect and very serious in front of the Sandtorkai Bridge and probably rather astonished at the weird street names and the queer, harsh German spoken by his hosts. I was deeply impressed by his smart uniform and his whole appearance.

At last all the speakers had voiced their good wishes for the future, emphasized the importance of this historic occasion, been mindful of the reigning house, the old Hanseatic city, and many other things besides. Someone handed the Emperor a hammer; he took it, raised it and let it fall three times on the stones which the foreman had set in the tower on the bridge.

Those three strokes remained in my memory for years. From the moment they had sounded, Hamburg had surrendered her old right of exemption from duty and had become incorporated in the larger Union — eighteen years after the war with France, out of which the Empire had arisen.

A few minutes later the Emperor re-entered his carriage, bowed right and left and drove away. The great event of the year was over.

From that day onward I looked upon the world with different eyes. There is a vast difference between just *hearing* about an emperor and actually seeing him in the flesh. Power is an empty word until one has seen a display of power. Such a display was the laying of the foundation stone in the Free Port of Hamburg. I suddenly grasped the meaning of the word politics. I understood why people like Uncle Wieding grew excited when they discussed politics. I had made my first contact with a wider world.

To understand the after-effects on Hamburg of the solemn

occasion one need only to follow the history of a single shipping firm.

The Hamburg-Amerikanische Paketfahrt AG. (HAPAG for short), founded in 1847, had had to reduce their capital of 22,500,000 marks by 15,000,000 in 1877, having overcommitted themselves competing with the Adler Line. In 1886, two years before the Free Port celebrations, Albert Ballin took over the passenger traffic. He was a most gifted man, son of a Jewish shipping agent engaged in the booking of passages for emigrants. But even Ballin himself could not, singlehanded, have built up HAPAG into the mighty establishment it became during the ensuing twenty-four years.

Eighteen ninety-one saw the beginning of HAPAG's fast weekly service to New York and the inauguration of winter cruises for tourists; 1894 introduced the great P-liners (all the names of these vessels began with P — *Prussia, Persia, Patria, Phoenicia, Palatia*). These steamships were built for both freight and passenger traffic.

Between 1897 and 1900 HAPAG bought up the Hamburg-Calcutta Line, the Hamburg-Kingsin Line and the shipping firm of de Freitas with a Brazilian line. In 1900 the new fast liner *Deutschland*, 23.5 knots, was put into commission, to which were added in 1905 freight-and-passenger vessels of the *Kaiserin Augusta Victoria* class (25,000 tons displacement).

In the last few years prior to the First World War the three giants of the *Imperator* class followed in quick succession: *Imperator, Vaterland* and *Bismarck*, each one over 50,000 gross register tons.

The number of ocean vessels of this one line alone had risen from 26 to 194, the gross registered tonnage from 71,000 to 1,370,000. Instead of 500,000 cubic meters of goods the annual purchases now amounted to 8,300,000 meters, and instead of 48,000 passengers a year the liners now carried a total of 463,000 — nearly ten times as many.

I made the acquaintance of Albert Ballin, who had been president of HAPAG since 1899, during the First World War. Two years later, after the German collapse, he took his own life.

The tremendous advance and growth of Hamburg due to its incorporation into the Empire was soon apparent to everyone. International trade, industry and self-government was now the threefold slogan that made of the Hanseatic city on the northern bank of the Elbe the second largest town in Germany, and one of the largest ports in the world.

When, four years later, the Equitable decided to transfer its offices from Hanseatic Hamburg to the imperial capital Berlin, my father moved there also.

That was the beginning of a new chapter for all of us — for Father and Mother, because they had to accustom themselves to an entirely new kind of life; for me, because I made up my mind to stay on at the Johanneum in Hamburg, and for this purpose found board and lodging with a doctor's family in Wedel, the other side of Hamburg.

# IV

## CHOLERA IN HAMBURG

THE REMOVAL VAN containing the furniture, kitchen utensils and so forth had departed, drawn by hefty iron-gray Percherons with funny tufts of hair on hoofs and belly. Father, Mother and Oluf had left by the Hamburg-Berlin train; brother Eddy was studying medicine in Kiel and fully occupied with anatomy, jolly companionship and attractive blondes. I remained behind in Wedel, near Hamburg.

Every morning I went into Hamburg by steam train — an hour and a quarter's journey — and returned in the evening. From the windows of my compartment I could see the magnificent villas in Blankensee belonging to various shipowners, and the white sails of the yachts cruising on the lower Elbe.

In spite of the view, however, I was not really happy because of the mistress of the house my parents had chosen for me. She was a miserly woman, stepmother to the two daughters of a somewhat corpulent doctor, a friend of my father's student days whose first wife had died many years previously.

When my parents moved to Berlin they took the doctor's eldest daughter with them and I went to board with the family at Wedel so that I could continue to attend the Johanneum. From this exchange of offspring there sprang up a staunch friendship between my "foster sister" and myself which has endured to this day.

There was nothing wrong with the doctor. He was an easygoing sort of fellow who asked nothing better than to get into his pony trap and drive off on his rounds. If I were at home he would often ask, "What about it, Hjalmar — feel inclined to come along?"

I always felt inclined, so the two of us would drive all over the place.

"It's not comfortable at home," he would sigh, when we came to an attractive-looking pub. "Come along, let's have a grog." We would have one — or several according to how we felt and then drive on again.

His wife never bothered herself about me, but I put up with it. I was in the upper school, the masters addressed me in the third person, as is the custom in Germany among adults; in addition to compulsory Latin and Greek I had chosen Hebrew as my optional subject. I did not know whether I would ever go in for theology, but a variety of subjects never does anyone any harm — and later on we would frequently say — in fun — that the Hebrew language was by no means a bad preparation for a banking career.

Sometimes, it is true, I would be fed up with conditions in the doctor's house; on the other hand there was a magnet that kept me there — the youngest daughter.

She was not my first love. I had got over that in my Upper Fifth days. My first love had been a cousin in lower Saxony whom I had met at a wedding at the age of fifteen. I liked her so much that six months later I set out on a thirty-three-mile walking trip in order to see her again.

The doctor's daughter was a somewhat different story; my feeling for her could best be described as platonic. I wrote verses for her and kept my efforts hidden in a drawer. My thoughts wavered between her and the bicycle I intended to earn by private coaching. But before I could do anything about it the great Hamburg cholera epidemic broke out and upset all my plans.

Nine years previously Robert Koch — whom Germany at that time had honored as a hero — had discovered in the comma bacillus the cause of cholera.

Now there is a vast difference between seeing a picture of a comma bacillus in the newspaper and seeing a whole town succumb to this pestilence. No one in Hamburg imagined during that summer that things were not all they should be. Evidently, however, some traveler from India had brought the cholera bacillus with him and it spread throughout the city. In matters of sanitation the Hamburg of those days was very much behind the times. Crowds of human beings huddled together in the Old Town; ancient tenement dwellings, often with only one or two lavatories in the basement, inadequate drainage — refuse was mostly carried straight into the Elbe without any provision being made for sewers — in short, first-class scope for an epidemic. More than ten thousand Hamburgers fell victims to the defects of a one-sided administration which gave too much attention to business and too little to the welfare of the community. Between the great conflagration of

1842 and the Allied bombings of 1943, no other catastrophe of comparable dimensions had befallen the city.

The frightful part of it was the sudden spread of the epidemic; it was like an explosion. Only yesterday I had gone to town by train from Wedel, had written a Greek extempore exercise, and in the afternoon had returned to my doctor's house without the remotest idea of the ghastly danger to which, at that very moment, thousands of people were already exposed. The next morning I packed my school satchel, stuck my blue cap on my head and made my way over the uneven cobbles to the railway station. The stationmaster looked at me and beckoned me nearer.

"Well, Schacht, I suppose you want to go to Hamburg?"

"Yes," I said.

"Well, you can't," said the good man.

"Why not?" I asked.

He leaned forward slightly and his expression became very grave. "Cholera has broken out in Hamburg," he whispered. "All schools are closed till further notice. We have had instructions to send back any students coming into the city from outside."

I picked up my satchel and went right back.

"What shall we do now?" I asked the doctor. He glanced first at his wife, then at me. I took the hint, went to my room and packed a bundle not much larger than a Hamburg carpenter's knapsack. Then I went downstairs, made my farewells and said I would return when the schools reopened. My address was c/o Dr. Schacht, Friedrichstadt; would they please write to me there if they heard any news about the school.

Soon afterwards I was stepping out in the direction of Utersen. Bypassing Hamburg and the cholera I wandered through the countryside, past rich pastures and poor-conditioned fields, past marsh and high ground. The knowledge that I would not have to go to school for a few weeks outweighed any feeling of horror at the calamity that had overtaken the city. Youth is very self-centered.

It was, in fact, a terrible calamity. The civilian and the emergency military hospitals were very soon full to overflowing with the dying. A constant stream of mothers with children, daughters with fathers, husbands and wives thronged the advisory centers asking for help which those in authority were often unable to give. Residents in whole streets fell ill where contaminated water had seeped in through the defective pipes, while in the next street not a single person sickened. Unsuspected carriers may well have been responsible for the fact that in streets and districts where hitherto not one soul had succumbed, new centers of the disease suddenly developed and spread like wildfire. Relief trains were assembled and dispatched from Germany; young doctors from all over the empire poured into Hamburg and threw themselves with sublime courage into the fight against the Asiatic foe. Voluntary hospital nurses from the big charitable organizations offered their services. Many of them sickened; not a few died.

The epidemic lasted three months. It took six weeks before matters were sufficiently under control to admit of the schools reopening. Meanwhile ten thousand Hamburgers had perished from cholera. During those six weeks I stayed with my grandfather in Friedrichstadt.

It was late evening when I arrived at Friedrichstadt on the Eider. It was like coming home. I had already stayed with my grandfather twice — once when we still lived in Husum and the second time when I was twelve years old. I knew that in the interval my grandmother, whom I had admired immensely, had died. But Grandfather was still alive and in spite of his seventy-nine years, active and unchanged.

"Ah, there you are, my boy," was all he said by way of greeting. That was typical of the prevailing tone in our family. The Friesians are a taciturn race, fully occupied with the realities of life. If a member of the family turned up he had his own reason for doing so. There were no lengthy inquiries.

The housekeeper prepared a room for me and looked suspiciously at the small amount of underwear I had brought. I washed up and ran downstairs to Grandfather who was waiting for me at the supper table. Of course I immediately told him about the cholera. He was not happy at the news. To begin with, he was a doctor and it did not take much imagination to picture what a cholera epidemic meant in the narrow dirty quarters of Old Hamburg. Then, too, he feared that fear of the sickness would mean a lot of extra work for him. And he was right.

Friedichstadt is only some fifteen and a half feet above sea level. The Danish King Frederick III had allowed Dutch Arminians to settle there when they had repudiated Calvin's doctrine of predestination. Later, other churches had joined them — Reformed congregations, Mennonites, Remonstrants. Even Catholics who had been persecuted in Protestant countries found refuge here. I can never forget the Sunday mornings when the air was filled with the sound of all the various bells calling the faithful to worship. And no matter how greatly the preachers may have differed in their views, the bells all spoke the same language and were in harmony with one another.

Frederick III's humaneness had paid good dividends. Friedrichstadt owes its Dutch character to those Arminians — a character which has been preserved to this day: the dead-straight canals with their neat borders of stone or turf, the little bridges, the flower gardens and hedges. A further point is that Friedrichstadt lies in the middle of a real Friesian marsh setting.

Never again have I so appreciated my North German home as I did during those six weeks in the Eider neighborhood.

Despite his great age Grandfather was still a practicing parish doctor. A year later he was appointed Medical Officer of Health, but he never knew what to do with the title. Medical Officer of Health — what on earth was that? To his patients he was the parish doctor till the day of his death at the age of eighty-five.

At sixteen one looks at the world with different eyes. What I had not realized during my previous visit four years earlier, I now felt very distinctly: this was my real home, and Grandfather the connecting link between past and present. He was born in the year of the Battle of Leipzig and had witnessed the passing of almost an entire century. The whole toughness of his race showed itself in the way in which, unburdened by age, he handled his patients and, the day's work done, would get into a rough tweed suit and stroll for an hour around the market place with its many trees, smoking his long pipe and replying with good-humored grunts to the greetings of his fellow townsmen. Sometimes I think I have inherited my own toughness from this same grandfather, although in my case there is also a good dose of Eggers temperament that my grandfather lacked. In all his dealings he was calm, very deliberate, never excited or upset.

Of course I helped him in his practice. Much more interesting than sitting in my classroom at the Johanneum and estimating third-dimension curves. Above all, it was more human.

Part of his duties as parish doctor consisted in keeping the territory at the mouth of the Eider clear of suspicious intruders who, under certain circumstances, might import cholera from Hamburg. What steps he took I no longer remember. An essential factor was, however, his wide experience during his medical career. Although he certainly did not go to work according to the most modern methods, his district nevertheless remained free of the disease.

I remember one day when a chubby-faced, redheaded cattle dealer from Hamburg strode heavily into the consulting room. He was examined and given a clean bill of health. Somewhat relieved he took a deep breath, leaned confidingly against Grandfather's writing table and explained why he had been scared at this visit.

"You'll understand, Doctor," he said, "I've come here on business."

Grandfather blinked slightly, "All right, go ahead," he advised. "But see here, mind what I'm telling you. It's not easy to pull off a deal with our Eiderstedt farmers. Many a cattle dealer has tried his hand at it and after a bit he has packed up and left. By then the farmers have had his cash and he has had his experience."

During my previous visits I had learned from Grandfather some details of past family history. This time, however, I felt that he would welcome the opportunity of saying something about the province and the people to whom it gave birth. In the course of those six weeks I came by almost all the knowledge I possess about my family. Betweentimes, too, he was interested in my progress at school and asked whether I knew what I wanted to do. I said frankly that I hadn't yet made up my mind. Perhaps I might go in for medicine like Eddy — perhaps something else.

He did not worry. "We Schachts always mature late and live all the longer in consequence," he said. "You'll find out soon enough what you want to do. The wise man takes his time!"

I was much attracted by Grandfather's big bookcase where I discovered a complete edition of Hebbel's plays. We had studied some of them at school — not surprising since Hebbel's first work, *Judith*, had been written in Hamburg. Grandfather noticed the book in my hand, looked over my shoulder and tapped the pages with the mouthpiece of his long pipe.

"I knew him well," he said.

"Who? Hebbel?" I asked incredulously. He nodded.

"Certainly. He was the son of a mason in Wesselburen — between Büsum and Heide. At that time I was doing my year's practical training in pharmacology at the chemist's in Wesselburen and occasionally went home on Sundays. I came to know Hebbel during that year — he was writing church plays in Wesselburen, poor chap. He was very keen to learn Latin so that he could read the Latin authors, and I gave him lessons for nearly a year."

"You gave Hebbel Latin lessons?"

Once again he nodded. "Nobody so much as mentioned his name in those days," he said, "and nobody would have believed that he had a future. Poor devil, he was ambitious and full of queer stilted expressions. But clever — very clever. Later on Amalie Schoppe, the Hamburg author, took him back with her so that he might have a chance of fitting himself for real study. And study he did, but I don't think he was ever really happy. He was one of those people who think they can do everything. But that doesn't work. Look at our family — it took two generations to turn me into an ordinary G.P. That's the way of the world. But Hebbel wanted to get there all at once. He often used to write to me — his letters were a bit stilted and queer — he was like that. But very, very clever. And a great dramatist . . . "

I never would have thought that my somewhat dry old stick of a grandfather could have been so closely connected with poetry. Where were those letters? Had he kept them?

"They're somewhere among all the junk in the attic. You can look for them if you like. I haven't thrown them away."

I climbed up to the loft and hunted through the old boxes and chests. There were packets of letters in now faded ink. At last I found what I sought. Friedrich Hebbel's letters to my grandfather written when Grandfather was studying in Copenhagen. They were the same age.

I found the great dramatist's letters to my grandfather deeply moving. It must be remembered that when he wrote them Hebbel was a completely unknown young man with visions of the great outside world, but no prospects. Nevertheless his letters contain sentences such as the following, which became my guiding star:

If we cannot be together, if I am engulfed in the widest of circles and you in a narrow one, I shall yet leave a true and faithful impress of my whole being in works of the heart and the intellect, and you will always be a welcome guest at this repast — perhaps not an unwilling one — the more so, maybe, since you will have known the tree while it was still in the bud and have experienced its sharpest (though purest) flavor.

Grandfather must have noticed that I set particular store by the letters and also by a copy of the *Dithmarschen Messenger* which contained the first contributions from Hebbel's pen and which I had also discovered in the attic. So when one day I received a letter from the Johanneum saying that they had resumed activities, he made me a present of everything I had found. I thanked him, packed my bags, said goodbye and went back to Hamburg. The old gentleman remained standing in the doorway in his tweed coat, his long-stemmed pipe in his hand. I never saw him again. Six years later he was found dead in bed. The pipe had fallen from his hand and was still alight.

I returned to Hamburg where many men wore mourning bands on their arms and many women black veils. In the city great discussions were in progress; the Senate was blamed for not having troubled sufficiently about the well-being of the inhabitants.

In the home of my Wedel doctor I found the pretty daughter, the stout papa and the scraggy stepmother. Once again short rations were the order of the day. I thought longingly of Grandfather's good table, the big joints with their crisp crackling, the flat hot scones for breakfast, the sole, brill and turbot that his housekeeper used to fry in butter.

I resumed my studies and gave private lessons. At last I had saved enough to be able to collect the bicycle I had ordered. It cost me two hundred and fifty marks, a tremendous sum in those days. It was not so long since my mother had kept house for more than a month on that amount. But the world was on the upgrade, money was plentiful everywhere; progress was the watchword, earnings increased from day to day. The manager of the bicycle shop wrote in his order book: "Hjalmar Schacht, student, saved the money for his bicycle by private tutoring." I could not dream that the Opel firm would one day dig out this old book and publish that entry as a good advertisement for the business. But that was not until 1936 . . .

Any country lover will realize what a bicycle meant to a sixteen-year-old boy. I went for long rides to lower Saxony and Mecklenburg, up and down the Elbe. Then came the winter, and even my bicycle could not make up for conditions in the doctor's house at Wedel. My room was never heated, my intake of calories was insufficient. My exasperation was increased by the fact that every morning the washing water was solid ice. My country drives with the doctor became more and more frequent and many were the prolonged sessions and talks we enjoyed over steaming glasses of grog.

My liking for grog dates from that time, and the doctor's gray horse seemed no less appreciative of the intervals afforded by our visits to the bar parlor. If, in the course of his rounds, the doctor attempted to pass a village pub, the good creature refused to let him. Ignoring the reins, he would turn in at the entrance and there was nothing for it but to get out and have a pint. My doctor was a witty fellow with bright ideas, and during our drives together he was always in the best of tempers.

"What's the difference between high land and marsh land?" I asked him on one occasion.

He winked. "I'll tell you, my dear student," he said. "It's like this. If I drive down there through Hetlingen and my gray drops something, not a soul bothers about it. But if that happens up at Holm, a farmer'll come rushing out of the house, one on each side, with broom and shovel, and yell: 'That's my bit of dung!'"

I took advantage of the long winter evenings to write pages of verse to my adored one, the doctor's daughter. All in vain. The heartless girl refused to take me seriously and made fun of my poems. One day she seized her chance and locked me into a certain outside apartment. That was the last straw. I saw no reason to remain any longer in that house, gave notice — ostensibly because of a moldy cheese rind that my hostess had put up by way of sandwich for school lunch — and left. From one of my acquaintances I heard that a clockmaker and his wife living in St. George's were willing to board a grammar-school boy.

# V

## A MEETING WITH BISMARCK

ALTHOUGH NOWADAYS grammar-school pupils in the top forms have to tackle the differential calculus and organic chemistry I don't believe that we sixth-formers had an easier time. In my day the school set especial store by the behavior of the older boys. They were people of importance and were expected to behave as though they were already grown up.

Grave, stiff, dressed in dark suits, with white silk caps on our heads, we made our way daily to the vast building on the Speersort. But our gravity was sometimes deceptive. This became apparent when our old Headmaster, Hoche, was succeeded by a new man who was to have the effect of a fresh breeze on the somewhat leisurely ways of the school. The new Head, Schultes, was a first-rate man, only a bit too keen. The upper forms, which had grown large under Hoche's rule, were thoroughly riled by his keenness and determined to get their own back. There was to be a binge for the 1893 top-formers who had passed their final examination. At this party a *Bierzeitung* — a humorous gazette specially got up for the occasion — was read out. In it the "Muli" (the nickname given to the graduates after the examination and before they entered the University) unmercifully lampooned their school and their Headmaster. The new Head took the whole thing in the wrong spirit and left the gathering, obviously deeply offended.

Personally, I got along very well indeed under Professor Schultes. My interests were many and varied, particularly in the realms of intellectual subjects, as well as contemporary history, geography, languages and literature. Schultes liked that. He encouraged his pupils to tackle unusual subjects. Occasionally, when he asked a question that had nothing to do with the subject, he would look at me through his spectacles and say: "Come, come, Schacht, you know it!" Sometimes I did know the answer. Then he would grin with satisfaction. We got along very well together.

During those years I also learned a lot from Uncle Wieding, whom

I often used to meet on Sundays. We would go for a stroll along the river or forsake the town in favor of a country walk.

As a young man Uncle Wieding — a native of Hamburg — had fought in the battle of Idstedt. There cannot be many today who know what this battle was about. It decided the outcome of the fight between Schleswig-Holstein and Denmark. The Prussian General Willesen was beaten by a superior Danish force and compelled to retreat. All this happened near the little village of Idstedt on the main road between Schleswig and Flensburg.

Uncle Wieding had fought on the losing side. But before the battle had been completely lost he had done something that millions of others have done before and since: he had shot a Dane and killed him.

He took this incident deeply to heart. He was a civilian and a townsman through and through, and had not bothered his head over what might be expected of him once he was in uniform. Then came the Battle of Idstedt. Uncle Wieding, fighting mad like the rest, overcome by the general lust of battle, raised his rifle and fired.

"I saw the Dane I was aiming at. I saw my bullet hit him, saw him fall and lie there — dead. And in the same moment I realized: You have killed a man, another human being, made in God's image — like yourself . . . "

Uncle Wieding would never have killed a man of his own free will. He was inoffensive, good-natured, always ready to come to the aid of man or beast. What kind of unnatural mental confusion must have occurred to make such a man kill another in the heat of battle? What kind of battle was it anyway?

In spite of Uncle Wieding's shot the campaign was lost — but even after this sacrifice of blood the frontier between Germany and Denmark was not really settled. It was perpetually being shifted about by politicians — and it may continue to be shifted about, even now.

I don't think many men looked upon international history from the same standpoint as Uncle Wieding. Certainly Uncle Hermann Eggers, the first lieutenant, had no qualms of conscience whatever over the enemies he had dispatched during the War of 1870. People were beginning to envisage great things — technical progress, international markets, monster fleets and huge stocks of raw materials.

Ever since those walks with Uncle Wieding I have, for my own part, repudiated the idea that the problems of this world can ever be solved by violent methods.

There is frequent mention these days of "lost generations." The first lost generation of modern times were undoubtedly the Liberals who were done out of their opportunities thanks to the events of the fateful year 1888. Among these Liberals I include Uncle Wieding.

To my sixth-form period belongs also another meeting — this time with a man who was in every respect the complete antithesis of my gentle uncle. I am reminded of the torchlight procession staged by us older boys in 1893 in honor of the venerable Prince Otto von Bismarck.

Since the construction of the Free Port and the Customs Union with the Empire had turned out so advantageous for Hamburg, the inhabitants entertained a deep and warm respect for the Chancellor, which increased still further when Wilhelm II tactlessly dismissed Bismarck in 1890.

Bismarck was seventy-eight years old on April 1, 1893. For almost fifty years he had been a master of politics such as has never appeared since. He had created the empire of which we were a part — backed up by an emperor who had never let him down.

The forms which were to take part in the ceremony had already left by steamer for Friedrichsruh in the afternoon, each member armed with a torch of pitchpine. As dusk fell on that spring evening they formed fours and made ready to march off. I was class orderly at the time and as such was responsible for leading my section — I think it was the only time in my life that I held a semi-military rank. The original plan had been to give the orderlies magnesium torches, but later this idea had been discarded since the white glare of these torches would have dazzled the old gentleman and destroyed the general impression. So it came about that in addition to my pitchpine torch I had an unlit one of magnesium.

At last it was dark enough, and the huge procession of schoolboys, like some gigantic serpent, moved off toward the Friedrichsruh entrance gate. The torches were lit, and the millipedic column tramped across the gravel.

I glanced back and saw the faces of my schoolfellows enveloped in smoke, illumined by the flickering red lights of the pine branches. Then I looked ahead of me and saw the Chancellor.

He was wearing the uniform of the Halberstadt Cuirassiers, and stood erect in the archway, his left hand resting on the pommel of his sword, while from time to time he raised his right hand in salute. On his left breast gleamed the Iron Cross, First Class; the buttons on his uniform reflected the light from the torches and the dark material was almost completely merged in the background.

Someone behind me said, "The Iron Chancellor," and I have never been able to forget the description. There he stood, drawn up to his full height, tightly wedged into his uncomfortable uniform, a deep furrow between the bushy eyebrows, his asymmetrically shaped eyes under their heavy lids fixed keenly and earnestly on the schoolboys.

I was to see many a picture of him in later years, but none ever came up to that picture engraved in my memory.

A tremendous solemnity emanated from the old man, as though he alone foresaw how onerous and dark the future would be, how little reason there was to look forward hopefully to the coming century. Many decades later, when the significance of that era had become more apparent, I recalled again and again the penetrating, grave expression of the Chancellor's keen eyes. What had he tried to tell us by that look? A duty, a warning, a plea that we should not allow his work to be carelessly destroyed?

That same evening I returned to Wedel from Blankensee. The last suburban train had left long before we arrived back in Hamburg: an hour and a half's steady tramp lay ahead of me.

I trudged along by the Elbe, absorbed in recollection. I was not thinking of the Emperor Wilhelm II who, only a few years ago, had struck me as being so smart and well turned out; nor of genial, kindhearted Uncle Wieding: I could think of no one but Prince Bismarck.

For a single instant, in my position as orderly, I had had the feeling that the old man had been looking at me alone, that he and I were the only people there. It was only for an instant; then I had passed by and others saw the Prince and doubtless thought that he looked personally at each of them.

I longed desperately to do something to express my admiration for the Chancellor. Suddenly I felt a hard object against my arm; I looked down and saw the unlighted magnesium torch. Following an impulse I felt for some matches, lit the torch and held it high above my head as I tramped along the high road above the Elbe.

Below me ships' sirens hooted, red, green and white lights blinked, propellers threshed the water that hissed and foamed. I went on my way, paying an entirely personal torchlight tribute to Prince Otto von Bismarck, of which he would always remain in complete ignorance.

The sailors on the Elbe may well have thought that a lunatic had been let loose and was endangering the river traffic with his idiotic torchlight. Well, let them! Those sailors on the Elbe can have had no idea how the heart of a sixteen-year-old schoolboy can be ablaze with hero worship for an old man — a really grand old man.

Two years later my form was preparing for the final examination. As the authorities did not want any failures, all doubtful candidates were warned in good time to enter their names for a date six months ahead. In this way all nineteen of us passed.

As I have already mentioned, we were examined in groups on two successive days. Anyone who did well in a written examination was excused from the viva. Luckily this happened with my math test, in which I was so successful in the written part that I passed — which gave me great satisfaction. In Hebrew, too, I was exempted from the viva.

At last came the day when I found myself outside, my certificate in my hand. I went to the nearest telegraph office and wired home: PASSED FINAL EXAM SUCCESSFULLY   HJALMAR. Then I set about packing my things and sending boxes and trunks to the station. My nice clockmaker people wept a little and congratulated me warmly. They said that in a few years' time I should certainly be able to call myself Doctor. That, to them, was the essence of erudition.

I had no idea what I should be in a few years' time. Fritsch, my form master, had asked me a few days before the examination what I thought of becoming. Rather wickedly I said, "A professor like you, Professor." Fritsch, himself not lacking in irony, looked at me and shook his head, smiling: "I don't see you doing that . . . "

He was right — I never did become a professor. As yet I did not know what I wanted to be. But I had passed my final exam and was going to college. I was full of self-confidence and optimism while jogging back to Berlin in a fourth-class railway carriage.

There my enthusiasm was somewhat damped by my father who congratulated me on my success and added dryly: "But you really needn't have sent a wire. A twopenny postcard would have done just as well!"

"Still, it *is* his final exam, William," said Mother. But Father thought otherwise.

"Rubbish! It was obvious from the first that my son would pass his exam. There was no need to rush off and telegraph as though the skies had fallen . . . "

# VI

## AT THE UNIVERSITY

WHEN MY PARENTS first moved to Berlin in 1892 they rented a house in Charlottenburg. A few steps from the house was a field where cows grazed and one could buy a glass of milk fresh from the cow for five cents. Today the Zoological Gardens occupy the site that was so rural then.

As soon as he could afford it my father built himself a little villa outside Berlin at Schlachtensee, which has long since been incorporated in the capital. I still remember the flagstaff in front of the house with the American Stars and Stripes. Since he had acquired American citizenship while in New York, and at bottom was very liberal-minded, he took great pleasure in this little demonstration.

Here I spent the Easter holidays in 1895 and discussed with my parents and Eddy what career I should take up. My mother would have liked to see me go in for theology, but I had little inclination for that subject.

Eddy, in his fifth year as a medical student, persuaded me to follow in his footsteps. I was not altogether convinced that it was really my line but decided to have a shot at it.

During the three years I had lived on my own in Hamburg (up to the time I left school) I had grown independent. The severe upbringing at the Johanneum had had something to do with it. My father was quite pleased. He made me a modest monthly allowance, and unlike many fathers, did not attempt to interfere with my plans for the future. Later, too, when I frequently changed from one faculty to another and tackled subjects that seemed to lie poles apart, he invariably displayed great understanding and let me go my own way.

"Look around and choose whatever you feel is the right thing," he told me.

So when the Easter holidays were over I mounted my bicycle and

set out for Kiel with Eddy to register at the University as a student
of medicine. Kiel, the capital of the province of Schleswig-Holstein,
was in fact our home university.

My parents remained in Berlin with the two younger ones. Oluf
was a restless youngster, somewhat stubborn and not always straight.
William, the youngest, was my mother's acknowledged favorite.
He grew up the best-looking and the most good-tempered of all her
children.

Life at the University began differently for me than I had expected. Eddy was a devil-may-care young fellow, very intelligent,
quite unmoved by "exam nerves" — and very much one for the
girls. Now and again one of the charmers would deliberately set
her cap at him and for the time being he would be in a tight corner.
But it never lasted long. Eddy took life lightheartedly.

Outwardly we were very much alike and Eddy capitalized on this.
When, for instance, he had made simultaneous dates with two
girls he would send me to cope with one of them while he met the
other whom, presumably, he found the more attractive.

I was reading histology and osteology (the study of tissue and
bone) and beginning to tackle the structure and building up of
the human body. But no matter how hard I tried I couldn't work
up any real liking for the subject. So long as we were content to
preserve parts of tissues in paraffin in the histological laboratory
lecture room and cut them into the thinnest of wafers I could hold
my own with anyone. But when it came to analyzing our self-pre-
pared specimens under the microscope and determining whether we
were dealing with a lengthwise or crosswise muscular system, with
mucosa or submucosa, then I gave up. Whichever way I studied
it, one tissue looked just like another to me.

I began to cast my eye in other directions. An old enthusiasm,
to which I had given free rein while still in Wedel, reasserted itself:
I began once again to write verses and, alongside the study of medicine, to delve into the history of literature.

All this may sound rather confused. Actually, during my first
years at the University, I experimented in all directions until I
finally decided on political economy. My working terms of six
months each may be summarized as follows:

Summer 1895: Kiel. Medicine, Germanic Philology, History of
Literature. Winter 95/96: Berlin. Germanic Philology, History of
Literature, Journalism. Summer 1896. Munich. Political Economy

and Germanic Philology. Winter 96/97. Leipzig. Science of
Journalism, Political Economy. Summer 1897. Berlin. Political
Economy, Rhetoric. Winter 97/98. Paris. French, Sociology. Sum-
mer 1898. Kiel. Political Economy. Winter 98/99. Kiel. Political
Economy. Summer 1899. Kiel. Reading for Degree of Doctor of
Political Economy, Doctor of Philosophy (M.A.).

In four and a half years I attended five different universities; during the first seven terms I changed my university every term (every
six months) and experimented with subjects that had little to do
with each other.

I have always envied those young fellows who have gone straight
from school to the university, read half a dozen subjects and passed
one or two examinations at lightning speed. Usually, however, after
that final tour de force, they are finished, played out. Their ambition
is satisfied; they are content to sink into a pleasant middle-class
existence. They have proved that they are capable of satisfying the
demands of our civilization. The only other time we hear of them
is when their obituary appears in the newspapers.

To know what one wants, and to be able to steer straight for one's
objective, it is necessary amid the many opportunities offered by a
modern university to consult first-rate advisers, older friends and
favorable connections, and I lacked all these things. I stood alone
in the great hall and stared at the announcements on the black-
board: many of them conveyed some meaning, others again conveyed nothing whatever. It took me a long time to discover in what
department, which lecture room and which professors, I should
find what I was looking for. I didn't even know what I was looking
for; I was feeling my way; I made mistakes, miscalculations. It took
longer but the time was not wasted.

It was a very jolly first term. One of my friends was a member
of a wine merchant's family whose father sent him a present of a
small cask of Moselle. We took the cask, a basket of strawberries,
sugar, some assorted drinking vessels and went by ferry to Heikendorf on the Bay of Kiel. There we swam and afterwards made a
magnificent strawberry punch. When we boarded the last steamer
from Heikendorf at eight o'clock none of us could walk straight. For
some unknown reason I carried the empty cask under my arm and
was quite determined not to let it go. The first thing some of us
did when we reached Kiel was to take one of the crowd, who was
dead drunk, back to his room. I stayed where I was, still carrying
the cask, and leaned against a garden fence. Suddenly a bunch of

youngsters emerged from nowhere in particular, crowded around and burst out laughing. Still leaning against the fence I began to laugh too. I had no idea what we were laughing at; and it was only the next morning that my landlady enlightened me — the fence had just been freshly painted in bright green! My landlady had to remove the green zebra stripes from my jacket with benzine, accompanied by some plain speaking!

No less memorable was another trip that Eddy and I made somewhere about the end of our first month. We were both completely broke and made up our minds to look up our Uncle Hjalmar von Eggers, head of the sugar factory at Nykjöbing near Falster. We cycled to Lübeck, boarded the steamer for Falster and settled ourselves comfortably, having only just enough money for fares.

But the crossing lasted all night and we were hungry. Eddy went off to reconnoiter in the direction of the saloon and returned with the news that some excellent Danish Smørbrod was to be had at a very reasonable price.

"But we've only just enough for our fares," I objected. Eddy shrugged his shoulders.

"Let's eat, anyway," he said lightly. "The captain is sure to know Uncle Hjalmar — he'll stand us our fares till we get to Falster." That sounded right enough — after all, the captain couldn't very well throw us overboard.

We strolled into the saloon, ate Smørbrod and drank beer. At last we were full, and our purses empty. We went to the captain, introduced ourselves as Herr von Eggers' nephews and assured him that Uncle Hjalmar would settle the bill. The captain, who knew our uncle, made no objection.

On arrival we found Uncle Hjalmar just setting out for the races. He invited us to accompany him and we should have accepted with pleasure; unfortunately, the captain remained in the background expecting us to pay our debt.

When Uncle Hjalmar heard what we had been up to he cooled off considerably. He gave the captain the money for the journey, handed us a sum which just covered the return trip to Kiel and no more, and bade us a frigid farewell.

There we stood, in the morning sunshine, staring dumbly at each other; then we trotted across to the harbor and returned to Kiel much discomfited by our unkind reception.

"I imagined our aristocratic relative would have given us a warmer welcome," Eddy grumbled.

"If you hadn't guzzled all those sandwiches and beer Uncle Hjalmar would have been friendlier," I said. "But to start begging the moment we arrived — well, it does look bad."

"All right, no need to get mad," Eddy growled. "Those sandwiches and the beer were the best part of the whole trip."

And to tell the truth he wasn't far wrong . . . !

In July 1895 an event took place in Kiel which was scarcely less memorable than the laying of the foundation stone in the Free Port of Hamburg; namely, the opening of the North Baltic Canal by no less a personage than Wilhelm II. It was called the Kaiser-Wilhelm-Canal after his grandfather who had laid the foundation of the lock at Kiel-Holtenau the year before he died. From here the canal runs straight across country ending at Brunsbüttelkoog on the Elbe.

Warships from dozens of foreign countries were present; the German Navy was in full dress-ship, their crews in gala uniforms; all Kiel was ablaze with bunting. Launches carrying distinguished guests in naval, gold-braided uniform, bustled through the harbor, guards of honor of the Marines were drawn up at the landing stages. Germany, which in recent years had become Navy-conscious, was celebrating in Kiel an event that was to have far-reaching political consequences. First of all for the inhabitants themselves, the opening of this canal meant that Kiel was henceforth directly linked with the naval squadrons operating in the triangle of the North Sea. German liners need no longer go round by the Skagerrak and Kattegat; they were no longer dependent on the benevolent neutrality of the Scandinavian countries. The port of Kiel could thus become the second arsenal of the German Navy.

The new canal also acquired a far-reaching commercial-political importance. In 1913, eighteen years after its inauguration, and the last year of peace, goods to the value of ten million net registered tons passed through the Kaiser-Wilhelm-Canal in twelve months; in 1929 the total was more than twenty-one million tons. In that same year (1929) the Panama Canal averaged thirty million tons, the Suez Canal twenty-eight million. The Kaiser-Wilhelm-Canal was therefore not far behind . . .

Of course we spent the whole week wandering about the harbor, admiring the strange sailors from other countries, endeavoring to identify the various naval ensigns and studying with the greatest interest the extraordinary signals transmitted by the visitors, in daytime with semaphore flags, at night in Morse with flashlamps. These were the happy years of peace. No one thought of war. We stumbled over iron rivets on deck and listened to the explanations of our guides (whom I suspect of stuffing us with all sorts of yarns while keeping perfectly straight faces); we gazed in astonishment at the muzzles of the heavy-caliber guns projecting from the clumsy-looking turrets of the new dreadnoughts. But we never for one moment dreamed that they would ever be used in earnest; the very idea seemed incongruous. The world was making rapid progress; each year saw us all a step further on the upward grade. We already had internal-combustion motors; the first incandescent lamps were already in use; people were already talking of dirigible airships, the kind that my father had foretold by the light of the paraffin lamp in our Hamburg home. The world appeared fully occupied in producing all those miracles which year after year were being invented by technical and scientific experts.

No, we had no thought of war . . .

That same summer I went for a long cycle trip to Jutland, and visited my mother's sister — the one who had refused Uncle Wieding many years ago. Aunt Toni had married a Dane, Oerstedt by name, a Councilor of State and Lord Mayor. On my return journey I went to all those places where my peasant Schacht ancestors had lived and battled against inroads of the North Sea.

As a matter of fact this was no chance trip. On the way I came to a decision as to my future plans. Back in Kiel I said goodbye to medicine, studied the list of lectures and attended courses on the general history of literature. By way of filling in the remaining days of that summer term I unearthed the letters I had carried around with me ever since I had stayed with my grandfather in Friedrichstadt — the correspondence between Hebbel and the future Dr. Schacht.

I went through these valuable papers and arranged them in proper order, wrote an appropriate commentary and sent the whole thing to the *Magazin für Literatur* (Literary Review) — in those days a publication of high standing — which soon afterwards published my contribution.

Hebbel's actual letters traveled further afield and ended up in the Goethe-Schiller archives in Weimar. My work for the *Review* provided me with a certain incentive. Of course I could not expect to come upon and publish original letters from a famous German poet every day. But I had enjoyed this work so much that I stuck to it for the time being.

At the end of my first term I returned to Berlin and attended every course of lectures on Germanic philology which could possibly be crammed into a single timetable.

At the same time I joined a students' literary society, the Academic and Literary Union. While the society fought no duels it gave much satisfaction. Dr. Franz Ullstein was also a member of this circle; so was Arthur Dix, the future editor of the *National-Zeitung*.

Through Dix I was inspired to follow yet another trail. That was in my third term, which I spent in Munich. He suggested that I should attend the course of lectures on political economy given by the famous political economist Lujo Brantano. I acted on this advice and found the lectures so enthralling that I promptly abandoned Germanistic philology and devoted myself entirely to political economy.

In those days political economy was looked upon as a very second-rate subject. "All the fools and failures practice Economy" was the opinion of lawyers, theologians, doctors and philologists, the old inhabitants of their Alma Mater; and by that they meant political economy.

From Munich I went for a term to Leipzig to Professor Karl Bücher in order to study journalism — a territory which had attracted my attention for some time and about which Professor Bücher (a former editor of the *Frankfurter Zeitung*) had written.

Nowadays this is nothing unusual. But during my career as a student newspapers were still regarded as a necessary evil and a journalist — to quote Bismarck — as "a man who has mistaken his calling."

Unfortunately it soon became evident that Karl Bücher set store only by those students who wanted to take their doctor's degree and were prepared to spend several terms under his tuition. Since that was not my intention I returned to Berlin. But I did not sever my active connections with the press on that account. The year before I went to Leipzig I had already experienced the desire to take up journalism. How was a newspaper created? What sort of men were they who by day and night supplied and remodeled the news that filled the pages of the morning papers?

During my second term in Berlin it dawned upon me that it was idiotic to write about "the paper" when one had no practical knowledge of how a newspaper was produced. I had discussed this idea with my father, who had shown himself to be very open-minded. After all, he had had me christened after one of the most famous newspapermen of the United States. And he himself had been a journalist.

"What have you in mind when you speak of practical work on a newspaper?" he asked.

"I'd like to work for a few months at least in a newspaper office," I explained.

He thought this over. "I could have a talk with Dr. Leipziger," he said. "He is the head of the *Kleines Journal* — admittedly it isn't one of the leading newspapers! But still — we have business dealings with him — I will see what can be done, if you're really eager."

That was in January 1896 when I was just nineteen. On his way to the office next day my father called on Herr Leipziger and told him what I wanted to do. Herr Leipziger, who had a high opinion of my father, replied that I could start on February 1 as an "unpaid assistant" on the *Kleines Journal.*

"Tell him — as an ordinary unpaid assistant," said Leipziger. "We pay no special attention to students . . . "

# VII

## AN UNPAID ASSISTANT ON THE *KLEINES JOURNAL*

"HAVE YOU ever written anything?" enquired the head of the local news department, Herr Fürstenheim, when I presented myself at his office on the morning of February 1. He spoke in a loud, sarcastic and somewhat condescending voice.

I was nettled. Had I ever written anything — of course I had! Whole volumes!

"What?" asked Fürstenheim curtly.

"Poems," I said.

I had even had poems published — one, to be exact. And in order to have these verses printed in the *Weiner Dichterheim* I had had to pay five marks. The *Wiener Dichterheim* was supported by poets who paid to have their verses printed.

"Ha! Poetry!" barked Fürstenheim. He rummaged in an untidy heap of papers on his desk, pulled out a slip and said,

"Go along to the Weidendamm Bridge — it's half completed — and write me twelve lines — understand? No more."

Nothing simpler, I thought, took the slip of paper and set out for the bridge.

I could easily have written two thousand lines about this magnificent bridge. I could have described the gulls disporting themselves and reflected in the muddy Spree, the red-nosed children standing on the bank looking on at the workmen; the workmen themselves, and their tools. But Herr Fürstenheim had not asked for two thousand nor even for two hundred: no — he wanted just twelve lines.

I hurried back to the office and mulled over those twelve lines. I sat down and filled three sheets — I deleted a sentence here, another there. Suddenly an editor burst into the office and shouted:

"Herr Schacht, where's your twelve lines? D'you think the Berliners can wait till tomorrow morning for the *Journal* just so you can sit and write poetry?" He caught sight of the written sheets and snatched them from under my hand.

"Stop, stop!" I called after him. "My report isn't finished!"

"No time!" he replied over his shoulder and hurried off, waving my pages like so many captured standards. "Make-up can't wait."

I followed him and stared around the composing room. Everywhere were men with lengths of queer-looking grooved iron into which they were tossing letters with nimble fingers. The letters came out of little boxes standing on a desk. The compositors didn't even seem to look at what they were doing. Their fingers flew between boxes and composing clamp — just one or two more blanks in between the letters and they were already lifting the rows of type out of the clamp and placing them in the huge iron galley in which many other rows were ready waiting. From the next room came the muffled clatter of the linotype machines.

I was so fascinated by this sight that I completely forgot my report. Someone had snatched the half-finished copy out of my hand. Where was he? I looked around and saw the man who had made off with my pages. At the same moment he saw me, winked, nodded slightly and turned again to the make-up hands. In the meantime the latter had lifted one of the galleys and carried it, supported on their knees, from the composing table to a low stand. Here it was inked with a roller, a sheet of paper laid over it and brushed firmly on to the galley with a brush. There was a queer hissing noise as the make-up foreman pulled the page from the galley.

"Hm!" said Fürnstenheim, and scribbled something in green on the margin of the brush-proof, "not at all bad for a beginner — quite a nice little report."

I squinted over his shoulder and read my report on the Weidendamm Bridge. Then I blushed scarlet. There was not a single word of mine in it. The editor had written it up himself — after a brief glance at my notes. And I had to admit he had written it very well.

"That'll cost you a round of beer to square up," the make-up hand whispered. "Later, when the boss is gone!"

I nodded, and glanced quickly around. All the compositors and make-up men seemed to be grinning quietly. Only Herr Fürstenheim appeared to take no notice of anything that was going on.

I kept my eyes wide open during my time as unpaid assistant in Berlin, and learned just how a newspaper is produced. It was instructive and quite different from anything I had imagined. Everything that went to the making of the *Kleines Journal* seemed to me at first to originate in the most haphazard way: it was thrown together anyhow and combined according to formulas which, to me, appeared completely senseless. It took me quite a while to realize that it was not chance that was responsible for the birth of the *Journal*, but that, on the contrary, the editors knew very well what they wanted.

At their head stood Leipziger, staunch old Leipziger who on festive occasions sported a "Red Eagle Fourth Class" in his buttonhole. One might have supposed that a paper directed by him would have had radical tendencies. But no — Leipziger was a monarchist and would allow no aspersions to be cast on his beloved Hohenzollern. Palace doings were taboo so far as he was concerned; no invidious court gossip ever appeared in the pages of his *Journal*. The Red Eagle ribbon may have had something to do with it for Herr Leipziger was as proud of that as a French Minister might be of his ribbon of the Legion of Honor. Monarchs were, after all, full of wisdom!

So long as gossip had nothing to do with the court, there was no limit or restriction to Leipziger's enthusiasm. The *Journal* was a mixture of society scandal and American "yellow press" — the sort of thing that is nowadays contemptuously described as "pulp." The circulation was not large: it was printed at Büchsenstein's the printers and edited in the Friedrichstrasse in a house close to the Apollo Theater where we foregathered every day with renewed energy.

At Fürstenheim's instigation I would go out and about Berlin every day and would return with small reports. I visited societies for the protection of animals, rabbit clubs, annual gatherings of Allotment holders and Hairdressers' Guilds, variety performances and circus shows. It was not always easy to obey this reporter-muse when one had been accustomed to the somewhat highbrow seriousness of the university. Sometimes I managed to strike the right note. Then Fürstenheim was pleased and said so. More often, however, I perpetrated reports that were right outside the framework of the *Kleines Journal*.

"Too hifalutin," Fürstenheim would say in his Berlin dialect. "Y'must learn to write popular stuff, Herr Schacht." Or: "Who d'you think'll be interested in that rubbish, Herr Schacht? Didn't anything else happen at the dance?"

"The chairman made a speech," I replied condescendingly.

"Well, wasn't it interesting?"

"Really, Herr Fürstenheim, I can't think of anything that might have interested anyone."

He looked at me out of the corner of his eyes, blinking like an owl in sunlight. His voice took on a sarcastic note. "So! Y'can't think of anything? But y'must think of something, Herr Schacht, or you'll never make a journalist. People aren't interested in your opinions but in th'kind of thing they enjoy reading in the paper. That's th'kind of thing you've got t'write."

I have never had better journalistic advice. Everybody — myself not excepted — expects his newspaper to write the kind of thing he enjoys reading.

After I had been there a few weeks Herr Falk, the *feuilleton* editor, would give me an occasional play to write up, which meant three marks "exes" and a complimentary ticket. In this way I went to the theater free, and since I never missed a play during my student days, these write-up assignments were very welcome. At that time there were two outstanding men of the theater in Berlin — Otto Brahm and, somewhat later, Max Reinhardt. Of course in the Academic and Literary Union we would discuss the theater for nights on end. Reinhardt's new stage technique has become a matter of history, but Brahm's work is known only to the initiated. Under these two men Berlin leaped to the forefront and became one of the foremost stage cities of Europe. The theatrical style of the Vienna Burgtheater school was superseded in Berlin by the new realistic style.

In those days the shining lights of the Berlin theater were actors and actresses such as Matkowsky, Kainz and Agnes Sorma, dramatic critics of the stature of Theodor Fontane and Paul Schlenther, playwrights such as Hauptmann and Sudermann.

Nor was the lighter side of the theater less well equipped. There were the new operettas modeled on the French vaudeville or English musical comedies: works by Paul Lincke staged at the Apollo Theater and by Victor Hollaender at the Metropol. There would be an unassuming original Jewish comedy in some side street or other where Berlin dialect and Yiddish had full scope. Then there were the Berlin low comedians such as Bendix, that prince of funny men, and the famous Thomas who would rattle off their nonsense before a riotously appreciative audience all out for a good time. For an entire day Berlin would roar with laughter at these jokes * — the next day there would be fresh ones. And the

---

* Unfortunately, like so many jokes in all languages which depend on puns and play on words, they are completely untranslatable.

whole town would be humming the melodies of Lincke and Hollaender.

Much that I learned as unpaid assistant in Berlin I was able later to turn to good account.

Of course my ambition was one day to fill a front page with my contribution. Every true journalist is an inveterate, unremitting hunter of what, in present-day American, is called a scoop. My chance came when I was nearing the end of my apprenticeship.

By then I had already realized that first and foremost my work boiled down to what the French call *mise-en-scène* — the setting. A journalist can "set the scene" of every story in such a way as to create an atmosphere of sensationalism.

A rival newspaper had published a short account of an accident in the Spandau State Works. Fürstenheim read the report and dispatched apprentice Schacht out to Spandau to write up an original story for the paper. I went by train, blew my "exes" on a first-rate dinner in a restaurant adjoining the factory and subsequently started on my enquiries. They were highly successful: I had no difficulty in obtaining all the information I wanted so I boarded the train and returned to Berlin.

In the editorial offices all was quiet; the editors had gone home, the compositors were busy completing the front page. I seized my chance. This time I was wiser than with that first day's report on the Weidendamm Bridge. I sat down at my table, told the make-up hand to hold the page open and began to write. From time to time a messenger would arrive, take away my completed page and hurry off with it to the composing room. By the time I had finished I had written an *entrefilet* in grand style.

Next morning when the citizens of Berlin opened their *Kleines Journal* the first thing to catch their eye was a three-column headline on the front page:

## TERRIBLE DISASTER IN SPANDAU!

Underneath was the description of a fatal accident in Spandau's State Factory. An event which could easily have been dismissed in six lines under Local News.

That evening I had to stand the editorial department a round of beer, and was promoted from apprentice to journeyman. Shortly afterwards I resigned my position on the *Kleines Journal* and went to Munich. A year later I was back in Berlin studying rhetoric under Professor Dessoir. Since then I have never taken any further active part in journalism.

Years later when I had completed some exhaustive research among the records of a certain newspaper I wrote an essay on the press in *Conrad's Yearbooks*. This article, entitled *Statistics of the German Press*, has since been frequently quoted. In addition I used the knowledge I had acquired in the writing of several other articles on the history of the press which appeared partly in the *Grenzbote* (Frontier Messenger) which at that time enjoyed a considerable reputation, partly in other periodicals.

I have never regretted those days. On the contrary I was always glad that, at the opportune moment, I entered this important field of our public life. And I took not a little  pride in the fact that I discovered it, so to speak, off my own bat.

# VIII

## PARIS AT THE TURN OF THE CENTURY

HERR DESSOIR, Professor of Rhetoric, knew how to create public speakers. When I first went to him I had no knowledge whatever of the art of public speaking. Of course I had already heard such speakers; for example, my masters at the Johanneum, my professors, the candidates of the political parties. They had always seemed to me to say just whatever came into their heads at that particular moment. Dessoir made us realize that public speaking is an art.

He began by initiating us into the mysteries of logical speaking; he warned us against such descriptions as "an old, aged man," "a dark, coal-black horse," which might give rise to unexpected hilarity; and after he had given them a sound theoretical foundation, let his budding orators deliver speeches before the rest, in the course of which his gentle voice would frequently interrupt with such instructions as:

"Your words must be joined by a silken thread. At present your speech sounds as though it had been put together with wire staples."

Professor Dessoir succeeded in imparting to his students the art of picturesque language, of employing the right imagery at the right moment, of resorting if anything to understatement and letting his hearers guess the rest.

I have never been able to indulge in what is described as "flowery language." The Friesians are people of ready wit who take great delight in caustic verbal disputes — even when they proceed very calmly. I have never lost my enjoyment at debates and discussions with points demanding quick repartee, and my friends often said that if anyone wanted to do me a good turn he would attack me vigorously.

I spent the winter of 1897–98 in Paris. Officially I was enrolled at Berlin University. But I wanted to learn French and felt that the quickest way to acquire the best French was to go to France.

So I arranged for my allowance, made my way to the Anhalt railway station in Berlin and took the train for Cologne.

How times have changed! In those days the only question that presented itself to a student wishing to study in France was whether or not he could obtain a letter of credit from his father. The "transfer problem" had not yet been invented; difficulties with foreign exchange were nonexistent. It was not even necessary to procure a visa from the French Consul . . . The German money that one took along could be  exchanged at any bank without the slightest trouble. The French had gold francs, the German gold marks. Both were stable currencies; one hundred marks equaled one hundred and twenty-five francs. Anyone in possession of this amount could manage quite well for a month if he lived economically.

I took my seat in the train, read the paper for a while, then put it down and let my thoughts wander. There were one or two questions that I had to decide — the most important entitled Luise Sowa.

I had met her during the summer holidays the previous year when I returned from Munich. She was the daughter of a police inspector living in the same neighborhood as my parents.

Luise was dark, lively, with a dainty figure, and most attractive — especially to me. I met her on the tennis court, where she wore a long skirt after the fashion of the day. We played together in the mixed doubles, I took her home and met her again soon afterwards.

Gradually we came to know one another better and would go for longer and longer walks together on the shores of the Schlachtensee. Eventually I was invited to her home. After that Luise received an invitation to my parents' house. My mother was very much attracted by the girl and made no secret of the fact.

Luise and I took part in an amateur performance in Schlachtensee and raised one hundred and twenty marks for the Red Cross. My parents were among the audience and they and Inspector Sowa between them were responsible for resounding applause.

But in the autumn of 1897 there was no question of marriage. Luise and I had known each other for a year. All the same it seemed to me sometimes as though our relationship would never develop into anything further. I was in the middle of my university studies and still feeling my way, trying out any new activities in the university, and was simply not in a position to think of a family. Luise represented an unsolved problem in my life. I had seen what early marriage on insufficient means could do in the case of my parents.

I thought over all this while the train rattled through the depressing turnip fields of the fertile Magdeburg plain. Gradually it grew dark, a guard came along with a taper, lit the gas, drew the curtains and proceeded on his way. I took up a French grammar and began to study the irregular verbs. In my corner, one eye on the box in the luggage rack above, I sat and studied till my eyes ached. At last we reached Cologne. I picked up my luggage and looked for a third-class compartment in the Cologne-Paris night train.

I shall never forget the journey across Belgium. When we started there was one other passenger in the compartment who slept as soundly as I did. But these pleasant conditions underwent a change at the frontier. A party of men pushed their way in, took possession of a window corner and began to play cards.

Still half asleep, glancing up from time to time at my luggage, I remained in my corner wrapped in my coat and watched the men. The game appeared to afford them endless enjoyment although it was the simplest thing in the world. One of the players kept the bank. He drew three cards and laid them face upward on the table so that the other players could note their colors and values. Then he turned them over and mixed them very dexterously. Finally he raised his hands and asked for one of the three cards. His opponent pointed to a card: the card was turned up. If the caller had guessed rightly he received twice the amount of his stake from the bank. If he had called the wrong card his stake went into the bank. I found it as easy as A.B.C.; I staked — and lost my entire month's allowance, except for twenty marks.

That was the first and last time in my life that I ever gambled. Later, as Director of the Danat Bank, I saw how my co-directors gambled incessantly on the Stock Exchange. I have never gone in for it. While my colleagues' abstracts of account were as thick as fair-sized novels, my deals could be entered in one small volume.

I had gone to Paris with the object of going to the College Libre des Sciences Sociales and attending lectures on sociology. At no time during my life did I appreciate the social sciences so warmly as during that first month in the French capital.

Later I was to laugh over that incident in the night express, but it was no joke at the time. For a whole month I did not feel in the least like laughing. While I read Victor Hugo's *Les Misérables* in order to improve my knowledge of the language, I fully appreciated the circumstances in which these poor souls subsisted on bread and water, since I too had somehow to eke out my existence on twenty-five francs and limited credit.

When the lean month was over and a fresh supply of cash arrived from Germany I began to explore the great city. In those days I looked upon Paris with different eyes from those with which I considered it later at the time of the Young Plan. It still retained some of the splendor of the Third Empire. People came there from every country — partly for the sake of the good food and wine, partly on account of the fashions and the attractive women. Brazilians and Chinese, Americans and Dutch, Australian sheep farmers and Indian maharajas flocked to Paris, the center of the fashionable world. Jacques Offenbach's light operas were still being performed; women's dress was essentially feminine, the celebrated Cul de Paris just come into being. Compared with Berlin, Paris was a city of opulence. Berlin was sober, industrious, intimate, middle-class, slightly international and very "Prussian"; Paris was cosmopolitan, intoxicating, smart, somewhat snobbish and not at all Prussian. Nearly thirty years — a whole generation — had come and gone since the War of 1870 and the great Communist revolt. No one spoke of the war. These were the prosperous years just before the turn of the century. The idea of revenge appeared to be dead.

Although during those years I took no interest whatever in high-level politics there was one topic which it was impossible to ignore, a topic which affected contemporary French thought and split the country into two opposite camps — the Dreyfus Case.

The whole world knows the story of the Dreyfus Case. Dreyfus, a captain of artillery of Jewish origin and a native of Alsace, had been thrown into prison three years previously and in 1894 was sentenced to be deported for life to Devil's Island. Even at that time there were numerous people who maintained that the captain was the innocent victim of a political intrigue and had been unjustly condemned; he had been made the scapegoat of an attack calculated to strengthen French anti-Semitic feeling. In France at that time clerical partisans, Nationalists and Anti-Semites, were hand in glove in the struggle for power ever since the downfall of the Nationalist General Boulanger in 1889. Dreyfus had already been three years in prison when I was studying in Paris, and Emile Zola, France's most famous novelist, was demanding a revision of the sentence. He wrote an open letter to the President of the Republic under the heading *J'accuse!* which appeared on January 13, 1898, in the newspaper *L'Aurore*. Zola's letter had the effect of a bombshell. It is not uninteresting to know that Georges Clemenceau at that time brought great pressure to bear on *L'Aurore*. As was to be expected, there was strong opposition to the publication of *J'accuse* from Nationalist circles. There was a minor local revolt in Paris when it became known that, because of his letter to the President, Zola had been sentenced to a year's imprisonment and a fine of three thousand francs. The people of Paris organized protest marches directed partly at Zola's enemies, partly against the Dreyfusards. Zola was forced to flee to England but was permitted to return to Paris eighteen months later. But by means of his letter he had at least succeeded in inducing the French courts to reopen the Dreyfus Case, though many years were to pass however before the Jewish captain of artillery was finally vindicated. It was not until 1906 that he was acquitted by the Court of Cassation, reinstated with the rank of major and soon afterwards, at his own request, placed on the retired list.

I should have liked to be able to state that I had been intensely interested in the Dreyfus Case and that I had followed every phase of the drama which unfolded itself under my very eyes. Unfortunately it is not true. I took no slightest interest in politics and was only anxious to take the fullest possible advantage of my stay in Paris.

Nevertheless I can say now that two problems crossed my path at a very early stage, problems with which I had later to contend for years on end in my capacity as Minister and member of the Government. The problem of anti-Semitism which, before the turn of the century, played so significant a role in France that people would take sides and come to blows in the public streets. And the problem of Franco-German relations which reached one of its culminating points in the person of the man whose name I first heard in connection with the revision of the Dreyfus Case — Georges Clemenceau.

At Easter in 1898 I returned to Berlin, the richer by quite a few experiences. I had studied French and sociology — above all, however, I had experienced some of the things that are sometimes of the greatest importance in one's young days. And in Berlin Luise Sowa was waiting for me. We resumed our walks by the Schlachtensee; I told her about Paris, about the elegant fashions and the smart restaurants. Toward the end of the Easter holidays I went to Kiel to work for my degree of doctor of philosophy. My attitude to Luise had become more casual. I was up to the eyes in work and had no time to bother about girls. She appeared to understand this. When we met again in the long vacation we broke off our somewhat premature engagement. She seemed to realize that at present I was unable to think of anything but my future career. We parted good friends, without reproaches but also without promises for the future. I did not see her again until five years later.

# IX

## DOCTOR OF PHILOSOPHY

I TRAVELED to Kiel having decided to take Newspapers as the subject of my thesis for my doctor's degree. Nowadays there is nothing especially revolutionary about that. Institutes of journalism exist in connection with several German colleges.

But it was different then. Wilhelm Hasbach, Professor-in-Ordinary and of Political Economy at the University of Kiel, had no use whatever for newspapers. My first interview with him was not exactly encouraging.

Hasbach was a big man with reddish hair, steel-blue eyes that could flash like lightning from behind his glasses, and a pepper-and-salt beard. He was forty-nine years old and was reputed to be a hypochondriacal eccentric.

"Why did you come to Kiel?" he asked aggressively when I had introduced myself. "I suppose you think it will be easier to take your doctor's degree here?"

I said that Kiel was, so to speak, my own university — besides, my brother had passed his M.D. here. He appeared completely uninterested.

"Not counting political economy," he said grimly, "I have only had doctors of social philosophy in my university. You are the third."

"What subject had you thought of for your thesis?" was Hasbach's next — and decisive — question. I cleared my throat and said:

"Well, sir, I am interested in journalism. The subject I had in mind was The Economic Significance of Newspapers."

The suggestion did not find favor with Hasbach. "Newspapers?" he said frowning. "Rubbish! That's not the kind of subject for anyone taking a doctor's degree. I believe after all that you have come here in the hope you'll find it an easy job!"

I began to feel anxious. "No, I didn't," I said. "If you know of a better subject for me, sir, of course I am prepared to work on that . . ."

"Are you?" he answered shortly, glancing sharply at me. He went to his desk and began to rummage among his papers. My heart sank. A seventh-term student who approaches a university professor-in-ordinary takes the trouble to acquaint himself beforehand with the latter's work, so I knew that Hasbach had published two titles: *The English Working-men's Insurance System 1883* and *English Agricultural Workers During the Past Hundred Years, and the Enclosures Act (1894)*. Neither subject interested me in the least. Would I have to proceed on those lines?

Luckily it didn't turn out as bad as that. I was unaware that, at that time, Professor Wilhelm Hasbach was at daggers drawn with a political economist in Heidelberg. The subject of the dispute was whether or not the English commercial system could be classed as theoretical and related to political economy. The Heidelberger said yes, Hasbach retorted no. At the moment he was very much taken up with this quarrel. The Kiel professor knew of course that for a well-authenticated refutation it was necessary to obtain evidence which could only be extracted with considerable trouble from the records. It must have occurred to him while he was foraging in his desk that I was the very man to draft this counterblast against the Heidelberger commercialist. At any rate he turned to me in quite a friendly manner, motioned me to sit down, and said:

"Listen, Herr Schacht, I might be able to provide you with a magnificent theme for your doctor's thesis, but it would probably involve your going to England. Could you manage that?"

I thought of my time in Paris and said I could. Why not? In England it should be possible to live very cheaply.

"Read through this," said Hasbach and handed me the volume by his Heidelberg opponent. "I think one could produce a whole lot of arguments against it, assuming one could investigate the writings of the commercialists on the spot, that is to say, the British Museum in London . . ."

Like many other professors, Hasbach occasionally exploited his students by making them tackle the problems of their instructor. Since, however, this had always been the case there was nothing to be said. I accepted Professor Hasbach's assignment for my doctor's degree and set myself to study his opponent's book.

The subject of my task was *The Theoretical Quality of English Commerce*. As Hasbach had prophesied it necessitated traveling to England. I made the journey in January 1899, a year after those exciting days in Paris. I kept my traveling expenses as low as possible, going by cargo boat to Hull for twenty marks, staying in

London a fortnight and returning to Kiel by the same route. In spite of this, of course, I needed more money than usual. Luckily I found a financial backer in the Editor-in-Chief of the *Kieler Neueste Nachrichten,* who entrusted me with the art and dramatic criticism of his newspaper.

I had been a member of the Berlin "Academic and Literary Union," had studied Germanic philology and history of literature for several terms and had already worked in a newspaper office. The chief editor was pleased with my style and my approach to art criticism. We became acquainted during my last term and this afforded me the advantage of regular auxiliary work on a first-class paper, for the *Nachrichten* under my friend's energetic direction was more in the style of a general gazette.

Unfortunately, as so often happens, the publisher of the paper held different views from those of the editor. He did not like my criticisms and raised objections to them with the chief editor, who backed me up. But the publisher stuck to his opinion that I was too young and inexperienced for such an important position.

Matters came to a head one day over an exhibition at which I had praised the work of a very young painter. The publisher who disliked this young artist's work said that my write-up was biased and prejudiced. The editor told me about this.

"What had I better do?" he asked.

"Why not submit the notice in question to an impartial group such as the Kiel Art Club for their opinion," I countered. "If they consider that I'm too young for the post I will gladly resign . . ."

He acted on the suggestion and sent the notice to the Art Club without telling his publisher. Two days later we received their reply. The Club was of the opinion that this criticism, and others by Herr Schacht, were objective, impartial, and written with adequate knowledge of the subject. They could find nothing against him.

Armed with this letter the editor betook himself to the publisher who thereupon withdrew his opposition.

It might perhaps be appropriate to mention the name of the artist who was almost the cause of my leaving the *Kieler Neuesten Nachrichten.* At that time he was very young — just eighteen years old — and his name was Max Pechstein.

Sometimes, while dividing my attention between English Commerce and the local theater I could not help recalling my first term at Kiel. It was only four years ago but it often seemed as though I had grown twenty years older since then. In that first term while I was laboring over bones and tissues and writing reams of verse, I did not dream that in a few years' time I should be writing a serious work on English Commerce. On the contrary I sincerely believed that I was destined to be a poet. One of my friends was a musician who possessed the gift of being able with consummate ease to jot down tunes on any bit of music paper. Together we dreamed of collaborating sometime in the writing of an opera, or at the very least an operetta. He badgered me so persistently that I laid aside my anatomical efforts and drafted a libretto based on Grimm's fairy tale of "The Princesses Who Danced Their Shoes Into Holes." Unfortunately it had precious little action, consisting only of a sequence of lyrical scenes loosely strung together. My composer friend set the lyrics to music — and there our dream ended: the masterpiece was never performed. But at least I could boast of having, at one period of my life, written an operetta! Many decades later I was reminded of this "youthful indiscretion" in a most amusing way, of which more later.

So, at intervals, I recalled that first term. I remember how the *Wiener Dichterheim* had published my first poem for which I had had to contribute five marks toward expenses, and how proud I had been when I saw my full name printed underneath the twelve lines of verse. I sent a few copies of the little magazine to my friends and basked in the thought that I was now a poet with published work to his credit.

No — I am by no means an outstanding lyric writer — nor was I even in my callow youth. The moral, didactic element invariably obtrudes. And, as a matter of fact, I earned my first fee as a journalist not with a poem but with an aphorism — "Eating keeps body and soul together — drinking tears them apart . . ." Certainly no heaven-inspired flash of genius! But the editor of *Jugend* (Youth), to whom I sent this gem of wisdom, paid me two whole marks for it!

The art notices were more in my line. They demanded critical knowledge besides carrying decidedly better fees.

My trip to London was short and uneventful. Since then I have visited the English capital many times, occasionally in very dramatic circumstances.

On this occasion I stayed in a boardinghouse in Tottenham Court Road. I had chosen it because it was not far from the

British Museum. I had only to cross Bedford Square to reach the entrance to that vast building from whose shelves I obtained and consulted the works of mercantile authors ancient and modern: John Hale and John Stuart Mill: Locke, Hume and the remarkable Daniel Defoe, known to children the world over as the author of *Robinson Crusoe*. To them it is an adventure story, while in fact it constitutes a broad outline of a primitive economy — a delineation, so to speak, of political economy.

As I had only a fortnight at my disposal I was fully occupied and in consequence saw but little of the city. After breakfasting on milk, bread and butter, I went straight to my seat in the huge reading room, made copious extracts from the old books, left the Museum about midday for lunch and returned immediately to work till closing time. Then I dined, went for a short stroll and then to bed. Once or twice I went to a music hall, a favorite English entertainment. On Sundays I took long walks in Hyde Park. The English Sunday was a very dull, uninteresting affair.

London in January is a dreary city. The streets are usually shrouded in thick fog through which the sun rarely penetrates; the air is raw, cold and often filled with soot fit to choke. Life in Victorian London, especially in winter, could not compare with that in Paris at the turn of the century. I began to understand why wealthy English people bought villas on the Mediterranean, in Amalfi, on the Côte d'Azur. London is the most unsuitable spot in the world in which to spend a fortnight in winter.

My doctor's thesis eventually comprised one hundred closely written pages copiously sprinkled with footnotes. In order to strengthen and justify the professor's campaign against the theoretical quality of the mercantile system I had confirmed every sentence with quotations from the English originals. Only one half of the work, therefore, was in German: the other half was in English.

When I had made a fair copy I handed it to Professor Hasbach and entered my name for the oral examination. I think he was pleased with the work.

The oral examination took place in August 1899. I still remember it well because it was connected with a very curious conversation.

Officially, it must be noted, I was not taking my degree as doctor of political economy but as doctor of philosophy. Consequently I was obliged, if only for form's sake, to be examined by a philosopher. Philosophy was compulsory.

I had passed the oral examinations in other subjects without any trouble, but I anticipated the examination in philosophy with a certain amount of anxiety. I have never been a lover of intellectual speculation. I like mulling over problems; I enjoy having hard nuts to crack. But they must be practical problems capable of solution by practical means.

The professor in charge of this most learned of all the sciences greeted me kindly and invited me to sit down. He questioned me on the subject of sundry philosophers: I did know a little about them. In some instances I remembered fragments of theories associated with those particular names. I stammered something, then relapsed into silence. The professor scribbled jerkily on his writing pad and frowned. Suddenly he looked up sharply, stared past my left ear and asked: "What it that?"

I turned quickly, following the direction of his gaze. It would not have surprised me to see the ghost of the founder of the university emerge through the wall. But there was no ghost — only a plain brown cupboard in a corner of the room. The professor repeated his question: "What is that?"

"A cupboard," I said.

"Right." The professor of philosophy was relieved. I knew what a cupboard was. But now came the critical question: "What is that cupboard?"

Do you know what a cupboard is? I had never thought about it before. I used a cupboard to put my clothes in but that was all I ever did with it. I had never stopped to consider it one way or another.

"Well!" said the professor impatiently. "What is this cupboard?"

He sounded irritated — I had to give some sort of answer.

"Brown," I said.

"What else?" he said. "Don't you notice anything else about it?"

"Square — that is, cubiform," I stated.

"What else?"

"Wooden," I ventured. The philosopher behind me snorted.

"Man alive!" he exclaimed testily, "the cupboard is spatial!"

I stared at him uncomprehendingly. He began to laugh, louder and louder, pulled a handkerchief from his pocket, wiped his eyes, took his pencil and crossed out all his remarks.

"Oh, this political economy," he said somewhat resignedly. "What do you really know about philosophy?"

I knew a little and quoted Locke and Hobbes and one or two other passages from my thesis.

"That will do, thank you."

Somewhat mortified I went home — and quite uncertain as to

the result of that examination. Would the professor of philosophy upset all my plans at the last minute? Declaring that one could not possibly confer the degree of doctor of philosophy on a man who did not know even the elementary principles?

This uncertainty lasted two days. Then a messenger arrived with a letter from the university.

I had been awarded the degree of doctor of philosophy.

This time I did not make the mistake of sending my father a telegram. I packed my things, dispatched them to Berlin and followed a few days later.

All that winter I lived with my parents and attended the Schmoller Training College, where I continued my studies in political economy, and in the evenings went to the play or light opera.

By now we had really reached *fin de siècle*. An old century was nearing its end, a new one stood on the threshold. By now I had learned to look upon Berlin as home. Berlin was neither purse-proud nor exclusive like Hamburg. It was pleasant, witty, brilliant, mischievous — and human. The tolerance displayed by the kings of Prussia had invested the city with a special character of its own. Malicious tongues sometimes declared that Berlin was, in fact, not German at all, but a colony of foreigners — French Huguenots, Dutch Remonstrants, Oriental Jews, Polish conspirators and Italian *Carbonari*.

At any rate nobody was ever asked whether he was a "Berliner by birth." If he was in Berlin he was a Berliner.

On New Year's Eve 1899 we were sitting in the villa at Schlachtensee drinking hot punch my father had brewed. Just as it used to be in the old days, and yet — so much had changed.

"Finish your drinks so that I can fill them up again," said my father. "In twenty minutes it will be nineteen-hundred . . ."

"Good heavens!" my mother exclaimed and set down her glass on the table. "Nineteen-hundred! Do you remember, William, how we got married? That was twenty-seven years ago! What a lot we have experienced since then . . ."

I looked at her. Her hair had turned gray. For twenty-seven years she had toiled with her hands for her family's sake; she had scrubbed floors and washed linen, she had cooked; she had watched by her children's bedside, and always she had had in mind the future destiny of her four sons.

My father must have been thinking the same thing. He removed his cigar, looked at Mother, cleared his throat, replaced his cigar and began to fill the glasses. When he had finished he removed his cigar for the second time and did something he very rarely did. Since the evening when he had returned home with the Equitable Life Insurance job in his pocket he had never again kissed my mother in the presence of the children. Now he leaned forward, gave her a kiss and stroked her hand.

"Yes, Mama," he said, "twenty-seven years. And now we have grown-up sons. One is a doctor, the other a philosopher. We wouldn't have thought it possible . . ."

Oluf and William stared, wide-eyed.

From outside came suddenly the sound of gunfire. Somewhere a clock began to strike; bells pealed, people shouted at each other along the street that ran through the pinewood. We raised our glasses and drank to one another in silence.

# X

## COMMERCIAL TREATIES

THE NEW ERA seemed to be governed by domestic affairs. Economic problems loomed more and more in the foreground.

I was studying political economy at the Schmoller Training College and one of the men who at that time exercised considerable influence upon me was Professor Schmoller himself. Gustav von Schmoller (he was awarded a title in 1908) belonged still to the nineteenth century — one of those great Liberals who, politically speaking, never quite managed to "get there," but whose work has nevertheless borne fruit.

Schmoller was a "socialist *doctrinaire.*" He had been born six years after Goethe's death and had certainly never experienced in his own person the struggle of the industrial workers and those who had migrated from the country to the big cities. It was this lack of personal experience that imparted to his words a theoretical flavor completely summed up in the expression "socialist *doctrinaire.*" The working classes, in process of organizing themselves into the Social-Democratic Party, preferred officials who had risen from their own ranks. They wanted no "middle-class socialism."

But the actual period of political industrialism came to an end with the turn of the century, as did the period of large-scale capitalism. The starting point of this development dated from Bismarck's lifetime when the Chancellor had succeeded in carrying through his great work of Social Insurance between 1881 and 1889, which had been introduced to the Reichstag by an imperial message. The socialist *doctrinaires* had a considerable share in this social achievement.

At that time there arose the grotesque situation when the leaders of the Social-Democratic Party ranged themselves against these laws — solely because they originated, not among the workers but in titled and middle-class circles.

But the results of this legislation soon became apparent and helped greatly to relieve the tension in the social atmosphere, for in 1908 there were already in Germany thirteen million people insured against sickness and twenty-four millions against accidents. And those insured persons without exception came from the ranks of the impecunious masses of our people.

In proportion as the hardships of this first industrial period were overcome the pronouncements of the middle-class social reformers gained weight. Among them was Schmoller. While the workmen's leaders sought to gain power for their own class by means of organization, the middle class reformers were seeking a new social ethic. Man's moral responsibility for his fellow man was their first commandment.

From the kindly old man who, during a lifetime, had watched with attentive eyes the change in the social structure of his time, I learned that all true reforms must proceed along the path of evolution, of natural unforced development backed by understanding and good will.

In addition to his *Year Books* to which I often contributed, Schmoller published a series on political economy. One day he sent for me.

"I have read the thesis you wrote for your doctor's degree," he said, "and I should like to publish it in book form. But for this you would have to translate the English quotations into German."

He made the suggestion just when I was in process of securing a position. I didn't want to be a burden on my father any longer; besides, I should have to earn the cost of the printing expenses. My monthly allowance as a student had always been scanty but I had lived within it and could start my career unencumbered by debt. In subsequent years, too, I never had any debts, not even during the period of inflation when owing money was a very paying game.

The prospects of obtaining a job were not unfavorable. It was just at the time when numerous economic organizations began to take shape and wanted to bring their business interests to the notice of the public and of the government. Opportunities for economic secretaries and syndics were improving.

I answered an advertisement in a professional newspaper and received by return an invitation to an evening debate sponsored by a Dr. Vosberg-Rekow. This gentleman was manager of a "Central Office for the Preparation of Trade Agreements," a circle comprising several large-scale manufacturers interested in export. Vosberg-Rekow was an adept at inducing his members to contribute handsomely to the funds out of which the Central Office — to say nothing of himself — made their living. He was a highly intelligent man with an extraordinary gift for handling his fellows, though his character and technical knowledge were not quite on the same level. But a brilliant persuasiveness of manner concealed his essential superficiality.

I took part in the debate, and since I had absolutely no experience I did my best to turn my recently acquired university subjects to good account, my aim being to outdo other competitors who were present. Actually I obtained the appointment that same evening, but for a somewhat different reason than the one I had anticipated. Vosberg-Rekow came up to me and said: "If it suits you I shall start you off with a salary of one hundred marks a month. You are the only one here who has turned up in a dinner jacket. I like to see my staff take a pride in their appearance."

My job as clerk in the Central Office for the Preparation of Trade Agreements is the only one in my life for which I ever applied. In all my subsequent positions it was invariably others who applied for my services by reason of my qualifications and experience. In later years I have always steadily refuted any complaints I heard about how hard it was for young people to get on, how many obstructions were placed in their way. The demand for efficient staff is always far greater than the supply. More than anything else an employer is on the lookout for the hard-working reliable man who, like the messenger to García, will see the job through to the end.

Schmoller was disappointed when I told him I had no time to translate my thesis into German. I had neither typewriter nor stenographer. Half my thesis consisted of English quotations; I should have had to rewrite the whole thing and translate them all. My new job left me no time for it. Only the customary three hundred copies of the thesis were printed and these now lie buried in the libraries to which they were presented.

The eighties witnessed the start of Germany's great economic upheaval. It was beginning to be recognized that German soil alone could no longer provide sufficient agricultural produce wherewith to feed the growing population. Germany would have to import grain and furnish the necessary currency by means of industrial exports.

This was the occasion for political resistance on the part of farming circles who demanded the imposition of protective tariffs against the cheap foreign grain. It was the beginning of the contest between Germany's export trade and competing foreign industrial countries for possession of the world's markets.

General von Caprivi, who succeeded Bismarck as Chancellor, summed up Germany's situation in the following impressive words: "We must export either men or merchandise." The whole of Central Europe from the North Cape to the Gulf of Taranto was in similar plight: the produce of the land no longer sufficed to feed the increasing population. Even the most prohibitive tariffs would have been powerless to alter prevailing conditions. Emigration or export became the decisive question. Germany chose the second road: the price of her increase in population was the risk of conflict with other countries. She emerged victorious from the economic struggle for an adequate share of the world's markets: she failed to surmount the concomitant political danger.

That this struggle was not always pursued by Germany with the right political weapons has been brought home to us by the after-effects of two world wars.

While I was still at Schmoller's Training College yet another authority — Professor Hans Delbrück, editor of the *Prussian Year Books* — approached me with a request that I would write for him. For ten years I contributed book reviews and articles for this important monthly. Next to Schmoller, Hans Delbrück has been my most valued teacher, and to him also I owe a debt of gratitude for more than one decision during my period of growth. Delbrück was no socialist *doctrinaire* but a politician intensely interested in Germany's political development. He counted himself as one of the Liberal-Conservative groups, though on many questions he maintained a highly independent and non-party attitude.

Writing for the *Year Books* gave me the opportunity of defining my attitude to current questions of mercantile policy. In my first article (February 1901) I had already given expression to two ideas in regard to the dispute over the "bread racket" and the "prohibitive tariffs." The first was that the consumer would put up with a higher tariff on grain, which the farmers considered essential, and could afford to do so provided this tariff were counterbalanced by safeguards, by extension of the export trade and by the gradual rise in wages which might consequently be expected. The second idea was that, even more important than the actual tariff level, was the reciprocal fixing of tariffs over a considerable period, which would permit the uninterrupted development of stable conditions in the various economic circles. "The essential question," I affirmed, "is whether we can obtain new trade contracts in spite of a higher duty on grain; *not* whether, and to what extent, the duty on grain will increase the price of bread. If we do obtain new trade contracts despite a higher tariff, then we may confidently assume that we can look forward to a further period of economic prosperity which will also enable us to eat high-priced bread."

The articles which I published during those years leave no doubt as to my fundamental concept of economic policy — a concept I have maintained throughout my life.

The development of the highest and most efficiently organized productivity seemed to me then, as now, the best — indeed the only — means of bringing the greatest possible improvement in the welfare of the masses. To achieve this it is necessary that economics be kept free from political disturbances. External arbitrary action in matters of commercial policy, and devaluation of currency are as disruptive as internal strikes and lockouts. War and class hatred have always seemed to me the scourge of economic life.

The improvement in the social conditions of the masses has always been a matter of primary importance to me; and this I evinced in an article I contributed to the *Prussian Year Books* in December of the same year. In this article I emphatically supported the principle of a foreign trade policy which encouraged the processing and finishing industries because they provided more work for German brains and hands than in the raw materials and semimanufacture industries. A cargo of pig iron, for example, destined for abroad is less desirable than a cargo of fine textiles of the same value. In the first instance the greater part of the proceeds goes into dividends, in the second to wages. The "heavy" industries represent capital, the "light" industries represent labor.

In the same category is an article dated October 1902 in which for the first time I put forward the idea of industrial trusts as opposed to the usual cartels. A cartel is a collection of industrial concerns manufacturing the same goods, and agreeing among themselves to keep the prices as high as possible. A trust, on the other hand, embraces those enterprises concerned with the production and manufacture of the same material from the raw material to the finished article. I pointed out that the first object of this vertical aspect of production is to reduce production costs and increase consumption. This reduction in costs admits of a reduction in prices, leading to extended and lower-priced consumption, which is the aim of every industry.

"The cartel is a drug, the trust is an elixir," I declared, categorically.

It is significant that Germany's economic problem today is exactly the same as it was when I described its earliest visible stages more than fifty years ago. I wrote: "The problem of mercantile policy that we have to solve is at bottom a problem of population policy. We have to provide work for the millions of German workers who live on German soil and arise in endless succession from the womb of their motherland. Today these masses can no longer be maintained by the cultivation of grain or the production of semi-manufactured goods: the only way to provide them with work is to absorb them into intensive agricultural small-scale undertakings on the one hand, and into processing industries on the other. We have one factor at our disposal in unlimited measure: the intellectual and manual labor of human beings; we must endeavor to expand and develop this factor in such a way as to give us a lead over all other nations, who are not capable of competing against us with nothing but cheaper foreign raw materials."

In October 1908 the opening sentence of an article ran: "The work of economic policy is based on two fundamental requirements: the highest possible economic production and the fairest possible distribution of the results of such production." The article was by way of introducing an exhibition featuring the electrical industry. In this case I had no recourse to official statistics but was obliged to rely solely on private information, because as yet there were no such things as official electricity statistics. In this article I pointed out the colossal waste among the concerns engaged in electrical generation, whereby the innumerable little local electric works had the last word. I was able to prove that not only the prices for light but also the prices for power fluctuated between sixty and seventy pfennigs per kilowatt, and the small communal generating stations were the most costly, not merely on account of their limited capacity, but also because they were a welcome source of taxation for the communal authorities. By contrast I advocated a concentration of production in large generating stations with the aim of cheapening consumption, bringing electric economic policy under a single state leadership and combining public control with private enterprise. I am glad to say that later development of electric generation has proceeded along the above lines.

In 1901 I transferred my activities from the Central Office to the newly established larger *Handelsvertragsverein* (Association for Mercantile Contracts). On the Board of Administration were the directors of most of the principal banks and a very considerable proportion representing the export trade and shipping companies with whom I achieved personal contact. There were merchant princes from the Hanseatic cities such as Achelis of Bremen, chairman of the Norddeutscher Lloyd, and Adolf Wörmann of Hamburg, one of the German colonial pioneers. I was in touch with practically all the Chambers of Commerce and economic associations and even more closely with the economic press. As I myself was responsible for the publication of the Association's *Bulletin* I joined the Berlin Press Union and remained a member until its demise under Hitler.

At the head of the Association was George von Siemens, the founder and first director of the Deutsche Bank, with whom I was in close collaboration several hours a day until his death in 1901.

The elucidation and journalistic presentment of my economic ideas gave me great pleasure. A less pleasing feature, however, was the fact that the Association's propaganda work proceeded on less rational lines, and the campaign for trade contracts was of necessity conducted at mass meetings with the aid of political slogans.

During those two years I had to speak at innumerable meetings of economic groups and trade union assemblies, and thereby gained practice not only in delivery but also in discussion. But I found the exploiting of such work for party political ends unsatisfactory.

When in 1901 I was asked to stand for the Reichstag at the general elections I declined and left the field open in favor of a colleague who was eventually successful. I became more and more deeply interested in purely economic questions. I have stuck to this all my life and have steadily avoided one-sided party politics. That does not mean, however, that I have refused to take part in public life. For years I was on the committee of the Young Liberals' Association where the younger disciples of the National Liberal Party were wont to congregate. This group embodied within the National Liberal Party a strongly progressive tendency which was often a source of annoyance to the older party bosses.

# XI

## I MEET SOME OF THE BIG BANKERS

THE ASSOCIATION FOR MERCANTILE CONTRACTS proved a very important factor in my upward progress. Not only did I make the acquaintance of the outstanding economists of the day, but they on their part were able to see me at work, and my method even at that time must have acquired a fairly definite character.

I remember a conversation with Georg von Siemens on the subject of a colleague whose erratic ways obviously got on his nerves.

"Look, Herr Schacht," said Siemens, "this is how your colleague works —" and his index finger hop-skip-and-jumped across the table. Then he withdrew his hand abruptly and looked at me. "And this is how you work." This time his finger sped in a single energetic movement over the surface.

Since I had obviously not made a bad impression it was a foregone conclusion that in due course sundry members of the Board of Management should approach me with offers of employment, not all of which were tempting, though more than one appeared very interesting.

Thus it happened that Prince Ernst Günther of Schleswig-Holstein, brother-in-law of the Emperor Wilhelm II, sent his adjutant to see me one day and invited me to a conference.

The Prince received me at his Berlin residence and for half an hour stood chatting with me, smoking a cigar, giving me the impression of a quiet, almost shy personality. His idea had been to appoint me administrator of his property and financial affairs — certainly a most honorable position but not one which would have really satisfied me.

Early in 1903 I had the opportunity of entering an important South German Chamber of Commerce in the capacity of syndic. Shortly afterwards old Emil Rathenau invited me to join him at the Allgemeine Elektrizitätsgesellschaft (A.E.G., General Electric Company). I was tempted to agree. But a third offer attracted me still more. Waldemar Müller, a privy councilor and a member of the board of the Dresdner Bank, offered me a post in that undertaking.

I felt that employment in one of the big "D" Banks would afford me the widest scope to acquire the greatest possible insight into economics. The principal German banks were not merely concerned with deposit and current accounts, as was the case in England; their activities covered an immense range including the financing of industrial undertakings, the acceptance and disposal of shares and bonds of industrial works, transport firms, parishes and communities, provinces and entire states.

My actual appointment had a humorous flavor. I sat opposite Müller who asked me the fateful question: "How much have you been earning up to now, Dr. Schacht?"

"Eight thousand eight hundred marks a year," I said, not without some pride. Three years previously I had started on a monthly remuneration of one hundred marks.

"*How* much?" he queried incredulously. I explained: "Six thousand marks as manager of the Association, two thousand eight hundred from journalism." Müller shook his head.

"Why, even our chief clerks don't earn as much," he said. "I can't possibly pay you more than one of the bank's chief clerks!"

"Pay me what you consider fair, sir, and don't worry. A year hence I feel sure you will be paying me the same as I have been earning hitherto."

He agreed. And my prophecy was also fulfilled.

My work in the Dresdner Bank brought me more than ever into personal contact with pretty well all the most important bankers of the day. My connection with Georg von Siemens had already provided me with my first acquaintances. Georg von Siemens had been one of the great initiators of collaboration between banks and industry. In 1868, while quite a young man, he had gone to Teheran at the request of his famous cousin Werner von Siemens to participate in the construction of the great Overland-Telegraph system of the Indo-European Telegraph Company. It is certainly thanks to this first experience of the East that Georg von Siemens turned his attention to Turko-Arabian affairs with outstanding success. Anyone who has once come under the spell of the East can never tear himself away.

On his return Siemens, together with Bamberger and Steinthal, founded the Deutsche Bank. Once, on a subsequent occasion, he remarked mockingly that when the bank was founded he had first to look up in the dictionary the difference between "paper" (that is, bills for discount) and "money" — two conceptions which are familiar to every bank employee. It cannot have done his bank any harm, however, for in the course of the next thirty years it became the greatest undertaking of its kind in Germany.

It was the principal rival of the Discount Company, which by reason of its past history was more steeped in tradition and therefore probably somewhat more ponderous. At the time when I was already president of the Reichsbank it was absorbed by the Deutsche Bank; in addition to these two banks was the third D-Bank, the Dresdner, under the impulsive direction of Eugen Gutmann who, with all his daring, always succeeded in steering his ship safely through the chances and changes of business so that today it stands as firmly as ever; while the fourth D-Bank, the Darmstadt, first amalgamated with the National Bank under the title of *Danat* and finally gave up the ghost in the crisis of 1931, being taken over by the Dresdner Bank.

We have to thank the leading bankers of Berlin for many an apt remark which has passed into economic history, not only *bons mots* but observations that frequently concealed a deal of truth. One of the best-known ripostes dated back to Georg von Siemens. Somebody once asked him what he would do if all the bank's customers were to withdraw their money simultaneously. With his everlasting cigar between his lips Siemens retorted dryly:

"I shall go out on to the balcony, turn round and show the people my backside." A pungent answer to an absurd question: it is highly unlikely that everyone would suddenly want to withdraw all their money from a perfectly sound bank. What would they do with the money? At best they would deposit it in other banks and from there it would again be redistributed. Hoarded money is no good to anyone since it achieves no business turnover — which, when all's said and done, is what money is for.

My chief, Eugen Gutmann, was not merely a very clever and resourceful banker, but a man whose generous nature benefited not only the bank's customers but also the staff. After I had successfully concluded my first difficult bit of business — the negotiation of a big foreign loan on the Berlin Stock Exchange — he handed me a thousand-mark note as a special bonus. That was my first *mille*.

One of the leading bankers who rendered outstanding service to German industry was Karl Fürstenberg, owner of the Berliner Handelsgesellschaft. This company had never gone in for branch offices: its one and only establishment in Berlin concentrated its energies on maintaining contact with a large number of German industrial undertakings and participating in the financial transactions of several foreign countries. For instance, the introduction of Serbian loans on the Berlin Stock Exchange can be traced back to Fürstenberg. His company was concerned in all the biggest foreign deals, among them incidentally the negotiating of the Russian loans, introduced by Mendelssohn & Company's banking establishment in Berlin. This was a limited liability company in which the partners were responsible to the extent of their private means. That is why, on one occasion, Fürstenberg replied to a man who addressed him as "Herr Direktor": *

"I am not a manager. I am responsible *for* the management."

He disliked titles and outward show. His supposedly best *bon mot* was in connection with that "Hibernia" case of which more later. An emissary from the Imperial Court called on him and enquired whether Karl Fürstenberg set greater store by an Order or a Title.

"A title," said the banker.

"What sort of title had you in mind?" asked the other.

"There is only one title you could give me — and you can't give me that."

"But what sort of title is that?" enquired the emissary.

"Konsistorialrat!" ** said Karl Fürstenberg. He was a Jew and never attempted to conceal the fact.

Another highly esteemed banker of that time was Franz Urbig of the Diskontegesellschaft (Discount Company). He had started as Clerk of the Court and by his exceptional ability had worked his way up to a managership. For a long time he had been with the German-Asiatic Bank in China; the financing of the Chinese Shantung Railway was principally in his hands.

In my own Dresdner Bank Henry Nathan was remarkable for his efficiency. He belonged to that category of bankers who had risen in their profession without any influence from outside. I have never met another bank manager who was so well informed on such a

---

* Manager, *not* director. The German word for director as we understand it is V*erwalter*.

** The nearest English equivalent would be "Ecclesiastical Councilor" — literally "Councilor of the Consistory."

variety of subjects as Henry Nathan. Whereas the majority of managers were wont to specialize in this or that department there was no single bank transaction that Henry Nathan could not have mastered practically in every detail.

The above mentioned men represent an essential section of the older generation of leading bankers in my young days. It is due to them that Berlin achieved a position in the world of international finance and banking on the same level as London, New York and Paris. It is due to them also that the Berlin Stock Exchange acquired an international reputation, and its quotations and turnover were regarded in the same light as those of other Stock Exchanges.

Today people are all too prone to disparage the importance of Exchanges in matters economic. It was of course unavoidable that there should be widespread gambling on the Exchange. But that should not cause us to underrate the significance of a capital market, organized according to Stock Exchange rules, for the financing of a country's whole economic system.

# XII

## THE DRESDNER BANK

My APPOINTMENT to the Dresdner Bank could be traced to the experiences of that establishment in the crisis of 1901. At that period the Leipziger Bank, an old highly respected Saxon institution, had crashed through granting excessive credit to an adventurous industrial undertaking.

The whole affair was typical of a bank crash caused by reckless extension of credit. The factory that actually managed to achieve the ruin of a financial establishment such as the Leipziger was the Kassel Residue-Drying Works, and its foundation must surely have been sponsored by harebrained speculators instead of engineers. The idea was to utilize the residue of wine and brandy distilleries, and for this purpose the management borrowed considerable sums from the Leipziger. When, later, it transpired that the Works was not functioning the directors of the bank furnished additional funds to maintain production. The result was complete collapse, a run on deposit accounts by the bank's customers, and finally an announcement that the Leipziger Bank was insolvent.

That was where the enterprising Georg von Siemens came in. Together with his Deutsche Bank he took over the Leipziger on very favorable terms and within twenty-four hours had opened a new branch of his bank in the selfsame offices. The customers who received their money calmed down, the run on the bank ceased — so did the Leipziger Bank.

The Dresdner Bank, officially established in Saxony, was heavily involved in this crash. Confidence in Saxon undertakings had suddenly vanished; the press began to focus its attention on the third largest bank in Germany and criticized it severely. But Eugen Gutmann, the managing director, succeeded in bringing his ship safely through the storm, and the outcome of the affair was a desire for closer contact with the public.

Nowadays the importance of such a duty is recognized and provision for public relations made by all the bigger undertakings. At that period, however, it first fell to my lot in the Dresdner Bank and I tackled it with a will.

Among the newspapers whose attitude to the Dresdner Bank was particularly critical — and not always strictly impartial — was the *Berliner Morgenpost*. No sooner did the Dresdner Bank offer any shares or bonds than one could be sure some disparaging comment would appear in the *Morgenpost*. The publishers on the other hand were very glad to receive advertisements of such shares and bonds from the various banks for their advertisement columns. The *Morgenpost*'s critical attitude to the Dresdner Bank, therefore, in no way prevented the paper from steadily canvassing for bank advertisements. When I realized this I determined to bring matters to a head and categorically refused to insert any further advertisement in the *Morgenpost*. Since I felt myself to be in a very independent position I took this step without informing my management. I had not long to wait for results. A letter of protest from Louis Ullstein, the head of the publishing firm, was received by my board and I was requested to furnish an explanation to Eugen Gutmann. I asked him to leave the conduct of the affair in my hands and he agreed. I immediately announced my intention of calling upon Herr Ullstein.

The house of Ullstein was at that time a power in the world and the name of its head carried considerable weight. All the same I was not disposed to submit to intimidation.

I had first of all to listen to a lecture by Herr Ullstein in which he explained that one could not well refuse to advertise in so important a newspaper as the *Morgenpost* and continue to do so in the other papers. I interrupted this homily by remarking that other papers were essentially less prejudiced against the Dresdner Bank.

"It is part of the freedom of the press to be as critical as their editors think fit," said Ullstein loftily. "In addition, Dr. Schacht, you should know that the advertisement and editorial sections of a newspaper are two completely different departments which have nothing to do with each other."

If he imagined he had caught me out he was mistaken. I replied with an argument of the validity of which I remain convinced to this day.

"What would you say, Herr Ullstein, if in certain Berlin advertising columns you inserted an advertisement 'Buy the *Morgenpost*!' and immediately below someone regularly followed it with — 'The worst newspaper in Berlin!' Would you continue to spend good money advertising in those columns?"

"But that is not the same thing," he said, somewhat astonished.

I went on: "How can you expect me, Herr Ullstein, to let expensive insertions appear on the third page of the *Morgenpost*, advertising the issue of shares or bonds, when on the fourth page your financial editor refers to these same issues as being an inferior investment?"

I was in a strong position and he recognized it. Of course I knew as well as he did that the advertising and editorial departments of a newspaper are two quite different pairs of shoes. For years I had made an intensive study of journalism and I knew that this dependence on the advertiser is a canker at the heart of the free press. But to go into all that would have been much too complicated. I preferred to keep to simpler more efficacious methods.

And I achieved my object. Peace was restored and maintained between the publishers of the *Morgenpost* and the Dresdner Bank. Later I was on excellent terms with Ullsteins. Apart from anything else Franz Ullstein, Louis's brother, had been a member of my Club in our student days. It is an indisputable fact that Ullsteins have done a tremendous lot to establish the reputation and importance of the German press. I was genuinely glad when the news reached me that they had resumed work in 1951.

A second task that fell to my lot in the Dresdner Bank was the preparation of prospectuses for the issue of securities to be offered on the Stock Exchange. Anyone wishing to have shares or bonds officially quoted on Berlin Exchange, i.e., under state supervision by a sworn broker, was obliged to have these securities approved by the Office of Acceptance on the Berlin Stock Exchange. For this purpose his bank representative would submit a prospectus for publication which must contain an exact description of the species and character of the securities as well as of the issuing establishments; that is, industrial, transport or commercial undertakings, provincial and other public corporations, mortgage banks.

These prospectuses often ran into half a dozen printed pages and the greatest care was taken to see that all particulars essential for the assessment of the securities concerned were included. They were compiled, therefore, in closest touch with the issuing undertaking or corporation in question.

In this way I became connected with a large number of such establishments; I learned to read and evaluate balance sheets and clear up ambiguities; I got to know how the various undertakings managed their business affairs; I became absorbed in municipal and national budgets and gained an insight into the administration of public monies. During my thirteen years with the Dresdner Bank we did not issue a single prospectus that I had not prepared.

I soon became so experienced in my particular province that smaller banks occasionally approached my board and requested that I might prepare prospectuses for them. One result of these activities was that a few years later I myself was elected a member of the Acceptance Office.

In addition to this branch of public relations and the preparation of prospectuses I chose a third occupation in which I could put my previous learning to practical use. Each of the big banks possessed at that time a so-called record office in which were stored the business reports of most of the limited companies, budgets of public corporations and similar material.

Since my Paris days I knew that some of the principal French banks, in addition to this special material, collected and made use of general economic data. Within certain limits the record keepers of the German banks had likewise launched out in this direction. My ambition was to enrich the Dresdner Bank's collection of literature relating to political economy and make use of it in the interests of our clientele. I began with the publication of monthly surveys of the development of German — and some foreign — economic systems which I had put together in the form of short statistical summaries. These reports were regularly enclosed with letters to our customers and were soon the subject of enthusiastic comment. Nowadays this sort of economic information is published by all the big banks as a matter of course. In addition to purely statistical surveys there are market reports and reports from other countries dealing with economic conditions abroad; tips for the export trade and similar relevant data.

But however interested I might be in all these things, my overwhelming ambition was to go in for the actual practical side of the banking business, and a few years after I had entered the bank the board granted my request. For a whole year I was allowed to work in every department of the bank in succession in order to become thoroughly at home in actual banking practice. Nor did I drop any of my usual work: I simply doubled my working hours by making use of the early morning before we opened, the midday break and the evening after closing time to tackle those matters generally dealt with in normal office hours. I saw precious little of my family and enjoyed little sleep during that year, but by the end of it I was familiar with every department of the banking business. In the course of those months I not only worked at correspondence and bookkeeping and learned how to safeguard and administer stocks and shares, but also acted as cashier and served the public over the counter, discounted bills and calculated foreign drafts — in short there was no section of the bank that I had not been through once.

The final feature of this apprentice year was attendance at the Stock Exchange. I had to learn to find my way about this witches' cauldron! I was of course not entirely unfamiliar with the rooms and the general goings on: my work on the prospectuses had already involved my visiting the Stock Exchange. Now, however, I learned how to buy and sell securities, how to deal with brokers and with customers.

The Berlin Bourse was a magnificent building. At midday hundreds of dealers in stocks and commodities assembled in the three vast halls. In the center were the enclosures behind which the sworn brokers would determine the prices according to the supply and demand. Along the walls were the tables of the banking houses and commodity buyers. On busy days it was pandemonium; when we were slack we beguiled the time with talk and jokes.

I have always emphasized the essential need of the Stock Exchange. It is an organized market that keeps money in circulation and makes possible the financing of domestic undertakings through the sale of securities. Where there is no efficient Stock Exchange the whole economy suffers from lack of financial opportunities. This affects not only commerce and industry but also public bodies who depend on the negotiating of loans. I have never had any use for the speculative activities of those people whose one ambition is to buy securities cheaply and sell them again as quickly and as dear as possible. Throughout my whole life I have eschewed any kind of Stock Exchange speculation.

The most popular media for speculation were the time transactions which did not have to be settled until the end of the month and consequently afforded the opportunity of making a profit on a deal — whether purchase or sale — by a second sale or purchase. Although I can look back today on fifty years' banking I can say with satisfaction that I have never concluded such a transaction on my own behalf.

Not least among the huge losses we suffered through the collapse of 1945 must be reckoned the elimination of the German — and particularly the Berlin — Stock Exchange. It is not only our entire German economy which is affected by the loss of this capital-market organization, but communities, the Federal Republic and German public corporations. We are hampered at every turn by lack of money for the most urgent investments, and any funds that may be available or that can possibly be raised are dissipated and frittered away for want of a central market organization. Even greater perhaps is the loss of international influence and prestige which German Exchanges enjoyed prior to the catastrophe of the World War.

It is due to my year of apprenticeship in the banking business that at the age of thirty-two I was already nominal manager of the Dresdner Bank and was promoted to branch management.

A particularly happy occurrence — so far as I was concerned — was the conclusion of a deal in 1905 between the Dresdner Bank and the New York Banking firm of Morgan & Company. On our side the negotiations were in the hands of Eugen Gutmann's son-in-law, a member of our board. His name was Hans Schuster; he was of Swiss nationality; his father was the celebrated builder of the St. Gotthard Railway. He probably owed his position in the Dresdner Bank to his marriage with Gutmann's daughter, who was not only a beauty but an extremely gifted woman.

One morning Schuster sent for me.

"Dr. Schacht," he said abruptly, "I propose to go to New York on the bank's business and need a secretary. Would you care to come along?"

No one was more delighted than I, nor did I withdraw when Schuster questioned me as to my knowledge of English. My reply was perhaps rather more confident than strictly accurate. The desire for a glimpse of yet another section of international political economy was mingled with curiosity as to the country to which I owed my Christian names of Horace Greeley.

Among the passengers on the outward voyage were distinguished artists of whom Caruso is probably the only one to be remembered. I must be one of the few remaining Germans who can still boast of having played shuffleboard with Caruso. I was beaten by the man with the famous voice.

Schuster was no stranger to the United States and therefore had no reason to prolong his stay in New York. He was kind enough, however, to give me a Sunday off so that I might see the Niagara Falls which in those days were among the few American sights really worth seeing. Since then many others have been added to their number. One day Schuster devoted to going to Washington to pay his respects to President Theodore Roosevelt, and I was invited to accompany him. Then, on the occasion of my trip to Washington in 1933, I was able to tell President Franklin Roosevelt that I had visited his uncle in these same rooms twenty-eight years previously.

But even greater than the "Thundering Waters" of the Indians and the "Thunderer" at the White House was the impression made upon me during the seven days I spent in the offices of Morgan & Company. The firm at that time was still housed in the old low corner building on Wall Street. The entire office was contained in a single room on the ground floor in which were dozens of desks where the employees worked, a small room for the department heads being screened off from the whole by glass halfway partitions. No question of visitors being formally announced, no waiting, or ante-rooms. Anyone who saw that a principal was disengaged could walk right up to his desk. Relations between heads and employees were very informal and free-and-easy without thereby lacking in respect.

The principals took their meals together in a small room where Schuster and I joined them, an intimate association which enabled me to meet them all. So far as I know, not one of them is alive today. The last time I saw Morgan's son, Jack, was in 1930 at The Hague, and that first-rate fellow Thomas Lamont at Heidelberg in 1934. I spent four months working with Jack at the Young-Plan Conference in Paris in the spring of 1929. Despite his kindness and charm he never attained his father's greatness.

In 1905 when Schuster and I were in New York old John Pierpont Morgan was at the height of his fame. By his unparalleled far-sightedness he had guided the firm to a position of extraordinary wealth and influence. I once asked him to what he attributed his firm's amazing rise. His reply was entirely characteristic of the man and throughout my ensuing years of work I have invariably found it a good guide. "I have always," said Morgan, "had faith in the economic future of my country."

In outward appearance he was a giant, broad-shouldered and of Herculean stature. His son Jack inherited his figure. His somewhat rough-hewn face was characterized by an unusually large, fleshy nose. I have only seen one other nose like it and that was August Thyssen's before he had it operated on. The contrast between that Cyrano-like nose and the wise kind eyes was all the more astonishing. Everyone who talked with Morgan came under their spell.

One of the most interesting examples of business which at that time were being carried on in Germany was the attempt by the State of Prussia to acquire a controlling interest in the Hibernia Coal Mines. The reason for this was probably the desire to secure the coal output for the State Railways on terms which would be unaffected by fluctuations in prices. Müller-Brackwede, at that time Prussian Minister of Commerce,* entrusted the Dresdner Bank with the confidential task of buying up the Hibernia shares for the Prussian Treasury according to Stock Exchange procedure.

Although the job was carried out with the greatest secrecy and as unobtrusively as possible there was no concealing the fact that there was a regular buyer for Hibernia shares. The prices of the shares rose gradually, but steadily. The Berliner Handelsgesellschaft, which conducted all the Hibernia financial business, began to smell a rat. Karl Fürstenberg was not so devoted to the government as all that, nor was he the man to stand quietly by and let a brother banker make off with the Hibernia Company. It was far too important a deal to allow Eugen Gutmann of the Dresdner Bank to get away with, so, together with other banks who were interested, he began to buy and before long there was a race, and no one knew which of the two banks would eventually acquire the controlling interest. The financing of the purchases gave rise to difficulties — not for the Dresdner Bank which was able to draw on state funds, but for the Handelsgesellschaft and its associated banks.

Then Karl Fürstenberg came to the rescue with an idea that amounted to a stroke of genius. His group's holding of Hibernia shares was turned into a limited company, Herne G.m.b.H. With these shares as security Herne G.m.b.H. issued a 4 per cent public loan, with the proceeds of which the banks were able to resume their activities.

When matters came to a climax Fürstenberg was found to be victorious. The controlling interest was and remained in his possession. The government made the best of a bad job and closed the matter by investing Herr Karl Fürstenberg with the Third Class and Herr Eugen Gutmann with the Fourth Class of the Order of the Red Eagle.

Another financial transaction in which I took part in the Dresdner Bank was especially typical for it shows how, in the Germany of that time, banking and industry co-operated to further the export trade.

The matter concerned the erection of the first big electric power station on the Witwatersrand in South Africa. A company had been formed in England whose aim was to exploit the gigantic water power of the Victoria Falls on the Zambesi, and the General Electric Company (A.E.G.) in Berlin had been asked to investigate the

* The equivalent of president of the Board of Trade.

project. It turned out that to put in a turbine plant installation at the Victoria Falls and a long-distance connection from the Falls to the mining district of Johannesburg simply would not pay. On the other hand, utilization of the vast quantities of Witwatersrand coal by means of a steam plant promised to be economically successful. The Victoria Falls Company therefore entered into a contract with the A.E.G. for the erection of a power plant on the Witwatersrand coalfield, while the company retained its attractive name as bait for future shareholders. The necessary capital was raised in Germany by means of a loan issued by the Dresdner Bank and the A.E.G. order paid for out of the proceeds. The company has greatly increased its scope and still functions as a distinctly paying concern, while the immense masses of the Victoria Falls continue their headlong descent unmolested, as before.

# XIII

## THE NEAR EAST

IN SPITE OF the bicycle on which I spent such a disproportionately large sum as a fifth-former in 1893, my favorite exercise all my life has been walking. It is thanks to the walking tours I have made during my life that I am able, at the age of seventy-six, to smoke my daily cigars with impunity and remain untouched by all the diseases of civilization usually attendant on a sedentary existence.

As a third-term student I followed up the end of my stay in Munich by a hike right across the Alps as far as Milan. Important as this feat appeared to me at the age of nineteen, it was a mere stroll compared with another tour in 1902, from Vladikavkas over the Caucasus to Tiflis, on to Echmiadzin, the seat of the Armenian patriarch, and back again over the icy Caucasus by the Becho Pass to the Black Sea port of Novorossisk.

Of the three Oriental trips I made between 1902 and 1909 this was by far the most strenuous and at the same time the loveliest. Paul Rohrbach had organized it and collected a group of nine young fellows. One of them was Hello von Gerlach, the only deputy who had been sent to the Reichstag by Friedrich Naumann's National-sozialer Verein (National Social Union) in 1896. The remaining six were likewise members of Naumann's set. There is a delightful and graphic account of our expedition from Rohrbach's pen in some old back numbers of *Die Zeit*, the first magazine published by Naumann between 1901 and 1903.

Paul Rohrbach, the well-known journalist and politician, was at that time thirty-three years old and a friend of Naumann whom I also knew. Friedrich Naumann and his teacher Stoecker were Evangelical social reformers, but while Stoecker was a conservative, Naumann betook himself and his ideas to the liberal-minded groups. After the First World War Naumann exercised considerable influence in the drafting of the Weimar Constitution. He died in 1919. One of his surviving pupils is Theodor Heuss, now President of the West German Federal Republic.

I have never belonged to Naumann's set even though I was intimate with one or two of them. A group whose purpose is to bring
together such opposite sections of society as industrial workers and
members of conservative circles must realize clearly that such an aim
is incompatible with the policy of "not wishing to give offense."

From the point of view of party politics it is difficult to reconcile
such conflicting ideas as conservative Christianity, monarchist tradition, national self-assertiveness, tolerance, liberal-minded progress
and social justice. It was therefore inevitable that Naumann's followers should very quickly split up among the various political
parties. His own pupils landed up partly among the Social Democrats, partly among the Freethinkers or other more right-wing groups.
The men belonging to the Naumann set were decent, well-intentioned fellows whom one was glad to number among one's friends,
but their mentality was not such as to inspire passionate enthusiasm.

Rohrbach's description of our travels began as follows:

"From Berlin to the Caucasus there is now no end to civilization.
It is true that the thread grows thinner and thinner . . . but it still
holds — as far as the railway extends." Written in 1902 this sentence
contains some pointers which today seem to us very prophetic.

Hello von Gerlach was throughout the trip the life and soul of
the party. Although older than any of us, as years go, he remained
indifferent to cold, hunger and the frightful cloudbursts that repeatedly drenched us; even the loss of his knapsack, stolen by some
long-fingered rascal, was not sufficient to upset his usual good temper
for more than a minute or so. When I met him again many years
later I was shocked by the changes that the war had wrought. Old,
embittered and lonely, he was engaged in working out queer radical
social programs and had quite lost touch with the outside world. He
was a wonderful companion, firmly rooted in the peaceful years before the war . . .

Rohrbach had begun by studying theology. In addition to an
extensive education he had a keen eye for realities. Midway between
Russia and Turkey, those two great world-philosophic antagonists
of medieval times, he took careful note of all fortifications and drew
my attention to the wretched state of the batteries along the Turkish
coast — which I was later to see for myself. I was astonished at the
perspicacity with which he sized up the chances of those two opponents on the shores of the Black Sea.

"Nowadays [1902] a Russian fleet could occupy the Bosporus and
take Constantinople before the Western Powers even knew that the

Imperial Fleet had left Odessa," he remarked once. The three miserable vessels which at that time constituted the Sultan's entire fleet would have had little chance of withstanding an attack.

This was before the Turkish Revolution by which conditions on the Bosporus were radically altered. When only six years afterwards I visited Turkey I found that a start had already been made of a new, energetic policy under the leaders of Young Turkey. The "Sick Man of Europe" had begun to recover.

The memory of that Caucasian tour remained with me for a long time. When a year later I married, my wife wanted me to tell her some of the details. Didn't we have some funny experiences?

"Oh yes," I said. "The funniest thing that happened on that trip was meeting a Russian mining engineer who was prospecting for silver. He joined us in a drink and sang Russian songs. Then he insisted that we should sing German songs with him. Unfortunately he knew only one, so we all sang it over and over again."

"And what was the song?"

" 'Die Wacht am Rhein'! Imagine it — in the middle of the icy Caucasus . . . !"

Nowadays it sounds like a profoundly serious fairy tale . . .

After this mighty journey my next trip — to the Balkans — in 1906 was a mere stroll. I had asked my father to come with me. We went through Montenegro, Bosnia and Herzegovina. I was twenty-nine years old at the time and had successfully concluded my first banking deals. While we were wandering through these countries which to us western "progressives" seemed very behind the times, my mind was on economic problems. "At bottom they are the same as ours," I remarked eventually to my father.

"Think so?" he asked. "I have the impression that they're still living in the good old days. Plenty of handicrafts, few factories, bad roads, hardly any railways, and no banks."

"Yes," I replied, "that's true. Outwardly everything is very different from what it is at home. But take the fundamental problems. They're more in evidence here because they're simpler. There is less luxury among the ordinary folk, fewer superfluous possessions. But at bottom they are human beings like you and me! What they don't provide themselves they have to buy. That's why they're eager to earn money. The mountain peasant sells his cheese in order to buy grain for bread. The sheep farmers sell the wool and buy food with the proceeds. Admittedly food is cheaper than with us, their wants are fewer — therefore they need less money. But they do need *some* money. It's exactly the same with transport. They have to move their goods from one place to another — therefore they build roads. There isn't the same turnover of goods as in our industrial Germany, so they are able to let their roads remain in worse condition; but they can't do without them. They have their holidays and their bad seasons — therefore they must make some kind of planned provision . . . just like us. Everything is the same as it is at home — it's only the standards that are different."

"If you put it like that," said my father, "you'll find your fundamental economic problems even among the bush Negroes."

"I'm convinced I should find them among the bush Negroes," I said. "Civilization creates no new problems — it merely intensifies the age-old ones, the eternal problems of mankind . . ."

When in later years I was confronted with economic tasks that seemed to be very complicated and obscure, I would picture to myself how those same problems would appear to primitive peoples. I would recall my remarks about the Balkan nations and the Caucasian tribes, and after a while I would invariably come back to what I might call the Fundamental Factors of Political Economy. The structure of the problem became clear — and with it also the possibility of tackling it.

A permanent reminder of that summer trip to Bosnia was a Bosnian costume which I had had made to measure and wore at the Berlin Colonial Ball. It made a great impression on account of its genuineness. The Bosnian knee breeches fit very tightly at the waist, but are cut very wide lower down, so that they are enormously baggy behind. No Berlin tailor would ever have achieved such a work of art. On the other hand I should hardly have found a Bosnian costume that fitted me, at a theatrical costumer's. I had been strolling through various bazaars in Sarajevo — little booths with a roof but no front wall. As I was passing a tailor's stall it suddenly occurred to me to ask him how long he would take to make a costume.

"When are you leaving?" the tailor asked.

"The day after tomorrow," I said.

"I can let you have it by then," said the expert, and took up his tape measure. "Come inside, sir, I'll measure you right away. Please take off your breeches."

I took off my breeches and he measured me. The news spread like wildfire that a visitor from far-off Germany was in the tailor's shop, standing in his underpants. The inhabitants of Sarajevo felt that was too good to miss.

Whether the Bosnian tailors always require so much time for taking measurements or whether this one was unwilling to spoil his fellow countrymen's enjoyment on this one-and-only occasion, I have never been able to discover. Anyhow, I stood for a long while in my scanty attire in front of a large crowd who lost no opportunity of contributing good advice. But the costume was well worth the prolonged measuring. It fitted perfectly. With chibouk * and fez I need not feel ashamed of appearing at the Colonial Ball . . .

In 1908 I had joined a Freemason's Lodge. Freemasonry runs in my family. My father belonged to an American Lodge. My great-grandfather, Christian Ulrich Detlev von Eggers, was one of the Masonic notables of the Age of Enlightenment.

Neither the ceremonies of admission to the old Prussian Lodge Urania zur Unsterblichkeit in Berlin, nor my later experiences in Freemasonry have ever been able to convince me that my German Lodge was a dangerous international organization which compelled its members to submit to some satanic ritual. That kind of thing is part of that unpleasant gossip invented by certain people who gamble on the stupidity of the masses and their love of creepy stories. The Freemasons were once a community — a community which set its face against any kind of religious intolerance. Their warlike actions date back to the Age of Enlightenment. When the struggle was over, the importance of the Freemasons also diminished. What the Lodges preserved was the law of humanity and of friendly social activity.

That the Freemasons in other countries did undoubtedly sometimes take an active part in politics I learned during a trip to Turkey with Rohrbach and Ernst Jäkh in 1909. My Berlin Lodge had given me the address of a chemist who was a Freemason and lived in Salonika. As I could not get my bearings I went into a shop on the main street and asked the way to the chemist's house. In less than ten minutes the shop was full of dozens of men, all of them Freemasons, who asked what they could do for me. At one stroke I had made contact with numerous inhabitants of this foreign city. This turned out to be very useful; my new friends initiated me into the background of the Young Turks Movement and their war against the absolute Sultan-ship of the Porte.

In this way I learned that all the leaders of the Young Turks were Freemasons and their secret meetings took place under the protection of the Lodge — the only place where they were safe from spies.

* Long-stemmed Turkish pipe.

The incident made me thoughtful. I recognized that Freemasonry, — not, admittedly, in Germany but in other countries — is sometimes used for political purposes and I understood the reason for the dislike of Freemasonry in certain circles. Nevertheless I must once again emphasize that conditions in Germany are different. The Freemasons in the Old Prussian Lodges supported the idea of the preservation of the state through the monarchy.

From Salonika our road led to Constantinople where we met most of the leaders of the Young Turks.

What I did bring back with me from this trip — in addition to a Turkish Decoration and a multitude of impressions — was a most unpleasant malaria which, curiously enough, did not attack me until after my return, when it did so with a vengeance. As the doctors were at a loss to know what to do about it my condition grew worse from day to day and I narrowly escaped blackwater fever. Luckily my brother Eddy came and took charge of me and dismissed the three right honorable Berlin specialists who had been treating me. Together with Philalethes Kuhn, the celebrated authority on tropical diseases who was sent by Rohrbach, Eddy managed to set me on my feet again. I have never had a recurrence of the trouble.

# XIV

## MY FAMILY

On the tenth of January, 1903, I married Luise Sowa whom I had met at the Tennis Club seven years previously. We had become engaged when I was nineteen and she twenty-one. Then, when I returned from my term at the university in Paris, more than a year later, we broke it off; we both realized that I was too young to commit myself. Our position was very similar to that of my father and mother — our acquaintance was followed by a long separation.

When after a lapse of five years I saw Luise again in the autumn of 1902 I already had an excellent position. I was earning more than my father and there was nothing to prevent my starting a family. Luise attracted me as much as she had done the first day we met. We resumed our walks by the Schlachtensee, skated together there, and were soon officially engaged.

By that time Luise's father had died. Inspector Sowa had for years served in the immediate Imperial entourage in Potsdam and, apparently during that period, had acquired an almost morbid distrust of all mankind. At any rate he kept an eagle-eyed watch on his two daughters. So long as he lived Luise and I had to resort to any amount of subterfuge to be able to meet in peace. There are times when a Prussian detective inspector's unswerving sense of propriety can be very trying to a courting couple.

When we met again there were no further obstacles to a short engagement. Luise the practical started looking around for somewhere to live. When she had found a flat in Berlin-Friedenau that appealed to me we settled the date and were married, twelve days before my twenty-sixth birthday.

The first year of our married life proved fairly eventful. I exchanged political economy for banking — and in November our first child, Inge, was born.

The changeover to banking meant that I had to work very hard and had little time for my first family. In the morning I went by bus

— later by electric tram — to the Dresdner Bank, came home in the evening and sat down at my desk to write my book reviews and articles for the two *Year Books*.

I don't think that as a husband I can have been easy to live with. It was not in my nature to settle down to a comfortable middle-class existence. Even today I am ambitious. In those days I was constantly on the lookout for some new line, or occupied with my own ideas.

Luise displayed great understanding and appreciation of my work. She possessed the gift of being able to adapt herself easily to any circumstances; she was an excellent housewife and deeply interested in all my doings. When, later, I abandoned my private life for politics and public service she took these changes in her stride. The slender, dark-haired tennis player and skater of earlier years became with the passing of time a very distinguished and quick-witted society lady. Her hair went gray early — a silvery white that made a striking contrast to her dark eyes and eyebrows.

Ours was a very companionable marriage. We visited friends or invited them to our home; now and then we gave a dance; we went to evening parties and regularly attended the Press Ball, one of the biggest social events of the year. In the summer we went for outings in the neighborhood of Berlin, and during my holidays traveled in France, Belgium, Holland, the Mediterranean countries and even, on a later occasion, the United States.

In spite of these pleasant interruptions, however, the basic theme of our marriage was work. I have already mentioned that six years after joining the Dresdner Bank I became nominal manager and was now joint branch manager, while at the same time holding an additional appointment in the economic section. Our son Jens had been born a year previously. Both these events led to our building our own house — a small villa in Zehlendorf with a large garden, where we lived for fifteen years.

After the First World War our family circle was increased by the marriages of my two brothers. Eddy, the doctor, had married a Swedish girl, whom he later divorced, and I helped to care for his children. Eddy somewhat resembled our grandfather, who also did not bother overmuch about his sons' education.

About the same time my younger brother Oluf returned from Africa. Oluf, who took entirely after the Eggerses, had likewise married and until the outbreak of war had been an engineer in the Cameroons and South Africa. His long stay in the tropics, coupled with war service, had ruined his health. I found him a job in Berlin, but he did not remain in it for long. One day he entered his car and with his eldest son went for a drive out of Berlin. Out in the country he pulled up suddenly, got out, sat down in a ditch and a few minutes later was dead of a stroke.

As Oluf was by no means well-to-do the care of his children fell to my lot.

When I went to India in 1939 I took Eddy's eldest son Sven with me. He had considerable literary talent and wrote good verse, novels and short stories. Later he came up against the National Socialist laws, was arrested, thrown into Mauthausen Concentration Camp and perished there in 1944. The fact that his uncle was Minister at the time did not help — on the contrary. At that time I was looked upon with suspicion by the party and the Gestapo.

Our marriage, though a successful one, was not without its disagreements, though at first they did not unduly affect us. Luise had inherited from her father that narrow Prussian outlook which can sometimes develop into bigotry. I myself, however, had been brought up to proceed on more diplomatic lines and to show consideration for other people — so long as questions of principle were not involved.

None of this need have disturbed our pleasant family relationship had politics not intervened. Already my very Right-wing Radical wife had reproached me when I subscribed to the first draft of the Young Plan. Later, when Hitler came into power, she was one of his most wholehearted and devoted adherents. From the very first I had followed his movements with a keenly critical eye; but she refused to hear a word against him. Matters eventually reached the stage when she would pass on, in Berlin society, any disparaging remarks I had made at home. Even when I pointed out that by so doing she was endangering my life she did not cease. Finally I took the decisive step and obtained a judicial separation.

That was in 1938 when I was already looked upon as a suspect by the party on account of my antagonistic pronouncements. Throughout those months I acted as leader of the coup d'état which was frustrated by the Munich Conference. I plotted with Generals von Witzleben and Halder in an attempt, by a bold stroke, to thwart the government's disastrous policy. During that period it was necessary to weigh every word. Any careless statement by my wife could have sent me to the gallows.

Thus I lived apart from my wife during the last years of our marriage, although we often met and talked. Then she became seriously ill. I went to see her a week before she died and had an affectionate talk with her. That was during the war. The doctors didn't know what was wrong; she was in a hospital in South Germany and seemed fairly comfortable. I had hardly returned to Berlin when I received a telegram telling me of her death. We had been married thirty-seven years.

Each of my two children of this first marriage followed a different path. Inge went to a girls' school and after passing her final examination proceeded to college and studied political economy in Heidelberg. She was a typical Schacht — the name, be it known, comes from the Plattdeutsch dialect word *Schaft*, implying that those who bear it are tall and slender. At twenty-six she married Dr. Hilger von Scherpenberg of the Foreign Office, who today is a Permanent Secretary in the federal government.

My son Jens, seven years younger than Inge, took his final examination from the Arndt Grammar School at Dahlem and spent a few terms at the university, but switched over to a business career. He had two years to begin with in the banking firm of Mendelssohn & Company in Berlin, then a year in the States with the First National Bank of Chicago, then with the Flick Combine and subsequently with the Gutehoffnungshütte Combine.

In the war he served as an officer. During the last few days prior to the capitulation he was on short leave. Some older friends who foresaw the inevitable end tried to keep him in Berlin, but his sense of responsibility and esprit de corps would not allow him to do so. He returned to his company and was taken prisoner with his men. Brother officers of his who eventually came back reported that Jens would share the microscopic extra rations which came to him as an officer with the men of his company, pushing them through the barbed wire. When the Russians took the prisoners from the camps and drove them on the long forced march to the East he must have perished from exhaustion. I never heard of him again. He was quiet, reserved, very clever, and would have made an outstanding economist.

The family life of a public man should not, in itself, have anything to do with his memoirs. Discrepancies will always arise between what is described as simple domestic happiness and higher duties in the life of any man who, above and beyond the confines of his family circle, is concerned with the welfare of an entire country.

It was only under the emperors that Romans, to whom public life meant everything and the family very little, began to scrutinize the family circumstances of their statesmen — and the period of decadence had already set in.

Proof that during the early years of my married life my thoughts extended beyond the office of a bank manager was furnished many years later by a friend. He recalled that one day we had been discussing our future and I had disclosed my aims as follows:

"I would like to enter public service one of these days — provided I were materially entirely independent. I won't be one of those officials who are forever oppressed by the knowledge that their business existence depends on their strict obedience to the orders of their superiors. As an official I want to be able at any time to retire again into private life should I become involved in questions of conscience in the course of my duties . . . "

This conversation took place during a trip to Turkey on one of those marvelous Oriental nights when one's surroundings are unfortunately alive with vermin. All my life I have had a horror of every kind of bloodsucker. In the Caucasus, on the Black Sea, in Turkey — no matter where — I preferred to sleep on deck or under a tree, even on the coldest nights, rather than share my sleeping quarters with lice and fleas. Recalling these impressions had driven the conversation with my friend clean out of my head. But I am quite prepared to believe that I did say something of the sort. Material dependence implies intellectual servitude. A man who merely obeys orders loses his pleasure in independent work, his creative ability, his zest, his best qualities.

I have often been accused of ambition, as though that were a fault. I have always had a great ambition to do something worth while, not for my own personal advantage, but above all for the common weal. I have never made any secret of it; indeed, it must have been noticeable at an early stage, for in my final report at my grammar school was written: "Feels he is called to higher things." And it is true that in pursuit of these "higher things" family and friends always come off badly.

# XV

## GERMANY'S TURNING POINT

HERE ARE a few pleasant recollections of the last years of peace. One of them is the trip in the cruiser *Magdeburg* in 1913 at the invitation of the Admiralty. I had written an article in honor of the Emperor Wilhelm II's Silver Jubilee for Admiral Löhlein, which was published in the *Marine-Rundschau*. The invitation was his way of saying Thank you.

My Baltic cruise lasted a week. The memory of it is saddened by the fact that the *Magdeburg* and her hospitable commander were sunk shortly after the outbreak of war.

Another pleasant memory is of the visit of a group of forty distinguished Turks whom I shepherded on a tour through Germany. Thereby hangs a tale.

After my trip to Turkey, which finished up with a bad attack of malaria, Jäkh, Rohrbach and I had founded a German-Turkish Society of which I was chairman. Its object was to establish personal relations between Turkish industrialists, businessmen, higher officials, leading German economists and interesting personalities in our cultural life. We actually managed to invite forty prominent Turks for a four weeks' tour through Germany. The climax of the trip was a reception at Friedrichshafen on the shores of Lake Constance where, with the aid of public contributions after the air disaster at Echterdingen, Count Zeppelin had built the new airship *Hansa*.

Thanks to seventy-three-year-old Count Zeppelin, the tour proved an unforgettable experience for everyone. None of us had ever flown before. It is easy to picture the faces of the Turks when we suddenly saw "Germany from above."

The world was still in the throes of the controversy as to whether aircraft should be "lighter than air" or "heavier than air." The Wright brothers had succeeded, a few years previously, in remaining in the air for a few hundred yards in their motor aircraft. When the Zeppelin was supreme master of the air, motor aircraft were still in a very primitive state. It took World War I to bring about a change. All the deeper, therefore, was the impression we gained from our flight in the airship *Hansa.*

At the luncheon arranged by Count Zeppelin for his guests after his successful flight the Turks gave free rein to their enthusiasm. The Count was in the best of spirits and told us a great deal about the good and bad luck of his experiences with airships. He spoke, too, of the German people's willing sacrifices, and of the national fund which had resulted in not less than six million marks.

"Of all those who contributed to the fund," he said, "one small boy gave me the greatest pleasure. The youngster sent me three marks and wrote that he had received this money for notifying the fire brigade in the nick of time and so preventing an outbreak of fire by smashing the glass of a fire alarm." And he added, "That's something I've wanted to do for a long time!"

That highly successful tour with our Turkish guests had an amusing sequel where I was concerned. Kriege, at that time Secretary of the Turkish Section in the Foreign Office, was instrumental in procuring for me the Order of the Crown, Third Class. Such an award, however, could not go through without the relevant bureaucracy — in this instance the German Minister of Commerce. He, for his part, took the view that the award of so exalted an order to so young a banker (I was thirty-four at the time) was excessive. Kriege stuck to his guns. If it wasn't to be the Order of the Crown, Third Class, then at least it should be the Order of the Red Eagle, Fourth Class. But even that seemed to the Minister of Commerce too great an honor. He said he was prepared to award me the Order of the Crown, Fourth Class, instead of the Order of the Red Eagle. By this time, however, I was no longer interested. I refused the order point-blank and in consequence have never been the recipient of a Prussian order, apart from the Iron Cross (II).

By contrast, when in later years I was in a good position the most varied orders were showered upon me, especially in the case of official visits abroad. When I traveled through the Balkans in 1936 a French journalist declared that my journey was in the nature of a "small-scale commercial crusade." * "You are mistaken," I replied, "it is a large-scale 'crusade.'"

* The correct translation of the German word *Kreuzzug,* the only sense in which it is generally used, is "Crusade." Its *literal* meaning, however, is a "procession of crosses," and it is in this sense that the author uses it as a play on the word "cross," referring to the many orders bestowed upon him.

Most amusing were the highly attractive Chinese orders. Carved out of red and green jade they presented a very pleasing and artistic appearance. I experienced the same kind of thing with the Italians as with the Prussians. On one occasion Ambassador Attolico told me that all the German ministers had now visited Italy and there was an earnest desire that I should come to Rome. I consented, on condition that I did not receive any order. Attolico smilingly intimated that that would be impossible. My Italian visit never came off, and I have never been the recipient of an Italian order.

Once only in my life I went hunting for precious stones — not actually with pick and shovel but by taking a share in an emerald mine in South America. It happened in this way: in 1913 I received a visit from one of the partners in a firm of jewelers at Idar-Oberstein, whose brother-in-law was a friend of mine. He told me that he owned the concession for the reopening of the El Chivor emerald mine in Colombia which for years had been lying idle. He himself, he said, had found magnificent emeralds there, in no way inferior to those from El Muzo. Would I be interested in the reopening of the mine? The stones he showed me were certainly very fine. Since my visitor was known to me as an honorable and trustworthy person I managed to interest one or two of my acquaintances. Between us we raised the necessary capital for the prospector's expedition.

We persuaded Privy Councilor Scheibe, the famous chief mineralogist of the Berlin Geological Institute, to go out to Colombia as our expert. His reports were not unfavorable. We were feeling very hopeful when the First World War intervened. And there was our professor-and-privy councilor stuck fast in Colombia. Further financing by means of foreign exchange became impossible. A North American syndicate acquired our concession.

We consoled ourselves at the time for the loss of the emeralds by recalling the legend connected with El Chivor.

Three hundred years previously a Spanish adventurer had arrived in Colombia. His journeyings hither and thither all over the country brought him to El Chivor, a little Indian village in the middle of virgin forest. There he noticed that on feast days the villagers adorned themselves with exquisite emeralds. The source of the stones was carefully withheld from him so he proceeded to make advances to the chief's daughter, winning her confidence with promises of marriage — and she let him into the secret. The Spaniard dug up quantities of stones and took them to Bogotá, the capital, where he amassed a huge fortune, calmly jilted the Indian girl and married into one of the wealthy families. Retribution was not long in coming. On a certain occasion when he came down from Bogotá to El Chivor for some more emeralds he found that the Indians had diverted the course of a mountain torrent that flowed near the shaft, and the stream had buried the mine deep under masses of rock and tree trunks from the virgin forest. The Indian girl, however, laid a curse on him: "Cursed be thy wealth. Cursed be thou, thyself. Cursed be the emeralds of El Chivor. They shall lose their color and sparkle and he who weareth one of these gems shall curse thee, as I curse thee."

When the Spaniard returned to Bogotá where he had sold many of the emeralds it turned out that these stones did not keep their color or their sparkle. He was exposed as a fraud, driven out of the community and perished miserably.

I am quite ready to believe that the above is only a fairy tale to explain why the mine was once again abandoned after it had been working. At any rate the little emerald I possess as a memento of my jewel mine has retained its old sparkle and color to this day.

The loss of El Chivor is a mere fraction of Germany's losses in foreign securities during World War I. This is brought home to me more and more clearly whenever I have occasion to dip in to a little booklet that I wrote at that time. The year in which the Emperor Wilhelm II celebrated his Silver Jubilee was also a memorable one for the Dresdner Bank — now established forty years during which time it had risen to be the third of Germany's principal banks. It was in honor of this fortieth anniversary that I wrote the above mentioned booklet, entitled *Germany's Economic Resources*, describing the rise both of my banking firm and of my country.

The work summed up the results of the past forty years. The figures speak for themselves: my contribution consisted in having assembled them in reasonable sequence. Whoever read them would obtain a clear picture of the growth of German economy under the Empire. From the continental, intensely agricultural Germany of forty years previously had evolved an industrial and commercial state which was beginning to spread its feelers all over the world.

An essential feature of this process had been the rapid accumulation of capital in Germany which had enabled our country to reach out far beyond her own borders and to participate in the economic development of other countries and continents. German banks had made timely loans to big North American firms and by the purchase of shares and issues of bonds had acquired an interest in North American Railways.

Another successful German financial activity was the big cable companies which laid telegraphic cables between North America and Europe. German shipping had created a fleet of the most modern type of merchant vessels, not only tramp steamers but regular liner services to America, Africa and Asia.

In proportion as our international trade relations developed, branch establishments of affiliated companies and German banks sprang up abroad. The Dresdner Bank founded the Deutsche Orient Bank with establishments in Constantinople, Cairo and elsewhere, and the Deutsche Südamerikanische Bank with branches in the Argentine, Brazil and Chile. Earlier still the Deutsche Bank had founded the Deutsche Ueberseeische Bank. Domestic developments likewise showed how greatly the structure of our life had changed. Between 1870 and 1910 the population of Germany had risen from a full sixty million, an increase of exactly 52 per cent. Comparative figures show that the British increase in population during the same period was 37 per cent, the French only 8 per cent. In 1911 the National Debts of these three countries stood as follows: Germany — 317 gold marks per head. England — 330 gold marks. France — 666 gold marks — the two last computed from their respective currencies.

For military purposes the contribution per head of population in 1912 was: Germany — 21 marks. England — 32 marks. France — 27 marks.

Wages at Krupps's had risen by nearly 100 per cent since 1880. Sugar consumption (always a sign of general prosperity) had increased by 300 per cent; cotton had doubled.

Thanks to the chemical industry German agriculture too had been able to increase output enormously. In 1912 the harvest in Germany was 21 Doppelzentner per hectare as against 14 Doppelzentner in France and Austria-Hungary.

German coal output had increased sevenfold in the past four decades.

As a market for foreign goods Germany played a considerable part. She absorbed a larger proportion of British exports than either France or the U.S.A. In 1910 the international port of Hamburg was second only to New York in respect of tonnage.

The emigration figures were particularly impressive. The peak year was 1854, when a quarter of a million Germans left the country. After that numbers temporarily declined, but rose again in the sixties and reached a new peak in 1870 with more than a hundred and twenty thousand emigrants. After the German victory in the Franco-German War there was a sharp downward curve which touched bottom in 1876–77 with only twenty thousand emigrants. Immediately thereafter, however, the situation deteriorated and in 1880 the emigration figures again totaled a quarter of a million a year. After that the numbers steadily declined, to rise again for a brief interval in 1890 — presumably as a result of the agricultural crisis — and then dropped to a minimum. It is unlikely that more than twenty to twenty-five thousand Germans left their homes each year between 1895 and 1915.

It is owing to the industrialization of Germany and the policy of long-term trade agreements that the emigration fever abated after 1890. On the other hand a new problem arose; namely, that Germany's steady advance in the world's markets aroused the antagonism of those older industrial countries who were the first in the field and felt that their chances in the market were being threatened. That applied first and foremost to England.

Confronted with this new danger there was one chance of appeasement; namely, to engage in colonial activities. Old Bismarck can hardly have realized that it was a turning point in German destiny when the increasing population made industrial development inevitable. His whole policy was too deeply rooted in those days when the countries of Europe were not yet faced with problems of food production. This must assuredly have been the reason why Bismarck, very late and very hesitatingly, gave his support to Germany's first attempts at colonial activity. As a result, Germany's colonial administration has never managed to provide a remedy for the problems automatically created by Germany's industrial progress.

The former conception of colonial policy is nowadays completely discredited, and rightly so. Precisely on that account it is all the more essential, I feel, to emphasize the fact that Germany's colonial administration has never been directed towards any imperialistic goal. The German colonial force, which existed for the purpose of maintaining order, never exceeded a total of six thousand men in all the German colonies together. In neither of the two European wars were natives of the German colonies employed in battle, whereas native divisions from North Africa and India fought in large numbers with the Allies in Europe. German administrative and economic achievements in our colonies have been the subject of the highest praise by foreign connoisseurs. Even after Germany's defeat in two world wars her reputation has been preserved among the natives, despite the fact that these colonies had been in German possession for only twenty-five years.

Nowadays I learn more than I did formerly from the booklet I wrote for the Dresdner Bank's celebrations. Within two decades the European situation had radically altered. Politically and economically Germany had become a Great Power; England had emerged from her "splendid isolation" of Victorian days and was engaged in creating a strong network of alliances and agreements, directed against Germany. French loans amounting to billions contributed to the Tsar's military preparations in Russia. Bismarck's system of treaties had once meant that Germany was secure against all surprises. Now, however, she had fallen into an "isolation" which was anything but "splendid."

It is not my business in this book to describe how this isolation was achieved. At that time I was firmly convinced that there would never be war.

# XVI

## THE FIRST WORLD WAR

THE OUTBREAK of war came as a surprise to me as it did to all Germans. Right up to the eleventh hour every reasonable person still believed that the Sarajevo incident would remain a localized affair. Only when columns of soldiers came marching down the street, accompanied by cheering and weeping crowds; when the first tidings of disaster reached us from East Prussia and premature news of victory from the West, were we compelled to realize that a war of continental proportions had broken out. What Bismarck had always tried to prevent had come to pass — Germany was fighting on two fronts.

I had no conception of what such a war would be like. Since the day when a military surgeon major had examined me and rejected me as unfit for service on account of "acute myopia," I had taken no further interest in military doings.

Moreover, there were two institutions of which, all my life, I stood in considerable awe: one was the military, the other was officialdom. A captain or a government official to me represented huge beasts who, in some incomprehensible fashion, contrived to make life difficult for civilians.

During the first weeks after the declaration of war it was not possible to determine any economic changes. Financial policy adapted itself easily and smoothly to war conditions. Not until the first year was well under way did more serious problems arise. That was the beginning of never ending anxieties over raw materials and food supplies; and the steadily rising financial demands of the national economy, which had had to switch over completely to war requirements, gave us bankers many a headache.

Walther Rathenau, later Foreign Minister, was the first to raise the question of raw material supplies. Only then was the official machinery for the procuring and allocation of raw materials and food supplies set in motion. The dreadful word "control" so closely related to "bondage" was to become a permanent addition to our dictionaries. From 1914 onward new controls were constantly being imposed — gold, foreign exchange, metals, sugar, rubber — anything . . .

Moreover it was not more than two months before the war had me in its clutches. In October 1914 I was asked whether I would be prepared to take over the duties of banking administration in Occupied Belgium. Of course I accepted, and was therefore installed as administrator of the bank in Belgian Occupied Territory.

I remained there in this capacity from October 1914 to July 1915. Unfortunately I had never mastered the fundamental principle of the Army; that is, never, under any circumstances, to attract attention. I attracted the attention of my superiors in Belgium on account of one or two unusual ideas which were to give me a lot of bother and unpleasantness.

One of the problems of the Occupation was how to induce the Belgians to remit the Occupation costs in cash. During the first months the military simply commandeered whatever they wanted, which gave rise to difficulties for the Occupying Forces as well as for the population. It was essential to replace this irregular procedure by something different. Major von Lumm, the head of the Finance Department and a member of the Board of Directors of the Reichsbank, had had the bright idea to replace the existing Belgian coinage by a new currency. I considered this unnecessary, but could do nothing to prevent it. It now fell to my lot to organize the payment of Occupation costs by means of negotiations with the Belgian Société Générale. I succeeded in making the Belgian officials understand the advantages of cash payments over haphazard requisitioning. Above all, I pointed out, it would be possible to maintain the country's trade on an orderly basis if all goods were paid for in cash.

The Belgians objected first and foremost on grounds of foreign policy. The government had emigrated to London. Consequently the Belgian State, as such, could not be involved. I suggested instead by way of solution that the nine Belgian provinces should issue a loan exceeding the amount of the Occupation costs. The proceeds of this loan should realize a sum sufficient to cover these costs. My suggestion was eventually accepted after a good deal of discussion — I assume with the tacit consent of the Belgian Government in London, for despite all military precautions there was constant underground communication between the Belgian representatives in Brussels and the government in London.

The next step was to induce the German military authorities to agree to this plan. Of course commandeering, pure and simple, suited the military far better than proper methods of payment. In this respect I don't think there is anything to choose between the soldiers of one army and another. Requisitioning can never be so strictly controlled as payments from fixed capital.

Major von Lumm, therefore — very smart in his uniform of the Munich Life Guards — took me along to a meeting of the military authorities where I felt rather out of it as the only civilian in mufti. The rest were covered in gold braid and devastatingly impressive! Herr von Lumm left it to me to introduce my plan and defend it.

Then the nine provincial governors had to append their signatures to the agreement. In this connection some final difficulties arose. These men were fully aware of the heavy responsibility they were assuming vis-à-vis their people and their government when they consented to sign. I had fixed the monthly payments at forty million francs. At the last minute one or two of the governors tried to persuade me to reduce this amount to thirty-five million francs. The negotiations threatened to break down. I could understand the Belgians — they wanted to get as much as they could out of the deal — perhaps even they were anxious to provide against the contingency that the Germans might one day depart, and be able to prove that they had saved their country sixty million francs a year. But I wasn't able to let them off. I asked Herr von Sandt, the chairman of the civilian authorities, to give me a little time, and explained to the Belgians that if my suggestions were not accepted I should turn any further procedure over to the military. This argument was effective. We obtained the Belgians' signatures to a document guaranteeing payment of Occupation costs amounting to over four hundred and eighty million francs for the first year of the war.

In the subsequent years of the Occupation, after I left Belgium, it was no longer possible to obtain the signatures of the Belgian governors to further bonds, which, on the contrary, were signed by German provincial administrators in Belgium.

In the beginning the Governor General of Occupied Belgium was von der Goltz-Pasha — Field Marshal General Colmar von der Goltz, who had been awarded the rank of Pasha for his many years' service as organizer of the Turkish Army. He was typical of a Prussian officer of the old school — of great personal courage, intensely honorable, very human though somewhat reserved, correct, and with a great sense of duty. In addition he had an exceptionally good brain.

I had known him since 1911 when I was chairman of the German-Turkish Association and we had taken those forty distinguished visitors from the Land of the Crescent on a tour through Germany.

I didn't see why I, as a civilian, should be deprived of the privilege of frequenting the Officers Club which had been established in the Brussels Casino. I quickly had it rubbed into me that that was a typical civilian notion and that the staff officers clung tenaciously to their exclusiveness, especially when stationed at base.

"Impossible!" said Major von Lumm when I told him I intended to eat at the Officers Club. "It would be necessary to obtain the Governor General's permission."

"Right!" I said, "then let's ask him!"

"Out of the question!" von Lumm protested. "What are you thinking of? We cannot trouble the Governor General with a request of that kind. Perhaps we might consult Herr von der Lancken, the head of the appropriate department of the Foreign Office."

We duly consulted Herr von der Lancken who likewise raised considerable objections to a civilian frequenting the German Officers Club in Brussels. Von der Lancken also was of the opinion that so important a personage as His Excellency, Field Marshal General von der Goltz-Pasha, Governor General of Occupied Belgium, must certainly not be bothered with the request of an ordinary man with no title higher than that of Doctor. I began to grow impatient.

"Gentlemen," I said, "since you both have such objections you will perhaps allow me to approach von der Goltz direct."

"But — will the Governor General receive you?" they asked, as with one voice.

"My dear sirs, I know von der Goltz very well, but I didn't want to go over your heads."

As I expected, Goltz received me very cordially. Before I could get out a word about my request he said: "You'll dine with me this evening at the Casino, of course?" I turned up on the dot. To no small astonishment of my superior and some fifty other officers, Goltz had me sit on his right and engaged me in lively talk.

In the course of conversation he asked me about a little adventure I had had when I arrived in Belgium. He already had the official version, but wanted me to give him further details. So I told him the story.

Before I left for Brussels, Secretary Lewald of the Ministry for Home Affairs called me up and asked me if I would look after a lady during the journey. She was going to Brussels to inspect a house that belonged to her. Lewald had described her over the phone as a charming person (he was known as somewhat of a ladies' man) — a certain Princess X, with the *grand style* of a real society lady — if now and then some quiet gambling went on in her house — well, she looked the other way.

I looked after the Princess on the journey to Belgium, but kept my distance — she was a bit too much made-up for my taste. Moreover, since she tended to be rather too "forthcoming" I put up at another hotel in Brussels and thenceforth only ran across her once or twice in the anterooms of various government offices. She really was a woman of great charm and elegance. Small wonder, then, that all the men she had to do with fell for her. In addition, she had a letter of introduction to the Governor General from old Frau Krupp so that she obtained permission without any difficulty to take little gift packages to the troops who were besieging Antwerp.

I was flabbergasted when, on the evening of the second day, a German police officer in mufti came to the hotel where I happened to be sitting with an Austrian friend — a member of the bank's Board of Directors — and asked if I could speak to him privately for a minute. I followed him into the corridor. The police officer enquired whether I knew Princess X and who the visitor was in my room.

"I accompanied the Princess on the journey to Brussels at the request of a member of the Ministry for Home Affairs. The gentleman in my room is an Austrian and works in the same department of the bank as I do."

"Then I regret, Dr. Schacht, that I am obliged to arrest you. Please come with me."

I followed him without further ado and was ushered into the presence of a lieutenant of the German command who awaited us in the Princess's hotel. Of course I was able in a few words to establish my identity. The lieutenant apologized. It was obviously a case of mistaken identity.

I was curious. "For whom did you mistake us — my friend and I?" I asked.

The lieutenant then told us the story of Princess X. This charming and fashionable lady of the "upper ten" was the daughter of a petty municipal official somewhere in the Rhineland. Her unusual beauty had enabled her to form a liaison with an officer of princely rank who had strayed slightly from the path of virtue. The prince had married her and had had to leave the service, but had been reinstated following the outbreak of war.

The German military police had informed Brussels, somewhat late in the day, that Princess X was a member of a theatrical company which had already made the acquaintance of German courts of law. Espionage was suspected, since the Princess for no apparent reason had collected field-post letters from the troops at Antwerp with the intention of taking them back with her to Germany. Not only was this forbidden but it somehow didn't tally with the character of this particular princess. Actresses are not usually so interested in the needs and anxieties of the lower classes. The Princess had frequently been seen in the company of two men (so ran the Berlin report): one of them tall and fair, the other an Austrian.

Now of course we saw daylight. I had accompanied the Princess, I was tall and fair, and in my hotel room was my Austrian friend from the bank.

When we had had a good laugh over this mix-up the lieutenant asked me to assist him unobtrusively in arresting the Princess. At his request I called on the lady the following morning and had lunch with her in the hotel dining room. During lunch the lieutenant happened to come up to our table and I presented him to the Princess. He sat down; I made myself scarce at the first opportunity and left the Princess with him.

Life in Belgium would in the long run have been very boring and depressing had it not been for Ulrich Rauscher, a fresh lively Württemberger from the Foreign Office. He was free-and-easy and witty, an excellent companion. Many years later he was appointed German Ambassador in Warsaw. We went about a lot together. Unfortunately Rauscher was a bit too fond of his drink which sometimes proved too strong for his resolution; he was apt to become garrulous in his cups.

We were both inclined to be somewhat censorious. But when Rauscher had raised one too many he really did overstep the limit. There was a winter's night when I had taken him home — not for the first time. Next morning he must have had an attack of conscience, for he sent me the following verse, by hand:

> There comes a point when drinking breeds
> A Tippler,* fuddled fore and aft.
> Then for his overflow he needs
> A deep, discreet, and lengthy Shaft.*

* Word play on both their names. Rauscher — tippler, boozer, from "*einen Rausch haben*," to be tipsy, tight. *Schacht* — a shaft (long, deep opening).

I seized a pencil and, while the messenger waited, wrote on the other side of the sheet:

> *If you feel that drinking's "great,"*
> *Drink until you can't see straight.*
> *For to me you'll always matter*
> *(I'm "lengthy," "deep," and never chatter).*
> *But, when in your senses fully*
> *Speech and mind no longer "woolly,"*
> *Give me just a hearty grip*
> *Of your paw in comradeship.*

Rauscher was a writer with a remarkable sense of style. His experiences in Brussels during the Occupation period were later published in book form under the title *Belgium Yesterday, Today and Tomorrow.* He sent me a copy with the following inscription:

> *We've been through this together, lad,*
> > *What with old Lumm and Lancken.*
> *Who sticks that job may well be glad*
> > *Of his daily forty franken.*
> *He'll sweat himself to death an' all*
> > *To do the work he's hot on;*
> *He's lucky who can still recall*
> > *What we've long since forgotten.*

During the first months of the war in Occupied Brussels several professional colleagues gathered from Berlin and Frankfurt in the banking department of the military government. Paul von Schwabach was there, Ernst von Mendelssohn-Bartholdy, Hans Fürstenberg, Willy Dreyfus, young Weinschenk and many others. One day the son of the Hamburg banking firm of Behrens Sons turned up unannounced at von Lumm's. The conversation, at which I was present, was characteristic.

"What are you doing here in Belgium, Herr Behrens?" enquired von Lumm, stiff and standoffish.

"I wanted to offer you my services, sir."

Lumm was not enthusiastic. "I am not in need of your services. We are overstaffed in any case. Incidentally, how did you come here?"

"In my car."

Von Lumm displayed signs of interest. "You have a car?"

"Yes, sir, a Rolls-Royce."

Lumm opened his eyes. "A Rolls-Royce? Very well, you can stop, but the Rolls-Royce must be at my disposal."

"With pleasure, sir."

Lumm had a knack of exploiting his colleagues, but they paid him back. When the war was over and we quitted Belgium, one after another disappeared secretly in his car without notifying his chief. Eventually Herr von Lumm had to make the homeward journey in a third-class compartment packed like a sardine tin.

When I was there he was at the height of his power. Since he was not possessed of much business sense it so happened that, as time went on, my own work and that of my Austrian friend Somary became more and more conspicuous. That annoyed him, for he couldn't bear anyone else to be noticed. One day he told me quite frankly that he intended to fire Somary.

For a moment I was thunderstruck at such treachery. But after I had slept on it I went to Herr von Lumm and told him that under these circumstances I no longer entertained that confidence in him which was indispensable to successful co-operation, and wished to resign my post. He could not very well refuse. But the look he gave me boded no good. I should have realized that he was not the man to take a rebuff lying down.

With the introduction of the new banknotes (von Lumm's idea) the burden of their distribution (that is, their exchange for German marks) fell on the Military Commissariat. The Deutsche Bank had a branch in Brussels and applied for a very considerable delivery of these notes, which came in handy in their dealings with their Belgian customers. Whereupon the Dresdner Bank asked me to procure a supply of Belgian notes for them so that they might not be behind when doing business with their customers. I submitted this request in person to the Chief of the Commissariat who agreed without further ado.

All this had happened in February 1915 and Lumm, of course, knew about it. Now, in July, he suddenly brought the matter up again. It was, he said, an improper action on my part to represent the interests of the bank that had sent me to Belgium. I replied that if I had been guilty of improper action I would request that a disciplinary enquiry be instituted against me. That, unfortunately, was not possible, retorted Herr von Lumm with a spiteful smile, as I had resigned two days previously.

I applied to the Imperial Ministry for Home Affairs and requested that the matter be investigated. The result was a pronouncement that no blame whatever attached to me.

I mention this insignificant occurrence because it was later brought up against me. When, in 1923, I was about to take up a government post my opponents sought to discredit me politically by spreading a rumor that I had been guilty of sharp practices in Belgium. Whereupon Stresemann, who at that time was Chancellor, instituted a fresh enquiry into the case from the documents in the possession of the Ministry for Home Affairs and also contacted the remaining living witnesses. The result of this second enquiry tallied with that of the first. Stresemann conveyed the information to me in a very kind letter.

At the time of this intrigue Field Marshal General von der Goltz was no longer in Belgium. He had applied for a command in Turkey. In 1915 he succeeded in bottling up the British under Townsend in Kut-el-Amara. He died of typhus in Baghdad on April 19, 1916.

Von der Goltz was typical of the nonconforming element on the German General Staff, a man widely read and of many and varied interests. He was a combination of military expert, commanding officer and strategist. His individual and obstinate outlook not infrequently brought him into conflict with his superiors; on one occasion he was even temporarily placed on the retired list on account of his book *Léon Gambetta and his Armies* which quite openly touched the weaknesses of the General Staff on the raw. His rather heavy face with the short mustache, the mouth with its drawn-down corners, the wise eyes behind steel spectacles, have all remained in my memory. My brother Eddy, who served as surgeon major in Turkey under Goltz-Pasha, had the sad task of embalming the Field Marshal's body for the last journey home. The wheel of life sometimes has queer ways of coming full circle.

# XVII

## APPOINTMENT AS DIRECTOR OF THE BANK

MY ACTIVITIES were not affected by Herr von Lumm's intrigue in Brussels. Immediately after my return to Berlin I resumed my work in the Dresdner Bank. My old chief, Eugen Gutmann, intimated that I would be appointed a regular member of the board at the earliest opportunity. That I had done some successful work as deputy manager in Occupied Belgium had doubtless more than a little to do with it.

At home I found my wife and the two children in none too easy circumstances. Food had grown scarcer. Milk for children was unobtainable. So I did what hundreds of thousands of Berlin working-class families had done earlier. I started a vegetable garden and acquired a nanny goat which my twelve-year-old daughter had to learn to milk. Of course there were other ways of adding to the scanty food supplies, but they were less commendable. The usual "wangling" was not in my line. I had to submit to cultural and mental interests being crowded out by the material difficulties of wartime housekeeping.

Toward the end of the year — since my promised appointment to the board appeared to be held up — I enquired how matters stood and Gutmann rather hesitatingly disclosed that his son Herbert, who was a member of the board, had opposed my nomination.

"The best thing you can do," he said, "is to have it out with Herbert." Which, of course, I did without delay. Herbert Gutmann was naïve enough to give me the reason for his opposition.

"If you come on the board, Dr. Schacht, I am afraid you will very soon take all the syndicate business away from me."

By syndicate business is meant the collective activities of several big banks which as a rule are too extensive for any one bank to tackle alone, or which concern clients who deal with more than one bank.

My answer to Herbert Gutmann was short and to the point. I laughed.

"If you're scared, my dear Herbert, I'll clear out."

That same day I told the members of the board that I intended to leave the Dresdner Bank. There was a certain jarring atmosphere toward the end of my time there which both parties regretted. I had been with the Dresdner Bank for thirteen years — from 1903 to the end of 1915 — and had acquired my first knowledge of banking matters and won my first spurs there. I remember these thirteen years as some of the most satisfying years of my life and my relations with my old colleagues have consistently remained on the best possible footing. I was conscious of some satisfaction when someone later told me in confidence that Eugen Gutmann in particular had greatly regretted my leaving and has subsequently said to his colleagues: "You did a very stupid thing when you let Schacht go."

"What do you think of doing now?" my wife asked. "You always burn your bridges without knowing where the new road leads."

"My dear, the main thing now is not whether one is well or badly off from a material standpoint but whether one can preserve one's individuality. I am not in the least anxious about our future; but first of all I will go and report to the War Office."

Scarcely was I registered with the local detachment of the Home Guard when a new call arrived. The report of my resignation from the Dresdner Bank had quickly spread and Herr Witting, a privy councilor and chairman of the Supervisory Board of the Nationalbank für Deutschland, approached me with the offer of a seat on their Board. The Nationalbank was in the second rank of the big banks in Berlin, immediately after the so-called D-Banks. It had a capital of ninety million marks. It had no branches; against that however it was a member of several syndicates with the other big banks and for this reason was regarded with special esteem. After a brief discussion I signed my agreement with the bank, which once again diverted me from military duties in train, at base or with the Army Administration.

A few days after I had signed on for my new job Karl Friedrich von Siemens — head of the Siemens Combine — asked me to come and see him, and offered me the vacant post of Financial Director. This new offer caused me some regret because, had it arrived simultaneously with that of the Nationalbank I should probably have decided in favor of Siemens. Now, however, I had committed myself, and was obliged to decline with thanks.

The fact that all banking activities were concentrated on the support of the war effort meant that our duties were more uniform than in peacetime. There were no foreign or big financial transactions. Even during the war, however, interesting work did crop up. In my present position as one of the governors of a bank I had occasion to realize how, in every instance, personality counts far more than capital.

One day, very soon after I had taken over, a big businessman of my acquaintance sent in his card in a sealed envelope since he wished his visit to be as unobtrusive as possible. He was a customer of the Dresdner Bank and had called there on a matter of business. When he learned that I had left he declined to discuss the question with anyone else and brought his proposition to me because he had had previous experience of my unbiased attitude and my business methods. Personal confidence counted for more with him than the mere question of money.

Very much the same thing happened with Prince Hohenlohe's agent who one day asked for help. Prince Hohenlohe-Chringen, together with Prince Fürstenberg, had been a member of the so-called Princes' Combine which, in an effort to compete with big business in industrial and financial matters, had incurred heavy losses. After the winding up of the Combine, Prince Hohenlohe found himself in debt to the Deutsche Bank to the tune of some ninety million marks, and he obviously felt that they had not treated him properly. He stuck to his determination to sever his connection with the Deutsche Bank but he evidently had difficulty in finding another bank to undertake his affairs, either because the credit commitments were too high or because another bank feared that to do so might prejudice their relations with the Deutsche Bank. I was attracted by the magnitude of the task with its possibilities of consolidating the Hohenlohe undertaking. With the object of sharing the assignment I made certain first of all that the Barmer Bankverein would co-operate, and in order not to disturb our friendly relations with the Deutsche Bank I went to see Mankiewitz, the manager in charge of the business. I explained to him that the Prince was determined to sever his connection with the Deutsche Bank in any case, and that the only way to avoid unpleasantness was for the assignment to be taken over by a bank with whom his establishment was on friendly terms. This plain, straightforward statement did not fail to make an impression. The Nationalbank undertook the commission and was able to clear up the muddle very quickly during the following months through the sale of part of the Prince's property.

Yet another instance of an awkward situation being smoothed out by frank personal discussion. At that time the Deutsche Bank and the Diskontegesellschaft (Discount Company) had a difference of opinion as to which of them would be likely to achieve a controlling interest in the Deutsche Erdölgesellschaft (Petroleum Company). In this connection the Nationalbank was a member of the same combine to which the Discount Company also belonged and, for purposes of voting at the general meeting, always placed any available shares at the latter's disposal. For some reason unknown to me one of my colleagues on the board had promised our shares to the Deutsche Bank — a violation of all custom and also of our pledge to the Discount Company. By means of personal discussion and a straightforward exposition of the facts I was able to persuade the Deutsche Bank to relinquish the shares in question — an action which restored our reputation with the Discount Company. My colleague, however, was obliged to resign from the board of the Nationalbank.

While I was fully occupied with my sometimes irritating, sometimes satisfying job, the great tragedy of the war was unfolding at the Front. On my way from the banking quarters of Berlin to catch my train for home at the Potsdam Station I would pass the long queues of people in front of the shops with the badly lit windows, catchpenny articles and ersatz goods which now replaced the former magnificent displays and excellent quality. Women newsvendors cried the latest battles, advances and retreats. Coal supplies were becoming increasingly difficult. Shivering men and women hurried through the streets; everywhere were people with rucksacks and shopping bags bent on snaffling food supplies in the outlying districts. I was reminded of the poverty-ridden years of my childhood. I too had known what it was to hurry through the streets in order to buy a twopenny bucketful of coal. In those days there was plenty of coal but not enough cash. Now it was the other way about: money was plentiful, while supplies grew scarcer every day.

The general distress and misery of the war years paved the way for a complete reconstruction of Germany's social system. In vain the banks did all they could to maintain the monetary system on lines which experience had shown to be commercially sound, decent and therefore socially acceptable. The influence of the banks on the general economy declined in proportion as war profiteering began to flourish.

One of Germany's most far-reaching errors in the First World War was her mistaken fiscal policy. She endeavored to meet the colossal costs of the war by an appeal to the self-sacrificing spirit of the people.

"I gave gold for iron" was the slogan for the surrender of gold ornaments and jewelry. "Invest in War Loan" ran the appeal to the patriotic sense of duty of all classes. Issue after issue of War Loan was offered for subscription and transformed the greater part of German private fortunes into paper claims on the state. Our enemies, especially Britain, took another line. They met the cost of the war with taxes aimed primarily at those industries and groups to whom the war spelled prosperity. Britain's policy of taxation proved socially more equitable than Germany's policy of war loans, which lost their value after the war was over and proved a bitter disappointment to the self-sacrificing investors. The actual war profiteers however had a free hand. To have friends at court among the appropriate military authorities meant, for shrewd speculators, an opportunity to effect large deliveries at enormous profits. "Wanglers" on both sides of the German frontiers reaped a rich harvest importing low-quality food-stuffs from neutral countries. On one occasion during the war Albert Ballin, managing director of the Hamburg-Amerika Line, entered the lounge of the Hotel d'Angleterre in Copenhagen where a crowd of profiteers were eagerly gesticulating and haggling. He turned to his companions and said: "I estimate that that bunch between 'em would be good for thirty years hard labor."

It wasn't so much the big business firms that went in for profiteering, but predominantly the traders, the new-rich, the grabbers, sharks, the something-for-nothing type. Anyone who had proved himself capable of building up and maintaining an industry, with all its economic fluctuations, even in peacetime, is less interested in colossal wartime profits than the good-for-nothings who imagine they can make their pile during the turbulent years of war.

Among the many serious businessmen who gave of their best may be cited Albert Ballin. When I went to see him in his Hamburg office in 1916 and read the firm's proud motto, My Field is the World, we were both inclined to wonder whether this motto would live up to its implication. Ballin was confident. He relied, as I myself did, on the common-sense economic outlook which would prevail, even if the war should not end in a decisive German victory.

"You'll see, Herr Schacht, the businessman's sound judgment will win through. The wartime mania for destruction can be combatted only by general economic co-operation. In wartime, feelings of hatred and revenge are rampant. But when the ordeal is over, businessmen will once again be able to have their way. Politicians can't be so crazy as to perpetuate the miseries of war."

Ballin was mistaken in his belief. The politicians *were* crazy: businessmen never had a chance to speak their minds. Ballin never got over his self-delusion. A patriotic German Jew, he asked nothing better than that German achievement should contribute in economic co-operation with other countries to the advancement of the human race. When he realized that his hopes were in vain he took his own life.

Another conversation of that same year that also sticks in my memory is one with old August Thyssen, a man whose name became a legend even during his lifetime. One of the most outstanding figures in German industry, he had risen from a small manufacturer to be the owner of the largest German coal and steel combine. Small of stature, with a white mustache and pointed beard, he looked from a distance like Lenin grown old. Right up to extreme old age he possessed a restless creative energy, an amazing capacity for organization and an inexhaustible fund of new ideas.

Although he was easily the richest private individual in Germany all his actions were characterized by the utmost thrift. Of unassuming appearance he would travel third class on the railway and often stayed in second-rate hotels. Carrying his own bag he would frequently walk from the station to the hotel and bargain about the price of the room, afterwards entering his name in the visitors' book — August Thyssen, a signature that might be worth millions.

Thyssen was a consistent supporter of "vertical" business methods by which everything, from the raw materials of coal and ore to the polished piece of ironwork, passed through successive stages of manufacture. For that reason alone he interested me particularly, for as a young man I had stood out against the "horizontal" cartels which had maintained prices at high levels and had supported the "vertical" building up of industry which had for its aim the cheapening of consumer goods for the benefit of the masses.

Although August Thyssen presented the most unassuming exterior and deliberately avoided any ostentation in his private activities, he knew on the other hand how to keep up appearances in princely fashion. Long before the war, as one of the staff of the Dresdner Bank I had stayed with him at Schloss Landsberg, his country place. The numerous stately rooms contained many paintings by old masters; a series of Rodin sculptures adorned the hall; around the castle were well-kept lawns where proudly strutting peacocks aroused us betimes with their harsh screaming voices. Silver, table linen, indeed the entire establishment, bore the imprint of the authentic *grand seigneur*.

Thyssen was a past master of credit. The big banks vied with one another to obtain his custom. With those directors whom he took into his confidence he would correspond in his tiny close handwriting not always easy to read. But anything he wrote was treated with utmost respect. The advances on bills of exchange of which Thyssen was wont to avail himself did not always conform to Reichsbank commercial bills, but he made use of them because they were the cheapest. One could not always tell at first sight whether a bill was destined for payment of a goods transaction and therefore a genuine commercial bill, or whether it would simply be used as an accommodation bill to obtain cash (monetary) credit. When in 1911 it was realized that part of the coal in the Saar district could be converted into coke, August Thyssen and Hugo Stinnes, together with the Dresdner Bank founded the Saar-und-Mosel-Bergwerkgesellschaft (Mining Company). August Thyssen took up ten million marks' worth of shares, Hugo Stinnes ten million, and the Dresdner Bank one million so that, in the event of differences of opinion, it might play the part of arbiter. When the agreement had been signed Thyssen remarked to Stinnes:

"Now, Herr Stinnes, we must each pay in the ten million marks we have taken up. So I'll make you a proposition. I will issue bills to the value of ten million marks to you which you will then accept, and the Dresdner Bank will discount those bills."

These were of course not commercial bills but out-and-out "accommodation" bills. Stinnes replied: "But, Herr Thyssen, I have never yet put my signature to an 'accommodation' bill!"

"Then I'll make you another proposition, Herr Stinnes. You issue bills to the value of ten million marks to me and I will accept them."

I don't remember how the matter worked out. But one thing is certain — the Dresdner Bank credited the amount.

During the years of inflation when the issue of emergency money * had become a widespread nuisance, Thyssen was of course interested. One day Herr Schlitter, the director of the Deutsche Bank, was going by car with Thyssen to a meeting. On the way Schlitter plucked up courage and began:

* TRANSLATOR'S NOTE. The term "emergency money" in this connection refers to the later private currency issued and has nothing to do with the above somewhat doubtful transaction by Thyssen and Stinnes.

"Herr Thyssen, we have such a quantity of your emergency money in our safes. What shall we do about it?"

Thyssen was silent, apparently deep in thought. Only when he was about to alight from the car did he turn to Schlitter with the words:

"You are quite right, Herr Schlitter. What *shall* we do about it?"

One may have one's own opinions of these financial methods, but they had a powerful effect upon German economy. Thyssen undertakings counted among the most efficient, and technically, at the highest level. Both from an industrial and a business viewpoint they were brilliantly organized and have contributed materially to the fall in German production costs. They have provided work, wages and food for tens of thousands of German working-class families.

With all his urge to expand and develop on progressive lines, Thyssen never lost his capacity for cool-headed judgment. He had nothing in common with those war-obsessed Pan-Germans who dreamed of extension toward the adjoining industrial Western countries.

In 1916 I called upon him and let myself go on the subject of some of these big-business individuals, their craze for expansion, and their assumption that we should win the war and achieve a hundred per cent victory. Thyssen looked at me long and gravely; then he spoke one sentence: "But supposing, Herr Schacht, that we don't win the war?"

# XVIII

## THE FOUNDING OF A PARTY

I WAS FORTY-ONE years old when the First World War ended. On the day that the Emperor abdicated, that revolution broke out in Berlin, and the German representatives set out on their reluctant journey to Allied Headquarters to negotiate the Armistice, I entered politics for the first time. I became joint founder of a party which in the next few years was to play a considerable part.

My reasons for engaging in political activity were very simple. Throughout the whole of the last year of the war Germany was already in a state of invisible revolution, restrained only by the iron discipline of war. Strikes, heated arguments in factories and Parliament, protest marches — all these were signs which could no longer be ignored.

We cudgeled our brains as to what the new Germany would be like and which was destined to emerge from this process of revolution. There was no doubt that there would be a swerve to the Left. But would it be as definite as in Russia where, after a brief struggle, the extremists had prevailed against the moderate groups? Would Germany, in short, turn Bolshevik; would Lenin — as he had already intimated — establish his ultimate headquarters not in Moscow but in Berlin?

The danger was there. No one could foretell how matters would develop once the bounds were broken. Since August 1914 too much political dynamite had accumulated in cellars, backyards and tenement houses: what was to be done?

One of the meeting places for people who, despite the generally prevailing distress, still found time to tackle these questions, was the "Nineteen-fourteen Club" — a very significant name. It had been founded during the last year of peace. I often went to the Club and slept there now and again when work kept me too late at the bank. There I met kindred spirits — solicitors, journalists, businessmen, bankers. All were filled with the same anxiety: What was one to do?

My reply was: "We must prevent the 'moderates' in Germany from falling victim to the extremists. We must endeavor to form a mighty reservoir of all those elements who, without being extremist, are dissatisfied with present conditions. We need a middle-class Left which will throw in its lot with the organized workers in the coming coalition government." These deliberations led soon afterwards to the founding of the German Democratic Party.

Meanwhile there were increasing signs that the end might come at any moment. On November 3, 1918, the sailors of the main fleet started to mutiny. Spartacist elements had infiltrated the lower decks and hoisted the Red Flag. The revolution began to spread through Germany like wildfire. Workers' and Soldiers' Councils sprang up from nowhere and took over local authorities, this seizure of power being accompanied often enough by murder and looting.

During the early days of November 1918 Berlin prepared for civil war. Barbed-wire entanglements appeared in the streets, barricades were erected from overturned vehicles. Shots whistled through the streets in the center of the town and sent civilians scuttling indoors. No one appeared to have any authority: an armed mob stood ready to seize the helm.

November 9 was the day on which Prince Max of Baden announced the Emperor's abdication, even before the Emperor himself had decided on it. But he was confronted with a *fait accompli*. His General Staff persuaded him to bow to the immutable decree of fate. But was it really immutable? It is said that on his deathbed Hindenburg, whose advice the Emperor finally accepted, was seized with remorse. From a subjective point of view he was undoubtedly convinced that he did right when in 1918 he advised the Emperor to relinquish his throne. It may well be that fifteen years later he bitterly regretted this step when he realized what had happened to his country as the result of no longer possessing a monarchy.

Toward midday on November 9 I came out of the Hotel Esplanade with a friend and saw the first lorries drive across the Potsdamer-Platz filled with heavily armed Red troops. It was a curious sight. People passed by the lorries looking depressed and indifferent — they did not even glance at them. The Red revolutionists shouted, brandished their rifles and generally threw their weight about. In among them, before and behind, the usual midday Potsdamer-Platz traffic carried on. A very curious significant scene, expressive of Germany's disrupted condition — revolution in lorries, apathy in the streets.

In the face of this incident we changed our direction and made for the Reichstag with the object of finding a member who would enlighten us as to the situation. The great government building was deserted and lifeless. Our footsteps re-echoed as we continued our ghostly progress through the long corridors. At last we reached the abode of the Liberal Group: the door was locked, the key was on the inside.

"There must be someone there," I said, and knocked. No one answered. I knocked again.

Inside the room a quavering voice asked: "Who is it?" I recognized it at once — it was Stresemann's voice. At that time he was the leader of the National Liberal Group in the Reichstag.

"Dr. Schacht," I said.

The key turned in the lock. Stresemann's round face was visible in the doorway. He bade us enter.

"Have you any recent news?" I asked, looking round the room.

"Revolution," was Stresemann's terse reply with a weary gesture.

"And the Emperor — our Army — the Government — the Police . . . "

"I don't know," said Stresemann, "I'm the last remaining man in the Reichstag." His voice sounded hollow in the empty room, usually full of animated conversation and not looking half as big as it did now. Stresemann's face was gray, his eyes tired, his mouth pinched. He drummed on a table with his fingers.

"And what will happen?" I asked.

He shrugged his shoulders. "Ebert will probably do something," he said. "Now is his chance. His party is the strongest. If he doesn't succeed . . . "

It was obvious to me that the situation in Germany was in a complete mess. And as I have never been one to give in without a struggle I said:

"We *must* do something, Herr Stresemann. If the Left gets the upper hand, well and good. But we must start a middle-class Left party so that the Socialist majority don't have everything their own way."

"A middle-class party with Left-wing tendencies," he said. "Yes — that might be a way out."

We left him.

At the time I knew as well as anyone that the great hour for the Socialist parties had struck. Their persistent efforts for a negotiated peace, the workers' tremendous contribution to Germany's blood-

sacrifice and last, but not least, their promises of social improvements would attract masses of electors to their ranks. That would
lead to extreme opposition from the Right — as in Russia — which
might well develop into a war between Red and White. We must
act quickly if we were to achieve anything.

On the afternoon of November 10 we gathered in a large darkly
papered study at the Berlin residence of Dr. Theodor Vogelstein,
where the noise of street traffic penetrated but dimly. How long we
sat and talked there I no longer remember.

From the start it was clear that, for the founding of a political
party, the co-operation of the press was essential. But which press?
We called up Dr. Theodor Wolff of the *Berliner Tageblatt* at the
Mossehaus. Wolff immediately agreed and promised to co-operate.
A few hours later Wiesner and Stein of the *Frankfurter Zeitung* had
declared their readiness to place their paper at the disposal of a new
party on middle-class Left-wing lines. With these two newspapers
in the background our prospects appeared somewhat more favorable.

We finally decided to form the GDP (German Democratic Party)
on November 11, the day on which the Armistice was signed in the
Forest of Compiègne. Five days later Theodor Wolff drew up the
basic proclamation which was accepted by all of us. We were
joined by the liberal-minded deputy Fischbeck who undertook to
act as chairman of the Executive Committee. A draft program by
Dr. Paul Nathan was agreed to in principle, but proved unworkable
in practice. As time was short and certain members showed an
inclination to waste precious days in fruitless discussion I called
for an "electoral manifesto" which constituted the public announcement of the birth of the new party. This was followed at short intervals during the next few days by pamphlets addressed to definite
sections of the population. They were all of a provisional nature,
but endeavored to broadcast the aims of the GDP in all quarters.
Even my "electoral manifesto" was a program dictated by the needs
of the moment which could furnish only a broad outline of the
tendencies of our group. But it seemed to me at the time essential
that we should do *something* to further our objective. I recall especially one sentence of this manifesto: "The peoples of Germany will
be able to develop their special characteristics independently and
freely . . . "

One of the company — I think it was Count Bethusy-Huc —
smiled faintly when he read this passage and said:

"That sentence is typical of you, Herr Schacht. It's obvious that you come from the oldest farming republic in Germany."

"I don't get your meaning," I said.

He laughed. "Those were the words of a Dithmarschen farmer — not a Berlin banker. And you say you're no republican?"

He was alluding to an incident that had taken place when Theodor Wolff read out his proclamation which began with the words: "We are republicans . . . "

"Stop!" I interrupted. "I can't sign that. I'm a monarchist."

General astonishment. How, the others demanded, could a monarchist be a co-founder of a democratic party?

"Gentlemen," I said, "there are quite a few constitutional monarchies in the world which are democratically governed. Do you know the difference between republic and democracy? One is a type of state, the other a form of government. Democracy can be conservative, or liberal, or socialist."

Theodor Wolff gave in and began again. This time the sentence ran: "We base our standpoint on republican principles . . . "

I signified my agreement. What else could I do? At the moment, nothing. The Emperor was in Holland, the German Monarchy had ceased to exist . . .

But what confusion can be caused by catchwords! If anyone mentions democracy nowadays most people immediately connect it not only with a republic but also with a leftist political attitude. They mistake the type of State — that is the external construction — for the political content of the State. Democracy signifies the manifestation through the government of the political will expressed by the free vote of all citizens and the decision of the majority within the existing state construction. This political will undergoes changes as the result of experience and according to the trend of economic and cultural developments, as well as those of foreign policy. If the word democracy were synonymous with any leftist determination, that is to say with socialism or liberal radicalism — it would lead to political cyrstallization. Democracy is a philosophy of life only in so far as it signifies that the country must be governed according to the will of the majority. But democracy is no hard and fast directive for a definite philosophical course of action. The political comprehension of the majority can change, and does change, as the result of experience. Throughout the course of history democracy has prevailed under republican oligarchic and monarchical types of state. It has even contributed on occasion to the temporary investment of the government with full dictator powers.

The surmises we had entertained in connection with the formation of the GDP came to pass. The Social Democrats failed to obtain a majority in the National Assembly at the Elections of January 19, 1919. The GDP secured seventy-four seats, and at a critical juncture ensured that socialist theories were not applied in too one-sided a fashion. The Social Democrats were compelled to form a coalition government with the middle-class Left.

The GDP produced two ministers who helped to establish a gradual and continuous political development in place of an extremist upheaval. One was Hugo Preuss, the expert on constitutional law who had played a decisive part in the working out of the Weimar Constitution; and Walther Rathenau, who in 1922, as Foreign Minister, enabled Germany once again to take part in negotiations to resume her trading activities as a result of the Treaty of Rapallo.

I myself was very pleased with this success. Party political activities had no attraction for me. I declined to stand as a party candidate and in fact only participated in it for a short period.

I have never in my life been afraid. During the revolution in Berlin I did not change my style of clothing, nor did I wear dark glasses, and I continued to go about Berlin every day. In the brief interval between the revolution and the National Assembly I made several public speeches in which I spoke my mind plainly. The public were by no means always friendly. But they realized that I was not afraid.

On one occasion only was I prevented from speaking. It happened in Vienna before a packed house. Spread about in the front rows were some fifty rowdies who set up such howls and catcalls when I appeared that I had to abandon my speech. I was one against fifty. Behind them were three thousand citizens who had come to hear about the German Democratic Party's program. These three thousand allowed themselves to be terrorized by fifty hooligans instead of throwing them out. Freedom without order spells ruin to any democracy.

On another occasion I addressed the German Officers Association. This organization had invited six groups to send one speaker each to a meeting, each speaker to have twenty minutes in which to present his current program in detail to the audience, his place in the proceedings to be determined by lot. I drew Number One, stepped on to the platform and was immediately conscious of an icy atmosphere of antagonism emanating from the audience. If I did not want to waste my breath I must do something within one minute to jolt them out of their "superior" aloofness.

"Ladies and gentlemen," I began, "I am speaking as a representative of the GDP which, as you must surely know, is the party of the *Berliner Tageblatt* (*Hear, hear*), the party of Jewish high finance (*Quite right*), the party of the Golden International (*loud cries of Quite right*)." I paused deliberately; then went on.

"You see, ladies and gentlemen, these idiotic phrases are by way of preliminary remarks in order to determine the kind of audience I am addressing . . . "

The officers were taken aback and probably somewhat abashed. They leaned forward and listened attentively. No one tried to interrupt.

This speech marked the end of my active participation in GDP affairs. I retired once again into my bank and devoted myself to my work. In the ensuing period the Democratic Party did not fulfill the promise of its magnificent beginning. It did not understand how to carry its principles into effect; its representatives were no fighters. Many sturdier political parties increased their toll of voters at the expense of the GDP.

But on January 19, 1919, in the hour of revolution and of the relaxation of all civil control it did fulfill the task of assembling the liberal-minded elements among the German citizenry and endowing them with a voice against the socialization program of the German Socialist Party.

I resigned when, years later, in connection with the expropriation of the aristocracy, the party attacked the fundamental law of private ownership.

# XIX

## MEMBER OF THE WORKERS' AND
## SOLDIERS' COUNCIL

ONE OF THE most incredible chapters of my life is entitled: "Dr. Hjalmar Schacht — Member of the Workers' and Soldiers' Council," and the scene is laid in Zehlendorf.

The revolution in Zehlendorf started with the chairman of the Parish Council sending out invitations to the inhabitants to attend a meeting in the big hall of the Grammar School. There he made a speech which for sheer crass gobbledegook beat anything I have ever heard. The Parish Council, he said, had prepared a cheap popular lunch in an open-air restaurant situated on the borders of Zehlendorf, right on the arterial road from Berlin. When the revolutionary hordes came pouring out of Berlin they would be attracted by this cheap lunch, appease their hunger and by the time they entered Zehlendorf itself would be as tame, so to speak, as lions in a state of repletion.

The idea that Berlin "Reds" would come dashing out to Zehlendorf with about sixpence in their pockets in order to partake of a popular lunch tickled me immensely. Needless to say, not a soul came rushing out to Zehlendorf. The city's large well-heated assembly rooms proved far more attractive to the crowds than a popular-price lunch in a suburb.

Someone else, however, did turn up — actually during the chairman's speech. His name was Göhre and he was one of the Social Democrat members of the Reichstag. With a movement of the hand he dismissed the chairman from his position at the table, took his place and announced in a loud voice:

"Now — it's *our* turn!"

The meeting was struck dumb. The chairman made himself scarce, the voices died away. I watched the proceedings, not without a certain irony. The people of Germany have never been able to resist a man who forces his way on to the platform.

Now Göhre was anything but a man of violence. I knew him

personally: he was what is known as a bit of a softy, a good-natured fellow — a theologian, clergyman, and a man of high principles who had joined the socialist movement as far back as 1890 by way of the Naumann set and their National Social enterprise. He was fifty-seven years old and a member of the German Socialist Party (GSP) which, on the very day he spoke to us, had appointed him Under-Secretary of State for War. (No one was better qualified to testify publicly to the pacific intentions of the GSP than the said newly appointed Under-Secretary of State for War.)

Carried away by the historic occasion, Göhre let his enthusiasm get the better of him, became too big for his boots and announced that the sovereign power was now vested in the two German Socialist Parties — the GSP who were in the majority, and the Independent Socialists (IGSP).

The speaker had got so far when I interrupted him: "I assume that this sovereign power is valid only until the National Assembly proclaims the Constitution!"

Göhre was silent for a moment; there was a murmur of voices in the audience. Surely it was very presumptuous to interrupt such a great man at such a great moment?

"Yes," Göhre then said — perhaps somewhat nonplussed but perhaps also convinced — "yes — but only until the National Assembly!"

It was very important to make the revolutionary government realize as soon as possible that they were only a stop-gap. At that time everyone hoped that elections for the National Assembly would result in a different state of affairs. And our hopes were justified.

Much gratified I sat down. This was on November 10, 1918. That same afternoon I went to Berlin and discussed with my friends the formation of the Liberal Left-wing Party.

But first of all there was an unexpected sequel to the Zehlendorf meeting. When Göhre had finished, a Workers' and Soldiers' Council was elected for the parish and community of Zehlendorf. Those soldiers who were present nominated their man, the second representative was determined by acclamation. My name was called the greatest number of times, so from that moment I became a member of the Zehlendorf Workers' and Soldiers' Council.

A third representative had yet to be elected from among the ranks of the Workers.

"Will members of my own party please stand up!" pleaded Göhre.

Three men stood up, one of whom was quickly chosen. The "government" of Zehlendorf was now in a position to function.

"Government" in the Town Hall was not made easy for us. It was Sunday and not a single official was present. The cupboards containing official documents were locked, the tables bare. I was vividly reminded of the period of occupation in Belgium when von Sandt was supposed to take office as Civilian Governor in Brussels, and looking round the empty room, exclaimed: "How can anyone begin to rule here? There isn't even any revenue!"

In order, however, to signify our good intentions we drew up a proclamation to the people of Zehlendorf which appeared, proudly signed by all of us, in the next number of the local paper. The Workers' and Soldiers' Council did not meet again. Our proclamation will doubtless have found its way into the local archives. All the rest of the doings we turned over to the existing officials.

The successful result of the elections in January 1919 did not mean that the Socialist danger was eliminated. On the contrary, the war within the Left-wing Socialist ranks was only just beginning — the struggle for power between GSP, IGSP and the Spartacists.

In order to understand the situation one must know that the government at that time was in the hands of a Council of People's Delegates. These included not only the majority-Socialists Ebert, Scheidemann and others, but also two Independent delegates. The Independents leaned strongly toward the radical aspect of socialism; that is, toward Karl Liebknecht and his Spartacus League, backed up by the revolutionary naval divisions of Kiel.

On November 25, 1918 the Council of People's Delegates had decided to summon a national assembly with powers to formulate a constitution, and thus establish themselves on the basis of a parliamentary republic. This decision was confirmed between the tenth and the twentieth of December, 1918, by the National Conference of Workers' and Soldiers' Councils, thereby ensuring that there would be no "Russian Revolution" in Germany.

Following this there was a split in the ranks of the Independents. The Left Wing amalgamated with the Spartacus League on January 1, 1919, as the German Communist Party (henceforth known as the GCP). The majority-Socialists who desired to govern, not according to the Russian system of Soviets but according to political and civic methods, became the protagonists of the fight against communism.

About Christmas 1918 there was a dangerous rising among the People's Naval Divisions surrounding the Palace in Berlin, and shortly after New Year's there were fierce battles in Berlin's newspaper districts. Temporary volunteers, former officers and battalions of Social-Democratic workers made common cause against the menace of bolshevism.

On one occasion during this period of upheaval, when Germany's fate hung by a thread, I stood at a window in the Hotel Kaiserhof and watched the deployment of the Social-Democratic Trade Unions summoned by Ebert hold the Wilhelmstrasse against the Spartacist demonstrators by sheer force of numbers. A mighty torrent of humanity poured into the Wilhelmstrasse — workmen, artisans, humble townsfolk — any and everybody who supported the Trade Unions and Ebert's policy of law and order.

All at once the Spartacist masses streamed out of the Mohrenstrasse, advanced at right angles on the Trade-Unionists, collided with them and pulled up short. Recriminations followed, then blows. Suddenly, from the Spartacist direction something flew through the air and fell among the Trade-Unionist ranks. The dull thud of an explosion reached me, and I knew that it was a hand grenade. It had an immediate sobering effect. The Spartacists withdrew, the others clustered around one of their number who lay on the ground — dead. The hand grenade had burst in full force, penetrating the abdomen. An unknown victim — a single member of an army of men and women who, at a summons from their party leader had come pouring out of all the tenement-houses in Berlin to preserve decency and order.

Matters did not stop at this one death. In March 1919 the revolution was responsible for the loss of twelve hundred lives in Berlin alone. The decision of the Socialist majority to rule Germany with the help of Parliament and not by means of a dictatorship consolidated our position at the time as a Western Power, but at the cost of fierce fighting and bloodshed throughout the country.

Defeated in war and rent by internal strife, the German people in 1919 fought a lonely fight which since then has developed into a world problem of front-line importance and inflicted a severe rebuff to bolshevism.

Following this effort — which benefited not only the Germans themselves but also the Poles, Czechs, Finns, Esthonians, Letts, Hungarians, Rumanians and Bulgarians — Germany, willing, work-loving and more addicted to order than most other nations, could have achieved her own peace within the world but for the appearance of another specter, not from the East this time, but from the West; namely, the reparations demands of her former enemies.

I went through my own private experience with reparations at a very early date — long before the time when I officially strove for their cancellation. But before I go further into this matter I will explain how reparations came to be imposed in the first instance and why they were entirely lacking in common sense.

With this object I must ask my readers to view the war not, as is customary, through the eyes of a soldier but through those of a businessman.

Every modern war begins with whatever means are available and finishes with weapons which, at the beginning, were undreamed of.

From a purely external point of view the First World War started in much the same way as the war of 1870 — patriotic songs, rifles hung with flowers, bright colored uniforms and that mixture of deadly earnest and surface gaiety which takes possession of men when confronted by death. The equipment of troops was so primitive that during the early months of the war French soldiers (so I was told later) included in their already bulky battle kits bundles of firewood that they might be able to cook their own meals in camp. When armies set forth in August 1914, fighting was still pictured mainly as an affair of bayonet charges and shooting at close range. Four years later strikes and revolts among the civil population of Britain, France and Germany indicated that the incessant drain on the nations' economic resources was in itself responsible for the collapse of the war.

Conditions in the countries of both groups of belligerents appeared to be fairly similar. Albert Ballin had hoped that the war would end in a complete political fiasco which would give businessmen a chance of enlisting the voice of reason on their side. That hope might even then have been realized. That it was not was due to the intervention of a third, extra-European Power in the progress of the war. The United States at the beginning threw in their economic potential and later their armies to Europe, thus deciding the war in favor of the Entente Powers.

It is not for me to go into the reasons for the entry of the United States into the war. It is a fact, however — as I wrote later in my book *The End of Reparations* — that in so doing she assumed a political responsibility with which, at that time, she was not yet fit to cope. This is not, in my opinion, an unfair criticism. Many Americans have condemned America's political defection after the war far more harshly than I have done.

According to human reckoning the war was bound to end in general exhaustion. The map of Europe would presumably have needed only slight alterations. This same general exhaustion, this obvious senselessness of technical warfare would presumably have given rise to profitable enlightenment on both sides. The best thing that could have happened from the standpoint of world history would have been for the first technical war to have ended in a stalemate.

The reparations demands of the Allies after World War I aroused national resentments, and resentments are not a good foundation for a peaceful foreign policy. Both Right- and Left-wing extremists made capital out of the increasing political bitterness, the growing economic distress in Germany, till in 1932 they eventually created a situation where the only question was whether the Left or the Right would be the first to achieve its object. Two simple calculations go to show that:

The Communist Party, which had entered the Reichstag on June 6, 1920, with two seats, possessed exactly one hundred seats on November 6, 1932 (twelve years and five months later), and with twenty votes behind the GSP, was the third biggest party in Germany.

Hitler's National Socialists, however, who under that name had stalked into the Reichstag on May 20, 1928, with only twelve deputies, had nearly two hundred seats in 1932, and had become the strongest party in Germany.

The politicians, who had brought about this situation by their astronomical demands on the Reich, who refused to be dissuaded from their economic folly, today disclaim all responsibility and wash their hands of the whole business.

The war also claimed its victims from my own immediate family. My brother Oluf died as the result of an illness contracted during the war years. Our youngest brother William — fair-haired, lovable, my mother's favorite of all her children — had been killed in the Battle of the Somme. The news of his death in that ghastly western carnage of men and materials had affected my parents deeply. Whenever I had time I would go over to Schlachtensee and take one of the children along to see the grandparents — either Inge, now in her teens, or eight-year-old Jens.

Even at that time I was unable to ignore the political problems that were bound to arise after the war. The full extent of our losses had not so far been revealed. No one knew as yet that our own country had 1,600,000 dead and 3,500,000 war casualties — wrecked, maimed by the products of an industry we had all eagerly helped to build up. Anyone with eyes to see, however, would realize that after this war there could no longer be any question of an empire with its social problems unsolved; no old-style Prussian militarism (it had already met its doom on the battlefield and been forced to give place to the new technical methods of warfare); no division of electoral rights into three classes and no permanent order of society. The war had swept away all that. Something new must be found to replace the old and the outworn. What would it be like?

Such were Germany's domestic problems after her defeat in the technical war. It was not to be expected that our former enemies would be able to understand their full scope. But neither was it to be expected that they would so completely ignore Germany's struggle for her position in the West, as happened during the ensuing twelve years. I had a foretaste of it as far back as 1919. After a government had been formed in Germany I was called in to discuss with Allied representatives Germany's economic contribution to the victorious Powers. A deputation of industrialists and experts was sent to The Hague where an Allied Commission awaited us. My task was to go into the question of deliveries of potash and other chemical products.

Our reception reminded me vividly of illustrations in my school history books: *Persian Satraps receiving a Deputation from defeated Athens.*

A positively medieval arrogance characterized the members of the Allied Commission. Not only was there no question of chivalry — there was also a complete lack of common civility. I remember one occasion when not enough chairs had been provided for the Germans so that most of the German members of the Commission were obliged to take part in the discussions standing.

I made no secret of my disgust at this churlish treatment. My fellow members of the Commission were frankly nervous.

"For goodness sake, Doctor," one of them whispered to me. "You can't do that! You can't go lodging complaints!"

"I'll soon see if I can't lodge complaints," I said, and went across to the Allied general who presided at the meeting.

"We have been accommodated in the worst hotels; the food is wretched; we are prevented from going out; our movements are restricted and we are obliged to stand during the negotiations with our Allied partners." I was furious. "I would ask you if you please, General, to remedy these deficiencies."

"You seem to forget that your country lost the war," was the frigid reply.

I returned to Berlin the richer for the experience. Nothing that happened afterwards surprised me as greatly as it would have done had I not happened to attend that conference.

My visit to The Hague brought me up against the problem of reparations for the first time. It was to give me plenty to do in the years ahead.

At first I admittedly devoted all my attention once again to bank matters. For by now a new specter brooded over Germany which concerned the country's domestic situation as well as the reparations demands of our former enemies: the inflation of German currency.

# XX

## INFLATION

THE YEARS 1920 to 1924 are still known as "the period of inflation." Although few people can explain the meaning of the word it has come to signify many things for whole generations.

To all who still remember it, the period of inflation stands for the hunger blockade, the surrender of real values to foreign powers, political outlawry; regrouping of the population; the rise of obscure figures to sudden wealth. To the hitherto wealthy classes it meant loss of capital; to the well-to-do, the moderately comfortable and the small man it spelled ruin. In government and official circles it signified corruption, political jobbery among the parties, the Wehrmacht (Defense Force) and the ministries. Increase in child mortality, in crime; the young crippled with rickets, the old dying before their time. All this and much beside is summed up in the expression "period of inflation."

Inflation is loss of capital in its widest sense. The Latin word signifies "blowing up"; in its narrower sense therefore it signified the blowing up of a currency. In Germany this is easy to grasp from a statistical point of view: at the end of the war the mark was worth about half as much as at the beginning of hostilities. A gold mark (the standard on which the paper currency is based) was worth 2.02 paper marks. But in November 1923 a gold mark was worth one trillion paper marks. This is how it appeared in figures: 1,000,000,-000,000.

Within five years the German Reichsmark had sunk to a five hundred billionth of its value. At the end of the war one could, in theory, have bought five hundred billion eggs for the same price as that for which, five years later, only a single egg was procurable.

Such comparisons are mere juggling with figures. But for the one-and-only breadwinner of a family they represented not juggling with figures, but direst need.

We do not find the word *Währung* in other languages. There is *monnaie* or "currency"; that is, funds in cash or in circulation. Our German word expresses, in its deepest sense the significance of money as a means of payment. It must endure (*währen*), it must last, it must possess stability; i.e., it must preserve its value. Before bank-notes or paper money were invented, payment was made in material goods which did not change their value. The Latin word *pecunia* derives from *pecus*, a head of cattle, and dates from the time when flocks and herds constituted the medium of exchange with which other goods could be obtained. The most widespread means of exchange were *Buntmetalle* or precious metals — gold, silver, copper. Of these, as the result of thousands of years, gold has established itself as the favorite and achieved its position as the most precious means of payment. Through all the paper money operations the value of gold as a standard has never altered.

Since the introduction of paper money by modern states the critical task of monetary policy has been to preserve the value of such money. The purchasing power of money must remain the same throughout the passage of time. It is only by means of a stable currency that the system of barter has been superseded. When a worker nowadays receives his pay envelope at the end of the week he must be able to feel that he can buy as much with it the following week as he did in the past one. He must be able to save until he has sufficient to purchase a piece of land, or build himself a hut or cottage.

The introduction of banknotes or government paper currency has been made feasible only because the state or the central bank have promised to exchange the paper money for gold at any time. To ensure this possibility (that is, the redemption of paper by gold) at any time must therefore be the aim of all issuers of paper currency. Any state or central bank which deliberately or carelessly flings away this possibility is guilty of a crime against its citizens. Were a private individual to do so he would be branded as a defaulter and a cheat.

In former times there have been states that have gone bankrupt as a result of bad management; the deliberate manipulation of currency, however, has become a familiar feature only of the most recent history. As a result of two world wars, many countries were reduced to desperate financial straits and looked upon devaluation of currency as the only way out. This deliberate devaluation was usually preceded by a natural decline in the value of paper money. When a nation's expenses exceed its income and it has to try and meet its commitments with such a quantity of paper money the value of paper money declines.

Such was the situation in which Germany found herself as the terrible outcome of World War I. And not only Germany. Other nations did not escape inflation, or devaluation of paper currency. But Germany was the hardest hit. It was the masses in Germany who suffered most under the inflation. In matters of money — as indeed in all matters of business — the educated section of the population grasp the devaluation process more quickly than the uneducated masses. Anyone who was alive to the signs of approaching inflation could safeguard himself against losses in paper currency by the purchase of assets which, by contrast, would maintain their value; for example, houses, real estate, manufactured goods, raw materials, etc. This wholesale recourse to real values enabled not only the well-to-do but also and especially the unscrupulous to preserve and even possibly to increase their assets.

As a result of this struggle for self-enrichment and financial self-preservation, based on exploitation of the ignorance of the masses, every aspect of business life became vitiated. All savings activity ceased. Those unable to find any real values spent their money as rapidly as possible on pleasure. The creation of new capital goods and new production projects declined for lack of the necessary capital; the banks were no longer in receipt of their former steady flow of savings and cash deposits. As devaluation spread so its rate of progress accelerated. Those who were no longer able to meet even their daily needs — the laboring classes, officials and people with fixed incomes — were seized with a tremendous unrest and increasing bitterness. The payment of enhanced wages in paper money had no effect — on the contrary, the more paper currency was spent the more rapidly its value declined.

Many business firms took to paying their workpeople with foodstuffs. But that was only an imperfect and partial emergency measure. Firms requiring capital for business and investment adopted the practice of issuing bonds in respect, not of money, but of coal, electric kilowatt-hours, potash, cement, and so forth which constituted the real value of such bonds.

The distress engendered by inflation was immeasurably enhanced by the reparations demands imposed by the victorious Powers in spite of the misery prevailing in Germany. Enormous deliveries in goods were required, most of the proceeds from exports received in foreign currency went to swell the war payments. Any foreign securities or shares in businesses situated in neutral countries and still in German possession had to be included in the tribute instalments as they fell due.

Since it was impossible even with such vast sacrifices for Germany to pay the reparations imposed upon her at Versailles, reprisals were instituted against her in 1923 in the shape of the military occupation of the Rhineland in defiance of the Versailles Treaty. The population reacted to this violation of justice with every kind of passive resistance, refusal to work and sabotage. This in turn made fresh heavy demands on the government which had to continue pouring wages and salaries into the occupied area without receiving any commensurate return.

In 1923 the progress of devaluation achieved a really terrifying momentum. The demand for treasury notes was so great that the Reichsbank was unable to issue anything like the required number. In addition to the Reichsbank there were several private presses engaged in the printing of treasury notes for ever increasing denominations. The day was rapidly approaching when the price of a tram ticket was a billion-mark note. Many municipalities and industrial firms took to printing their own "emergency money" to meet their expenses. The Reichsbank could not refuse to accept this emergency money or to treat it as of equal value with their own notes. It became impossible to control the issue of emergency notes. The entire circulation of notes and coin was reduced to chaos.

During the whole of that period, that is, from early 1919 till toward the end of 1923, neither the Reichsbank nor the government made any effort to establish a stable currency. The Board of the Reichsbank took the view that it was useless to attempt to stabilize the mark so long as it was uncertain how much Germany would be able to pay in war damages and so long as no agreement had been reached on that point with the victorious Powers. It was difficult to counter this view, which was shared by the government. A stable currency which would have met not only the country's internal economic needs but also the colossal foreign commitments was in truth impossible.

There was, however, another possibility — one which I expounded and urged in a number of articles published in various newspapers, notably the *Berliner Tageblatt* and the *Vossische Zeitung*. It went to my heart to see how devaluation served only to enrich the sharpers and those "in the know," while the lower classes watched their incomes dwindle and their savings disappear. I suggested the introduction of a coinage based on gold, but in correspondingly restricted quantities, which would enable the worker to estimate the (daily decreasing) value of his paper money wages. Further, this coinage based on gold would be of valuable assistance in the export and import trade.

This suggestion was followed up to a point when an issue of small dollar coupons was launched in the middle of 1923, which at any rate served to stabilize part — though admittedly a very small part — of the money transfers and demonstrated the gap between gold coinage and paper currency.

During 1923 the conditions of the masses grew so much worse that Communist movements increased to an alarming extent. Political unrest developed to a point where the stabilization of money became a vital necessity if the whole country were not to collapse. If one realizes that these money tokens (notes) were sent in gigantic bundles by truck and railway wagon to cities and provinces; that in order to produce one currency note more working time was required by papermakers, engineers, printers, lithographers, color experts than was represented by the value of the finished article, it may be possible to understand the whole crazy setup during that period, which played havoc with the nation's most valuable capital — the working power of the people.

# XXI

## WITH THE DANAT BANK

Soon after I joined the Nationalbank für Deutschland one of my fellow members, as already mentioned, was obliged to resign from the board which now consisted only of my colleague Wittenberg and myself. Wittenberg handled the current business while I was entrusted with the larger credits and syndicate transactions. We were short of a manager for the entire securities department and it therefore became necessary to appoint a third member of the board. On the urgent recommendation of some members of my Supervisory Council I allowed myself to be persuaded into inviting Herr Jakob Goldschmidt, a partner in the banking firm of Schwarz, Goldschmidt & Company to join the Board of the Nationalbank. Schwarz, Goldschmidt & Company was one of the most active firms in the securities market and their senior partner Goldschmidt was reckoned one of the most capable men on the Exchange. He joined the Board of the Nationalbank in the middle of 1918 and during the ensuing decade developed into one of the most prominent figures on the Berlin Stock Exchange and one of the most discussed members of Berlin's banking business.

It soon transpired that Goldschmidt and I differed completely in temperament and, unfortunately, also in our attitude to banking policy. Although we were outwardly on good terms I very much disliked his speculative methods. Within a very short time he started to acquire securities amounting to considerable sums on the bank's account which resulted sometimes in gains, sometimes in losses. His strong suit was to gain a footing in most of the big incorporated companies by means of these parcels of securities and thereby obtain their trade for the bank. He would likewise instigate and carry through amalgamations and other combines among the big companies, all of which, it is true, greatly enhanced the importance of the Nationalbank and brought plenty of new business but which on the other hand made excessive demands on the bank's resources.

Incidentally he overlooked the fact that these same resources consisted not only of the bank's own capital, but even more of customers' deposits.

Goldschmidt always tended more to bulls than to bears — a common failing among speculators. Bulls are those who count on a rise in prices, bears or "fixers" those who expect a fall. Doubtless it is inherent in human nature to be governed to a greater extent by optimism than by pessimism.

The first major setback occurred with the military collapse toward the end of 1918. It was apparent that Goldschmidt's speculative activity — when it went awry — was accompanied by considerable "jumpiness."

It soon became evident, however, that the need to extend the foundations of the Nationalbank was urgent. As a result Goldschmidt negotiated the amalgamation of our bank with the Deutsche Nationalbank in Bremen which meant a corresponding increase of capital and the adoption of the branch system.

Aided by the continued progress of devaluation, Goldschmidt in the course of the ensuing years succeeded in appreciably extending our connections with the big industrial and transport concerns. Once again, however, the discrepancy between the level of securities commitments and the capital available very soon became apparent and in 1921 therefore Goldschmidt achieved a new amalgamation, this time with the Darmstädter Bank.

I was not at all enthusiastic over this amalgamation because the consequent extension of the money basis might prove an inducement to Goldschmidt to continue his speculative banking policy. My attitude to banking was governed first and foremost by a sense of responsibility for the safeguarding of customers' deposits and for the conduct of normal credit and securities business on behalf of our customers; but not for engaging on one's own account in speculations involving considerable risks. Nevertheless the big transactions negotiated by Goldschmidt, which at that time naturally made big profits, secured for him the full support of the Supervisory Board, some members of which were glad to participate in Goldschmidt's activities.

I remember a meeting of the board at which Goldschmidt presented one of his big deals, supported by one of the members who remarked, in tones of admiration, on why anyone troubled themselves over all the small transactions when it was only big ones such as this that achieved big profits. I had frequently issued warnings against speculative banking policy. During a pause in the conversation, therefore, I arose and quoted:

" 'When no single voice re-echoes in support of one defeated, then will I for Hector witness' . . . Where would you be, gentlemen, with your big deals if it were not for the deposits of our many small customers whose money alone makes the financing of such big deals possible. The first duty of a bank, in my opinion, is to ensure the safety of the deposits for which the bank is responsible."

In view of our straitened situation I could not oppose the amalgamation with the Darmstädter Bank, but I no longer took any pleasure in management. This state of affairs contributed largely to the fact that when two years later I left the bank I did so without regret. Since the amalgamation the establishment was known as the Danat Bank and subsequent developments unfortunately proved that I had been right. The bank crisis of 1931 was brought about by the collapse of the Danat Bank under the direction of Jakob Goldschmidt, when the bank was no longer in a position to repay their customers' deposits on demand.

I had frequently to blame Goldschmidt for his failure to grasp the duties of one of the major deposit banks and the corresponding responsibility vis-à-vis the depositors. On the other hand due allowance must be made for his gift for achieving financial combinations. Unfortunately he was unable to keep within bounds or preserve the right balance between the end and the means. This trait was the more regrettable as Goldschmidt was in himself a charming personality, heart and soul devoted to the cause of Germany's economic recovery.

Goldschmidt was not popular with his colleagues in the other big banks, not only on account of his competitive methods, which occasionally verged on ruthlessness, but also because his whole outlook did not fit in with that of responsible big bank leadership. This was brought home to him very forcibly when his bank was faced with the crisis of July 1931 and none of his colleagues stood surety for him or came to his assistance.

I think I can claim to have described Goldschmidt *sine ira et studio*, and may therefore be allowed to quote the parody of an extract from the Prologue to Schiller's *Wallenstein* which went the rounds after Goldschmidt's departure:

You know him well, the author of keen quotations,
Idol of "bulls" and scourge of "bearish" gamblers,

Dame Fortune's bold and enterprising son
Who, on inflation's pinions borne aloft,
Swiftly attained the highest peak on 'Change,
And, still insatiably bent on speculation,
Fell victim to that all-consuming craze.


The less pleasure I got out of my work in the Danat Bank the more I turned my attention to public economic questions. Next to problems of monetary policy I was most deeply concerned with the question of reparations. The enormous costs incurred by the First World War — in contrast to earlier wars — may well have been the reason for the astronomical figures at which the Allies assessed payment of war damages. The first sum published amounted to four hundred and fifty billion marks and originated with the French Finance Minister Monsieur Klotz. In Paris, at the end of January 1921, about half that total had been decided upon. It was to be paid yearly, beginning at the rate of two billions and increasing to six billions annually over a period of forty years.

There followed lively discussions with Germany, and international conferences as to the final amount of reparations to be determined. Today everyone is agreed that the reparations demands made absolute nonsense from the standpoint of political economy. At that time, however, the politicians responsible had no real idea how such demands could be met, nor of their eventual economic repercussions.

As early as 1921 I took the opportunity during a first postwar visit to Paris to air the reparations question — in particular the possibility of their economic implementation — with certain members of the French Government with whom I managed to get in contact, among them the Finance Minister Monsieur de Lasteyrie; but without achieving any result. Reparations were finally fixed at one hundred and twenty billions.

The development of inflation in Germany, and the Allies' costly occupation of the Rhineland, had made it abundantly clear how little could be expected as regards payment of such fantastic reparations. Shortly afterwards, in May 1923, I had the chance of discussing reparations problems in London with the representatives of a British industrial combine, the Commonwealth Union, under the leadership of a lawyer named Allan Smith. His deputy, engaged in the electrical industry, was of German origin and had changed his name of Hirsch to Hirst. Here too I was up against a general dislike of Germany; nevertheless the discussions were conducted on a basis of great impartiality and personal courtesy.

All those present appeared to agree as to the desirability of reviving Anglo-German trade. Certain political questions, such as the joint guarantee of the eastern frontiers laid down at Versailles, the internationalization of the Rhine railways, the separations of the Rhineland and so on were quickly dropped as being either unprofitable or politically detrimental; the main theme of the discussion was the level of reparations. The German Government had indicated a maximum of twenty billion marks as being all that Germany could afford.

"Twenty billion marks is much too little," declared one of those present; "that's not a fair offer."

"It may seem little to you, gentlemen," I said, "but at any rate it is fair. We have no wish to embark on a policy of dishonesty. It is precisely because we are willing to pay that we mention a sum which we assume we shall be able to pay. It would be easy enough today to suggest a higher amount if we base this suggestion on the premise that later the impossibility of such payments will become evident, and if we do not shrink from the accusation that we had given a promise which we were unable to fulfill."

"The German policy of taxation is too lenient," was the opinion. "The directors put everything into their businesses instead of paying taxes."

"You are aware, gentlemen, that we are suffering from the most frightful inflation. In the face of a daily sinking monetary value, any tax policy is illusory. So long as we have not succeeded in re-establishing a stable currency there is no prospect of being able to calculate our revenue from taxation on a workable basis, still less of being in a position to pay reparations. As regards the financing of businesses from their own resources, surely we must all rejoice if our industry — rendered backward and out of date by the war — can be set on its feet again. Without this industry there is no hope either for German exports or for payment of reparations."

On the afternoon of that first day I met Mr. McKenna, one of the cleverest of leading British bankers, and a former Chancellor of the Exchequer. When I told him of the morning's discussion he smiled thoughtfully. "The German proposal of twenty billion marks is far too high. Since Germany can only make payment by means of exports, she would be compelled to export to such an extent that British industry would suffer intolerably."

Among Allied economists MacKenna was probably the first to recognize the so-called Transfer Problem which has governed all reparations and economic action during the following decades. It is very easy to decree, on paper, that one country shall pay billions to another. On the one hand this problem affects the debtor country inasmuch as it must raise the amount of the debt by taxation and labor. On the other hand it also affects the creditor countries, since payment cannot be made in the currency of the debtor country (in Germany's case in Reichsmarks) but can only be accepted in gold or in goods. German marks can be spent only in Germany; but to export German goods in such vast quantities means severe competition for the other countries.

My visit to England ended the following day with a luncheon given in my honor at the Automobile Club — a sign, at any rate, that my presence and my explanations had met with appreciation and understanding. Those in Allied circles were beginning to realize the need to debate the question of reparations from an unbiased economic viewpoint as well as the necessity for restoring order in German currency. Government negotiations in the ensuing months resolved themselves in a decision to call an economic conference to discuss these questions. It met in 1924 in Paris under the chairmanship of the Chicago banker Charles Dawes, and is known to history as the Dawes Conference.

# XXII

## THE SECRET OF THE STABILIZED MARK

In THE SUMMER of 1923 the inflation misery in Germany reached its climax. Five years after the end of World War I found Germany in the grip of a fever that threatened to undermine her last vestige of strength. In Saxony, Thuringia and Bavaria riots broke out everywhere. Hitler was tub-thumping in the South. The Communist-Social-Democratic Zeigner Government in Saxony gave the Red Terror a free hand. In Hamburg street riots raged all day and fifteen policemen and sixty-five civilians were killed. The danger of a Communist upheaval was imminent.

I felt it my duty to evacuate my family from this hell's kitchen and pack them off to Switzerland so that I myself might not be hindered by personal considerations were I to be drawn into the whirlpool. So I offered my two children the chance of perfecting their knowledge of French. My thirteen-year-old boy was sent to school in Lausanne and my twenty-year-old daughter interrupted her studies in Heidelberg to attend Lausanne University.

Everyone was agreed that the Communist peril could be averted provided the fight against the French Occupation of the Ruhr were ended (this being the principal cause of the rapid inflationary progress) and a stabilized currency established. For three years the most widely different plans for stabilization had been under discussion without coming to any definite decision. The Stresemann cabinet finally resolved to put an end to the Ruhr dispute and concentrate on an attempt to stabilize the national currency.

Stresemann's political merit in this late summer of 1923 cannot be overestimated. He wasted no time on theoretical propositions. His aim was to create such a position in internal affairs as would ensure a sufficient majority in favor of stabilization. Furthermore he succeeded in enlisting Allied interest and co-operation to establish order in German financial and economic affairs. This co-operation led to the convening of the group of international experts which met in January 1924 and has become famous under the title of the Dawes Committee.

Success depended on the ability to achieve a union of Right and Left in a joint monetary policy. In this connection the political Right, which had particularly strong ties with agriculture, played an outstanding part.

Agriculture had so far derived considerable benefit from the inflation in so far as the latter had enabled farmers to repay their debts with the debased currency, because the German law supports the principle that mark equals mark. This meant that debts which had been incurred in gold marks could be paid by means of equal nominal amounts in debased paper marks. In addition, the agricultural community used their paper marks to purchase as quickly as possible all kinds of useful machinery and furniture — and many useless things as well. That was the period in which grand pianos were to be found in the most unmusical households.

The agricultural circles felt themselves to be masters of the political situation, though, from a political point of view, they were no friends of Stresemann whose seat was far removed from them on the Liberal benches in the Reichstag. But Stresemann knew how to capture them.

He gave his blessing to a currency plan put forward by the Conservative German-Nationalist member Helfferich, a plan which provided for a so-called Roggenmark (Rye mark). Several big undertakings had already conceived and adopted the idea of issuing bonds payable not in paper money but in kind (a ton of coal, a hundredweight of potash). Helfferich went further: he issued tokens for one hundred marks which were payable with a certain quantity of rye and remained valid for that quantity. It could not, of course, be described as a stable currency for the price of rye varied according to consumption and harvest, but the differences in value did keep within the bounds of the highest and lowest prices for rye.

Helfferich endeavored to exploit the Roggenmark plan to the advantage of his party by entrusting the issue of the tokens not to the Reichsbank but to a central bank institution shortly to be established and whose administrative force would be chosen for the most part from among agricultural groups. It is easy to understand that these groups would have acquired a strong influence in German economic affairs.

Naturally the idea met with stormy opposition from the Left. After much argument a compromise was reached in the shape of the so-called Rentenmark. In theory this Rentenmark was to be equal to the gold mark, but would be covered by a cautionary mortgage on the whole of German landed property, so that any given sum in Rentenmarks could be exchanged at any time for a like sum in mortgage bonds. Even this was obviously no guarantee for stability of value, for such a mortgage bond would fetch only fluctuating prices on the Stock Exchange. In the meantime something had to be done.

Under pressure of this "had to" Stresemann succeeded in obtaining a two thirds majority in the Reichstag which gave the government full power to decide as it saw fit in currency matters. So the Rentenmark became law. A special Rentenbank was founded; but the Reichsbank also came into the picture, for the distribution and loaning of Rentenmarks was entrusted to the board of the latter. Such was the situation when I was called upon to carry out the currency reform in a practical manner.

On the morning of November 12, 1923, the Minister of Finance, Dr. Luther, summoned me to an urgent consultation. Dr. Luther was an absolutely first-rate executive. Before he took over the Finance Ministry he had been Lord Mayor of Essen and had discharged his duties in exemplary fashion. He was likewise fully equal to his post at the Ministry of Finance, but did not feel able to cope with the task of reforming the national currency and looked about for a specialist in that line.

Now in attendance on the board was a certain very stout commissionaire, one Müssigbrodt * by name, who nevertheless, on account of his zeal and activity, had earned for himself the secret nickname of "old busybody." Feeling that he must do something to help me, he asked: "Will you not be requiring your red case, sir?"

The red case was a leather portfolio which accompanied me on all my journeys and to all conferences. It contained whatever documents and other papers I might be needing at the time. On this occasion, however, I did not require it. I shook my head. "No thanks, Müssigbrodt, no red case today."

I was not altogether unprepared for this discussion with the Finance Minister. I knew that two other members of the banking profession had already been approached with the request that they should take over the attempt at currency reform as Commissioners of

---

* TRANSLATOR'S NOTE: A singularly inappropriate appellation: it means "bread of idleness!"

National Currency. Both had declined. So I had a pretty good idea of what Luther was aiming at.

Luther very briefly laid his suggestion before me. My first question was: "Herr Luther, why don't you undertake it yourself?" He gave his reason, namely that he was already overworked.

"Why did the two other bankers, whom you approached first, refuse?"

"They probably did not feel equal to it. Indeed one of them was naive enough to say he would take on the job after the introduction of the Rentenmark. But that is to miss the point completely. It is this very introduction that is of vital importance."

"Why don't you let the Reichsbank carry out the currency reform?"

"You know well enough, Herr Schacht, that the president of the Reichsbank, who in himself would be quite capable of tackling the business, is not on very good terms with the government or the President of the Reich."

I certainly did know it. The government, and likewise President Ebert, had more than once given Havenstein * to understand that he should retire. But Havenstein held a life appointment, and before he did retire he probably wanted, among other things, to make sure that his successor would be someone who held the same views on currency questions as he did. It was no secret that he wished Herr Helfferich to succeed him. But the appointment rested with the President of the Reich and Helfferich was not the man to whom the government, or Ebert himself, would have given their confidence.

I considered the matter. Although, in principle, I was prepared to switch over from the private to the public service of the national economy I was aware that I looked upon the Rentenmark solely in the light of an emergency measure to be superseded as soon as possible. For me the only real solution was the reinstatement of the gold mark; and this could never be done through the Rentenbank but must be accomplished by the Reichsbank.

"I would ask for a few days in which to think over the matter thoroughly."

"I regret most sincerely that that is utterly impossible. You will have to decide today and take over the duties of Commissioner for National Economy immediately."

"What authority does the post carry?"

Luther explained. I should have a free hand in all matters touch-

* President of the Reichsbank.

ing the question of money and credit, and would be in direct contact with the government bypassing the various ministries.

"Would you agree, Herr Luther, to my informing you of my decision this afternoon? I shall have to come to some arrangement with my colleagues and my bank."

"If you accept by this afternoon I shall be quite satisfied."

I went back to the bank, thought over my plans and told my colleagues that I intended to accept the government post if the bank would release me from my agreement. They could not very well dissuade me, for it would have been difficult for the bank as such to oppose the government offer. It is also possible that among my colleagues were one or two who did not object to my departure. No public man can ever hope to escape traducers, and in my case the usual scandalmongers came out later with a tale of a large sum which the bank was supposed to have paid me by way of compensation. The truth is that at no time did I stipulate for, or receive, any compensation whatever.

At the same time that I left the bank I also resigned all my advisory positions. It was the custom for all banks to strengthen the relationships between their directorate and their clientele (where the latter consisted of joint stock companies) by the co-opting of leading bankers on to the companies' advisory boards. Their first duty was to cultivate credit and financial relations with these establishments and also to advise them. With the passage of years it had become usual to represent these advisory posts as remunerative sinecures. But, apart from the fact that the reimbursements attached to these positions were not always paid to individual bank officials but were remitted to the bank as a whole, these jobs were by no means exempt from work and anxiety. It was not possible to leave such duties to subordinate members of the staff since they nearly always involved responsible and immediate decisions, and the result was a big increase in the number of advisory posts undertaken by leading bankers. I myself, in the course of years, had achieved a total of about seventy. According to my secretary's evidence, I spent no fewer than one hundred nights in the train in one year in order to fulfil my advisory engagements — which may give some idea of the work entailed.

Next morning, November 13, 1923, I entered upon my duties as Commissioner for National Currency. Curiously enough, the number thirteen has frequently played a part in my life. On March 13, 1924, I founded the Golddiskontbank. May 13, 1927, was "Black

Friday" on the Berlin Stock Exchange. On January 13, 1931, I arrived at Scheveningen for The Hague Conference. On July 13, 1931, Chancellor Brüning summoned me to a consultation on the bank crisis. November 13, 1923, was also the day on which Stresemann finally succeeded in getting a law passed investing him with full authority, with the aid of which he suppressed the various attempts at insurrection and rioting throughout the country.

Four days previously, that is, on the evening of November 9, I had been sitting drinking beer with Stresemann whom I had known for twenty years and discussing the economic situation with him. Our conversation had been suddenly interrupted by a report from the Foreign Office informing Stresemann of Hitler's attempt at a National Socialist Putsch in Munich.

Up to this twelfth of November, when I burned my boats, I had been very happy in my private life. I had my family, my groups of friends, a decent income, a comfortable home; I could share my business anxieties with equally responsible colleagues. In short, had I not been driven by the urge to help my country I should probably have ended my life in comparative peace and comfort. But I was never able to rid myself of anxiety for the welfare of my people. I never considered my banking career in the light of a money-making business; rather I desired to use my activities as a banker in order to help German economy. I realized that Germany was in danger of succumbing to communism and felt it was my duty not to shirk a task which, as I hoped, lay within my power to fulfil.

Since my wife was in Lausanne I was not able to talk things over with her: all I could do was to acquaint her with my decision, which meant that I also had to do without her advice. A lonely road lay before me. Politics claimed me, whether I would or no, without the backing of any one political party. True, I was still a member of the German Democratic Party, but I had never felt warmly attracted to it. Nothing was further from my mind than to allow my views and convictions to be influenced by party considerations. So far as politics were concerned, it was obvious that I should remain a "cat that walked by himself." My work was political economy; but political economy changes with the passage of time and does not accommodate itself to party-political ideas.

My change of work meant also a complete change of social surroundings. The one person who made this change with me was my trusty secretary, Fräulein Steffeck. Her knowledge of English was perfect, as the result of many years' residence in South Africa; she was better at typewriting than at shorthand, but had a real aptitude for organization, was most discreet and displayed great tact in dealing with people. My office from now on was situated in the Ministry of Finance, and her transfer to that ministry gave rise to some difficulties, as was evident from my conversation with the head of the Personnel Department. "I am bringing my secretary with me," I began. "Where can you fit her in — I mean as regards salary scale?"

"The salary scale for our secretaries is two hundred marks per month."

"That seems to me much too little; when Fräulein Steffeck was with us in the bank she drew six hundred marks per month. What is the salary of the Commissioner for National Currency?"

"Four hundred marks per month have been allotted as the salary of the Commissioner for National Currency."

"That is rather small compared with my income up to now. But I will make you a suggestion: Add my salary to Fräulein Steffeck's; then she will still have her six hundred marks. For my part I will waive my claim to a salary."

"Do you mean you will work here for nothing?" The official was obviously disconcerted.

"Yes — on condition that you pay my secretary six hundred marks."

My office in the Ministry of Finance consisted of one small room looking onto the back yard which had hitherto been used by the charwomen as a sort of housemaid's cupboard. But at any rate there was a writing table and a telephone.

Ten days after my appointment as Commissioner for National Currency the Stresemann government fell and its place was taken by the Marx cabinet. It made no difference to my position. Marx was certainly not a man of outstanding energy, but he was, on the other hand, a man of invariable kindness of heart and unswerving rectitude. Throughout the struggles of the next few months he gave me his discreet but unreserved support.

A few days elapsed before the necessary Rentenmark bills were printed. In the meantime the devaluation of the paper mark progressed rapidly. All previous efforts to establish a fixed price for the dollar on Exchange had failed. For weeks on end only a percentage of the foreign currencies bespoken by business circles could be covered, and then at the rate momentarily fixed by the Reichsbank. Against this, however, all foreign currencies, particularly the dollar, fetched far higher prices in black-market dealings. The Reichsbank had no choice but to participate in this increase for the first few days.

On November 20, 1923, the official rate was four trillion two hundred billion marks (4,200,000,000,000) for one dollar.

It is to the credit of the late Geheimrat Kaufmann, a member of the Board of the Reichsbank and their determining voice on the Stock Exchange, that he voiced the request that this rate be maintained. He may possibly have been influenced by the consideration that the peacetime rate for the dollar had been 4.2 marks. If, therefore, it was desired to transpose the paper mark to the old gold mark basis it was only necessary to leave out the trillion sign which made the transposition in bookkeeping amazingly simpler. Every odd-numbered amount would have meant unending work when it came to conversion.

The bankbooks were filled with zeros, which gave rise to many a joke, the most pungent of which was attributed to Karl Fürstenberg. He once asked an acquaintance why the Discount Company had added two stories to their building and was told it was because of all the zeros which required more and more space. Whereupon Fürstenberg is supposed to have retorted: "I always assumed that the zeros in the Discount Company were housed on the first floor." The Board Rooms were on that floor.

The official rate on Exchange remained at 4.2 trillion while during the last week in November the dollar fetched up to twelve trillion marks in the black market.

In the course of those November weeks Germany was in a curious position with three separate currencies, so to speak, existing side by side — the paper mark, the Rentenmark and — theoretically — the old gold mark, which it was my aim to reintroduce in practice through the Reichsbank.

Two enemies of stabilization remained to be defeated — the black market and the emergency money issued by many public corporations and private businesses. This emergency money was on an equal footing with the paper mark, and so long as the former could be paid into the Reichsbank stabilization was not possible. In this instance there was no question of the Reichsbank exercising control over money that was issued: the emergency money was foisted upon it from outside. The time had come to put an end to the system, "Everyone his own Reichsbank."

The first step taken by the Reichsbank was to announce that from now on no more in-payments of emergency money would be accepted. This meant that there was no reason for the corporations and businesses concerned to issue any more emergency money. For such money, if no longer accepted by the Reichsbank and no longer on the same footing as the paper mark but based solely on the credit of the issuing firms or municipalities, would no longer be accepted by anyone.

This decision on the part of the Reichsbank aroused a storm of indignation among all those groups to whom the emergency issues had spelled such wonderful profits. The reason for this indignation, especially in the industrial districts of Rhineland-Westphalia, lay partly in annoyance at the knowledge that profits from the emergency money would henceforth steadily diminish, partly also in the embarrassment experienced particularly by certain municipalities who had placed orders and undertaken investments, expecting to be able to pay in emergency money. But by now it was no longer a question of advantages or disadvantages to this or that interested party, but of the stabilization of money for the whole country.

A discussion with representatives of the Reichsbank was arranged to take place in the Town Hall at Cologne on November 25, 1923, sponsored by leading municipal and business groups of Rhineland-Westphalia and under the direction of the Lord Mayor of Cologne. I took part in this meeting in my capacity of Commissioner for National Currency. It is easy to imagine the tension with which not only the groups involved, but the public as a whole, looked forward to the results of this discussion.

For a good three hours on end one speaker after another addressed the meeting. Each of them had only one request; namely, the reacceptance of emergency money by the Reichsbank. It was a tremendous disappointment to me that not a single voice was raised which either understood or admitted that reacceptance of emergency money would mean the complete fiasco of any attempt to stabilize currency. Indeed, every speech was characterized by absolute distrust of the success of that scheme. It proved yet again, not that a big meeting is incapable of understanding a given situation but that it can never result in a decision to act. Had it been possible to discuss the matter with each individual separately one or other among them might perhaps have been won over. But at a mass meeting every vestige of comprehension was doomed.

A storm of supplications, appeals and threats beat upon my nerves like hailstones without making the slightest impression on me. I allowed all the speakers to proceed without a single interruption. Finally, however, I rose to my feet and said: "Gentlemen, for the past three hours you have been doing your best to talk me round.

I am quite willing to admit that the stopping of emergency money will mean unpleasantness, embarrassment, even considerable difficulties for you. Nevertheless none of your arguments carries weight against the need to restore German currency to its position as a stable currency. I regret that so many among you have voiced doubts as to whether the stabilization of the mark would be successful. To that I reply that the stabilization of the mark will be successfully carried out irrespective of whether difficulties may arise in individual cases. The great mass of German working folk must be able once again — thanks to a stable currency — to feel the ground firm under their feet. Consequently, I will now bring this discussion to a close with the irrevocable declaration that the Reichsbank will adhere to its decision to refuse emergency money. You will have once more to accustom yourselves to budgeting with fixed figures."

Such action did nothing at first to increase my popularity. But neither had my respect increased for the general economic and political attitude of those present. My satisfaction lay in the fact that the stabilization of the mark was successful and that these same groups who, on that November afternoon, had attacked and rejected me were obliged, in a few months, to admit that I had taken the right way.

The second decisive blow to be struck was aimed at the black-market traffic in foreign exchanges.

The success of this blow was due mainly to the fact that although the Rentenmark was introduced as a legal measure, it did not receive the status of legal tender and the distribution of Rentenmark loans was made through the Reichsbank, not through the Rentenbank. These were the two angles from which the Reichsbank was able to reaffirm and develop its function of sole responsibility for monetary policy.

The expression "legal tender" implies the right of every person to settle his debts with this money, and the obligation of every creditor to accept the same in payment. If the Rentenmark did not possess this qualification, nobody could be compelled to accept the Rentenmark as legal tender.

Curiously enough, the gamblers in foreign exchanges had overlooked this characteristic of the Rentenmark. The buying and selling of foreign bills of exchange, particularly the dollar, was carried on for the most part by so-called term transactions. The purchase agreement was concluded at the day's ruling price, while the payment was completed only at the end of the month, the so-called ultimo.

By the November ultimo the black-market dollar rate had risen to exactly twelve trillion marks for one dollar. It now transpired that many of the gamblers in foreign exchanges had not sufficient money to meet their commitments for the November ultimo. The Reichsbank was swamped with demands for credit which had formerly been honored without any trouble. Now however the Reichsbank refused to grant credit to the speculators. Nevertheless it announced its willingness to buy every foreign bill, but only at the official price of 4.2 trillion marks to the dollar, as fixed on November 20. For many speculators there was nothing for it but to sell their foreign bills back to the Reichsbank, so that whoever had bought dollars at the rate of twelve trillion marks was obliged to surrender them to the Reichsbank at the rate of 4.2 trillion. Which meant that they lost eight trillion marks on every dollar!

This "bloodletting" gave the gamblers such a shock that a fresh large-scale speculation in foreign exchange against the official Reichsbank rate was not to be expected for some time to come. With the defeat of the foreign-exchange speculators and the stopping of emergency money the first round in the battle for stabilized currency had been won. But I knew that fresh struggles would follow.

Among the many communications I received in my official capacity, a considerable proportion consisted of requests for employment in my department. Everyone had expected that with the establishment of a Commissioner for National Currency there would arise a new, comprehensive authority. I have never engaged a single employee or official. My secretary was and remained my sole assistant. Later, she was occasionally asked by reporters how I had carried on my activities as Commissioner for National Currency. To one of these questioners Fräulein Steffeck replied:

"What did he do? He sat on his chair and smoked in his little dark room at the Ministry of Finance, which still smelled of old floorcloths. Did he read letters? No, he read no letters. Did he write letters? No, he wrote no letters. He telephoned a great deal — he telephoned in every direction and to every German and international place that had anything to do with money and foreign exchange as well as with the Reichsbank and the Finance Minister. And he smoked. We did not eat much during that time. We usually went home late, often by the last suburban train, traveling third class. Apart from that, he did nothing."

# XXIII

## PRESIDENT OF THE REICHSBANK

IF THE TWENTIETH of November constituted a milestone in the history of the stabilization of the mark by the fixing of the dollar rate at 4.2 trillion paper marks, it also brought yet another fateful occurrence. On that same day Havenstein, president of the Reichsbank, died quite unexpectedly.

The discussion as to Havenstein's successor concentrated essentially on two individuals. One was Karl Helfferich, Bank Director and representative of the German National Party in the Reichstag. The other was Hjalmar Schacht, Commissioner for National Currency and joint founder of the German Democratic Party. From the technical viewpoint Helfferich's former career as a professor was in his favor, coupled with the fact that he had written several scientific books and articles on the monetary system. Schacht had to his credit his recent immediate monetary success as Commissioner for National Currency. Both men could look back on a professional banking career.

At first I took no part in the discussions on the subject of Havenstein's successor. But when criticism became a matter of personal abuse I gave tongue.

The Board of Directors of the Reichsbank, as a body, was entitled to express its expert opinion on the candidates for the presidency of the bank. They had long been aware of the late president's wishes in this respect and, as was only natural, they desired to give effect to these wishes by appointing Helfferich. Nevertheless, for some unknown reason, they allowed themselves to be misled into casting aspersions on my personal reliability in reference to the passage of arms I had had with Herr von Lumm in Belgium in 1915. The Brussels incident was not of course aired frankly and impartially but was the subject of disparaging hints and innuendoes. Fortunately, however, Stresemann in his official capacity as Chancellor had, at my request, caused the Brussels affair to be thoroughly investigated weeks before my appointment as Commissioner, and I could point to his letter as a complete vindication. So that little intrigue failed in its purpose and my candidature went forward.

A conference to which I was bidden by President Ebert may possibly have served to turn the scales. Hitherto I had been only slightly acquainted with Ebert. Now the opportunity presented itself for a fairly long discussion on political economy during which I realized with great pleasure how little this man was bound by party-political prejudice.

"You know, of course, Herr Schacht, that professionally speaking we cannot regard Herr Helfferich as less well qualified than yourself. On the other hand it is very natural that we should accord preference to a man whose general outlook tends essentially more to the Left than in Helfferich's case."

"I am most grateful, sir, for your good opinion. Unfortunately I must confess that, although I take my stand as a broad-minded Liberal I am not in any sense a Social Democrat. From the standpoint of economic policy I am all against exaggerated state bureaucracy and I expect an improvement in our economic situation first and foremost from the unhampered development of private enterprise."

Ebert brushed my objections aside. "In my opinion, whether you are a Social Democrat or not has nothing whatever to do with the present case, nor whether from an economic view you incline more to socialism or liberalism. You have made a successful beginning with the stabilization of our currency. But it is only a beginning, and it will require further unremitting effort to restore our monetary system to a position of definite and permanent stability, and to keep it so. The question I must therefore put to you is this: Do you feel confident that you can carry through this work of stabilization to its final conclusion?"

I did not hesitate. "I have most carefully considered and examined the ways and means of pursuing my stabilization policy. I am confident that I can carry through this task to a successful conclusion. And you may rest assured that I shall devote all my energies and all my knowledge to this end."

We shook hands warmly and Ebert terminated the interview saying: "Right! You will be hearing from me again."

Some fairly heated arguments ensued. The verdict of the Reichsbank Board was definitely against me. With three exceptions the consultative group of the Reichsbank Central Committee — to which about forty prominent members of the business community belonged — expressed themselves unfavorably. But these pronounce-ments carried no weight save as professional opinions. The decision rested with the government and the federal council and, in the last resort, with the President. With only one dissident vote — that of Bavaria — the federal council was solidly in my favor and on December 22, 1923, I received the document, duly drawn up, and signed by President Ebert, appointing me to the post of President of the Reichsbank for life.

I had told my wife as little as possible about the preceding bicker-ings and arguments. Now, however, I telephoned the news of my appointment — which would once again involve a distinct change in our mode of life — and left immediately for Switzerland to spend Christmas Eve and Christmas Day with my wife and children.

In our two rooms at the pension we celebrated Christmas with candles and a Christmas tree; we sang our German Christmas songs and read the Christmas Gospel; and if it was not quite the same as being at home, being together made it as enjoyable as possible.

We arrived back in Berlin on December 27. I had all my papers transferred from the "darkroom" at the Finance Ministry to the bright, airy presidential offices in the Reichsbank. Then I called on the vice-president, Herr von Glasenapp. I had a question to put to him and my subsequent activities would depend upon his answer.

Glasenapp was a Prussian official of the old school with a first-rate legal training, of exactly the same type as Havenstein. His family ranked among the lesser Pomeranian nobility. He was probably better informed than Havenstein had been on matters of monetary policy and had won considerable esteem in international discus-sions in which German interests figured. In his dealings with others he was cheerful and unaffectedly courteous. Though somewhat limited by the prejudices of his surroundings he was yet sufficiently unbiased to bow to wiser judgment and more valid reasons. He had literary tastes and had been of great practical assistance to his eldest son — who later became a well-known authority on India — with his metrical translations from the Sanskrit.

"Herr von Glasenapp," I began, "I have just dropped in to ascer-tain from you whether the Reichsbank has any plans for the definite reintroduction of gold currency, and if so, what they are. I assume you are in a position to give me some information on the subject."

A pleasant, if somewhat embarrassed, smile was followed by the statement: "The bank has no plans or activities in view, Herr Presi-dent."

"That is what I thought, Herr von Glasenapp; in fact I did not anticipate any different answer. Nevertheless it compels me to post-pone taking office for a few days. Before I do so I want to call on the Governor of the Bank of England and discuss both the German and the international currency situation with him."

There followed a lively exchange of telegrams with the German Embassy in London. I enquired whether my visit would be agree-able to Mr. Montagu Norman, the Governor of the Bank of Eng-land, and if so when it would be convenient. I was anxious that our interview should take place at an early date. The answer arrived promptly: I should be very welcome and if possible should come immediately. I agreed to start for London on the evening of Decem-ber 30.

Before recounting my first visit to the Bank of England as presi-dent of the Reichsbank (a visit which was not without significant results) I should like briefly to describe the concluding stages of my taking over at the Reichsbank.

On my return from London at the beginning of January I called a meeting of the Board of Directors. "I take this opportunity, gentle-men, of welcoming you as my colleagues. Today I enter upon my duties as president of the Reichsbank, and am aware that I do so despite your unanimous desire to the contrary. I entirely appreciate your attitude, for until now you have scarcely known me. For that reason I should also understand it if you preferred not to work with me provided a position of equal status were obtainable elsewhere. I will gladly be of assistance to any of you who desire to transfer to such a position. On the other hand I, for my part, shall bear no resentment on account of your hitherto prevailing attitude toward me personally, and shall be happy to see any of you in the Reichs-bank who will continue to co-operate loyally with me. I would ask you therefore kindly to let me know by tomorrow morning whether you prefer to make a change or are willing to work with me. Good morning, gentlemen."

Whereupon I retired to my office. Within half an hour Herr von Glasenapp appeared with heightened color to assure me, on behalf of all the directors, that they were ready to co-operate loyally with me.

"Thank you for this assurance, Herr von Glasenapp. I realize from it the sincere attachment which the members of the board entertain for their work at the Reichsbank, and am convinced that our work together will develop on lines of cordiality and mutual trust."

And in this I was not disappointed. My relations with my colleagues on the board became and remained in every respect satisfying, confidential and friendly. This was due not only to the uprightness of character of all concerned but also to the fact that every one of my colleagues was fully equal to his task, which was to try each of them severely in the ensuing years.

The first meeting with the forty members of the Central Committee passed off in somewhat lighter vein. According to the statutes the Board of the Reichsbank was obliged to convene a monthly session of the Central Committee. I hadn't given a thought to this regulation when on the morning of January 30 my personal assistant brought to my attention the fact that the prescribed meeting had not been held that month.

"Then get busy and call the monthly meeting for tomorrow, the thirty-first. Notify the foreign members by telegram."

Next morning every member of the Central Committee was present in the great Kaisersaal (Hall of the Emperors) of the Reichsbank — so called because of the three life-size portraits of the three Emperors (Wilhelm I, Friedrich III, Wilhelm II) that adorned the walls. The room was so planned that for social receptions it could be made to connect with the adjoining presidential residence. At one evening party I was strolling through the Kaisersaal with the wife of President Ebert. She glanced with a somewhat surprised expression at the paintings and said with a smile as attractive as it was significant: "So you still have the emperors' portraits here!"

"But of course! It is not the duty of the republic to wipe out Germany's past from the pages of history. But if you will kindly turn round you will see the bronze bust of your husband at the other end of the room."

It was in the Kaisersaal, then, that the members of the Central Committee had solemnly gathered when I entered, in my everyday suit. I nodded to several acquaintances, sat down in my chair and asked everyone also to be seated.

"Gentlemen," I began, "I have the honor to welcome you here as your new president. I know, of course, that with a few honorable exceptions all of you voted against my appointment. This fact proved exceedingly useful during my visit to London at the beginning of this month, because it enabled other countries to recognize that the economic policy hitherto pursued by the Reichsbank will undergo a drastic change. You will have the opportunity of forming your own opinion of this policy in the course of the next few weeks and months. For today it may serve to close the meeting, unless one of you has anything to say."

The three members who at the time had voted for me grinned contentedly when one of my principal opponents, a very well-known Berlin banker, asked leave to speak and on behalf of all present made the customary apology and declaration and assurance of loyalty. I acknowledged them gratefully and brought the meeting to a close.

# XXIV

## THE BANK OF ENGLAND

AT EIGHT O'CLOCK on New Year's Eve, 1923, my train glided into Liverpool Street Station. I had arranged with Herr Dufour-Feronce, Councilor to the German Embassy, that he should meet me at the station and accompany me to my hotel. Before we left, my secretary had asked me if there were any further material I wished her to include. By way of a joke I had said: "Put in *Brockhaus*, Volume B — there's something about the Bank of England in it." Fräulein Steffeck took the joke seriously and when we reached our London hotel presented me with *Brockhaus*. She had to take it back to Germany — unread!

Dufour was at the station to meet me as arranged. I was not a little surprised to see, standing beside him a tall man with a pointed grayish beard and shrewd, discerning eyes, who introduced himself as Montagu Norman, governor of the Bank of England. He shook hands warmly and said in English: "I am most heartily glad to see you: you are sincerely welcome. I'm especially pleased that you were able to follow up my invitation so quickly. I have only come to welcome you but I won't keep you any longer as you must be tired. Come and see me, will you, at the Bank of England tomorrow morning at eleven o'clock."

"But Mr. Governor, tomorrow is New Year's Day — surely you won't be going to the bank tomorrow?"

"That doesn't matter. I want to have a talk with you as soon as possible and I shall expect you at eleven. I hope we shall be friends."

Dufour accompanied me to the hotel. I expressed my pleasure and appreciation that my English colleague should have taken the trouble to come and meet me, especially on New Year's Eve and at such a late hour.

"Oh," said Dufour, "Norman is very keen to make your acquaintance. He will certainly discuss matters of vital importance with you and you can count on his sincere understanding. When I told him you were coming and said I hoped you would get on well together he replied: 'I *want* to get on well with him.' "

Dufour was not a career diplomat. He came of an old Huguenot titled family which for generations had been highly esteemed in the Leipzig business community. After the First World War certain influential politicians had felt that the old style of career diplomats would benefit considerably from the introduction and absorption of outstanding business elements. Several personalities from the business world, therefore, who were considered suitable, were appointed to the Foreign Office and to various diplomatic posts abroad. Among the few whose appointment could be classed as successful Dufour took first place. Not only was he a clever farsighted businessman, but he possessed a vast fund of general knowledge and the innate tact — the result of family tradition — lacking in so many businessmen who had been pushed into the Diplomatic Service — a man of the highest social principles and thoroughly reliable character. In international circles he was entirely at home, whether from a linguistic, social or business standpoint. The way he backed me up during my visit to London made my task appreciably easier.

I certainly did not make light of that task. Only a very few members of the government realized the important results my visit might have on Germany's immediate policy. Our struggle for the establishment of a stable currency was by no means over. Economically we were completely exhausted. The meeting of the Dawes Committee was imminent. Everything depended on being able to rouse the Allies to an understanding of our position, and to create a friendly atmosphere. In this connection my London discussions would not be without influence.

In the Carlton Hotel where we were staying New Year's festivities were in full swing. The rooms were full of men and women in tails and full evening dress. I was not in the mood for dance music, champagne, crackers and confetti. Feeling somewhat anxious I turned in early.

Next morning, the first day of the New Year, I became more intimately acquainted with Norman. Our conversation proceeded in friendly fashion, even when dealing with very serious essentials. I was completely frank with him regarding our situation. The discussion soon focused itself on the most vital point, namely Germany currency.

"Have you any definite plans for safeguarding your currency in such unstable circumstances? Or are you awaiting the decisions of the Dawes Committee? You know that they intend to tackle the question of the stabilization of German currency first of all?"

"I shall of course be very pleased, Mr. Governor, if the Dawes Committee will co-operate in stabilizing German currency. But I don't want to rely on their decisions alone. Above all, I don't want to wait until these decisions come up for discussion — that may take months. Even if the Committee gets to work quickly you know that their decisions will have to be ratified through the various political bodies of the countries concerned. Such ratifications take up a lot of time and give rise to many complications. Furthermore, I am of the opinion that we should not rely only on others. We ourselves must act, and in view of the unstable economic situation we must act quickly."

"From your reply I may assume that you have plans of your own. What are they?"

"First and foremost, as soon as the Ruhr dispute is ended it will be necessary to set German industry going again. For this we need to create opportunities for credit, opportunities which will enable foreign trade to be conducted on a stable monetary foundation. But at present I lack the means to achieve this."

"So you are looking for foreign credit? I hardly think you will obtain it at the moment in any appreciable quantity. It is pretty safe to assume that the other countries will await the result of the Dawes Committee before they proffer financial assistance."

"My plans are not limited solely to obtaining credit. I intend to found a second credit bank in addition to the Reichsbank, a bank based entirely on gold. This bank will make loans only against bills of exchange, and will give preferential assistance to those German industries which are able to resume export trade. Supposing for the sake of argument I call this bank the Golddiskontbank." (Gold Discount Bank.)

"How do you reckon to procure funds for this bank?"

"I picture this bank starting with a capital of two hundred million marks. This capital will be entirely in foreign currency, let us say in pounds sterling. I believe I shall be able to raise half of this capital in foreign currency in Germany itself. The remaining half I should like to borrow from the Bank of England."

"Are you purporting to make the Bank of England a shareholder in the Golddiskontbank?"

"No, not that. I should like to obtain from you a loan for the

Reichsbank of one hundred million marks in pounds sterling for three years. With this money the Reichsbank will take over the second half of the capital of the Golddiskontbank."

Norman was silent while he considered the matter. The idea of the Golddiskontbank was something quite new to him. With his limited knowledge of German economy he was unable immediately to appreciate the scope of the effectiveness of such a bank.

"Who will be the directors?"

"The management of this Golddiskontbank will be solely in the hands of the Reichsbank."

"Who will borrow from the bank?"

"Having regard to the preponderance of Rhineland-Westphalian industry in the German economic system, and also to the severe damage suffered by the Occupation of the Ruhr, the loans will chiefly be used, so far as the Occupation of the Ruhr permits, to finance Rhenish-Westphalian industries."

"For such a project two hundred million marks could not possibly be sufficient."

"Naturally I have thought of that, and I should like to enlist your agreement and your support for a further project. As this is essentially a question of obtaining funds to meet deliveries of raw materials and for the export of goods, I believe that the bills which the Golddiskontbank will accept will be a suitable investment for the London money market. I would ask you therefore to be so good as to allow these bills to be offered in the English market."

Another pause. Norman was aware that without the authorization of the Bank of England such bills would never be taken up by British bankers in any appreciable quantity. He seemed hesitant. Then I played a third card.

"Mr. Norman, the Golddiskontbank will be an issue bank which will issue banknotes based on its gold capital of two hundred million marks. I intend to issue these notes in pounds sterling."

"You mean to issue notes in Germany in a foreign currency?"

"At first glance the idea may strike you as extraordinary. But if a firm of exporters uses foreign currency in the course of business why should I not use foreign currency in my dealings with them?"

Silence again while Norman thought this over.

"And just think, Mr. Governor," I went on, "what prospects such a measure would afford for economic collaboration between Great Britain's World Empire and Germany. If we desire to establish European peace we must free ourselves from the limitations imposed by mere conference resolutions and Declarations of Congress. Economically, the European countries must be more closely linked. Somehow, somewhere, we must make a practical start in that direction."

Norman listened with visibly growing appreciation and interest.

"You have some very remarkable ideas there, Mr. President." He began to take kindly to my plans; we discussed a whole lot of supplementary questions and problems.

"Well, Mr. President, I think that's enough for today. I shall give all these matters my very careful consideration. Please come along tomorrow at ten o'clock. Then we can proceed further."

I was quite excited when I returned to the hotel and told Dufour about our conversation.

When I arrived the next morning I realized at once that my arguments of the previous day had not failed to impress Norman. He was in the best of humors and asked me to stay to lunch after our talk, as he wanted me to meet the members of his Board of Directors and some of his close colleagues. He signified his intention also of discussing my proposals that very day with influential City men and hoped to be in a position to give me a definite answer on the morrow.

"Today I should like to tell you about another matter, Mr. President, and ask your opinion. I have had a letter from Monsieur Finaly, president of the Banque de Paris et des Pays-Bas. He informs me that a French Banking Syndicate, together with a group of Rhineland Bankers and with the consent of the German Government, intend to set up their own central bank in the Rhineland which will issue their own banknotes independently of the Reichsbank. Monsieur Finaly asks me to mention some London banks who might be prepared to join this Franco-Rhineland Syndicate. I should very much like to know, Mr. President, whether you are aware of this plan and what you think of it."

Unfortunately I was aware of it. I have no wish to go further into the regrettable separatist tendencies which were at work in the Rhineland and the Palatinate in 1923 and which are painfully impressed on the memory of the German people. I am the more unwilling to do so because some of the persons who sympathized with these tendencies — or at any rate were not opposed to them — are still active in public life. I had hoped that the cessation of the Ruhr dispute would have enabled Stresemann to put a stop to these proceedings. That, however, had been possible only in the political sphere. In the economic field the separatist efforts had continued. The government's inability to help in the rapid and practical re-establishment of economic life of Rhineland-Westphalia, and the efforts of Rhineland business groups to obtain any sort of assistance, had finally resulted in this distressing situation. The Marx cabinet had allowed itself to be misled into surrendering to pressure from the interested parties and granting permission for the establishment of an independent Rhineland issue bank with Allied capital participation.

That much I knew. What I did not know until now was that preparations for such a separatist bank were already so far advanced that Anglo-French negotiations for its rapid completion were well under way. My reply to Norman's enquiry was hesitating and obviously could not entirely conceal my mental attitude.

"Mr. Governor, I am aware that the German Government has given its consent to this bank project."

"I have no doubt that the French statement regarding the German Government's consent is conclusive. However, I am not greatly interested in that consent. What does interest me is what the Reichsbank thinks about it."

I breathed again. "The Reichsbank's attitude is entirely clear and unequivocal. The Reichsbank is definitely opposed to this and to any similar project which seeks to restrict its own supreme power in matters of currency within the German Reich."

"Thank you, Mr. President. That is good enough for me. And now let's go to lunch."

There was little of the modern office about the rooms sacred to the Board of Directors: on the contrary a pleasant private atmosphere prevailed. Norman's study was furnished in massive mahogany. It was the same in the dining room where everyone connected with the directorate was wont to foregather at lunch time. The rooms were all lofty and spacious but it was necessary to work by artificial light throughout the day for the surrounding streets were narrow and the houses opposite took away a great deal of light. In 1924 the bank had not yet been rebuilt and still retained much of its old-fashioned character which had earned for it the nickname of "The Old Lady of Threadneedle Street."

With inward pride Norman took me over the vast building and, with some emotion, into an inner courtyard resembling a Spanish patio, in the center of which stood the memorial to those members of the bank who fell in the First World War. I was deeply impressed by this memorial, which represented St. Christopher wading through the river with the Christ Child on his shoulder.

During lunch I was introduced informally to all the members of the Board of Directors and the management. They responded in completely unselfconscious and friendly fashion, which contrasted pleasantly with former meetings with Allied circles in Paris and London. It was evident that Norman had already told them something about me. Mentally he towered above the entire assembly. The governor of the Bank of England is elected annually for a period of one year. For twenty years Norman was invariably reelected, unaffected by the changes in the British Government.

With the passage of years my relations with Norman developed into a genuine friendship. As a young man he had studied music in Dresden and retained the happiest memories of his stay in Germany. For all his characteristic mellowness and outward calm he was a man of great personal determination and tenacity of purpose. In his younger days he had fought in the Boer War and still spent many of his holidays in South Africa. He had made many trips to America where he enjoyed more than one highly prized friendship. He was in constant correspondence and frequent personal touch with the presidents of many foreign central banks.

When my daughter Inge's third child was born Norman stood godfather. He came over to Berlin for the christening and held the child — who was given the names of Norman Hjalmar — over the font.

We resumed our correspondence after the Second World War. By then he had retired and was in poor health. I wanted to go over and see him, but was unable to obtain an English visa and it was a great grief to me that I was refused one, even to attend his funeral, as I had not yet been officially denazified. Norman himself would not have cared.

# XXV

## THE CENTER OF SEPARATISM

NORMAN and I continued our conversation the following morning.

"I have gone into your proposal most thoroughly and discussed it not only with my board here but also with my banking friends in the City. Do you really think you can raise one hundred million marks in foreign currency in Germany?"

"I am convinced that I stand a very good chance of it."

"Then I am prepared to make you a loan from the Bank of England for a period of three years, for the purpose of establishing the Golddiskontbank."

"I am deeply grateful to you, Mr. Governor. I take it that I should have the right to repay the loan before the expiration of that period?"

"There would certainly be no objection to that."

"What rate of interest does the loan carry?"

"We will reckon interest at flat rate of five per cent."

When one remembers that at that time interest in Germany was in the neighborhood of ten per cent, even for financially sound debtors, it is easy to appreciate that this rate was a great concession. I accepted without further ado. No mention was made of guarantee or security. Norman was satisfied with an ordinary simple undertaking on the part of the Reichsbank

"Mr. President, I and my friends have gone further into the question of the possibility of discounting your bills in the London market. A group of London bankers is prepared to accept bills to the value of several hundred million marks, provided they are endorsed by the Golddiskontbank, so that you may count altogether on half a billion working capital for your bank."

Once again I expressed my deep gratitude; I saw my Golddiskontbank as a certainty, which at the same time would afford me the opportunity of giving a good "boost" to Rhineland-Westphalian industry.

But Norman had yet another surprise in store for me. "Before you leave London," he said, "I would like to show you the letter I sent to Monsieur Finaly in Paris yesterday." He handed me the carbon copy of his letter — scarcely more than twenty lines in all. In the most courteous terms he acknowledged the receipt of Finaly's letter and added that, as regards the proposed central bank in the Rhineland, the Bank of England set less store by the German Government's approval than by the opinion of the Reichsbank. In this connection Norman felt that he was justified in assuming that the Reichsbank was opposed to the project. As a result he regretted that he was unable to give Monsieur Finaly the name of any English bank that would be willing to join the French syndicate.

I handed the carbon copy back to Norman. I was deeply moved, for I realized at once that this letter meant the deathblow to Rhineland separatism. It was not from any political resentment that certain business groups in the Rhineland had agreed to support the project of an independent foreign-aided central bank, but from sheer necessity since their economic system, lacking both money and credit, was no longer able to find employment for the workpeople under their charge. But that did not lessen the political damage which would be caused by giving way to this necessity.

My secretary and I left the Bank of England with feelings of deep thankfulness for the deliverance that had been vouchsafed us. Norman accompanied us as far as the entrance to the courtyard where our car was waiting to take us to the station. The usual London fog had given place to snow, with thick flakes falling from a lowering winter sky under the light of the street lamps. Norman came up to the car, took a rug from the front seat and spread it over our knees. Then he waved goodbye from the steps as we drove away into the darkness.

"I have never seen you so cheerful," said my secretary Fräulein Steffeck as, from the stern of our ship, we watched England disappear in the fog.

If I had imagined that the establishment of the Golddiskontbank in Germany would be an easy matter I was doomed to severe disappointment. Opposition arose in the first instance from the business community in the Rhineland who were determined to establish their own central bank and regarded the president of the Reichsbank as their enemy. Hugo Stinnes went so far, in the course of the next few days, as to advise the German Government that the Rhineland businessmen must decline to have any dealings with me. But for better or worse they were compelled, in the first instance, to deal with me.

Scarcely was I back in the Reichsbank when I received a call from the Chancellery inviting me to attend a conference with representatives of Rhineland industry on the question of the Rhineland Central Bank. The Chancellor, Herr Marx, took the chair; there were also present Herr Luther, the Minister of Finance, some permanent heads of departments, and four leading figures from the Rhineland business community. The last named had come to the conference in a somewhat exultant frame of mind: had not the French as good as promised to furnish some of the necessary capital? Furthermore, leading Rhineland politicians had succeeded, only a few days previously, in bringing about the discharge of Herr Bracht, the Prussian Secretary of State, who had defended Prussian interests in the Rhineland with courage and tenacity. Under pressure by these political forces it had been necessary to remove Bracht from office.

The Rhineland deputation opened the conference with a lengthy description of the hopeless economic conditions in the Rhineland, and the urgent request that in accordance with French desires, the government would now execute an official deed ratifying their consent to the establishment of the Rhineland Central Bank. The arguments brought forward seemed to me weighty but not sufficiently convincing. During these speeches I jotted down the following verse * and passed it around among my colleagues on our side of the table, causing a good deal of quiet amusement:

> *The Rhinelanders, with white-hot ire,*
> *At Bracht and Schacht direct their fire.*
> *Bracht's efforts have been curbed,*
> *Schacht remains unperturbed.*

The Chancellor then called upon me to speak. I agreed that the Rhinelanders had described the situation correctly, but emphasized the need for self-help. Nor did I hesitate to point out the political consequences which would inevitably arise from our acceptance of French aid.

---

* *Des Rheinlands Wut ist glutentfacht,*
  *Teils gegen Bracht, teils gegen Schacht.*
  *Bracht ist schon abgeschossen,*
  *Schacht ist noch unverdrossen.*

"Unfortunately," countered the opposite camp, "the government has so far not been in a position to help us. Our program of self-help can only go forward if supported by French capital. Or do you know any other way, Herr Schacht?"

"Yes, there is another way."

I then proceeded to unfold my plan for the Golddiskontbank in all its details. The one item I kept back was Norman's letter to Finaly; nor did I ever once breathe a word of it in the course of ensuing developments. This is the first time I have referred to it after a lapse of thirty years. I did not do so at the time because I realized something that the Rhinelanders could not know — namely, that the French had begun to get cold feet.

The deputation of course raised a whole lot of objections to my plan, which they described as unfeasible, and, when I had demolished these objections, they finally persisted in their contention that it would be utterly impossible for me to raise one hundred million marks in foreign currency in Germany, which represented the German half of the Golddiskontbank's capital.

This caused the Chancellor to ask me: "Herr Schacht, we have to come to a definite decision today whether or not to give official assent to the Rhineland Central Bank. Following the objections put forward by these gentlemen we can, I think, only come to such a decision if we are quite clear in our minds as to whether you can or cannot raise this one hundred million marks."

Since this government conference took place immediately on my return from London I had had no opportunity to put out any feelers or do anything about finding that hundred million. I had now therefore either to risk a government decision in favor of the Rhinelanders or to shoulder the responsibility for achieving the hundred million. So I said:

"Herr Reichskanzler, I undertake to find the hundred million marks and am confident that I shall be able to raise that amount."

"Under these circumstances, gentlemen," declared the Chancellor, "you will understand that, in view of the responsibility which the president of the Reichsbank has assumed, the government cannot feel justified in according permission for the establishment of a central bank in the Rhineland."

The deputation withdrew after expressing their dissatisfaction and disappointment.

During the days immediately following I arranged meetings with several banks and banking firms and within a few days had the satisfaction of ascertaining that the requisite amount of one hundred million gold marks had been subscribed in foreign exchange.

I was now able to proceed immediately with the establishment of the Golddiskontbank. It was necessary that the Reichstag should pass a bill to this effect. A draft of the bill was prepared by us and submitted to the Reichstag by the government, whence it passed to the usual committees for discussion. Here I met with further opposition. The Conservative element, who had already shown considerable disapproval over the Rentenmark question, suspected that their influence would be still further restricted and deputed Helfferich to enter the lists against me. One of his contentions was similar to that which I had raised in connection with French participation. He feared the effects of foreign influence on the management of the Reichsbank. I was able easily to point out that capital participation in an undertaking, as envisaged by the French — particularly with a foreign majority — could very well achieve such an undesired effect. But in my case it was simply a matter of an ordinary straightforward loan which I could repay at any time within three years. There could be no question whatever of any influence connected with the conduct of the Reichsbank.

Finally Helfferich said that he feared the interest on the loan would prove too heavy a burden and would be detrimental to the Reichsbank. "What rate of interest do you have to pay, Herr Schacht?"

My reply was received with obvious amazement; even Helfferich could think of no retort to my curt statement "Five per cent, Herr Helfferich." Everyone knew that at that time the normal rate of interest was double that amount and more. The debate in committee ended with a resolution that the bill for the establishment of the Golddiskontbank be submitted to a plenary session of the Reichstag.

But the trials and tribulations of the Golddiskontbank plan were not yet over, for in the meanwhile the Dawes Committee had met in Paris. Its members were not a little discomfited when they learned what I had been able to achieve in the interval from the point of view of monetary policy. Of course I had to tell them about the plan for the Golddiskontbank. They naturally wanted the credit for the final stabilization of German currency to be a feather in the Committee's cap, and did their utmost to keep putting off the actual establishment of the bank. It was inevitable that Germany's economy should suffer under this policy of procrastination — a state of affairs I was not prepared to put up with. So I had recourse to means which I frequently adopted in later years: I took refuge in publicity.

In a speech at Königsberg at the beginning of March 1924 I described the Dawes Committee's policy of delay and declared that I could no longer accept responsibility for the maintenance of the Rentenmark if stumbling blocks were continually put in my way. I incurred considerable displeasure on the part of the Committee, but I achieved my object — they withdrew their objections to my plan.

The Golddiskontbank was established on March 13, 1924. Right up to the collapse of Germany in 1945 it contributed successfully, as an auxiliary of the Reichsbank, to the maintenance of currency and to the expansion of German exports. The continued progress of stabilization due to the Reichsbank policy made it unnecessary for the Golddiskontbank to contemplate issuing banknotes. It is true that we did print Golddiskontbank notes payable in pounds sterling as discussed with Norman, but they were never put into circulation because in the interval, the Reichsmark had achieved, and thereafter maintained, its gold parity.

# XXVI

## MONSIEUR POINCARÉ

ON THE TWENTY-THIRD of January, 1924, I arrived in Paris at the request of the Dawes Committee. Instead of coming to Berlin they had preferred to discuss the German economic situation first in Paris, and my presence was required as a source of information. On the afternoon of my arrival I had to appear before a subcommittee under the chairmanship of the American, Owen Young. Anyone with experience of the years immediately following Germany's collapse in 1945 can picture something of the anti-German atmosphere of those earlier days and understand that I approached this new task with some inner anxiety.

Owen Young greeted me in true American fashion with a hearty handshake and the customary "How do you do." The Frenchman shook hands with obvious reluctance, the Belgian hesitatingly, the Englishman coolly. The sense of constraint vanished only when the Italian — Professor Flora from Bologna — shook hands warmly with a good old Austrian "Habe die Ehre." ("It's a pleasure.")

Then the examination started. The secretary of the subcommittee, a Belgian, had prepared a lengthy questionnaire. I don't know if that questionnaire was in any way comparable with the one we experienced after 1945, but so far as I could tell from a glance, the number of questions cannot have been much smaller. It would have taken days to answer all those questions, as the first of them, with their replies, showed. The practical American soon had enough of it.

"Gentlemen, we shall never get through at this rate. I think we should do far better to ask Herr Schacht to give us a coherent report on the economic and financial conditions in Germany as they were, and as they stand today."

Even at that time the Americans carried so much weight in international matters that no one ventured to object. I was in no sense prepared for such an eventuality, but conditions in Germany were of course so familiar to me that I declared, without any hesitation, that I was ready to do as the Committee asked. So for nearly two hours I gave them, extempore and in English, a detailed report. I described how Germany's resources had been drained dry by the war, the compulsory deliveries of materials, the Ruhr dispute, and inflation. I added an account of what, in the meantime, we had achieved on our own power. I told them of the Rentenmark, the Reichsbank, the Golddiskontbank, and concluded with the words:

"I think, gentlemen, I have given you an exhaustive report on conditions in Germany. I have only one additional request to make. My presence at home is urgently needed: the progress of the policy already begun demands it. I would ask you therefore to allow me to return to Berlin as soon as possible."

The effect was unexpected. The subcommittee expressed its satisfaction at my report but there could be no question at this stage of my early return to Germany. The measures I had meanwhile adopted in Berlin had been noted with the greatest interest. Up to a point, however, they proved disappointing, for after all the Dawes Committee had come to Europe with the express object of stabilizing German currency, and they now found that a considerable part of the work had already been accomplished. The impression must not be allowed to get abroad that in this important matter the work of the Dawes Committee was superfluous. So the public was informed that in the course of its first discussion with me, the Committee was most gratified to note that my ideas and aims coincided with those of the Committee and that further discussions would follow.

There was a distinct improvement in the atmosphere, though in the next plenary session I still felt like a prisoner in the dock. The members sat at a long semicircular table while I had to make my report from a kind of "stool of repentance" facing the semicircle. But I experienced considerable inner satisfaction from the fact that Germany had, by her own efforts, made a successful beginning on the work of stabilization and in so doing had aroused respect and established her position at future deliberations.

Being obliged to resign myself to a longer sojourn in Paris I began to pay a few calls, first and foremost on my opposite number, Monsieur Robineau, governor of the Banque de France, who received me politely. My second visit was to Monsieur Léon Barthou, chairman of the Reparations Commission, under whose aegis the Dawes Committee had been convened and assembled. I looked upon these two visits as matters of duty. Suddenly, I received a summons from the Chancellory to call on Monsieur Millerand, the President of the Republic. Millerand was reckoned a Right-wing Socialist with a reputation for opportunism. At our interview I found him fairly forthcoming in many respects, but in the long run of the same narrow political outlook I had experienced in Monsieur Barthou. During our half hour's conversation I failed to convince him that Franco-German understanding, which I described as an urgent necessity, could most quickly be restored by the closest possible economic connections. Millerand stuck to his lawyer's and politician's attitude where Germany was concerned.

This visit to the head of the French State, which I had not felt able to decline, did not make me anxious for any further talks with French politicians. In the meantime my visit to Millerand worried Monsieur Poincaré, the Prime Minister. Monsieur Barthou came to see me one day and tried to persuade me that I should also call upon Monsieur Poincaré.

"I did not come to Paris for political discussions, Monsieur Barthou. Naturally I called upon you in your capacity as Chairman of the Reparations Commission. If I visited the President of the Republic it was because he himself requested me to do so. I have no wish to take the first step in calling on Monsieur Poincaré. If Monsieur Poincaré wishes to see me it is for him to send for me. In that case it would of course be most discourteous on my part not to comply with such a request. And I have no desire to be discourteous."

"But Herr Schacht, you can understand that since you have called on Monsieur Millerand, Monsieur Poincaré attached considerable importance to a visit from you. Monsieur Poincaré is head of the goverment and therefore cannot simply overlook the fact that, while you have called on the President of the Republic, you ignore the head of the government."

"I haven't the slightest intention of ignoring Monsieur Poincaré. I am quite aware of Monsieur Poincaré's outstanding political position. But I am here once and for all as a businessman at the request of the Dawes Committee, and I have nothing to do with politics. The Dawes Committee does not come within the domain of the Head of the French Government but within your own domain, Monsieur Barthou, as Chairman of the Reparations Commission."

"But you don't understand, Herr Schacht! Monsieur Poincaré insists on seeing you."

"Then let him send for me."

"He can't possibly do that. Parliament would look upon such action on his part as most suspicious from a political point of view."

I stuck to my guns. It took two more days, with a lot of coming-and-going in which the French Foreign Office also took a hand, before I would give in. After all, Poincaré was the most powerful man on the entire Allied Council.

"I can assure you, Herr Schacht," concluded Monsieur Barthou when all the preparations were complete, "if you present yourself at the Quai d'Orsay at five o'clock tomorrow afternoon the Prime Minister will receive you immediately."

Punctually at five o'clock the following afternoon I arrived at the Foreign Office on the Quai d'Orsay where Monsieur Poincaré had his quarters. I was relieved of my hat and coat and taken into one of those luxuriously appointed rooms in Louis Seize style which appeals to us even today. A clock on the mantelpiece confirmed that the time was exactly 5 P.M. I waited five minutes; I waited ten minutes. I began to grow impatient and waited another five minutes. I remembered Barthou's promise that there would be no delay. I waited another three minutes. Then my patience gave out. I saw no reason to put up with discourtesy, even from the French Prime Minister. I asked the manservant to give me my hat and coat and to inform His Excellency that unfortunately I had been unable to wait any longer. The manservant tried to stop me, but I took my departure quickly. I had gone downstairs and had already crossed the forecourt and reached the sidewalk when I heard my name called. Two menservants, one in red, the other in black, came running after me and informed me that the Prime Minister had been entertaining some visitors but that His Excellency begged me to return. He would ask his visitors to wait and would receive me at once. Since I did not wish to be discourteous I turned back. Monsieur Poincaré was standing in the entrance to his study and received me at once.

A few weeks later the whole incident was featured in a satirical Paris weekly with the caption: *Dr. Schacht ne peut pas attendre.* (Dr. Schacht can't wait.)

My interview with Monsieur Poincaré lasted nearly an hour. To him also I expounded the German situation. I explained how utterly impossible it was for us to pay reparations totaling one hundred and twenty billion marks. I tried to make him see that Germany could pay only by exporting goods to an extent which would never be tolerated by other countries, least of all by France herself. I pointed out that such exports would stifle competitive industry in the Allied countries. Yet there was no other way of conveying the required amount of reparations from Germany to other nations.

It became evident that I had to deal with a thoroughly intelligent and highly cultured man. But it was equally evident that he was prepared to subordinate all other considerations to his political aims; for instance, to reduce Germany to a state of complete disablement and degradation. He continued to insist on payment.

"Mr. Prime Minister, you could affix a notice to every house in Germany, 'This house is the property of M. Poincaré,' without being one cent better off. To be the owner of houses in Germany would not help you one scrap. You would not even be able to transfer the rents from German currency into French currency."

Poincaré remained obdurate. He understood very well what I was talking about, but his one desire was to keep Germany in subjection.

I rose.

"I regret that in these circumstances it would be useless to continue our conversation. I shall leave this room far less hopefully than I entered it."

Our leave-taking was icy.

From a member of his entourage I learned during the next few days that Poincaré had declared that I was the first German who had told him in plain terms what Germany wanted, and the first person to break off a discussion with him.

I had, of course, to report in detail to our Ambassador in Paris and he in turn passed the information on to Berlin. The result was that the story of my visit to Poincaré, with all the attendant circumstances, spread rapidly. Our Ambassador was horrified at the stand I had taken and there was a good deal of head-shaking among members of the cabinet. Only General von Seeckt chuckled when he heard the story. I set greater store by the chuckles than the headshaking.

It took another eight years before the Allied politicians realized that the whole policy of reparations was an economic evil which was bound to inflict the utmost injury not only upon Germany but upon the Allied nations as well. Of the one hundred and twenty billions which Germany was supposed to pay, between ten and twelve billions were actually paid during the years 1924 to 1932. And they were not paid out of surplus exports as they should have been. During those eight years Germany never achieved any surplus exports. Rather they were paid out of the proceeds of loans which other countries, acting under a complete misapprehension as to Germany's resources, pressed upon her to such an extent that in 1931 it transpired that Germany could no longer meet even the interest on these loans. Finally, in 1932, there followed the Lausanne Conference at which the reparations commitments were practically written off. Of the prescribed one hundred and twenty billions a clear ten per cent had been paid. On the other hand each and all of the foreign loans made to Germany, amounting to a clear twenty billions, remained outstanding. The Allied Governments pocketed the ten to twelve billions reparations, but foreign private investors lost their money on the loans made to Germany.

But in 1924 at the time of my visit to Paris, the French people were obsessed by the delusion that they would receive billions and billions from Germany.

During that period I had to make a business trip from Paris to London for the day. My only chance was to take the night train and cross from Dieppe to Newhaven. As a German I was relegated to the end of the queue passing through the French passport control. When at last my turn came I was obliged to answer a lengthy enquiry form full of the most idiotic questions.

"Your name?"

"Schacht."

"Father's name?"

"Also Schacht."

Finally, when it became too much of a good thing I said: "Don't you ever read any newspapers?"

"Of course I do, sir," replied the somewhat astonished official. Up to now it was *he* who had asked questions.

"Then you should know my name. Haven't you read that I am in Paris on account of reparations talks?"

A smile spread itself over his face. He became more affable.

"Ah! So I can write under *Reason for journey* 'Payment of reparations'?"

"Yes, you can certainly write that."

# XXVII

## A PAINFUL RECOVERY

IT WAS UNFORTUNATE that my business with the Dawes Committee lasted so long. The Rentenmark could now be reckoned as legal tender, thanks to the willingness of the Reichsbank occasionally to accept the same at gold mark rates. Consequently, certain circles began to resume their practice of selling Rentenmarks abroad against foreign bills, not however, with the intention of using such bills to pay for imports but in order to replenish their hoards of stable securities. As early as February 1924 the Rentenmark was quoted below par, and was therefore at a discount which soon reached some fifteen per cent.

When I was once more able to take up my duties at the Reichsbank and realized that the mark was again having to stand up to speculation my colleagues and I took counsel together and decided on a drastic step. Fine speeches about maintaining the stability of the mark were completely useless. It was necessary to show the speculators that the Reichsbank did not stop at mere words, but meant business.

Once the public loses confidence in a currency, not even the highest rate of discount will scare off speculators. It does not matter if he has to pay ten, twenty or thirty per cent per annum if the value of the currency drops five, ten or fifteen per cent from one month to the next. It was no good therefore attacking foreign exchange speculators with higher interest rates: we should have to launch an attack on the supply of funds. We decided on a complete stoppage of credit to the business community on the part of the Reichsbank. We realized that such a stoppage would not only be most awkward, to say the least, but that it contained a certain amount of injustice in that it would hit the innocent as well as the guilty. We comforted ourselves with the thought that the stoppage would not last long but that the exchange situation would return to normal in the shortest possible time.

In order to set the necessary machinery in motion we resorted to a method which has subsequently often been copied in the political world. On Saturday, April 5, 1924, after the Stock Exchange had closed, we announced that as from Monday, April 7, the Reichsbank would not increase its total holding in foreign bills and would therefore not accept further bills. That gave the public a day and a half in which to familiarize themselves with the announcement.

The step we had taken was in direct contradiction to all the traditional rules concerning central banks. It was also probably the first time in economic history that a central bank deliberately refused to grant credit. According to traditional business principles the idea of a central bank was that the said bank should meet advances on bills at any time, and counteract an excessive influx of bills simply by increasing its discount charges. But, as already mentioned, no discount policy would avail to win a race against devaluation of currency.

The Reichsbank's action aroused absolute panic in the business world. The storm that broke over my head was a pretty complete hurricane. That any president of the Reichsbank should dare to resort to such measures, not only against all theoretical rules but at such short notice that nobody was able to take appropriate action seemed to the entire business world completely outrageous. But it was this same short-dated execution of our plan that was calculated to achieve the desired result.

I had to give the foreign exchange hoarders a shock and leave them no time to extricate themselves from their dilemma. It was not a question of material, but first and foremost of moral effect. People must understand once and for all that the Reichsbank would make use of any means to ensure the stability of the mark. If the German business community had given their solid support to the new currency from the beginning, the seventh of April, 1924, would never have happened. Now, however, matters had reached a point where we had to risk a trial of strength between the speculative interests of individuals and the upholding of the general interests of the German people. I was never for a moment in doubt that this defense of the general interest would earn for the Reichsbank the approval of the masses.

Meanwhile "destroyer of German industry" was the least opprobrious epithet coined for my benefit. The one reproach that I did take seriously was that of injustice toward decent business folk. For the rest, reproaches left me cold. By means of most careful treatment of our customers we began to counteract injustices during the days and weeks that followed. We did not decrease our portfolio but maintained it at the same level. Any money which came back to the Reichsbank from matured bills was used to grant credit to those businesses in special need of it. Since the Reichsbank controlled nearly four hundred undertakings and subsidiaries throughout the country this policy soon proved its worth. The hoarders, on the other hand, did not get their expired credits renewed, nor were they granted fresh credits. So they were obliged to resort to the same action which I had forced them to adopt at the end of November 1923; namely, to hand over their hoarded foreign bills to the Reichsbank in return for Reichsmarks.

The results of this action were surprisingly swift and surprisingly effective. Between April 7 and June 3, 1924, that is to say within fifty-seven days, no less a sum than eight hundred million marks in foreign exchange bills returned to the German Reichsbank. Since the last years of the war it had never been possible to satisfy all business demands for foreign bills. For months on end during the inflation period we had been able to meet only *one* per cent of such requirements. On July 3 the Reichsbank was able for the first time to meet all demands for foreign bills in full; and it continued to be in a position to do so until the financial crash of 1931 once again put a stop to it. Of which more later.

Abroad the moral effect produced by this painful but rapid process of recovery was astounding. It had been completed before the decisions of the Dawes Committee came into operation. Confidence in the management of the Reichsbank increased, not only in Germany itself but more especially in other countries. A second "epidemic" of inflation during those fateful months would have brought well-nigh irreparable damage to Germany. In all probability it would have encouraged the Allies to exercise appreciably greater intervention and wider control over German business and financial affairs. The decisive action of the Reichsbank and its complete mastery of a dangerous situation showed the world that Germany was in a position to resume her place as a financial partner. Once again our international credit rating stood at a satisfactory level. Germany's reputation as an honest businessman was saved.

The decisions of the Dawes Committee and the resultant policy are well known. They led to a reform of the Reichsbank which provided for a supervisory body consisting of seven foreigners and seven Germans in addition to the German board of directors and the German president. The British member of the Dawes Committee, Sir Robert Kindersley, and I were entrusted with the working out of the individual regulations within the framework of this politically determined directive. Good will on both sides resulted in a footing of mutual confidence which made it possible to keep the foreign influence on the management of the Reichsbank within reasonable bounds. The president of the Reichsbank was chairman not only of the German board of directors but also of the international supervisory body, which functioned for six years until 1930. On no single occasion during this period was there a question of unpleasant arguments or divergencies of opinion. No majority resolutions were passed. Our co-operation was harmonious from every point of view. There was an atmosphere of mutual trust among all the foreign members, many of whom became my very good friends.

I was on especially intimate terms with the Dutch representative, Professor Bruins, who was also Commissioner for the Printing of Banknotes; also with the Englishman Sir Charles Addis, the Swiss Professor Bachmann, the American McGarah and the Italian Signor Feltrinelli. Even with the Belgian representative Monsieur Callens and the Frenchman Monsieur Sergeant I was always on good terms. There was close collaboration too with Parker Gilbert who had been appointed Agent for Reparations on account of the Dawes Resolutions and whose duty it was to supervise the payments of reparations.

Taken all round the year 1924 was one of the most exciting of my career. It closed with the successful issue of the so-called Dawes Loan in Allied and neutral countries, from the proceeds of which eight hundred million gold marks poured into the Reichsbank in the guise of foreign bills, enabling the bank to tackle its further duties with an ample reserve of gold and foreign exchange bills.

I had reason to be satisfied with the result of my labors and I was particularly pleased at the recognition accorded by other countries. When it was all over I received a letter from Owen D. Young of the Dawes Committee:

Dear Mr. Schacht,

I have today found among my papers a letter which Mr. Bates [Secretary to the Dawes Committee] wrote to one of his influential friends in America. I cannot resist the temptation to quote you that part of the letter that refers to yourself. It expresses my own feelings exactly, as well as those of Mr. Bates.

"Since January of this year Schacht has been a tower of strength in Berlin in every sense of the word . . . In order to avoid another period of inflation he went to such lengths in refusing to grant credits that some failures resulted in individual branches of German industry. In spite of threatening letters, open criticism and political opposition he never batted an eyelid and displayed quite extraordinary courage."

And on the last day of the year I received a New Year's letter from Baron Bruno Schroeder, Head of the English Banking firm of Schroeder & Company, which contained the following words:

You can look back with pride on your activities during the Old Year, for I am convinced that had it not been for you the atmosphere would not have been created in London which was so needed for the reconstruction of our poor old country.

I experienced no little satisfaction at having contributed in some measure to the restoration of international confidence in Germany. Our credit stood once again on firm foundations. Now we had to make certain that we did not misuse this credit. In my own mind I was quite clear that for the reconstruction of her industry Germany would have to buy raw materials, foodstuffs and perhaps also certain machinery from abroad. To borrow from abroad for such purposes was a thoroughly commonsense action. But these loans must not overstep the bounds imposed by such necessity. Under the Dawes Plan we were committed to an annual payment averaging two billion gold marks. This debt had to be paid in foreign currency and this foreign currency could only be obtained by surplus exports. If we were also compelled to furnish instalments on interest and principal in foreign currency our annual indebtedness abroad would increase with every loan and force us to export in ever greater quantities.

From the first moment of my joining the Reichsbank I had emphasized the dangers of such indebtedness in all government departments to which I had access, as well as in public at home and abroad. The whole of the six years that made up my first period as president of the Reichsbank were taken up with the struggle for the limitation of our foreign indebtedness.

My opponents in this struggle were as shortsighted as they were numerous. They were to be found in the world of business, in municipalities and, not least, in government offices. The impoverishment in Germany brought about by the war was positively horrifying.

Industry was in desperate need not only for money for the purchase of raw materials; it cried out for capital to invest in the restoration and improvement of its means of production. To expect this capital to accrue from even the most economical management and from the thriftiness of the population was inopportune as well as waste of time. A much quicker result could be achieved from the proceeds of a foreign loan. In the course of the next few years a considerable proportion of big business had incurred debts on foreign loans.

To this was added another factor. The end of the war had been attended in Germany itself by revolutionary signs and had raised revolutionary politicians to posts of responsibility. Revolutions, how-ever, are kept within bounds only if the masses can perceive some outward advantages to themselves. Instead of making up their minds, after their defeat, to live and manage on the most modest and eco-nomical basis, everyone succumbed to the demands for increased standards of living and a good time in general. At the head and front were the municipal corporations with a preponderance of Social Democratic circles and those with similar tendencies. Many munici-palities took up loans in foreign currency which found ready investors abroad, especially in the United States of America, but also in Switzerland, Holland and elsewhere.

It was regrettable that in face of these attractions at home, the Social Democrats should have failed to realize that all foreign monies which did not serve to increase our production were bound to have a particularly adverse social effect. Foreign currency could be spent only abroad, which led to an increase in foreign imports, especially in finished articles. This means that German manufacturers of such finished articles would suffer which, in turn, would lead to unem-ployment.

Even if one could think that industry might be in a position to meet both interest and principal on these loans out of exports, this most certainly did not apply to public bodies whose income con-sisted not of export earnings but of taxes in German currency. Business as a whole had therefore to find the foreign bills to meet interest and principal on foreign public loans. Public authorities turned in their bills from foreign loans to the Reichsbank, for which the latter had to pay in marks. When, however, the moment arrived for public authorities to pay interest and principal in foreign cur-rency, the Reichsbank had to furnish the necessary foreign bills and received only marks in return. In this way public authorities were consciously acting in defiance of their business obligations — a fact that I once tried to explain to a young business friend by means of a humorous illustration. The young fellow had borrowed in English currency and invested in Danzig currency. When he asked me whether he had acted rightly I replied: "If you owe your creditor so-many hens you should not keep ducks."

In the course of years more than twenty billions in foreign currency came into the country, and our indebtedness increased by a like amount. Had this foreign currency remained in the Reichsbank the bank would have been able to repay them at any time. That, however, was not possible as by this time we had to meet our obligations under the Dawes Plan. Every year the Agent for Reparations claimed his two billion gold marks in foreign currency from the Reichsbank. The money which had come into the country in the form of foreign loans went out of the country to meet the payments under the Dawes Plan.

It was only possible to play this tantalizing but highly dangerous game as long as foreign loans continued to come into Germany. But directly these foreign loans stopped, payment of reparations under the Dawes Plan would also stop automatically. The foreign loans were therefore in the highest degree instrumental in prolonging the payment of reparations. Had we ceased sooner to accept foreign loans the question of reparations would have been settled much earlier. Instead, the political circles of the day persisted in encumbering Germany with foreign loans — and therefore with foreign debts — notwithstanding the Reichsbank's continual warnings; and the blame that attaches to them in this respect cannot be sufficiently emphasized.

Unfortunately other countries also failed to heed my warnings. International financial agents and banking firms positively vied with one another in urging Germany's acceptance of these loans. Foreign agents practically besieged captains of industry and municipal authorities with offers of loans. It was also impossible to pass the Adlon Hotel, Unter den Linden, without being buttonholed by some financial representative who would enquire whether there were no business or municipal concern to whom he could offer a loan.

Again and again the Reichsbank, in the interests of German currency, tried to persuade the government to grant the bank a right to veto the acceptance of foreign loans. The request was invariably refused. Chancellor Brüning was the first member of the government to admit in the autumn of 1931 that piling up of foreign debts had been a great blunder. But by then it was already too late. The bank crash had set in in July 1931. The victims were those thrifty foreign investors who, trusting to the recommendations of their banks, had subscribed to the German foreign loans.

By the spring of 1925 I felt that the currency situation was sufficiently under control to enable me to take a long-overdue holiday. With my wife and the two children we committed ourselves to the care of the SS *General San Martin* of the Stinnes Line which was to take us from Genoa through the loveliest part of the Mediterranean. It was one of those so-called conducted tours, stopping at various ports from which there would be excursions inland, and in the course of which one made many pleasant acquaintances.

I took advantage of the trip to explore the history of the Mediterranean countries with my children, from ancient times to the present day — not as "lessons" but in conversation about things the children themselves knew, what we saw and what our fellow passengers contributed to the discussions.

On my return to Berlin from our Mediterranean cruise I immediately became immersed in the struggle against reparations, a task that was to involve me in fresh anxieties and fresh work. But before I go further into that subject I must mention an amusing little incident.

One morning I found on my desk a gaudily printed piece of sheet music such as was fashionable in the early twenties. I opened it and to my amazement read: " 'Spielmannslied' (Minstrel's Song): Words by Hjalmar Schacht." It was, in fact, one of the poems I had written at the age of nineteen for a fellow student who was a musical enthusiast and had wanted to make it into a light opera. A firm of music publishers had somehow got hold of it and was obviously banking on the sensation that would result when it became known that the president of the Reichsbank wrote popular "hits" in his spare time. I was dead against that sort of cheap publicity and refused to allow my "Spielmannslied" to be published.

# XXVIII

## THE REICHSBANK FROM THE INSIDE

THE HOLIDAY which I took in the spring of 1925 had been well earned. Also, after the Reichsbank successes of the previous year, I believed that quieter times might lie ahead. During the period immediately following the events of 1924 I concentrated my energies on the internal development of the Reichsbank, doing everything in my power to maintain and consolidate the traditions of devotion to duty, diligence and service to our clientele. Every member of the Reichsbank was imbued with this sense of tradition.

The fact that we trained the oncoming generation under our own roof constituted by far the most helpful element. It is true that the Board of Management included several administrative legal experts who had joined us from outside. Beyond that, however, the higher grades were staffed by those who had graduated from the lower ranks. Anyone entering the Reichsbank as a young man had the chance of becoming a member of the board. Within this imperial institution the truest democracy reigned. Whoever came through his probationary period successfully was assured of a job for life. The same held good for the subsidiary staff who were not engaged in actual banking — the messengers, manservants and runners who were grouped under the heading of *Geldzähler*. Among them too tradition and appearance were maintained. They wore liveries of blue cloth with gilt buttons and red collars. Many of them had come to us from the Imperial Household after the dissolution of the Empire, and they were frequently called upon to assist at official functions. They knew exactly how to treat guests, how to look after the cloakrooms, handle china and wait at table. It was not unusual for other authorities and even private individuals to "borrow" some of our Geldzähler for their parties. Among these hosts, later on, was Adolf Hitler, who regularly fell back on men trained in our bank or in the Imperial Household.

Although these Geldzähler were not eligible themselves for an actual banking career, such openings were available for their children. There were several instances where the sons of some of our Geldzähler embarked on academic careers and even occasionally attained to some of the highest positions in the Reichsbank itself. The Geldzähler attached to my anteroom, Leben by name, had mastered so many subjects in English and French as a result of private coaching that I was able to take him with me regularly as my personal attendant when I went abroad. Not I alone, but all of us concerned in the management of the Reichsbank made a point of helping conscientious and efficient members of the staff to get on.

Our oncoming generation increased to such an extent that each new *Diäter* — the name given to beginners — had to have two years' practical business experience before we accepted him. The age limit for a new entrant was twenty-six. At first he was on probation for a period of several months, after which he had to pass a test before being transferred to the permanent staff. This probationary period also enabled us to form an estimate of his character and personal behavior. The test was arranged by a commission consisting of high-ranking Reichsbank officials.

Once the applicant had passed his test and had been accepted, a career in the intermediate grade lay open to him as Bank Inspector rising to Senior Inspector. After a few years, if he were sufficiently ambitious to desire promotion, the bank would grant him three months' study leave on full pay, at the end of which he would take his test for the higher grades. If he passed he became a *Bankrat* and could work his way up to a seat on the board. During my term of office quite a few members of the board had risen from the ranks in this way. A previous academic or non-academic education did not matter in the least. The whole of this democratic system was based not on political or social position but simply and solely on ability and character.

To this principle and its application I gave my enthusiastic support in two ways. First by being readily accessible to every member of the staff, from the charwomen and the office boy upward. Secondly, by persistently encouraging all my colleagues to express freely any criticism or disagreement whenever I discussed any proposed measures with them. "Yes men" never got any further with me. On the other hand, if anyone put forward a well thought out, well substantiated contention or suggestion he could count on my support. When Herr von Glasenapp retired and I had to appoint a deputy I chose a colleague who had risen from the ranks.

In addition to personal questions I turned my attention to any technical improvements which might serve to facilitate intercourse between the business world and the Reichsbank. Of these one of the most essential was the introduction of the telegraphic system of monetary transfers. The vital importance of such a rapid transfer system for monetary policy in general was forcibly brought home to me after the collapse in 1945. In the case of transfers from one German town to another (during the years before the transfer system in the provincial central banks resumed its normal working) four, five or even six days would elapse between the payment by the transferor and the crediting of the amount to the transferee. This meant that such sums were out of circulation for days at a time, being held up by the delay in transfer from one account to another. When one thinks that in peacetime the Reichsbank was wont to handle several billion marks a day one can picture the loss in interest occasioned by this dilatory system. The technical difficulties of the transfer system were considerable, because the question of security and abuse had to be carefully taken into account. These difficulties were however overcome, and it was possible, after the introduction of the telegraphic Giro to transfer any sum within two hours from, for example, Berlin to Munich or any other destination.

I never troubled about the technical execution of current transactions. My colleagues dealt with the assessment and allocation of loans. It may sound absurd, but I have never handled a single Reichsbank bill; and I have studied precious few documents. My desk was always empty. Years previously I had occasion to call on my predecessor, Havenstein, and found him submerged under piles of documents. I agreed with Harriman the American railroad magnate who was once shown over a bank in Vienna, including a room where a man was busy working surrounded by piles of papers. On enquiring who this man might be and being told that he was one of the managers, Harriman exclaimed: "Impossible! A manager should be able to sit with his feet on his empty desk and smoke a leisurely cigar!" The chief item on my desk was my ashtray and next to it a small bronze statuette of Frederick the Great under whose aegis the Reichsbank was founded.

In dealing with those problems which did concern me I received admirable support not only from my colleagues on the board but also from the Economic and Statistical Department. They had an extensive library, a voluminous collection of scientific material and a first-rate staff of sound political economists. This department had been established by my former enemy von Lumm, and I must hand it to him unreservedly that it was a model of its kind. The head of the department in my time was Dr. Nordhoff, an outstandingly conscientious and meticulous man and a past master in all currency matters. On countless occasions during the course of years I have had to speak on currency and political economy to audiences small and large. I invariably went through the materials for my speeches with the staff of the Political Economy Department, and as invariably asked Dr. Nordhoff for his criticism.

"You are the keeper of the bank's conscience, Dr. Nordhoff. Don't let anything pass that isn't absolutely foolproof."

"You know you can rely on me, sir."

Our official residence was immediately next door to my office and was looked after by the bank's domestic staff in exactly the same way as the offices. It frequently happened that I would suddenly come upon a workman or mechanic engaged on some job in our home which I had not known of beforehand. If by chance I ran across one of these unexpected visitors when on my way to the bathroom in my pajamas and dressing gown, as often as not I would be told: "Porter sent me up here to see to that there rotten pipe in the central heatin'. There's a leak somewhere, but I'll find it all right." We had practically no real privacy.

Although the number of business callers certainly grew no less, I made it a rule never to keep anybody waiting if I could help it. All appointments were punctually observed. If an unexpected visitor turned up without my having earmarked any time for him, Fräulein Steffeck would come in and plead: "Go and see him for a minute or two anyway — just to shake hands." Her tact and kindliness helped to make her a favorite with everyone.

The arrangements for our social life I was content to leave in my wife's most capable hands. She would tell me of her requirements for the evening, and all I needed to do was to give the necessary instructions. Perhaps there were guests staying in the house; or she was giving a musical party at which Margarete Klose would sing. Or again, we wanted tickets for the opera, for the theater, with a party of so-many friends. Our daughter would have invited some boy and girl friends and there would be dancing. Ministers, bankers, foreign visitors, diplomats came and went. Our evenings in Berlin were nearly always booked up with some kind of social function. Often, too, they provided an opportunity to discuss economic and financial problems after we had left the dinnertable.

Our domestic staff was well trained, but there were nevertheless occasions when they found themselves at a loss. Among our guests one evening was the papal Nuncio Pacelli, the future Pope. He was in full canonicals and, after the maid had taken his cloak, he extended his hand with the episcopal ring for her to kiss. But the good soul — a staunch Evangelical from East Prussia — hadn't the least idea what she was supposed to do and quite cheerfully shook the Nuncio's hand. He chuckled with enjoyment when he told us of the incident later.

After conditions in Germany had become more settled, the government began to encourage a certain amount of social life. The President and sundry ministers gave parties and dances which, outwardly at least, scarcely differed from the receptions of imperial days. It was of course primarily the duty of footmen and stewards of the household to see that everything went "according to plan," but most of them had remained in their jobs and been taken on by new employers in these more modern times. True, the dresses were much simpler and plainer than of old, and the subjects of conversation provided an even greater contrast. But in spite of a good many gaucheries, at which members of the old order looked down their noses, one was conscious of a general effort to re-establish a decent representative social order.

Many ministers of middle-class origin, and especially their wives, conducted themselves in a manner that can only be described as both dignified and attractive. Foremost among them were the President and Frau Ebert, and the unassuming fashion in which they took their changed circumstances for granted put to shame many members of prewar society. My wife was once present during a conversation that took place at a reception. Someone was expressing admiration for one of Giotto's paintings in the Pitti Gallery in Florence, and Frau Ebert observed how much she too had liked it. One of the other ladies was tactless enough to ask if and when the President's wife had seen the picture, to which Frau Ebert smilingly and quietly replied: "When I was a lady's maid and went to Italy with my employer."

# XXIX

## SOME ECONOMIC AFTEREFFECTS

WHEN I LEFT the *General San Martin* at Hamburg at the end of our Mediterranean cruise I anticipated a period of less strenuous work. Unfortunately, however, things didn't work out that way. The birth of the new Reichsmark had been successfully accomplished after hard labor, but there remained a good many afterpains.

Barely a fortnight after my return, I received a visit from the heir to a big industrial combine whose founder had died the preceding year and who was very anxious to discuss his financial situation with me. He showed me the balance sheet of his total assets. The figures were imposing, though they showed a heavy indebtedness. Nevertheless there was a considerable surplus of assets over liabilities, in spite of which I could only assume that he wished to go into the matter of his debts.

"I am glad," I began, "that you have managed to preserve the large fortune that your father left you. I take it you have come to see me on account of your debts?"

"As a matter of fact, sir, I'm dreadfully worried about them."

"Tell me some details."

"Among my liabilities are ninety million marks in bills of exchange and I haven't the necessary liquid resources to repay them."

"Well, I expect there's a way out."

"Unfortunately it isn't as simple as all that. You see, these liabilities are payable not in marks but in pounds sterling."

"You aren't trying to tell me that you owe bills of exchange to the tune of ninety million marks payable in pounds sterling! Who in heaven's name granted you such vast credits in pounds?"

"I had it from several London banks."

"When do the bills fall due?"

"In fourteen days."

I found it difficult to conceal my irritation and astonishment. "I know that you have inherited a heavy burden; I can also appreciate your probably not wanting to part with any of your property. If, however, you could maintain that property only at the price of such a crushing burden of debt, then it was an absolute duty to realize some of your assets and provide for a liquidity which would have saved you from landing yourself in such a hole as this."

"You must realize, sir, that I was not able to put this vast inheritance in order so soon after my father's death. Also, I had to consider my family's feelings; they would have raised objections even to a partial splitting up of our family property — out of regard for our father's memory, which is easily understood. For that same reason, too, I have tried to keep the property intact."

"I do understand that very well, and I sympathize. What I cannot understand — in my capacity as guardian of German currency — is how you could have incurred such a large proportion of these debts in foreign currency. To pay out ninety million marks in pounds sterling today — a year after stabilization — is no light matter, even for the Reichsbank."

"My English banker friends were always willing to grant these credits. But I fully realize now that I should not have allowed myself to borrow so much from abroad. The only thing I can do now is to apply to the Reichsbank for help."

And what could *I* do but tackle the business myself? A failure of the combine — even if due not to overborrowing but simply to illiquidity — was something I could not permit in the interests of German economy and its newly regained credit-standing abroad. I called a meeting of the four or five German big banks that dealt with the combine, persuaded them to grant the credit of ninety million marks and to co-operate in realizing part of the business. The Reichsbank, on the other hand, furnished the equivalent of ninety million marks in pounds sterling. The entire amount was settled in London on the date the bills fell due, to the great surprise of the City undertakings concerned. Heavy and unwelcome as this sacrifice was for the Reichsbank it was amply repaid by the impression created in London by this prompt settlement of so large a sterling commitment. It was a further proof for other countries that the Reichsbank was in complete control of the exchange situation and of the economic position of the Reichsmark in international trade.

The whole business afforded me the opportunity not only to press for the limitation of long-term foreign loans, but also to go into the question of the short-term loans granted by foreign countries to German industrial firms, insurance companies and banks.

During friendly conversations with some of the managers of the big banks I ascertained that the latter accepted current short-term loans amounting to considerable sums from foreign banking friends. The equivalent of these sums in Reichsmarks was loaned out to the banks' clientele. These transactions were carried out with the best of intentions on both sides. The foreign bankers were very glad of the higher rates of interest which they were able to obtain in Germany for their money; but many of them were also honestly keen to be of assistance to German industry; and the German banks which accepted these foreign monies must certainly have been even more encouraged by this good will. I was prompted, however, by motives that extended beyond these more businesslike considerations on the part of the banks. I therefore pointed out to some of the directors the particular dangers that I dreaded.

"You tell me," I said to one of them, "that you have received hundreds of millions in short-term foreign money. If, owing to some unexpected circumstances, you were suddenly asked to repay these amounts the Reichsbank would not be in a position to furnish them in foreign currency. Your colleagues in the other banks have also accepted similar amounts and, like yourself, rely — quite wrongly — on the Reichsbank in the event of a sudden demand for repayment. You are aware that, out of the incoming foreign bills, the Reichsbank has to pay out two billions a year to the reparations agent. The remaining stocks of gold and foreign bills would therefore never suffice to meet demands such as you would be compelled to make in the aforementioned circumstances."

"I see, sir; unfortunately you are right. I will discuss the matter with my colleagues on the Board. I am wondering whether we ought not to try to change our short-term foreign liability into a long-term loan through the issue of bonds."

"I would far rather you cut down a good proportion of your short-term foreign borrowing in general. But for the moment your suggestion would appear to be fairly opportune."

The result of these conversations was that some banks did actually issue bonds and raise a long-term loan abroad, with the proceeds of which they repaid their short-term foreign obligations.

But if I was still able to appreciate the desire of the banks to assist German industry by means of loans from the proceeds of foreign monies, I entirely failed to understand the action of several banking establishments who placed such proceeds at the disposal of the Stock Exchange for speculative security credits. It seemed to me monstrous that Stock Exchange gambling with foreign money should be maintained at the Reichsbank's expense. Again and again

I warned bank directors by word of mouth to put a stop to this scandal. I urged the banks to request their customers to deposit a good part of their money for the purchase of securities with the bank and therefore to effect such purchases on a purely credit basis. On one occasion I even went so far as to exclude from clearing-house business one of the big banks which had failed to comply with Reichsbank regulations — a measure that quickly brought it to its senses. Since, however, none of this really did any good, at the beginning of May 1927 I compelled the banks to exercise a drastic curtailment of credits to those of their customers holding securities. Unfortunately the banks gave notice of this measure without previously coming to an agreement with the Reichsbank and the sensational surprise led to a considerable drop in the prices of securities on the Berlin Stock Exchange on Friday, May 13.

This day went down in the history of the Berlin Stock Exchange as "Black Friday." Once again I was attacked from all sides. While I deplored the clumsy manner in which the measure had been carried out, the measure itself was a necessity. It probably contributed to the fact that the Stock Exchange disaster in New York two years later caused less damage on German Exchange than would have been the case had I allowed speculation to continue unchecked.

On the evening of that same "Black Friday" my wife and I were at a party in Potsdam. I sat next to our hostess who in the course of conversation told me, with every sign of distress, that she had suffered heavy losses on the Stock Exchange that day.

"But my dear lady, how did you incur such losses? What securities have you?"

She mentioned several very sound shares.

"But these are all first-rate securities. If they really did drop today their value as shares remains unaffected. And their price will rise again."

"But Dr. Schacht, I simply *have* to sell."

"Why is it so absolutely necessary that you should sell?"

"Well, you see, I bought my shares with a loan from the bank and now have to find the money. And as I haven't the cash I am obliged to sell these securities."

"My dear Mrs. Blank, if you do things like that, I'm sorry I can't help you. There's a little rhyme over the entrance to the New York Stock Exchange which is worth noting:

> *"He who sells what isn't his'n*
> *Must pay, or else he'll go to prison."*

"Black Friday" did not increase my popularity. Neither did my fight against foreign loans bring me any sympathy from the perpetually hard-up politicians and businessmen. Moreover I had formally and completely retired from politics in 1926 because, in the matter of the so-called expropriation of the princes the German Democratic Party had ranged themselves against the protection of private property. It is true that they abandoned this line after some consideration, but I had no wish to become involved in any changing political programs.

Under the Dawes Plan the president of the Reichsbank held office for a term of four years instead of for life. My first four-year period ended in the autumn of 1928. When the question of my re-election came up for discussion certain Left-wing papers had managed to spread the rumor that I was suffering from intestinal trouble which would make it impossible for me to accept re-election.

In defending myself against attack I have always relied more on deeds than on words. I therefore called up my daughter who was studying at Heidelberg University. "The annual assembly of the Union for the Study of Social Policy is being held next week in Zurich. I have said I will go and wondered if you would care to come along."

My daughter was delighted, packed a suitcase and attended the assembly with me until the weekend. From Saturday midday until early Monday morning there were no meetings. We got into a car and drove at top speed from Zurich to Lauterbrunnen in four hours and just caught the last train for the Eiger Glacier Station. There we spent the night, about 5660 feet up, after we had had a drink or two and danced a little and, incidentally, run across Frau Stresemann who happened to be staying there.

Next morning we took the first train to the Jungfraujoch, got out our ice axes, had ourselves roped together by the guide and started to climb to the top. I was fifty-one years old at the time and had done no climbing for more than twenty years. In spite of this I cannot say that I found the ascent more difficult than my daughter did. Only once, when crossing a crevasse, did the guide have to come to my assistance. Visibility was poor, but the lovely scenery didn't matter to me as much as my prowess as a mountaineer. I even found the mist quite pleasant on the ridge just below the summit, as to look into the abyss on either side might have made me somewhat unsteady.

We had reached the summit from the Joch in three hours. I was not in the least tired, neither was my heart affected. Indeed I was as fit as a fiddle, despite a difference in altitude of nearly ten thousand feet in under sixteen hours. After a short rest we descended, were back at the Jungfraujoch for lunch, caught the three o'clock train for Lauterbrunnen and sat down to supper in our Dolder Hotel in Zurich.

Like everyone else who has climbed the Jungfrau I had received the customary official certificate. I had it framed and hung in my anteroom at the Reichsbank, so that every caller could form his own opinion as to my state of health. The rumors soon died down.

In 1926 I acquired a property about seventy miles north of Berlin, not far from Rheinsberg and Neuruppin. Gühlen, with its well-wooded grounds, surrounded by lakes, became in truth a source of recreation for me. Time and again, when the day's work proved unusually trying I would call to mind my Gühlen motto:

> *No trouble so heavy, but Gühlen doth feel it.*
> *No wound goes so deep, but that Gühlen doth heal it.*
> *No attack is so sharp, but that Gühlen defeats it.*
> *No joy so profound, but that Gühlen completes it.*

# XXX

## CLOUDS ON THE HORIZON

THE PURCHASE of Gühlen soon proved itself to have been a wise and far-sighted move. A man in my precarious, semi-economic, semi-political position needed a home outside the capital; a fortress to which he could retire if the number of his enemies should become too great.

During the years following the inflation my part as president of the Reichsbank appears to me to have been first and foremost that of watchdog, keeping a sharp eye on our currency and seeing that there was no drop in market quotations. I took careful note of every slightest shift in the money market, every striking quotation below par of the new German mark. Any multiplication of danger signals meant prompt intervention on my part. Today it seems to me only natural that I did not always resort to gentle methods and that my opponents in the open market — who thought only of their personal advantage and never of the general welfare — should avoid me. No one defending a cause in which he believes will be able invariably to confine himself to soft words and kindly warnings.

In order to ensure that Germany intended to pay her reparations the Dawes Committee had installed reliable confidential agents in the Reichsbank and other German business establishments. These men, working under Parker Gilbert, the Agent for Reparations, practically controlled Germany's ability to pay. It was their job to see that the reparations instalments were punctually remitted.

But were we actually in a position to remit payments on reparations — to transmit over two billion German marks annually in foreign currency? We were not. Nevertheless we did it. And we did it by first borrowing from abroad the monies which we later paid out abroad.

Other nations lent us money — but through whom? The politicians? Certainly not. The politicians were engaged in vote-catching in their own countries, by promising their electors that Germany would pay vast sums in reparations. Economists and businessmen were wiser, more far-sighted than the politicians. They saw the great danger that threatened if a land such as ours was barred from international competition. They recognized that it would be healthier and more intelligent to give Germany an economic chance. At that time men like Montagu Norman did more for peace than any party-political leader whose "theme song," when addressing his followers, continued to be: "Germany Must Pay . . ."

In *The End of Reparations* (1931) I have furnished an exact statement of account of the money that flowed into Germany and the money that went out of Germany again during the six years following the inflation. Even then I spoke quite frankly of the spoils that had fallen to the other nations after the war, in the form of German property, *without* their being set down under the heading of "Reparations." They amounted to enormous sums. The German Colonies alone, which were allotted to "Mandatories," represented a value of eighty to one hundred billion marks.

But the politicians were not satisfied: they wanted hard cash as well. So they extorted the annual reparations payments.

The ultimate victims of this procedure were the foreign lenders. They loaned money to German firms, public companies, corporations, municipalities and towns. The Reichsbank exchanged these foreign remittances (bills of exchange) for German money; the bills of exchange however constituted the funds from which reparations were transmitted. In this way the foreign politicians obtained the money which foreign private capitalists had supplied to Germany in the form of loans and credits.

This method involved the newly revived German economy in the most enormous burden of debt. For with the long-term and short-term loans we assumed responsibility not only for the ultimate repayment of these amounts — we had to pay current interest on them. To the reparations was added the interest on the foreign loans.

Readers will now understand why, soon after I took over at the Reichsbank, I started to warn the public against excessive borrowing abroad, especially for such things as swimming baths, public pleasure grounds, libraries, sports grounds. In peacetime these are all signs of increasing prosperity, but they were not at all appropriate to our country, impoverished and crushed by war and postwar conditions.

But, as has always happened in history, my warnings did not tend to make me popular. Under its new political status — a republic instead of an empire — Germany had disintegrated into numerous small states, communities, districts, provinces, each competing furiously with the other in borrowing.

Along with this change the party-membership-book began to play its part and often enough replaced qualifications, efficiency, professional training. Party interests were a significant factor in the acceptance of foreign loans. Party representatives vied with one another in who could do most "for the people." Whoever achieved the most obtained most votes.

This combination of personal and general arguments, supposed to benefit everybody, took place quite openly. That, however, did not mean that the public saw through the little game. On the contrary — each individual considered, from his little standpoint alone, how the money from these foreign investments could help to raise the German standard of living. Collective liability without personal responsibility is a very dangerous game, which could not eventually remain hidden from Parker Gilbert, Agent for Reparations. He realized that Germany's payments of reparations were not genuine, that the country was paying her debts not with honest export surpluses but with borrowed money. It could be only a matter of how long it would take before Germany was no longer in a position to remit foreign currency.

The recognition of this fact led to a new conference, this time under the chairmanship of the American Owen Young, who had already played a significant part in connection with the Dawes Plan. The Young Conference which gave birth to the so-called Young Plan met in the spring of 1929. The whole of 1928 was devoted to preparations for this conference.

As early as 1927 there had been a session of the Friedrich-List Society, which I will briefly describe, for on this session fell the shadows of those coming events which were eventually to be brought up for general discussion by the Young Conference.

In connection with this session and in my capacity as president of the Reichsbank, I held a semi-official position within the government. I did not, therefore, contribute any public statements but made them to a closed circle of invited members of the Friedrich-List Society, among whom were representatives of the *Frankfurter Zeitung* and the *Berliner Tageblatt*. Both these papers had lent a helping hand when the German Democratic Party was founded in 1918. When, later, I left the party they ranged themselves against me. Nevertheless I believed that their representatives would recognize the difference between public statement of opinion and a private conversation. As matters turned out, however, my confidence was misplaced.

The main point of all my arguments in 1927 was that I categorically rejected the principle that there was any justification for the payment of reparations from an economic as well as from a political and moral viewpoint. I declared that I looked upon it as my duty to press unflinchingly for the removal of reparations; that I could not simply stand by and see the standard of living of German workers permanently lowered as the result of an annual burden of billions of marks.

Owing to a breach of confidence my words found their way to Paris and were destined later to play their part.

The year 1928 was taken up with preparations for the Paris Conference which was intended to re-regulate Germany's reparations debts. A great deal of detailed work was necessary; and a full share of it fell to the Economic and Statistical Department of the Reichsbank.

The Young Conference opened in Paris in February 1929, at the Hotel George V, a new luxury building better known to the younger generation as the place where Rita Hayworth always stayed.

The atmosphere was distinctly more friendly than at the Dawes Conference five years previously. Now we all sat at the same table, the Germans among the rest — Americans, British, French, Belgians, Japanese.

The president of the Reichsbank (myself) led the German delegation which in addition consisted of Vögler, General Manager of the United Steel Works, and his deputy, Privy Councilor Kastl of the National Association of German Industrialists, and my own deputy Melchior of the Hamburg banking establishment of Warburg & Company. In my immediate entourage were Director Blessing and my secretary Fräulein Steffeck of the Reichsbank.

America was represented by Owen Young and Jack Morgan, the great son of the even greater Pierpont Morgan. On the French side was Monsieur Moreau, president of the Central Bank.

Among our interpreters was the quite outstanding Paul Schmidt, who has recently achieved fame with his vivid book *An Extra on the Diplomatic Stage*.

The Conference was focused on two main questions. First, the level of the amounts that Germany would in future have to find to meet her annual payments of reparations. Secondly, what proportion of this amount could be transmitted in foreign currency without damage to the German economy.

The last question was the decisive one.

As leader of the German delegation I had prepared my plan of action. First of all I would endeavor, through the submission of thoroughly comprehensive material, to persuade the Conference to reduce the amount of reparations as much as possible, before proceeding to the question of transmission. The long-drawn-out discussion of this material soon led to a certain amount of exhaustion. Jack Morgan was the first to take a few days off which he spent cruising in the Mediterranean in his yacht. But the other participants also felt the need of relaxation.

Since Easter was now approaching I considered that we Germans too were entitled to a few days breathing space. I suggested therefore that each of the Allied experts should state the lowest demand he was in a position to make on behalf of his country. The suggestion was accepted, and enabled me to take a week's holiday with my wife visiting the castles of Touraine in the wonderful valley of the Loire.

When my colleagues and I met again at the conference table after my return from this trip, I discovered that my proposal had had the most astonishing result. The Allied representatives had in fact not once got in touch with each other on the subject of the amounts they had been asked to suggest. Each of them obviously feared the reproaches of his friends should his greed outstrip all limits. So it came about that, when the American chairman asked that the figures be made known and these figures were added up, individual demands were considerably larger than the total amount previously contained in the Dawes Plan, whereas the whole aim of the Dawes Conference was supposed to be to reduce the reparations debt. This result, which came as a surprise to each of those present, created a sense of bewilderment that ultimately gave way to general merriment and afforded us Germans a not inconsiderable moral uplift.

It made little difference, however, to the obstinacy of our opponents as the Conference proceeded. The French made no bones about resorting to underhand press methods as well as to valid arguments. One day I received news from Berlin that every French bank with outstanding debts in Berlin had suddenly called in these debts, or, if they had been incurred on an instalment plan or were due by a certain date, had given notice demanding full repayment. The fact that this happened without warning on one and the same day that all French banks were involved pointed to a concerted action obviously dictated by higher authority.

This action resulted in the rapid decrease of the Reichsbank reserves in gold and foreign bills, as other banks were obliged to call on the Reichsbank's stock of foreign bills to cover the repayment of the French debts. It was up to me to devise an immediate counter-stroke.

I went to see Parker Gilbert, who was in Paris a lot during the Conference, and told him what had happened, though of course he himself was *au fait* with everything that went on. It became evident during our conversation that both the French and Mr. Gilbert (if the latter had indeed approved the French action) were badly out in their reckoning. They had thought to force me into meeting them halfway in the matter of our indebtedness, whereas all they did was to play into my hands and afford me further argument against an overheavy burden of transmission.

"Do you consider the French action very dignified or politically expedient?" I asked.

Gilbert had no idea what I was getting at. He shrugged his shoulders and said: "You can't really be surprised. The French believe you are trying to get out of paying. They are evidently trying to show you what that would lead to."

"I can tell you in very few words, Mr. Gilbert, what that would lead to, and I think the French will very quickly cancel such measures. If the calling in of these — not very considerable — French debts at German banks creates an obvious menace to German currency such as we have seen recorded in the Exchange Market during the past few days; if German currency is shaken by the repayment, in foreign exchange, of borrowed capital, it is surely obvious that payments of reparations, such as the French still dream of, are simply out of the question."

Gilbert turned even paler than he usually was and showed signs of nervousness. I went on calmly: "If the French banks do not rescind their orders forthwith I shall express my thanks at the next session to the French delegation for having given me such striking proof of the impossibility of transferring the payments of reparations which they still demand."

The result of this conversation was that Gilbert said he would seek out my colleague Monsieur Moreau, president of the French Central Bank, and tell him the gist of my argument. The very next morning Gilbert called me.

"Herr Schacht, in connection with our conversation yesterday, I wish to inform you that the French banks are withdrawing their notices. I hope therefore that you will consent not to refer to the matter again at the Conference. I am sure you will agree with me that to raise the question would involve everyone in very unpleasant recriminations and react very unfavorably on the general atmosphere."

I had of course to admit as much myself. I was satisfied with my success and the subject was not mentioned at the Conference.

My trip through Touraine was the last pleasant episode during the Young Conference. The amusing incident of the individual demands put forward by each of the Allied countries was preserved in a delightful caricature in the French comic paper *Le Rire*. The story had got around very quickly. It was followed by very serious discussions within the Conference, which was nearing its end. Already disquieting clouds were visible on the horizon.

# XXXI

## I SIGN THE YOUNG PLAN

AFTER THE FAILURE of the attempt to evolve a new Young Plan based on the minimum demands of Germany's former enemies, the chairman very justly turned the tables on us.

"Now," he said, "it is up to the German experts to tell us what they think they can manage." To the question, when we would be able to submit a German memorandum, I replied: "At tomorrow's session."

We worked on that memorandum right through the night. We were clear enough in our minds as to the contents but it had now to be formulated and set down in absolutely watertight fashion.

Punctually the following morning we submitted our memorandum in German and English. It had been compiled by the four German experts working in complete accord with the officials who had been seconded to our delegation. I won't go into details of the amounts we quoted: they were still too high. But for the time being we could not possibly hope for the cancellation of reparations. It seemed to us more important to discuss those circumstances which would most strongly affect Germany's ability to pay.

This memorandum led to an explosion which set the entire political pack on our heels. The cause of the excitement was the sentence: "The loss of the eastern provinces handed over to Poland had reduced Germany's food-growing areas to such an extent as seriously to impair Germany's solvency." Whereupon the hostile press immediately set up a howl: "Herr Schacht demands the return of the lost eastern provinces!"

No less dust was raised by a second argument in this memorandum. We had written that we should have been in a position to increase our payments but for the seizure of our colonies, which deprived us of the chance of procuring raw materials from overseas with our own currency.

"Dr. Schacht wants the German colonies back!" yelled the enemy press, by which both instances were misrepresented, distorted, misinterpreted. Today there is no one who can fail to admit the validity of our arguments. As a matter of fact we had made no demands — we had only offered explanations and stimulated consideration.

The day on which we submitted our memorandum saw the beginning of the developments which led to my resignation from the presidency of the Reichsbank eight months later.

Had the antagonistic press in Allied countries been the only source of attack we could have dismissed the whole business with a shrug. But as so often happened in German history, it was our own country that stabbed its own representative in the back.

The experts working on the Young Plan had been chosen on the express condition that they voice their own opinions independently of their respective governments. This was undoubtedly done in order to avoid the impression that there was any intention of imposing another dictated arrangement on Germany. That much wisdom at least had been acquired in the past ten years. The various governments were thereby encouraged to send their best brains to the Conference; for without general instructions only the best brains could be expected to arrive at conclusions which would comply with their government's outlook.

Toward the end of May I had revisited Germany in order to form an impression of the general atmosphere. This personal visit had proved necessary because in Paris we were unable to speak freely over the telephone. Hardly had one of us lifted the receiver and asked for a German number than the French *table d'écoute* (tapping service) cut in. It was like a foretaste of future Gestapo methods. I was partly irritated, partly amused by this restriction on my personal liberty. Directly I heard the click of the eavesdropping service I would say in French: "All right, *table d'écoute*, you can clear the line. I shall most certainly say nothing that could possibly interest you."

Of course what we had foreseen came to pass: the Allies considered our figures far too low. So Owen Young, the chairman of the Conference, sat down and worked out a compromise suggestion halfway between the Allied figures and ours. The fact that the chairman himself sponsored this suggested compromise invested it with a corresponding importance and made a decision imperative.

During my visit to Berlin at the end of May I ascertained that the German cabinet was by no means unanimous in regard to this suggested compromise. The Minister, Wirth, tried to persuade me to shoulder the entire responsibility for the Young Plan figures. His view was that I should exonerate the government from any responsibility in the matter.

"Somebody's got to stick his neck out," he remarked dryly.

To which I replied in the same vein: "It won't be my neck, Herr Wirth."

All this was sufficiently depressing and unpleasant, but there were other factors, positively mortifying to the German participators in the Young Plan. The German Government did not hesitate officially to disown me as the spiritual parent of the Paris Memorandum.

I am speaking here only of bare facts without reference to any undercurrents. It is a fact that while we in Paris were wrestling for every German mark, Severing, the Prussian Minister of the Interior, declared in a public meeting that Germany could well afford an annual payment of two billion marks in reparations.

It is also a fact that hardly had I submitted my memorandum to the Young Conference when Tyrrel, the British Ambassador in Paris, addressed an enquiry to the former German Ambassador, Kühlmann (who was on a private visit to Paris), and protested against the so-called political demands which — according to him — I had made. Kühlmann had simply forwarded Tyrrel's complaint to Berlin without comment and without telling me. Stresemann, misinformed, thereupon declared to various Allied representatives that Schacht had no right to make such demands.

No one took the trouble to enquire exactly what had been said or written. The country left us in the lurch. This lack of consistency seemed even more incomprehensible abroad than it did to us. But they realized now, of course, that I was fighting a losing battle, not only against those Allies taking part in the Conference who were out to grab the largest possible slice of the German cake, but also against my own government.

Meanwhile the Conference had dragged on for nearly four months and the time was approaching when we had to come to a decision. I returned to Paris and, together with Vögler, called on the chairman of the Conference. We told him we were prepared to agree to the Plan as based on Young's proposals, but that we were obliged to put forward certain conditions. Immediately following this conversation we received the official telegram from the government urging us to agree to the Plan, which practically terminated the Conference. The Young Agreement was signed in Paris on June 7, 1929.

It would probably be impossible in any other country for a delegation entrusted by its government with important decisions affecting foreign policy, and endeavoring to safeguard the nation's interests, to be hampered in its efforts by party strife in Parliament and press. We were not to escape this misfortune. The Left was quite frankly prepared to accept any payment based on the Dawes figures. The Right, as always, was opposed to any payment of reparations. The *Vorwärts* of May 11, 1929, published a very biting caricature: Schacht in front, to the left; in the background two figures, one bearing a laurel wreath, the other armed with a machine gun. Underneath was the caption: "For us Nationalists the Paris situation is clear as daylight. If negotiations fail, Schacht gets a laurel wreath, if he comes to terms with our enemies — a machine gun at the ready."

The decision to agree to the Young Plan was not, of course, an easy one for me. I still considered the payment of reparations absolutely impracticable from an economic point of view, even under the Young Plan, and I expressed this conviction clearly when the Conference met in full session for the signing of the Agreement. If, nevertheless, I did sign, it was because I was convinced that this economic impracticability would very quickly become apparent and compel the reopening of negotiations. The Young Plan was in fact ratified by the respective governments in March 1930, and the Hoover Moratorium for Reparations was declared as early as June 1931.

It stands to reason that I had not overlooked the political consequences attendant on Germany's refusal to approve the Young Plan. On our willingness to sign depended the withdrawal of Allied Occupation Forces from the Rhineland, and the improvement of the entire international atmosphere.

Despite some pleasant memories, therefore, the general impression of that Conference period in Paris is somewhat gloomy. I remember especially a controversy with my colleague Monsieur Moreau of the French Central Bank. At a critical stage in the Young negotiations he suddenly reproached me with the words I had uttered in confidence to that intimate circle at the Pyrmont Assembly in 1927, and referred to the occasion of that conference. My opponents had obviously transmitted my observations to France.

"Herr Schacht, I regret that you do not mean to come to an understanding here," exclaimed Moreau. "Did you not declare in Pyrmont two years ago that you did not intend to pay any more reparations?"

I did not let myself be put out of countenance and replied in the same tone. "What I think, Monsieur Moreau, about the justification or otherwise of reparations is something we do not need to discuss here, but how can you assert that I have no intention of paying when we have just made you an offer of more than one billion six million marks per annum?"

He had no answer to that. But the thought that once again I had been denounced by my own countrymen rankled for a long time.

The final wording of the Young Agreement dragged on until June 6. The formal signing took place the following day in the Hotel George V.

I think everyone was aware of the "historical significance" of the hour — including, presumably, the Fates. Scarcely had we appended our signatures to the document and, as usual, congratulated ourselves on the mischief we had once more set in motion, than the curtains in one of the windows suddenly caught fire and burst into flame. The fire spread to the other curtains. The servants however rose to the occasion, tore down the flaming curtains and rolled them up tightly, so that the fire was extinguished. But the impression remained unforgettable. It did not augur well for the stability and permanence of our work.

Another bad omen arose over the resignation of my colleague Vögler. The fact that the Young Plan was about to be accepted and the amount in question was, naturally, discussed all over Germany, and aroused strong opposition, particularly in legal circles and in heavy industry. Probably Vögler did not want to expose himself to the criticism of his professional colleagues. He resigned his position under pretext of an unimportant subsidiary condition in the Agreement, though until then he had worked out every detail with me.

On the day of the signing I was reminded of some words spoken by our first-rate British colleague, Sir Josiah Stamp, on the first day of the Conference. "This is no economic conference," he had said, "but a political one." It was evident to each of us — with the exception of a few fanatics — that from an economic point of view the Young Plan was completely crazy. The decision whether or not to sign did not depend on the economic workability of the Plan. The question at issue was whether one was justified in refusing to sign, since to do so would give rise to the danger of serious new political entanglements; or whether, having signed, one should continue steadily to resist reparations in general until the occasion arose which would enable them to be put an end to once and for all. I had decided in favor of the second method. The Plan contained a number of paragraphs and clauses which, if cleverly handled, could be turned to considerable advantage. All that mattered now was that German politicians should take the experts' advice as the starting point of their own policy. But they did no such thing. They remained precisely as vacillating, as weak, as they had been during our deliberations.

In Germany the political discussion on the Young Plan continued to run its course. It was one of the links in the series of struggles against the burdens under which German economy continually groaned and which grew heavier and heavier especially when, in the autumn of 1929, the first signs of the approaching international crisis appeared in America. This crisis developed to an intensive degree within the German economy and led to that deflation which in turn resulted in the collapse of the existing German political parties. Had Germany refused to subscribe to the Young Plan it could have made no difference to this critical development: rather it would have most certainly had a detrimental effect on the situation.

The whole comprehensive problem inherent in the Young Plan negotiations confronted me once again in all its crass stupidity. I had gone straight from the Young Conference to join my wife at Marienbad. She greeted me at the station with the words: "You ought never to have signed!"

# XXXII

## A FAR–REACHING IDEA

THE YOUNG PLAN differed from the Dawes Plan in certain definite details. The responsibility for the transmission of payments now rested with the Germans, but a protective clause had been inserted for revision in case of emergency. The annual sum payable on account of reparations was reduced by an average of half a billion marks. The mortgages in favor of the Allies which had hitherto been placed under foreign control as security for payments of reparations were released. All foreign controlling bodies were withdrawn. The Reichsbank and the state railways were restored to purely German management.

When the Dawes Plan was evolved in 1924 it created a profound sensation because for the first time, instead of one-sided arbitrary action, the reparations problem had been discussed in circumstances usually associated with the drawing up of a contract. At the time that had constituted a decisive fundamental change in international politics. The Young Plan included a number of improvements but no sensational change, and the chairman of the Conference was perpetually on the lookout for some idea with propaganda value which could be introduced into the Young Plan. I was fortunate enough to conceive such an idea which I submitted one day to Owen Young.

I began by describing the reparations policy from its inception down to the present time. I was at special pains to explain why it had not been possible to pay the reparations debts out of export surplus. Not once in the course of the past five years had we achieved such a surplus. Rather, we had met all payments of reparations out of the loans made to us by other countries during those years, a system which could not possibly be continued for any length of time. The interest would increase our indebtedness year by year and the loans themselves would not always be forthcoming. It was necessary therefore to take decisive action to strengthen German export trade in order to achieve a surplus.

In addition to this general exposition of the situation I emphasized that the American policy of lavishing loans upon Germany had been an entirely mistaken one. Germany was an industrial country which even after the war was comparatively well equipped for industrial purposes, so that there was no necessity to incur such huge debts on that account. The economic history of the past decades had furnished convincing proof that loans should be used primarily to help the underdeveloped countries to make full use of their raw materials and gradually to become industrialized. Before the war the European capital markets had supplied the funds in connection with loans for the economic advancement of the underdeveloped South American and Balkan states and many other overseas territories. England, France, Germany and others had not been in need of foreign loans: on the contrary they had been creditors and suppliers of capital to underdeveloped countries.

Germany was now an impoverished country and no longer able to make loans to others. If the Allies really wished to help her to meet her reparations liabilities they should grant loans to the underdeveloped countries, and thereby put the latter in a position where they would be able to purchase their industrial equipment in Germany. No useful purpose would be served by allowing Germany to compete in existing world markets against other European industrial states as she had hitherto done. German competition in these spheres had been one of the main factors that had contributed to the end of world peace and to attempted settlement by war. The repetition of such a competitive struggle must be avoided, or its bitterness at least reduced by seeking to open many fresh markets which would afford to all industrial countries opportunities for employment and for disposal of their goods. Increased well-being of all nations was the fundamental economic principle by which peace could be preserved and future wars avoided.

Owen Young immediately asked whether I saw any way of putting my ideas into practice.

"I should not be telling you all this, Mr. Young, if I were not able to submit a practical proposal for the realization of my object. I would suggest that in the Young Plan you assume responsibility for all concerned for the joint founding of a bank through which, on the one hand, the reparations payments shall be distributed and which, on the other hand, shall be entrusted with the carrying out of financial operations offering to the underdeveloped countries the means of exploiting their natural resources and increasing their agricultural products. This financial aid will enable these countries to purchase all industrial equipment — especially in Germany — necessary for increased production. A bank of this kind will demand financial co-operation between vanquished and victors that will lead to community of interests which in turn will give rise to mutual confidence and understanding and thus promote and ensure peace."

I can still vividly recall the setting in which this conversation took place. Owen Young was seated in his armchair puffing away at his pipe, his legs outstretched, his keen eyes fixed unswervingly on me. As is my habit when propounding such arguments I was doing a quiet steady "quarter-deck" up and down the room. When I had finished there was a brief pause. Then his whole face lighted up and his resolve found utterance in the words:

"Dr. Schacht, you gave me a wonderful idea and I am going to sell it to the world."

All this happened in the late spring of 1929. Nearly twenty years later — while still under police supervision and obliged to receive my visitors in the modest country inn on Lüneburg Heath where I had been "confined" by the British — I read of a plan for world peace put forward by the United States Government under President Truman. The idea underlying Point Four of this plan — which before long was on everyone's lips — was that in order to promote universal welfare it was essential to assist those countries as yet underdeveloped with loans and supplies. It was a first-rate idea and met with a universally good reception. No one appeared to realize that it was a repetition of my suggestion of twenty years previously, although in 1929 it did not stop short at the bare suggestion but was formally incorporated in the Young Plan which envisaged the creation of a Bank for International Settlements (B.I.S.).

Had this statutarily appointed task been carried out, it would probably have had considerable effect on the world economic situation and contributed much toward a peaceful development. Unfortunately the executives of the B.I.S. did not devote their attention to this item of the program. Under the strong influence of the Allies, and especially of the French, they confined themselves to the administration and distribution of reparations payments and to the very useful promotion of co-operation between the central banks of the various countries. But since payment of reparations very soon ceased, their activity in this connection dwindled to nothing. The world economic crisis following the Wall Street slump of October 1929 also prevented any active measure on the lines I had suggested. The critical developments in universal political conditions likewise had a hampering effect. Had the B.I.S. when first founded immediately taken the initiative in the matter of financial aid to the underdeveloped countries it might possibly, after the Second World War, have occupied the position that the so-called World's Bank * now does in the U.S.A. The policy of the World's Bank not infrequently encounters political mistrust, whereas the B.I.S. would in all likelihood have been spared this adverse condition. Even today however one need not abandon the hope of future collaboration between the B.I.S. and the World's Bank.

My bank for international settlements remained the finest item of propaganda for the Young Plan. Our next job was to tackle the working out of the statutes of the B.I.S. Hitherto all international conferences dealing with the German economic and financial situation had been held outside Germany. On this occasion I was keen that Germany should be included. My suggestion that the conference should take place in Baden-Baden was readily agreed to by my colleagues. It was the first time that a German meeting place had been chosen.

We were in Baden-Baden for four weeks in October 1929. In spite of several petty discussions the work went pretty smoothly and, most important of all, in a completely friendly atmosphere. The famous watering place which had seen so many of Europe's crowned heads, so many equestrians in its well-known hotels was set in a forest ablaze with autumn coloring, behind which stretched the endless fir-covered hills and mountains of the Black Forest. After we had been deliberating for hours on end in the conference room at the Hotel Stephanie we would escape into the mountains in fine weather and relax after the day's exertions.

The chairman of the Baden-Baden conference was Jackson Reynolds, one of the leading New York bankers. The second American representative was Melvin Taylor, head of the First National Bank of Chicago. The French and Germans were again represented by the presidents of their respective central banks, while the chief British representative was Sir Charles Addis who had spent many years as head of the Hong Kong and Shanghai Banking Corporation and was now, among other things, a member of the Board of the Reichsbank.

In the meantime my idea of a Bank for International Settlements

* The full title is International Bank for Development and Reconstruction.

had met with such enthusiastic response from all those taking part in the Young Conference that soon there was not one among them who would not have liked to claim the suggestion as his own. As a result several of the countries concerned put forward requests that the bank might be established there; Belgium in particular hoped that Brussels would be chosen. For my part I felt that the political atmosphere in the western countries vis-à-vis Germany had not yet progressed sufficiently to induce me to support the Belgian claim, and I therefore suggested Switzerland.

There were no really essential differences of opinion during our discussions on the B.I.S. regulations. It was an outside occurrence that cast something of a blight on the proceedings. Right in the middle of the conference there burst the Wall Street crash.

When Jackson Reynolds approached the breakfast table one morning I felt compelled to remark, "Mr. Reynolds, you don't look very cheerful. What's the matter?"

"Haven't you seen the dispatches from New York?"

"Of course I have. But surely it won't hit you very much!"

"Unfortunately it hits me very seriously as I have large commitments on Wall Street."

A few minutes later Mr. Taylor came in with a beaming face, waving his daily wire from New York.

"Seen the reports from New York, Dr. Schacht?"

"Certainly. How has it hit *you?*"

"It hasn't hit me at all. When I left New York for Europe on a visit of several weeks I sold all my securities like the far-sighted man I am."

Jackson's face grew longer and longer, Taylor's grin broader and broader.

Both Reynolds and Taylor were great favorites as colleagues; but Taylor was the more cheerful nature whereas Reynolds took things somewhat more seriously though he was, too, an exponent of real American humor.

New York is inclined to take itself seriously and Reynolds was a typical New Yorker. Taylor on the other hand was a typical Middlewesterner, invariably good-humored and with the best intentions in the world. At that time when prohibition was the law in the United States, Taylor's home town, Chicago, was the headquarters of all bootleggers.

Taylor himself preferred a good bottle of German wine or a glass of Munich beer to apple juice. His birthday, as it chanced, fell on a conference day, so I bought a large bottle of the best Black Forest kirsch, tied a bunch of roses on the neck and presented the whole thing with a card on which I had penned the following verses, to be sung to the tune of Yankee Doodle:

> A *Yankee boy is trim and tall*
> *And never over-wet, sir,*
> *But prohibition, after all*
> *Is what he least aims at, sir.*
> *Yankee Doodle, guard your wit,*
> *Yankee Doodle, Dandy,*
> *Don't think it fair to prohibit*
> *Black Forest cherry brandy.*

Taylor was delighted with his present. "I swear to you, Dr. Schacht, I'll get this bottle through the customs without any bother," he declared. "My friends in Chicago shall also enjoy it." He was as good as his word. A year later I was in Chicago during a lecture tour. Taylor took me to a party where he told the Baden-Baden story in his best manner.

As the Conference ended, Jackson Reynolds, as chairman, adopted a curious attitude. He declared that he must deliver the report of the Conference to the presidents of the central banks of the participating countries before he himself could communicate its contents to the press. That would have meant that the report would have had to be sent by post to New York, Tokyo, and so forth, and that the waiting journalists would only then have been able to take cognizance of it. This aroused a storm of opposition among the journalists but Reynolds refused to budge.

Then one day I received a visit from Louis Lochner, well known to me as the Berlin representative of the Associated Press.

"Dr. Schacht, for days and weeks past we have been waiting here for the outcome of the Conference. It's surely out of the question that we should be sent home now without being informed of the result. The public everywhere is interested in it and now we are supposed to leave emptyhanded. It just won't do. Please help us to get hold of that report."

I thought the matter over for a few minutes before replying.

"I am not in a position to raise any objections to the chairman's perfectly correct attitude; all the same I'll do my best to help you." Then I went to Reynolds.

"Mr. Reynolds, I understand perfectly that, as chairman, you feel obliged first of all to deliver the report to the presidents of the various central banks. Naturally you won't object to their handing the report to the press. As president of the Reichsbank I would ask you, if you will, to hand me the report officially. I will not conceal the fact however that I intend to pass it on immediately to the press."

Reynolds smiled and said, "Obviously I cannot refuse your request, Dr. Schacht. You have every right to receive the report. If you on your part will assume responsibility for communicating it to the press, that is your own affair and outside my province. I herewith officially hand you the report."

We parted with friendly smiles and Herr Lochner secured his report.

At a press banquet some time later Herr Lochner recounted this incident in the course of his speech as a tribute to my understanding of a reporter's requirements. I myself was reminded of the affair only when my wife told me how, in 1945 when she had been without news of my whereabouts for months and I was in American custody, she had turned to Herr Lochner in Berlin, among others, to ask if he knew where I was. Herr Lochner sent his secretary into the anteroom where my wife was waiting with the message that as the wife of a "war criminal" he was unable to receive her.

# XXXIII

## I RESIGN FROM THE REICHSBANK

EVER SINCE 1926 when I resigned from the Democratic Party, the leftist press had adopted an unfriendly attitude toward me. It was not merely the fact that, in contrast to a certain section of the party, I stood firmly by the invulnerability of private property. I was *persona non grata* in liberal circles by reason of events such as that Black Friday which showed that I was not disposed to allow speculation to flourish unchecked. In addition, my pronounced German and social attitude on the question of reparations was something which got on the nerves of the opportunist politicians. And finally, my persistent warning against the luxury spending of public money, notably by municipal authorities, did not tend to increase the number of my friends.

Their hostility reached its climax when I found myself compelled to take a stand against the German Government's treatment of the Young Plan.

As in the case of the Dawes Plan six years previously the Young Plan contained a clause to the effect that the Plan must be accepted or rejected in its entirety. So that when — after the experts had subscribed to the Plan — several foreign governments began to make changes and to modify individual points in the Plan, it would have been the simplest thing in the world for Germany to refuse to have anything to do with such proceedings.

Instead, the German Government actually entered into negotiations with the governments of Poland and some other countries over some very important changes in the Young Plan. It was due solely to government officials who were friends of mine that I gradually became aware of these goings on after my return from Baden-Baden at the beginning of November 1929. Only a few weeks previously I had supported the government when, together with men like Severing, I had signed the proclamation against the popular demand. Now I had to look on while the German Government not only abandoned the Young Plan to which I had been a co-signatory, but did not even inform me of its intentions. That was the reason I prepared a memorandum on the impending deterioration of the Young Plan which I not merely submitted to the government on December 6 but published in the press on the same day. It came as a bombshell.

In this memorandum I pointed out that the German experts had agreed to the figures in the Young Plan only with the utmost reservation. Now, however, the Germans were being asked to waive claims to property and payment of supplementary sums which were fully justified and which far exceeded anything included in the Young Plan. The Plan provided for the replacement of all Germany's other commitments by the amounts determined in the Plan. It would be contrary to the provisions of the Young Plan for Germany to make voluntary payments or to forego claims to which she had formerly been entitled. This sentence referred specially to an agreement with Poland on the subject of liquidation in which Germany waived her claim to compensation for national and government property ceded to Poland. Germany was also expected to forego several hundred million marks which, according to the Young Plan, were hers by right, being the proceeds of the liquidation of requisitioned German property. I concluded the memorandum with a statement that such an adulterated and debased Young Plan was something to which I could never agree.

The memorandum aroused great excitement. The tension between the government and myself increased and a further event served only to intensify it.

Before the Young Plan was signed we had explained to the German Government that we would sign only on condition that the said government would agree to institute drastic financial reforms. Hermann Müller, the Chancellor, and Hilferding, the Minister of Finance, had also signified their assent. Unfortunately the exchequer was so depleted owing to extravagant financial policy that in December the danger arose that it might not be able to meet the salaries of the Civil Service. Once again, without telling me, Hilferding arranged with an American banking syndicate to grant a short-term loan. In the course of negotiations, however, the American banking firm thought it necessary to enquire from the Reichsbank whether the latter were in favor of the granting of such a loan, to which the Reichsbank replied in the negative. I informed Hilferding of the Reichsbank's attitude in this matter and at the same time told him that I did not intend to let him down but was willing to recommend the granting of a German bank loan of some hundred million marks if the Reichstag would pass a corresponding law guaranteeing repayment of the loan in three equal consecutive annual instalments, and if the government would abide by its promise to carry out the proposed financial reforms.

The Left-wing majority in the Reichstag were furious with me but they could not eventually refuse to pass the law I had asked for. The fact that the measure was known as *Lex Schacht* (Schacht's Law) showed that the general feeling toward me was definitely the reverse of friendly.

Hilferding resigned and with him also Popitz his Secretary of State who gave as his reason: "I consider this interference in national politics on the part of the president of the Reichsbank to be intolerable." I did not resent Popitz's attitude which, from his point of view, was quite understandable; and later we resumed our friendly footing.

Hilferding's post was filled by Moldenhauer, member for the German People's Party, an easygoing cheerful Rhinelander given to looking on the bright side of life. By a coincidence we all met, a few days after his appointment, at a New Year's Eve party in the house of some mutual friends. Someone asked Moldenhauer what a Finance Minister actually did, to which he replied jauntily in his rich dialect: "I spend the whole day governing till my head fairly spins."

But I must admit that Moldenhauer knew his job and was fully alive to his responsibilities.

The holidays at the end of the year were quiet and undisturbed. Our daughter Inge became engaged to Herr von Scherpenberg, Legation Secretary at the Foreign Office, and we fixed the date of the official betrothal party for January 12, 1930. But politics were in full swing during the first days of January and swept me along in their wake. At the beginning of the month the governments concerned met in conference at The Hague to ratify the signing of the Young Plan. Notwithstanding my memorandum of December 6 and my differences with the Ministry of Finance and the Reichstag; and although I had received no information whatever as to the government's intentions, they invited me to come to The Hague as soon as the negotiations had started.

At The Hague I was compelled to realize that all my efforts to see the Young Plan through in its original form were fruitless. Personally I had no intention of going against my convictions. I stated frankly that if the proposed detrimental modifications to the Young Plan were accepted I should be forced to consider, in my capacity as president of the Reichsbank, whether or not I would take up the post in the International Bank at Basle which had been provided for in the Young Plan. For the government, of course, that was a hard nut to crack. Moldenhauer tried to talk me round.

"Herr Schacht, you must know the difficulties your attitude is creating for the government. I venture to suggest — would you perhaps not consider it more fitting were you to resign your position as president of the Reichsbank?"

It must be remembered that, according to prevailing Reichsbank law, the president could not be officially deprived of his post before his term of office had expired. It is also worth remembering however that this proviso did not date from the beginning of foreign influence but from a German law of 1922 establishing the Reichsbank's independence of the government. Personally, I have always maintained that a proviso which stipulates that a Reichsbank president cannot be removed from office is politically intolerable, the more so as prior to 1924 the office of president had been a life tenure. My immediate reply to Moldenhauer's suggestion expressed this view.

"I shall resign my position, Herr Moldenhauer, if the President of the Republic urges me to do so: but certainly not at the desire of a temporary government."

Moldenhauer glued himself to the telephone and suggested to Meissner, the Secretary of State, that the President should express the wish that I should resign my post. He must have been somewhat taken aback by Berlin's reply. Meissner said he would never dream of even mentioning such a suggestion to the President, since the President was not likely to act upon it under any circumstances.

Government lawyers were then roped in. The Allies were assured that a German law would be passed which would compel the president of the Reichsbank to join the Bank for International Settlements (B.I.S.). One or two journalists asked me whether I would comply with such a law to which I smilingly replied:

"I am far too loyal a citizen to refuse to obey a German law. I reserve the right, however, to draw my own conclusions from such a proposal."

The position was hopeless. On March 3, 1930, I submitted a written communication to President von Hindenburg in which I had set down my views. On March 6, I had a long talk with him during which I once again repeated all my reasons for opposing the deviations from the Young Plan. I begged him therefore to appreciate the cause which led me to place my resignation in his hands.

The trend of our conversation is best shown in the following letter which President von Hindenburg sent me the same day:

My dear Mr. Reichsbankpresident,

I am sorry to learn from your communication of the 3rd inst. and our conversation of today's date your decision to resign your responsible position as President of the Reichsbank. As I have already told you, I deeply regret your decision. Since, however, my attempts during today's conversation to induce you to remain in office have been in vain, I must accept your decision as irrevocable.

To my request that you should at least postpone your resignation you replied that you would fix the date of your departure in agreement with the Board and the General Council of the Reichsbank, and that it made no difference to you whether your resignation took effect in fourteen days or three months; and I note here also that you promised to inform me of your eventual decision.

Further, in the course of today's discussion you agreed to comply with my request not to give to the public the same reasons for taking this step that you have given me in your letter; but that you reserved the right to choose what form they should take, as you felt it was your duty to lay before the public the real reason for your decision. I therefore reiterate my appeal to your patriotism and sense of responsibility, and my urgent wish that you will put before the public some other reason for your departure than that given at the end of your letter. I would especially ask you to delete the arguments relating to the "freedom of action" which, in your opinion, was granted by the Young Plan to the creditor nations, among which you expressly include Poland. To my way of thinking this is a misinterpretation which has so far been advanced only by the extreme opposition, but has not been supported by the French Government. Consequently it would be in the highest degree regrettable and prejudicial if you were to represent the mere statement received at The Hague (on a matter which moreover is justified under International Law) as a possible first step toward the imposition of fresh sanctions. I would likewise ask you to omit the observation at the end of your letter on the danger to our currency and the hints as to the possibility of fresh inflation, for such remarks, coming from so prominent a quarter, would prove highly injurious to our economy, causing flight of capital and difficulties in regard to loans.

I shall have occasion later to remember your valuable and outstanding work for Germany and your services to our country, when your decision — which I so greatly regret — has become an established fact.

Please accept this expression of my highest esteem and regard, and believe me,

Yours very sincerely
VON HINDENBURG

It goes without saying that the second part of my letter giving the reasons for my retirement was altered for public consumption. I had no intention of creating unnecessary difficulties for the government. Unfortunately I suffered thereby because my retirement was sometimes misunderstood even by well-intentioned people. Today there is no longer any reason for concealment. When the Hoover Moratorium came into operation the Young Plan perished — barely fifteen months after its birth.

The press and the Reichstag blamed me for making things unjustifiably hard for the government, to which Moldenhauer replied in the Reichstag in very honorable and dignified fashion:

"All our dealings with Schacht have been carried out on a thoroughly amicable basis, and I personally have never had any serious disagreements with him . . . Dr. Schacht's action is consistent with his feeling that he can no longer accept responsibility for the Young Plan. No one can dispute the fact that it is causing the government a certain amount of temporary embarrassment . . . I regret his retirement but I recognize that he has chosen the one path open to a man in his position."

It will be easily understood that I thought a good deal about the past years during this time. On October 19, 1924, a year after my appointment, the Federal Chancellor (Marx) had written:

Prior to the introduction of the Rentenmark on November 15 of last year the federal government was in need of the responsible co-operation of an outstanding expert on bank matters in order to carry out the measures determined by them. In response to this need you immediately placed your services at the disposal of the public a few days previous to this same November 15. The great importance of your co-operation in the expert accomplishment of the introduction of the Rentenmark, and the maintenance of the value of the new currency is something which the Government acknowledges with appreciation and gratitude.

With the highest regard and esteem, I am,

Yours most sincerely,

MARX

On October 22, 1924, my father sent me a letter of congratulation written in his unpretentious style, which I have kept as a memento:

Dear Hjalmar,

Mama and I send you our best and most loving congratulations on yesterday's address by the Federal Chancellor. All that I ever dreamed of and longed for in my youth, but have never attained, I now see realized in you, and together with Mama I rejoice that I have lived to see this day. We are proud of you and hope that you will enjoy the fruit of your labors for a very long time to come.

With much love,

YOUR PARENTS

# XXXIV

## ON MY OWN

I DID NOT FIND it easy to relinquish my office as President of the Reichsbank. In the six years and more during which I had been at the head of the bank, relations with my fellow directors, my colleagues, and all bank employees had acquired such a confidential character as to maintain, if not actually to increase, the bank's *esprit de corps* which had been famous from time immemorial.

In addition the policy of the Reichsbank during my term of office had been proved advantageous to the German economy, and the Reichsbank's reputation in the international world of banking had regained its former high level. We had kept up our connections, too, with the remaining principal central banks throughout the world.

My professional travels had taken me not only to European capitals but also repeatedly to New York where I had found a particularly kind friend and counselor in the late Henry Strong, then president of the Federal Reserve Bank.

Strong was a first rate connoisseur of finance and banking conditions in the United States and keenly interested in bringing the policy of the American money market into line with that of other markets. This purpose was further served by various meetings between us central bank presidents either in Europe or the U.S.A. Our gatherings in the skyscraper Federal Reserve Bank consisted of the heads of the central banks of New York, London, Paris and Berlin. These discussions were invariably characterized by complete harmony.

Even during the period of prohibition Strong did not despise alcohol. By way of returning his hospitality I sent him on one occasion a case of the finest (and headiest) wine of the Palatinate that I could find in all Germany. At our next meeting in New York he said:

"I still have a bottle left of your wonderful wine; you must come to lunch and share it with me." At lunch he raised his glass and welcomed us. "Gentlemen, this is a marvelous light Moselle Schacht sent me."

I was taken aback for a moment, and laughed. "Strong, if that's what you call a light Moselle I'll send you nothing but real spirits next time."

Another amusing incident arose from the fact that the Reichsbank maintained a not inconsiderable gold deposit in the Federal Reserve Bank in New York. Strong was proud to be able to show us the vaults which were situated in the deepest cellar of the building and remarked:

"Now, Herr Schacht, you shall see where the Reichsbank gold is kept."

While the staff looked for the hiding place of the Reichsbank gold we went through the vaults. We waited several minutes: at length we were told: "Mr. Strong, we can't find the Reichsbank gold."

Strong was flabbergasted but I comforted him. "Never mind: I believe you when you say the gold is there. Even if it weren't you are good for its replacement."

One essential problem I had unfortunately to leave unsolved when the time came for my return. This was the problem of the treatment of foreign loans to Germany.

In the face of this situation I urged: "There can surely be nobody in Germany who will allow autonomy and federalism to become an obstacle to a financial and monetary policy which will benefit the entire country."

Unfortunately I was mistaken: there were a lot of them. As a result the country's financial policy was heading for disaster. Even the letter written by President Hindenburg on April 2, 1930 — the day of my official departure — could not dispel my anxieties.

When during the fateful days of 1923 you were called to assume the responsible position of Commissioner for National Currency you played a decisive part in the overcoming of those circumstances which at that time constituted Germany's greatest danger. Among those who can claim the merit of having recreated a consolidated currency your name will always occupy the front rank.

In the six years and more that you have held office as President of the Reichsbank you have always considered it your foremost duty to maintain and confirm those things which had been brought into being by your far-reaching co-operation.

Fair words, honorable words. But alas! only words, which were powerless to avert the danger that threatened the whole of Germany and the German people.

On leaving the Reichsbank my wife and I finally moved out to Gühlen, the property I had acquired in 1926. Gühlen is part of the little town of Lindow so excellently portrayed by Theodor Fontane in his book *Wanderings through Brandenburg*. It lies some fifty-six miles north of Berlin.

During my student days in Berlin I frequently saw Theodor Fontane at the theater where he occupied an eminent position as critic. My admiration for him personally, for his novels led me later to acquire, at an auction, what to my knowledge is the only oil portrait of this great Prussian poet. It is the work of Hanns Fechner and now hangs in my study — a reminder of wonderful vanished days.

The old Brandenburg song, "Soar aloft, O red eagle, high over swamp and sand and over the dark pine forests," suits Gühlen. Here for the most part is typical Brandenburg sandy soil and pinewood, and in minor degree sour marshy meadows, pasture and agricultural land. Gühlen was no lucrative property investment. Once, when my daughter was asked where her father's estate was, she replied: "It depends on the direction of the wind." It was the less lucrative because the greater part had been cleared of timber during the First World War, the wood being needed for pit-props. Nearly a third of the ground had still to be replanted and had lain parched and desiccated since the end of the war. I embarked on intensive reforestation and planted at least three million trees.

Notwithstanding the poor condition of the arable soil and of the meadows and pastures I went in also for agriculture which involved considerable outlay. With the typical ambition of the townsman who wants to "show the farmers," I succeeded in carrying off the prize for milk while my pig-breeding activities soon provided the whole neighborhood with piglings.

It was not only the agricultural and forestry work that gave me pleasure — not even the brickworks which I maintained on a little island on the adjoining lake. I derived even greater enjoyment from walking and exploring — hours and hours in the woods with meadows in clearings and views over the lakes which surrounded the property on three sides.

This unique position was probably the reason for Gühlen's plentiful supply of game. I was no great huntsman, much preferring to preserve, and I always took my telescope when I left my gun at home.

In autumn the red deer were regular arrivals and the belling of the stags could be heard through the entire house. Among the more or less permanent wild population were roe deer, foxes, badgers, rabbits, and the wild boar must not be forgotten. The feathered folk included almost every species of hawk, foremost among them being the red kite; waterfowl such as herons, merganser, duck and diver. Our special pride was a pair of cranes which returned every year to their nest in the deep pool.

In the spring wild geese and wild swans flew over Gühlen on their way north and on one occasion even stayed with us for a short while. And once we had some rare visitors — a pair of wild swans that nested with us and a pair of real sea eagles — very seldom seen in the Mark Brandenburg — whereas the fishing eagle regularly frequented our lakes.

The house itself, framed by ancient oak, elm and pine trees, was situated right on the shores of the lake. Here, therefore, we took up our abode. We had many visitors at Gühlen — sportsmen, relations and friends from our own country and abroad. Nor did I sever my connection with the Reichsbank personnel. I had always encouraged any sporting activities among the staff, and the Rowing Club came on a boating excursion and spent a fine summer afternoon and evening with food and drink on our veranda. Political friends too were not lacking and afforded opportunities for many profitable discussions.

During the three years I spent at Gühlen I played no part in daily political doings, though I naturally took the keenest interest in all big and important developments. I tried to live a quiet life and to remain as much as possible outside public affairs, though outward appearances may not have conveyed such an impression of the idyllic peace and meditative aspect of rural existence. My daughter, in fact, used afterwards to testify to the exact opposite; according to her I would pace up and down the house and garden like a caged lion while consuming an endless succession of cigars.

But her description doesn't quite fit. Gühlen always did me good. And I always found time to commemorate in verse one or two amusing happenings during my walks, such as for instance, the following:

### THE LAST COCK PHEASANT

*Brer Fox reigns supreme in copse and cover,*
*Not a partridge remains the wide fields over,*
*And as for the pheasants — well, we're bereft;*
*A single old cock is all that's left.*
*The master vowed 'twas time to get tough*
*And show Mus' Reynard he'd had enough.*

*In fresh-ploughed furrow in fresh-tilled field*
*The iron trap is carefully concealed.*
*Next day, master goes to see who's present —*
*Blest if it isn't the last cock pheasant!*

### THE HERONS

*On one of those lengthy bars, hard by,*
*Where fishermens' nets hang out to dry,*
*There sit — as down the lake I go —*
*Five silvery herons all in a row,*
*Crouching, extending,*
*Ducking and bending,*
*Turning and leaning,*
*Puffing and preening.*
*Carefully threading his way through the quitch,*
*With ears a-prickit and nose a-twitch,*
*My dog approaches — stops — blah! in dismay —*
*All the birds have suddenly flown away.*

Actually I had no wish to bury myself in Gühlen. I constantly thought over the question of what I could do, as a private individual, to help solve Germany's problem. The world would have to realize that the burden of reparations imposed upon Germany was ruining not Germany's economy alone, but of necessity the whole world's trade. When the opportunity presented itself in the form of several invitations from abroad I devoted myself to this task of explanation in lectures which took me to Bucharest, Berne, Copenhagen, Stockholm, and above all, America.

My first visit was in response to an invitation from the Rumanian Government to speak in the Carolinum on the German economic situation. I held no commission from any official German quarter but started my lecture campaign on my own account, relying solely on my reputation as an expert in currency and economic matters.

After the lecture I took the opportunity to make a trip through the country with my friend Radukanu, then Minister of Labor in the Maniu cabinet. We traveled partly by small steamer, partly by car.

In the few days I was there I met a number of leading citizens, first and foremost their splendid Bishop Teutsch — then already advanced in years — the uncrowned but universally acknowledged head of the Siebenbürgen Germans. He was also the head of the Lutheran

Church to which the entire German population belonged. I had harbored so many bitter feelings on account of the inner divisions and lack of steadfastness of character displayed by the home population since the collapse following the First World War — and here was a section of the German people full of honest pride, conscious of their traditions, democratic, fearless — held together by their Christian profession.

Bishop Teutsch especially was a dignitary after my own heart, a morally unimpeachable personality, staunch of character and possessed of an authority dependent upon no earthly office or secular power. I place him on the same level with other church dignitaries of the various Christian denominations whom I have met in the course of my life: His Holiness Pope Pius XII, who as Cardinal Pacelli the Papal Nuncio was a guest in our house; Neuhäusler the Suffragan Bishop of Munich who, while in Dachau Concentration Camp under Hitler, was a true minister and father in God; and the late Bishop Wurm of Württemberg who stood by me in the internment camp at Ludwigsburg and throughout my denazification trial as an indefatigable champion of morality, justice and freedom.

# XXXV

## THE END OF REPARATIONS

THE SUCCESS of my lectures in the neutral countries left me no peace. I had to pursue my campaign of enlightenment right into the headquarters of our most influential political opponent. Ever since the conferences which had been held under the names of Dawes and Young it had become increasingly clear that the United States of America had become the decisive factor, economically and politically, in the destiny of Europe. I was bound to try to win the support of the population for my objective.

My son Jens had expressed the wish to spend a year working in America, so I took the opportunity to make the journey with him and my wife in the autumn of 1930. My friend Melvin Taylor had signified his willingness to take Jens for a year into the First National Bank of Chicago. I answered the enquiry of a New York lecture agency by signing up for some lectures on economic subjects and prepared about a dozen different talks in all.

Elections for the Reichstag were held on September 14, 1930. I went to the polls in the morning and caught the midday train for London. On our arrival the following morning we were astounded at the result of these elections. The National Socialist Party, which up till then had had twelve representatives in the Reichstag, had gained no fewer than a hundred and seven seats.

This result could be attributed to one thing only: the steadily worsening economic and social condition of the German people. Hitherto I had taken hardly any notice of the National Socialist movement. Not only was I very little interested in party politics as such, but my somewhat retired life at Gühlen and my lecture tours meant that I had paid scarcely any heed to Hitler's growing influence.

Now, however, the result of these elections afforded me a welcome opportunity of pointing to the consequences confronting Germany if the misery attendant on the payment of reparations were to be perpetuated. My friends in the City bombarded me with questions and began to give concrete expression on the Exchange to their mistrust of economic and political conditions in Germany. Naturally I had no wish to see German credit imperiled. I pointedly gave instructions for the purchase of German bonds quoted on the London Stock Exchange. My action at once became noised abroad and was not without its reassuring effect.

We remained in London a few days before boarding our steamer. The crossing was uneventful until, shortly before we landed, I was startled by a radio report from Berlin telling of negotiations between the German Government and a New York banking syndicate under the management of Lee, Higginson & Company. I was horrified. Once again the German Government was endeavoring to conceal the true economic situation by piling up fresh debts abroad. To a radio enquiry which I addressed to the government I received the reply that Otto Kiep, the German Chargé d'Affaires in the United States, would give me all the information on arrival. Although now a private individual I had acquainted my government with the purpose of my journey before I left, and I felt justified in requesting an explanation in order to avoid adverse reactions in America as a result of unwarranted statements.

Not only did the elections of September 14 yield one hundred and seven seats to the Right-wing Radicals; the Communist Party also had shot up from fifty-four to seventy-seven representatives. Both Right- and Left-wing radicalism had increased beyond all expectation. The Moderate parties, including the Social Democrats, had lost a total of one hundred and eighteen seats.

All the anxieties that had beset me during my time as president of the Reichsbank came crowding back. Did the German Government mean to continue its passive policy?

On my arrival Kiep gave me details of the loan negotiations, which were already as good as concluded. My friend George Murnane, partner in the banking firm of Lee, Higginson & Company, enquired what I thought of this transaction, which was to consist of a three-year loan repayable in equal instalments of one third over the next three years. I found myself in a regular cleft stick when he asked me if I considered that this advance was amply secured and whether it was a wise measure. My answer therefore was something after the following:

"You'll certainly get your money back, Murnane; whether it will be precisely on the dates agreed upon may be open to doubt. As to whether the loan can be described as a wise measure, I am not in a position to reply to that question, in view of its political character."

When I called on the lecture agency I was considerably astonished to find that instead of the eight or ten lectures agreed upon there was a perfect mountain of enquiries. I was particularly impressed by the fact that among the different subjects I had suggested some ninety per cent of the enquirers had chosen reparations.

During the ensuing fifty days I gave almost as many lectures, from New York, Philadelphia, Boston in the East to Los Angeles and San Francisco in the West. I spoke to audiences of students and professors, to economic associations of businessmen, industrial leaders and bankers; to numerous clubs and public meetings. During those fifty days I slept in forty-two different beds, twenty-two of them in Pullman sleepers. On several occasions I gave three talks in one day. My wife went everywhere with me.

All my lectures were given in English, and nearly all were followed by open discussion during which intelligent questions from the audience proved both stimulating and fruitful. I invariably preferred this volley of question-and-answer to the actual lecture itself for I am better at debate than at plain speechmaking. Moreover, debates afforded me greater opportunity of exploring the psychology of my listeners. Through public dinners and many private meetings I was in contact with innumerable Americans. Even today I run into many whom I met during that period.

The organization of these events was always most impressive. Most of the lectures took place immediately after some public dinner which at times would include as many as two thousand people. True, a certain monotony in the menu was inevitable: it was nearly always either a Lamb Dinner or a Chicken Dinner — mostly Chicken Dinner followed by ice cream. Any attempt to vary this sequence proved fruitless.

On my tenth evening when I was to speak in Philadelphia I said to the chairman as we went in to dinner: "Herr Wassermann, if we have chicken and ice cream again I shall strike!"

"Just a minute," said Wassermann.

He was back in a few moments with a long face and murmured: "Sorry, Dr. Schacht, it's chicken and ice cream."

In many debates I was asked about the significance of the National Socialist success in the recent elections. Later, at my denazification examination they tried to make out that I had spoken in favor of National Socialism during my American visit, which of course is nonsense. Rather I pointed to the National Socialist success as an example of the danger that would arise if further efforts were made to extort payment of reparations from the German people.

As a result of my lecture tour the local press throughout the country began to interest itself in the reparations question. Unfortunately I was greatly disappointed in the German Government's attitude. I had made it quite clear in my first lecture in New York immediately after my arrival that if payment of reparations continued to be enforced the time would come when transmission in foreign currency would no longer be possible. The first talk, in fact, was given before an invited audience of some six hundred representatives of New York's business community at the instigation of the German-American Chamber of Commerce. I was somewhat discomfited for a moment or so when, on mounting the platform, I found myself facing a microphone and the chairman's voice announced: "Please, gentlemen, be silent now, we are on the air." As I was speaking in English for the first time after a fairly long interval, and speaking extempore, I had to overcome a certain nervousness but managed to do so without any untoward incident.

The incident occurred afterwards when my remarks as to a possible stoppage of payment was published in the press in correspondingly sensational fashion. On the selfsame day, instead of contenting himself with describing my statements as those of a private individual, Dietrich, the German Minister of Finance, declared at a press reception in Berlin that Herr Schacht was not authorized to make such statements, which in no way represented the view of the German Government. I had never said they did and Dietrich's pronouncement was to a certain extent merely beating the air. But this personal disowning of me created the impression that it would still be possible to continue the payment of reparations — therein lay the mischief. Somewhat irritated I informed Kiep of my surprise at this revelation and its implicit mistrust and requested him to transmit this to Berlin. Early the following morning Kiep phoned me the government's reply to the effect that they had complete confidence in me. Such clumsy double-dealing made me furious and I telephoned Kiep, "Please cable back: Be damned to you."

Toward the end of my tour I received an offer from an American firm to publish the subject matter of my lectures in book form. Nothing could have pleased me more than this opportunity of consolidating the effect of my talks. A discussion arose with the publisher over the title. My suggestion that we should use Carlyle's "Down the Niagara and After" was rejected. Finally we agreed on the attractive title, *The End of Reparations*. Neither of us was afraid of anticipating an event which we confidently expected to materialize.

The book first appeared in New York, then in March 1931 in Germany, and was a big success. A London edition followed shortly afterwards and caused me no little amusement as the publisher declared himself unable to accept the American translation and must publish the book in English! I was reminded of the jesting words of an Englishman to his American friend: "Nothing separates our two nations except the language."

Fortunately I was not obliged to confine my campaign to public meetings. I had been able to have private speech with a lot of politicians. One of the most impressive occasions was my talk with President Hoover. Our acquaintance dated from the period of my activities in Belgium during the First World War when Hoover rendered yeoman service in the feeding of the Belgian population. He was by far the most distinguished American of our time and it was his misfortune that the world economic crisis which followed the artificial postwar boom should have occurred during his period of office. The fact that he was not re-elected President in 1932 can only be attributed to this event. Economic depressions are apt to be attended by political changes.

Our *tête-à-tête* at the White House lasted nearly an hour, during which I was able to acquaint Hoover with the devastating effects of the war tributes of which he showed himself fully appreciative. Between recognition and effective action, however, a certain interval was necessary. But when in June 1931, six months after my tour, Hoover suggested to the Allied Powers a moratorium for the Young payments, the end of reparations was assured.

On my return home I spoke in Bremen and Munich, always on the same subject, nor did I omit to report personally to Brüning, the Chancellor. The evening before the publication of my book and my departure for a lecture in Stockholm, I had another exhaustive discussion on the situation with Brüning and Pünder, his Secretary of State. I promised to send him the first copy of my book when it was published on the morrow.

Although I was on the best of terms with Brüning and although I had, and still have, the highest respect for his sterling character, his uprightness and frankness, nevertheless my visit to Stockholm brought me again into outward conflict with the government. To the question put by a Swedish journalist, "What would you do,

Herr Schacht, if you were to become Chancellor tomorrow?" I had replied, "I would make an end of payment of reparations that very day." The government shied away from this statement so promptly that once again they gave the impression that they still considered these remittances possible. Three and a half months later the payment of reparations ceased altogether.

# XXXVI

## MEETING WITH HITLER

DURING my absence the political influence of the greatly increased Radical parties — both Left- and Right-wing — had made itself effectively felt. It had become obvious that economic developments could not proceed along the same lines as heretofore. On Brüning fell the heavy burden of somehow maintaining the standard of living of the German population in the face of constant pressure from abroad and the results of the world economic crisis. This task could have been carried out only if the Central parties, including the German National and the Social Democrats, had backed up Brüning. Unfortunately they did not. As the strongest party, the Social Democrats refused to co-operate with the other central groups, so that the Chancellor was continually faced with the danger of a vote of no-confidence in the Reichstag. As a result Brüning was forced more and more to take the path of so-called Presidential Government which was constrained to reply, not on majority resolutions in the Reichstag, but on constitutional prearranged emergency orders issued by the President. The masses, already crying out against the prevailing misery, sided on the one hand with the National Socialists and their radical promises, and on the other hand with the Communists. It seemed as though before long political developments in Germany would admit of no way out save the transition of the government either to the Right or the Left Wing of the Reichstag.

In December 1930 von Stauss, a friend of many years' standing who had been on the board of the Deutsche Bank since 1915, asked me to dinner one evening to which he had also invited Hermann Goering. I was naturally pleased to have the opportunity of meeting one of the foremost leaders of the National Socialist movement. This dinner party of three discussed the universally burning topics of the economic situation, the rise in unemployment figures, the timidity of German foreign policy and all the other relevant questions. Goering turned out to be a pleasant, urbane companion, though he did not give me the impression of being especially conversant with any one subject. I could not possibly have deduced from the conversation anything that might have been described as an irreconcilable or intolerable political radicalism.

Consequently when, not long afterwards, I received an invitation to dinner from Hermann Goering and his wife I had no scruples about accepting, particularly since the invitation was accompanied by a note to the effect that Adolf Hitler would be there.

Goering's dinner party took place on January 5, 1931. Besides my wife and myself there were present Fritz Thyssen, Frau Karin Goering's son by her first marriage, and Dr. Goebbels. At that time the Goerings lived in a pleasant middle-class home, furnished with comfort and good taste without any sign of ostentation.

Frau Goering, a tall slender Swede with a most winning and kindly nature, suffered from a serious heart complaint. After dinner, an essentially simple meal of pea soup and bacon, she had to lie on the sofa where she listened to our conversation without taking any part in it.

Hitler came in after dinner. He wore dark trousers and the traditional yellowish-brown jacket — the uniform of the party. His appearance was neither pretentious nor affected — there was nothing about him to indicate that he was already the leader of the second largest German party in the Reichstag. After the many rumors that we had heard about Hitler and the published criticisms we had read of him we were pleasantly impressed by the general atmosphere.

Our talk quickly turned to political and economic problems. At this first meeting I learned what all of us experienced later, that in a discussion with Hitler his associates contributed only five per cent; Hitler himself supplied the remaining ninety-five per cent of the conversation. His skill in exposition was most striking. Everything he said he stated as incontrovertible truth; nevertheless his ideas were not unreasonable. He was obviously anxious to avoid anything that might shock us in our capacity as representatives of a more traditional society.

Goebbels and Goering maintained an impressive silence throughout and did nothing to underline Hitler's arguments. Since I had not come in order to sell Hitler my political and economic opinions I contented myself with taking note of his views and intentions. The thing that impressed me most about this man was his absolute conviction of the rightness of his outlook and his determination to translate this outlook into practical action.

Even at this first meeting it was obvious to me that Hitler's power of propaganda would have a tremendous pull on the German population if we did not succeed in overcoming the economic crisis and weaning the masses from radicalism.

After the experience of this evening I took the opportunity during the ensuing weeks of urging the Chancellor and other politicians with whom I was in touch to incorporate the National Socialists in a coalition government as soon as possible. Only thus, it seemed to me, could the complete transfer of power into the hands of this Radical Right-wing movement be avoided. In a coalition, so far as one could foresee, National Socialism might have been kept within reasonable bounds by having to share the responsibilities of government. When a year later the idea finally caught on, the opportunity was already past.

The remainder of 1931 brought a severe deterioration of the economic and financial situation which Brüning was unable to counteract without the backing of the whole of the Reichstag Moderates. Whether Brüning's resignation was due to this impossibility, to the standing aside of the Social Democrats or to intrigues on the part of the German National Party remains open to question. Probably it was a combination of all three.

The fateful decision of von Papen, Brüning's successor, to dissolve the Reichstag and proclaim new elections was the final factor that brought about Hitler's seizure of power. On July 31, 1932, 37.2 per cent of the German people voted National-Socialist and 14.3 per cent Communist. The position of the two fronts was now clear. The center of the Reichstag, from the German National Party down to the Social Democrats, had shown themselves incapable of shaping the nation's destiny. Words like military dictatorship and civil war began to creep into public discussions.

Throughout the years following the collapse in the spring of 1945 at home and abroad which put an end to the National-Socialist regime, the problem has been discussed over and over again and from every possible angle — who was to blame for the establishment of the Hitler regime. Party-political blindness has repeatedly led to the defamation of individuals accused of having prepared the way and served as a mounting block for Hitler. Against this must be realized once and for all that not a single one of the persons thus accused sided with the National Socialist movement prior to July 31, 1932. I myself had never, before that date, supported Hitler either in writing or by word of mouth.

After the collapse it was even accounted a crime — or at least as immoral conduct — to have had any personal contact with such a "criminal" as Hitler. This kind of entirely unproductive political outlook is practically unsound because those circles who today are loud in their denunciation of any dealings with the criminal actually sought and achieved contact with that same criminal in 1932. By way of illustration I quote a man upon whose moral character no one can cast the slightest aspersion.

My friend Paul Rohrbach, mentioned in an earlier chapter, held the view that one should have no truck whatever with an immoral man like Hitler and expressed this view in a letter to Brüning. Brüning's reply dated August 31, 1932, runs as follows:

> For weeks past I have been urged by persons who do not belong to my party not to refuse a discussion with National Socialist leaders. As long as negotiations were pending between the National Socialists and the government I could not bring myself to engage in such discussions for fear of upsetting these negotiations. Since, however, the government subsequently failed to come to an agreement with the N.S.D.A.P.* (a situation clearly foreseen by knowledgeable politicians at the time of the dissolution of the Reichstag) and following renewed petitions by patriotically minded people, I have signified my readiness to seek contact with them.
>
> Such a discussion would serve to determine whether it were anyhow possible to form a constitutional government, and I considered it my bounden duty to attempt it. I feel it is incumbent upon me now as heretofore, vis-à-vis all those who elected the President of the Reich, to spare no effort to consolidate the President's authority and prevent any straying along an unconstitutional path. You will see from this that my action is determined, not by any bitterness but by anxiety for my country.
>
> I am in entire agreement with you in your condemnation of the events at Beuthen and also of Herr Hitler's statements in this connection. If, nevertheless, you will raise objections to my having had discussions with leaders of the National Socialist Party you will have meanwhile gathered from the newspapers that even the government does not refuse to have dealings with Herr Hitler after his above-mentioned statements. As a matter of fact my activities in this matter are confined to this discussion. The actual negotiations are in the hands of persons connected with the Cen-

* *National Sozialistische Deutsche Allgemeine Partei* — Nazi Party.

tral party who have been expressly nominated by the party committees to conduct such negotiations.


The political necessity for coming to an agreement on the question of government with the National Socialist Party and its leader was admitted by all Central parties after the results of the election of July 13, 1932, had demonstrated that the National Socialists were by far the strongest party in the Reichstag. And despite a reduction in National Socialist votes in the second Reichstag election in November 1932 the fact remained that a majority in the Reichstag was no longer possible without the extreme Left or the extreme Right. The prospect of an alliance with the Communist Left aroused greater misgivings than with the National Socialist Right.

Prior to July 1932 one or two National Socialists had occasionally approached me and sought my advice on the grounds of my meeting with Hitler. Among them was Herr Keppler, Hitler's Economic Adviser, a mechanical engineer by profession and until then partner in a small glue factory near Heidelberg.

On another occasion Goering arranged that I should meet Röwer, later a *Gauleiter*, who in 1932 had become the first National Socialist Prime Minister in the Province of Oldenburg. Röwer had hit upon the remarkable idea of introducing a special monetary system in Oldenberg and operating all payments only by a transfer from one Giro account to another. I did not find it very easy to remain polite or serious in face of such nonsense. When I asked how Herr Röwer proposed to tackle, for example, payment of ladies' hosiery from Chemnitz — which even the Oldenburg country girls would not willingly forego, he replied: "Well, we shall just have to get hold of some Chemnitz currency." *

I very quickly broke off my conversation with Herr Röwer and his fellow specialists and wired Hitler the result of our talk.

Taken all round Karl Röwer wasn't a bad sort. He had run a small business in the Cameroons and had seen something of the world, which during the years that followed tended to make him very skeptical of his party's transgressions. One day when he was taking a walk

---

* For the benefit of readers not intimately acquainted with banking terms, the word *Devisen* used in the original means "foreign exchange" or "foreign currency." Röwer, whose ideas on finance were peculiar — to put it mildly — was in this instance proposing to treat a town in Saxony as though it were in a foreign country with a currency of its own. Needless to say nothing came of it.

in the Municipal Gardens in Bremen with the well-known indus-
trialist Franz Stapelfield he suddenly asked:

"How many trees would you reckon there were in this park, Franz?"

"That's a funny question," replied Stapelfield, looking round. "At
a guess I'd say about four hundred, Karl."

" 'Twon't be enough, Franz, to hang all of us."

Röwer just escaped being hanged — he died a natural death.

After several meetings with persons purporting to represent the
German economic outlook, including more than one conversation
with Gottfried Feder, I asked myself what would become of German
economy if such theories should ever be put into practice.

I began to wonder whether I was justified in continuing to keep
away from public affairs to such an extent as I had done till now.

# XXXVII

## THE BANK CRISIS

In March 1931 an event occurred which I could regard only as a storm signal. The largest bank in Austria, the Kreditanstalt, was no longer in a position to meet its foreign liabilities. It ceased its payments abroad and came under the trusteeship of its foreign creditors. It was a decisive shock to the system of the granting of international credits and it was clear that Germany could not fail to be affected by it. Foreign creditors began to call in the loans that had previously been made to Germany.

Matters now developed as I had always foreseen. Private firms could not furnish the necessary foreign currency from their own resources and were obliged to purchase them from the Reichsbank. The Reichsbank's reserves of foreign exchange and gold melted away at a terrifying rate. Since the amount of reserves was invariably published by the Reichsbank in its weekly returns every foreign creditor was able to follow the decline in gold and foreign exchange, which resulted in a steady increase in the calling in of loans.

On June 3, 1931, in the middle of a very heated economic and political atmosphere I had accepted an invitation to the White Hart near Dresden, which included all the so-called German Associations (clubs, societies, unions). It was, if I remember rightly, the last demonstration at which the representatives of laissez-faire monetary policy sought to defend their ideas.

I took the opportunity to address the meeting and pointed out that the very essence of banking advances demanded particular consideration on the part of creditors when faced with difficult times. The creditor should not aggravate the debtor's condition by compulsory calling in of loans, thereby actually creating an insolvency which would have been avoided by the exercise of a little patience.

I had hoped that the Reichsbank would have taken advantage of these expoundings to proclaim a moratorium and thus stem the unlimited withdrawal of foreign exchange reserves. Curiously enough the Reichsbank did not show sufficient understanding of the situation. A central bank can at any time cope with a rush on the part of its creditors by issuing more notes, thereby tiding the banks over the difficulty and enabling them to meet all payments. In the case of a run on payments in foreign currency the central bank is entirely dependent on its reserves of foreign exchange. The Reichsbank took the view that all foreign demands must be met as promptly as possible and the rush would then cease. The exact opposite happened. The more other countries realized the dwindling of the Reichsbank's foreign reserves the more they hastened to get their money back before those reserves were entirely exhausted — and the devil take the hindmost!

The complete collapse of the Reichsbank foreign exchange reserves coincided with the failure of one of the big banks. The Danat Bank was, of all the banks, the most heavily involved from the point of view of foreign currency. It was then severely hit by the collapse of the Nordwolle-Gesellschaft (Northern Wool Company) in Bremen, to whom the bank had made large loans. The Danat Bank was faced with the necessity of suspending payments.

I was sitting with my family on the evening of July 11 when the telephone rang. An urgent message from Chancellor Brüning begged me to come to Berlin.

When I arrived at the Chancellor's office next morning I found two stormy meetings in progress. In one room was a gathering of bank managers who were indulging in mutual recriminations over their financial situation and professional conduct. In another room, in an even greater babel, ministers, heads of departments, government and Reichsbank officials were debating on the appropriate measures to be taken. I was invited to take a seat on Brüning's right and for the first time I learned of a number of details revealing a state of affairs which, in my isolated existence at Gühlen, I had not imagined could be so dire. All the banks had been compelled to make colossal payments and were now jointly and severally faced with the impossibility of meeting their foreign obligations. The Reichsbank's foreign exchange was well-nigh exhausted. Other banks besides the Danat Bank had sustained heavy losses. The need for Germany to declare an immediate moratorium on foreign payments was now obvious. In addition the question of the Danat Bank's suspension of payment remained to be cleared up.

I have always held the view that in the matter of granting loans it is not only the debtor who should be held responsible, but the creditor should be deemed to share the responsibility for the security and liquidity of the loans. He must not allow Goethe's lines to apply to himself:

> *You let the poor man pile up debts,*
> *Then leave him to his misery.*

When, in 1929, the General Insurance Company of Frankfurt (FAVAG) got into difficulties, old Baron Schroeder, head of the well-known Anglo-German banking firm, approached me in London.

"Herr Schacht, in your capacity as president of the Reichsbank you must see to it, whatever happens, that I don't lose any money with FAVAG, that I get my loans back."

I pretended to be very surprised and replied coolly: "I have always thought, Baron, that assurance companies were not *borrowers*, but on the contrary acted as *lenders*. I don't understand on what grounds you made loans to FAVAG, particularly loans in foreign currency. Furthermore, I would ask you what interest and commission you have earned on these loans."

"Including commission I reckon we shall have made between eight and nine per cent."

"And what percentage would you have obtained if you had loaned the money in England?"

"About four per cent."

"Then please, Baron, deduct the overpayment of five per cent from the amount of the loan, and I hope you will manage to be satisfied with a correspondingly lower repayment of your advance."

In the present case, I pleaded that the Danat Bank's small creditors should be given a guarantee up to ten thousand marks for each individual account; but the larger creditors should be obliged to await the gradual liquidation of the Danat Bank estate. The small creditor, who was not in a position to keep tabs on the economic and financial position but relied on the reputation of the big banks, was to be protected; the large creditor, who should have closely followed the trend of events, would have to suffer the consequences of his actions.

My suggestion met with the most violent opposition from Herr Schäffer, Secretary of State in the Ministry of Finance (not to be confused with his namesake who later became Federal Minister of Finance). Herr Schäffer declared that intolerable damage would be inflicted on the prestige of the Reich if all foreign creditors were not satisfied. Shortly afterwards, thanks to the support of his foreign banking friends, Herr Schäffer was appointed liquidator of the

Swedish match firm of Kreuger and Toll, in which capacity he still resides in Stockholm.

The matter was settled according to Schäffer's ideas. On the other hand it was decided that the Danat Bank should no longer continue to function but should be liquidated. I left the meeting.

Once again a number thirteen followed this eventful evening and once again it proved a decisive day for me. On July 13 the Gühlen telephone rang. For the second time Chancellor Brüning asked me to come to the capital. Once there he begged me to accept the post of Reichs Commissioner and in that capacity to bring order out of the chaos of the bank crisis. I thanked him sincerely for this expression of trust.

"I have already held the position of Reichs Commissioner on a former occasion, Chancellor, although at that time also there was already a high-ranking official — namely the president of the Reichsbank — who would have been fully qualified to solve the currency problem with which I was confronted. At that time too I understood that, following the difference of opinion between the government and the president of the Reichsbank, the government should have resorted to the appointment of a special commissioner. Today, on the other hand, you have a president of the Reichsbank who enjoys the confidence of the government and co-operates harmoniously with the government. Today therefore he is the right man to see the banks through the crisis. The task which you set me comes by right within the province of the president of the Reichsbank."

Brüning seemed to hint that during the course of the bank crisis the Reichsbank had not hitherto shown much initiative or afforded him much support. The solution of the Danat Bank crisis was now in the hands of the government.

"That is a fact, Chancellor, about which I regret to say I can do nothing. The government's duty was simply to declare a moratorium on foreign payments. In my opinion the solution of the internal financial crisis was the Reichsbank's job."

Brüning appeared unsatisfied and again urged me to accept his offer. I maintained that we could not come to any decision over the head of the president of the Reichsbank. Nor would I budge an inch, even when President Hindenburg sent Herr Meissner, his Secretary of State, who conveyed the President's own wish that I would accept the position. I have always had a great respect for the old gentleman in his capacity of a soldier, but not for his political qualifications and decisions.

I went back to my retreat at Gühlen and took no further part in the shaping of banking circumstances. The Danat Bank was taken over by the Dresdner Bank to which the government was obliged to furnish substantial assistance. The failure of the Danat Bank and the clearing up of the crisis involved the country in a total loss of four hundred million marks.

I was not even informed of the extent of the Reichsbank's share in putting the national finances back on a sound basis. Shortly before the crash the president of the Reichsbank, Herr Luther, had flown to London, Paris and Basel in a last-minute attempt to obtain credit assistance, which could not be granted (as might have been foreseen) in view of the unavoidable moratorium on foreign payments. Only after the moratorium had been declared did the Allied central banks place a gold deposit of four hundred million marks at Luther's disposal. This was done through the medium of the Basel Bank for International Balance of Foreign Payments and carried an interest of four per cent.

World economy suffered yet another blow through the devaluation of the pound sterling which the British Government brought into operation on September 20, 1931. This was the beginning of the era of currency devaluations which affected and afflicted many countries, including the United States, and which was repeated at a later date by Great Britain. It was the death blow to trust and good faith in international monetary and credit dealings.

On the following day Vögler — my colleague on the Young Plan — called me unexpectedly and asked for information as to what steps Germany should now take. Should she retain her gold parity as hitherto (even though it existed only in theory so far as other countries were concerned) or should she follow the example of Great Britain and have recourse to devaluation? I tried to avoid answering his enquiry and once again referred him to the president of the Reichsbank as the man qualified to deal with it. When Vögler persisted, however, I finally told him over the phone:

"If I were president of the Reichsbank, Herr Vögler, I would board a plane for London right away. *Before* the crash such action was both useless and reprehensible. *Now*, however, there is the chance that we might reap considerable economic advantages from Britain if we agree to devalue. At the moment the British Government feels extraordinarily uncertain as to the result of the devaluation of the pound. They would certainly be prepared to grant us economic advantages if we were to justify and even buttress her action by devaluation on our part. But without attempting such a bargain, that is, without obtaining some equivalent, there would be no sense in Germany devaluing the mark."

Eight years previously I had endeavored to bring about a closer connection between the two greatest European economic powers by means of the issue of pound notes through the Golddiskontbank and my effort then had not been entirely unappreciated. Now, a second impulse might perhaps have carried the idea a stage further.

# XXXVIII

## THE HARZBURG FRONT

My wife suffered occasionally from heart trouble, which was why we spent the late summer of 1931 at Kudowa in Silesia, a spa specializing in heart complaints. There one day I received a telegram from the chairman of the German National Party, inviting me to attend a session of all nationally-minded parties and associations at Bad Harzburg with the object of taking a definite attitude vis-à-vis the government's policy. He asked me to report on the economic situation and I saw no reason to refuse the invitation.

I had learned from the newspapers that Hugenberg and Hitler had agreed to hold a joint demonstration and that one or two other groups also wished to take part.

In Harzburg I ascertained that representatives of several groups were actually present, united in opposition to the existing government but otherwise quite distinctly separate from each other. It was already apparent that Hitler did not appreciate the fact that the initiative had originated with Hugenberg, the leader of the German National Party. Hitler would spare no pains to avoid giving the impression that his adherents were marching under the German national banner. There was much talk, later, of the "Harzburg Front," but in reality this front never existed. If this apparent get-together is to be labeled the Harzburg Front it must be understood that it was born on the morning of October 11 and died that same evening.

My own remarks were brief, but to the point. "The fact," I began, "that a businessman with no party affiliation is able to speak to you today is a further sign that the purport of this assembly extends far beyond the framework of any party-inspired affair. The interests of German economy are indeed most vitally bound up with the ultimate success of the national movement. Production has shrunk by at least a third; huge unemployment figures appear permanent; a daily increasing toll of bankruptcies is simply an expression of our liabilities at home, just as the impossibility of repaying our foreign loans as they fall due is an expression of our liabilities abroad; our currency no longer serves to promote regular trade, but merely to conceal the illiquidity of our financial institutions and our public authorities. Such is the state of affairs in Germany today.

"Yet even more serious than these staggering facts are the wrong foundations underlying the hitherto prevailing system, its insincerity, its dubious legality, its lack of freedom of action. Our financial situation in particular has always been — and still is — far worse than has been suggested to the public.

"The program which a national government will have to carry out rests solely on a few fundamental ideas. It is the same program that Frederick the Great carried through after the Seven Years War: namely, to depend solely on our own resources; to extract from our native soil whatever can be extracted and finally to live frugally, to save, and to work hard for an entire generation."

My remarks certainly contained very sharp criticism of the government's internal economic policy, but a situation such as prevailed at the time invariably demands pungent criticism if a change is to be brought about.

I had intended immediately on leaving Harzburg to go with my wife to Meran. When I emerged from my sleeper at Munich the next morning I was confronted with headlines in the early papers: Schacht's Flight Abroad: Fear of Government Measures following his Harzburg Speech..

I came to a quick decision. I told my wife, who had come to meet me at the station, that we should have to postpone our journey for a day. Then I bought a ticket for the express train to Berlin which stops only at Nuremberg and Halle and would bring me back to the capital in six hours. In Nuremberg journalists came to my compartment with a published article by Herr Dietrich, the Finance Minister, expressing in the sharpest possible terms his disapproval of my Harzburg contentions. Two hours later I had my answer ready and handed it for publication to the journalists who were waiting for me at Halle. When I arrived in Berlin, yet another two hours afterwards, my explanation had already found its way into the evening papers. The press had done its work quickly and well.

I quite appreciated the fact that Herr Dietrich, the Minister of Finance, should have felt himself particularly hit by my Harzburg speech. But I had the satisfaction of knowing that my statements were later substantiated by the Reichsbank's official declaration.

Personally I was sorry for Dietrich whom I regarded as a thoroughly decent, experienced man. Strangely enough we came face to face again at my denazification trial at Ludwigsburg in 1947, and I had the pleasure of hearing from Dietrich's own lips that personally we had always been on excellent terms.

Dietrich most certainly realized the precariousness of Germany's financial and credit situation, but was unable to find a way out of the impasse. In Ludwigsburg he confirmed that in 1932 the burden of unemployment relief for the Reich alone, that is, without the addition of local relief, amounted to three billion marks which had had to be spent without any economic return. To which I was able to reply that my "Mefo" exchange * scheme of relief for creating work (which played an important part in my denazification trial) had never amounted to more than three billion marks per annum, but with this difference — that it was accompanied by a correspondingly increased production.

In December 1931, when taking my son Jens to Rostock University, I had a bad motor smash. Going at full speed, the chauffeur got onto ice like glass. The car overturned. My son and the driver were unhurt and able to get out of the car, but I had to be carried into a house on the main road suffering from concussion, and lay for two hours unconscious. When I came to I could not move my legs. I spent three weeks in the hospital until the brain had recovered from the loss of blood; after that I hobbled about on crutches for another two weeks at Gühlen till at last I had regained the full use of my limbs.

I did not bother about party politics. On June 1, 1932, Papen's cabinet went into action. When the cabinet was being formed there was only one occasion when I expressed an opinion and that was in reply to an enquiry as to who could be Minister of Finance, when I said they should choose Count Schwerin von Krosigk, hitherto Permanent Secretary in the Ministry.

Meanwhile unemployment figures continued to rise steadily. Efforts had been set on foot under Brüning, and continued by Papen, to create work through state relief in the form of so-called labor vouchers; but they could not affect conditions to any great extent because the ratio of such relief to the millions of unemployed was totally inadequate.

In the field of foreign policy, on the other hand, Papen continued

* For the explanation of this "telescope" name see p. 290.

Brüning's attempts to bring about the end of reparations, not merely *de facto* but also *de jure* by means of a treaty. Thanks to Brüning's preliminary work Papen succeeded in writing a judiciary *Finis* to reparations at the Lausanne Conference in the latter half of July. Had this success been made the subject of timely propaganda it might well have influenced popular opinion in favor of the Papen regime. Unfortunately such endeavors came much too late, for only a few days after the success at Lausanne the Reichstag elections — instigated by Papen — took place. They achieved the unprecedented result of two hundred and thirty seats for Hitler, making the National Socialists the largest party in the Reichstag. From now on no government could obtain a majority in the Reichstag without either the National Socialists or the Communists, who had managed to secure eighty-nine seats.

The following months were occupied with attempts to induce Hitler to participate in a coalition government in which, at most, he would take second place. In 1931, when I had recommended it, such an attempt might still have been possible. Now, as head of the largest party, Hitler demanded the lead. The absurd part of it was that this politician — already regarded with fear as a future dictator — was able to base his claim on the recognized principles of democratic parliamentary regulations, whereby the leader of the strongest party has at least the right to be entrusted with the attempt to form a government.

I had grown up from childhood with the democratic outlook. In my opinion the will of the people must always remain the supreme law of government, no matter whether the state in question were a republic or a monarchy. For this reason I regarded it as certain that a government under the chancellorship of Adolf Hitler could no longer be avoided if one did not wish to run the risk of military dictatorship and civil war. I was however opposed to both these possibilities.

After the uncertainty and feebleness of previous governments who had allowed unemployment figures to increase to six million, the election results of July 31, 1932, enabled me to look forward again for the first time to the possibility of an uninterrupted steady and energetic government. The motive that caused me to emerge from my hitherto zealously guarded retirement sprang from the many things I had learned from my occasional conversations with National Socialist political economists. If men like Gottfried Feder and Röwer were to gain control of the banking and monetary system,

I could see already that it would spell ruin for German economic policy despite the parliamentary strength of a Hitler Government. The work of the Reichsbank would collapse if threatened with a "featherweight" (*Federgeld*)* shadow currency or even a splitting up into local Giro currencies *à la* Röwer. I felt it my duty to prevent such a disaster. I therefore gave Hitler to understand, both by word of mouth and in writing, that if he came into power I would not refuse to collaborate with him. Later on this was brought up against me. But neither then nor later have I ever come across any suggestion for a possible alternative to Hitler's chancellorship.

When finally in January 1933 Hindenburg himself could see no other way out, he called a meeting of the leaders of all the Central parties to consult them as to a possible solution. None of those present had any proposal to make. Even Herr Wels, the chairman of the Social-Democratic Party, told the President that they would have to hand over the office of Chancellor to Hitler, in the hope that he would soon overreach himself.

There is consequently sound justification for the raising of the question: What were the circumstances that actually made possible Hitler's rise to this position of power? The answer was given in June 1934 by a leading Social Democrat, Victor Schiff, in the *Magazine of Socialism*, published abroad:

> If there is indeed a point on which there is — and on which there could be — no difference of opinion among us, it must surely be that Hitler owes his rise and his ultimate victory essentially to the world economic crisis; to the despair of the unemployed proletariat, to the academically trained youth for whom there is no future; to the middle-class businessmen and craftsmen heading for bankruptcy; and to the farmers threatened with a fall in agricultural prices. In this connection all of us have indeed been found wanting. It is true that we have rightly blamed the capitalistic order of things for the crisis, but beyond that we were not in a position to offer the masses anything more than mere socialistic phrases.

Anyone reading this pronouncement will, I think, understand my resolve to risk the attempt, under a strong government, to stem the

---

* TRANSLATOR'S NOTE: a play on Gottfried Feder's name. Feder means both "feather" and "pen," and Schacht's cleverly coined epithet is intended to imply that any "freak" currency introduced by Feder would have nothing solid behind it.

tide of economic misery and provide wages and food once again to the six and a half million unemployed.

After all efforts had failed to persuade Hitler to join a cabinet led by one of the Moderate parties, Papen once again resorted to the futile attempt to obtain a majority by means of new Reichstag elections. In these November elections the National Socialists did indeed lose thirty-four seats, but against that the Communist gains rose from eighty-nine to one hundred. It was quite obvious that, if Hitler did not come up to scratch, the electors' dissatisfaction would drive them to seek their salvation on the Left. Papen withdrew after the elections. The question began to crop up as to whether a military dictatorship would work after all.

The post of Chancellor went to General Schleicher, a suave, political general, more at home in the atmosphere of intrigue than on the parade ground. He had tried first of all to find another candidate for the Chancellorship and had got in touch with various individuals. He asked me too, one day, to come and see him and suggested that I should take over the job. Although I immediately decided to refuse I was interested to discover his political view of the situation and I asked him to tell me what his program was. His statements were so colorless that I had time to look around the room. It was every bit as devoid of character as the man's speech — without any personal touch, any sign of individual taste. The correct number of armchairs, some insignificant pictures on the walls, cold and unimpressive. Schleicher's mode of speech, though entirely soulless, was yet directed by the kind of intellect which seeks to win over its opponent and fails completely for lack of a single constructive idea or any kind of enthusiasm. He was the typical man-behind-the-scenes, cold but calculating. It must have cost him a great effort finally to take over the office of Chancellor and thereby to expose himself to public criticism. He pinned his last hope on a split in the National Socialist Party. When he expressed this hope in my presence I broke in:

"I think, General, that you underrate the iron discipline of the party so assiduously maintained by Hitler. Anyone who tried to speak out of turn he will freeze out without more ado."

On the day that Schleicher made his inaugural speech as newly appointed Chancellor I was dining with Seldte and others. While we ate we listened to Schleicher's speech on the radio. The longer he spoke the more our enthusiasm cooled. By the time we had arrived at the *bombe glacée* our frame of mind had sunk to freezing point. For sheer lack of ideas and psychological coldness Schleicher's speech was unsurpassable; it was the death knell of the Weimar Republic. Even he did not dare attempt a military dictatorship.

Three weeks later Hitler was appointed Chancellor by the President. I took no part in these activities, nor did I aspire to any ministerial position; I had hardly any contact with Hitler's party. When we met on one occasion in November 1932 I asked him whether he insisted on entry into the party as a condition of co-operation. To my great relief Hitler replied in the negative. I would never have accepted a subordinate position under his party jurisdiction. I wanted to preserve my freedom; I have never been a member of the party.

# XXXIX

## PRESIDENT OF THE REICHSBANK AGAIN

I saw Hitler only once during the first weeks after he took office, but it was on a very significant occasion. I happened to be in the room with a mere handful of his entourage when he made his first speech to the German people over the radio — that speech beginning "Give me four years." It seemed to me that for the first time I had an opportunity of seeing the soul of this man; I had the impression that the burden of his new responsibilities weighed heavily upon him. At this moment he felt clearly what it meant to be transferred from the propaganda ranks of the Opposition to a post of government responsibility. I beheld the outward and visible expression of an inward emotion which was not just "putting on an act" — it was the real thing. It served to strengthen my hope that it would be possible to guide this man into the path of righteousness.

During the negotiations over Hitler's appointment the President — and probably Hugenberg also — had resigned themselves to the necessity of having yet again to sanction Reichstag elections. These were fixed for March 5, 1933. Just why they had to take place is not clear. Not counting the Communists, Hitler's and Hugenberg's parties commanded a clear majority in the existing House. If, notwithstanding, Hitler still insisted on an election he must have cherished the hope (the more so since he had now attained to power) of achieving a majority for his own National Socialist Party. This would have resulted in a new situation which would have allowed him to form a purely National Socialist cabinet instead of a national one. The attempt proved a failure.

Quite unexpectedly I received an invitation from Hermann Goering to a gathering on February 25 at the residence of the President of the Reichstag which he occupied in his official capacity. I met a good number of industrialists, nearly all of whom were known to me and who had been invited by Goering to give financial backing to the Reichstag elections. I knew that most of those present were not adherents of the National Socialist movement. Yet they had not refused this invitation. Goering welcomed the guests and explained that the purpose of the gathering was to raise an election fund for the Right-wing parties. Then Hitler arrived and expounded his political views in so compelling a fashion that, to my great astonishment, when Hitler had finished, Krupp von Bohlen rose and in the name of the assembled guests expressed his complete willingness to support the Hitler Government. I was astonished because I knew that four weeks previously this same Krupp von Bohlen had turned down an invitation from Fritz Thyssen, where Hitler intended to address industrialists in Rhineland-Westphalia.

The company that evening subscribed a total of three million marks for the election fund. Hitler asked me to undertake the banking administration of this fund which I agreed to do. A tremendous lot has been written in after years to show how heavily in debt the National Socialist Party was at the end of 1932. On the basis of my experience with the Fund for the March elections I can only describe these allegations as ridiculous. Had the party stood in need of money it could at least have claimed its share of the three million. Actually this was not the case. Of the three million marks a total of two million four hundred thousand was utilized by the Right-wing parties, including the National Socialists. At the end of the elections there remained a balance of six hundred thousand marks. One must give the National Socialist movement credit for the fact that most of its propaganda was paid for out of the pockets of its own members.

The burning of the Reichstag occurred only a few days after February 25. Nowadays it should be quite clear that this action could not be fastened on the Communist Party. To what extent individual National Socialists co-operated in the planning and execution of the deed will be difficult to establish, but in view of all that has been revealed in the meantime, the fact must be accepted that Goebbels and Goering each played a leading part, the one in planning, the other in carrying out the plan. It is my own firm conviction that Hitler himself was genuinely overcome. To quote the words spoken later by the wife of a prominent party leader, Hitler's entourage wanted to "place the smoldering ruins of the Reichstag building on his breakfast table by way of a surprise." At any rate the Reichstag Fire furnished the welcome pretext for the final removal of the Communist Party from the political scene.

The task that confronted the Hitler Government was no easy one.

From their lowest level in the summer of 1927 the unemployment figures had risen tremendously year by year and reached their first peak in the winter of 1931–32. The following winter again saw a tendency to increase. The most heavily affected was the building industry in which nearly ninety per cent were unemployed. Without large state orders unemployment could not be eliminated, and such elimination could not be achieved without the most enormous expenditure. Factories stood empty, machines were silent, stores were rotting and workers standing idle.

It was only long afterwards that I learned that Hitler sent for Dr. Luther, the president of the Reichsbank, and enquired of him what amount the Reichsbank could contribute toward the creation of employment. After thinking it over Luther is reported to have mentioned the sum of a hundred and fifty million marks. If this report is correct one can understand Hitler's disappointment at the result of his discussion with Luther. The figure given by Luther would have been just sufficient to provide exactly four days and five hours' work for the total number of German unemployed at a wage of five marks a day — precisely as useless as the three billion marks unemployment benefit which had vanished like smoke in 1932.

In the middle of March 1933 Hitler sent for me and put the same question to me that he had done to Luther, without however breathing a word of his conversation with the latter.

"I am honestly not in a position, Chancellor, to mention any particular sum. My opinion is this: whatever happens we must put an end to unemployment and therefore the Reichsbank must furnish whatever will be necessary to take the last unemployed off the streets."

There was a short pause; then Hitler looked at me and asked: "Would you be prepared to take command of the Reichsbank again?"

I realized the far-reaching import of this question. I would have preferred it if Brüning had asked me the same thing in July 1931. Now, the question had been put before me by a chancellor with whose general outlook and propaganda, political fighting methods and even individual actions I frequently did not agree. Should I let such considerations influence me to the point of refusal, or should I devote my energies to the saving of six and a half million unemployed?

During the denazification trials to which I was subjected after Germany's collapse the same idiotic assertion was made again and again: "If you had not helped Hitler he would have failed in his efforts." I retorted with understandable heat: "I don't believe Hitler depended only on me. He would have found other methods and other assistance; he was not the man to give up. You, sir, would have been glad if Hitler had perished without my help. But the whole of the German working class would have perished with him, and even you would not have advocated that."

Since I was now given the opportunity of ending this unemployment, all other considerations must give way.

"I should not think it very fair, Chancellor, were I to be placed in a position that would involve Herr Luther, the president of the Reichsbank, being driven out of office."

"I don't expect you to do anything of the kind. In any case Herr Luther will not remain president of the Reichsbank. I have other uses for him."

"If that is so then I am prepared to resume office as president of the Reichsbank."

On March 17, 1933 — almost exactly three years since my voluntary resignation — I resumed office, this time under far more difficult conditions than at the end of 1923, and with far greater responsibility.

My salary under the Weimar Republic was two hundred thousand marks. In 1924 it had been fixed at the same level as that of the Agent-General for Reparations. There were obvious reasons why it should remain at the old figure. To my enquiry Hitler answered that he left it to me to fix my own salary. I declined his offer and asked for a triumvirate, consisting of the Minister of Finance, the Minister for Economic Affairs and myself. I suggested to this triumvirate that my salary should be fixed at thirty per cent of the former figure, that is, at sixty thousand marks, to include all my official expenses, and so it was arranged. My object was to set an example to the party bosses, that they too might keep their remuneration within reasonable bounds. Unfortunately they did not do so.

The first Work-Creation (Reinhardt) Program to be decided by the cabinet aimed at the repair and reconstruction of houses, factories and machinery. To this program the Reichsbank contributed the sum of one billion marks.

The second job to be tackled — and it was tackled very soon — was the construction of national *Autobahnen.** For this I sanctioned

---

* Highways for the use of motor traffic only.

an initial credit of six hundred million marks which, however, was to be repaid out of the National Budget. Within a very short time the State Railways Board took over the completion and running of the *Autobahnen*. With the object of making these highways pay, I had stipulated with Hitler at the beginning that road and rail traffic must work hand-in-hand with each other. Why this purpose should have been lost sight of later I am unable to say since in course of time, and after I had received back the six hundred million marks for the Reichsbank, I had nothing further to do with the *Autobahnen* construction.

After the collapse of Germany, national, provincial and county officials were constantly blamed for having so readily offered their services to that "criminal" Hitler. But under Hitler they now received a steady supply of funds which enabled them to carry out all the works in which they had long been interested and which previous governments had hitherto refused to sanction. Most of them experienced an upsurge of positive inspiration now that at last they were able once again to produce really worthwhile work in the districts under their administration. An analysis of the National Socialist "philosophy" was completely outside their scope: all they wanted was that the immediate effect of government activities should be to promote business and satisfy the population. Reports from individual districts and counties piled up, showing that unemployment had decreased or even been done away with altogether.

As regards the "philosophical" conflict of outlook, that had to be carried on at a higher level. That was the Reichstag's job. It was here I experienced my first big disappointment.

The combined Right-wing parties in the government comprised sixty per cent of the Reichstag, of which the National Socialists alone amounted to nearly fifty per cent. The Reichstag was therefore fully able to carry out the ideas of the cabinet. Only in decisions involving constitutional changes was a two thirds majority necessary. Undesired constitutional changes could not be carried through by the National Socialists alone. The non-National-Socialist Right-wingers and the remaining Moderate parties had it in their power to compel obedience to the rules of the constitution. Why, under these circumstances, an Enabling Bill was introduced on March 23, 1933, which should give the government authority to make constitutional changes, was and remains a complete mystery. The Reichstag surrendered its powers of control without any need to do so, thereby creating the legal basis for practically all the measures to which Hitler later resorted in defiance of the former constitution.

I attended that session of the Reichstag as a spectator on the platform, and saw with increasing disappointment how the Moderate parties threw away their own chances. It is to this law that Hitler owed his dictatorship. Among these deputies were a fair number of men who, by a curious coincidence, today occupy leading political positions in the Federal Republic of West Germany and who extol parliamentary democracy as the alpha and omega of the German constitution.

During the following months I was unfortunately compelled to witness how the Central parties pursued their self-debilitation to the point of suicide. One after another the Moderate parties disintegrated. The Reichstag deputies who had been elected by the people to represent the interests of the people repudiated the undertaking they had given to their electors; of their own free will they renounced their power and their influence without consulting those same electors. Democracy had dug its own grave.

# XL

## A VISIT TO ROOSEVELT

THE WORLD ECONOMIC CRISIS had been checked. The breakdown of international money and credit business had persisted for nearly three and a half years and in the United States the new government of the Democratic Party, which had been in office since March 1933 was pressing for a General Economic Conference which should bring about a solution of the international economic tangle. The Allied Powers agreed to call this conference in London. It took place in June and July 1933 and was attended by representatives of more than sixty countries from all over the world.

First of all by way of preparation for this World Economic Conference, Ramsay Macdonald had gone over to New York from Great Britain in the spring of 1933 for discussions with the new President, Franklin Delano Roosevelt.

Shortly before Macdonald arrived in New York Roosevelt astonished the world by devaluing the dollar by forty per cent — the same proportion by which Great Britain had devalued the pound sterling in September 1931. The reasons which urged Roosevelt to take this step were not, as in London, due to the country's financial needs. America possessed the greatest amount of gold; the dollar was the most stable currency in the world. Owing to the First World War the United States balance of payments had developed in most striking fashion in favor of the Americans. From the point of view of currency or financial policy there was not the slightest incentive to devalue.

If, despite this, America was still set on devaluation it was obviously because she wanted to reap the same commercial advantage that Great Britain had done from her devaluation of sterling. The first effect of monetary devaluation is always to lower the price of exports from the devaluing country. The British devaluation of 1931 contributed in corresponding measure to the increase of British exports. Roosevelt's aim was frankly to counter this artificially created preference in favor of Britain.

It is easy to imagine that the discussion between Roosevelt and Macdonald did not precisely lead to any pronounced harmony. Monsieur Herriot fared better. France had appointed him her representative at the World Economic Conference and sent him first as emissary to Roosevelt. French policy had always understood how to win the sympathy of other nations by focussing attention on the cultural aspect of her mission. For decades past Paris has been and remains the goal of every globetrotter who seeks artistic, intellectual and material recreation.

The German Government too had to send a representative to Roosevelt for the preparations for the World Economic Conference. I was chosen for this position. I arrived in Washington in May, accompanied by sundry government and Reichsbank officials. My stay there lasted eight days.

On the occasion of my first visit President Roosevelt received me on the terrace of the White House. He was a heavily built, handsome man of great stature. In company he was natural and unconstrained and possessed that kind of compelling politeness that does not wound only because it is always accompanied by a jest.

Together we went into his study where the sofa received the full impact of his two-hundred-odd pounds avoirdupois. This initial conversation was followed by three others, all of which took place in this same room. He was without doubt a political gambler in the grand style; highly intelligent and, for all his frankness, possessed of a certain reticence, a man who thought first of his position as leader of his political party and only second of his responsibilities in relation to the economic situation.

The diplomatic courtesies were punctiliously observed where I was concerned. First there was a big luncheon at the White House at which Roosevelt presided. On another evening Cordell Hull gave a dinner in my honor, and also in honor of the Chinese representative who likewise had come to take part in the preliminaries of the World Economic Conference. I met this Chinese gentleman for the first time in Washington and had many talks with him later in Berlin, where he called on me officially and was also a guest in our house. His name was H. H. Kung, brother-in-law of Chiang Kai-shek.

I am reminded of a little episode at that dinner. I was on Cordell Hull's right and on the left of the then Secretary to the Treasury. An orchestra as usual was dispensing music — as of course they invariably do in order to cover up any embarrassing moments in the conversation — when I suddenly became aware of a performance in an idiom completely new to me. At the end of the number Kung remarked: "That sounds almost like Chinese music."

My neighbor, the Secretary of the Treasury, turned proudly toward me and whispered: "That's a real feather in my cap. I wrote that piece especially for this reception to the Chinese delegate."

Roosevelt and Hitler came into power almost at the same time. Both owed their election to a previous economic depression. Both were faced with the task of resorting to state intervention to crank up the economic engine. But while Roosevelt was able to dip into a full purse Hitler's coffers were empty.

My first professional discussion with Roosevelt showed me that Herriot, who had left Washington only one day before I arrived, had managed to draw Roosevelt completely into the orbit of French interests, and I had much ado to convince him by describing conditions in Germany that German problems were essentially of more decisive importance than the French. Nevertheless I succeeded in doing so during other conversations. I began slowly to prepare Roosevelt for the fact that even after the abolition of reparations it would be impossible for Germany to continue the interest and amortization in foreign currency of the numerous loans which, notwithstanding my warning, had been made to our country between 1924 and 1930.

I seized the bull by the horns at a discussion which took place in his office, and at which the Foreign Minister Cordell Hull and our German Ambassador Dr. Luther were also present. I stated bluntly that in a very short time Germany would be compelled to cease payment of the interest on the American loans. Cordell Hull grew nervous. Luther fidgeted in his chair. I myself expected an indignant outburst on the part of the President. To our astonishment there was nothing of the sort. Roosevelt gave his thigh a resounding smack and exclaimed with a laugh: "Serves the Wall Street bankers right!"

The next day saw a little sequel to this incident. I was asked to call upon Cordell Hull in the State Department. In his buttoned-up frock coat he came forward solemnly and handed me an envelope with the brief words: "I am to give you this from the President."

I took the envelope and asked whether I should read the letter immediately, to which Hull replied in the affirmative. It was a very short note and consisted solely of the information that the President had been much shocked by my statement of yesterday. It occurred to me that the President had not experienced any shock until twenty-four hours had elapsed, but I naturally preferred to replace the note without comment. There was a brief, formal conversation before I took my departure.

Cordell Hull was the exact opposite of Roosevelt. Where Roosevelt had about him something of the modern manager who acts according to impulse and intuition, Cordell Hull seemed to have stepped directly out of the era of Abraham Lincoln. Lean, of middle height, with slightly bowed head and tightly compressed lips, he held himself always very erect, avoided any animated movement and preserved a totally uninterested countenance even in face of the most interesting topic. His old-fashioned frock coat was always impeccably buttoned. Round his neck he wore an old-fashioned stock. I have always pictured the typical Old Colonial Gentleman as being exactly like Cordell Hull.

Whenever I had a few hours' leisure I would leave the Mayflower Hotel and go for short trips through the city and out to the celebrated Mount Vernon. At that time Washington was not so overgrown nor so overrun with bureaucratic offices as it is now but was still a lovely residential city, with attractive Embassies in widely differing architectural styles, each country being at pains to create a bit of home even in the construction of its diplomatic residence. The German Embassy provided a regrettable exception. Since we had lost the former building through the war our Embassy was now housed in a rented building several stories high which certainly did not present any atmosphere of comfort.

When I took leave of Roosevelt in his private room he motioned me to the sofa and said: "You have made an excellent impression here because from every point of view you have spoken frankly and sincerely."

I thanked him and bade him goodbye in the hope that my visit had not been altogether in vain.

I was due to sail the next evening. The liners as a rule left New York Harbor after midnight. I was able therefore to accept the invitation of a Jewish friend who had asked me if I wouldn't come, just once, and talk to a group of his friends about the anti-Semitic attitude of the National Socialists. I was well aware that here was a subject with which I could achieve no result, be it handled ever so tactfully or so delicately. On the other hand I too felt the need at any rate to make an effort to discuss these anti-Semitic sentiments with Jewish circles — sentiments which had been artificially stimulated in Germany to a great extent but which had not once made their appearance in the rest of the world.

The friend who invited me was David Sarnoff, an outstandingly able, well-informed man on matters of international policy. He had accompanied the American Delegation to the Young Conference in Paris in 1929 and had shown himself consistently kind and helpful to us Germans. He had come to America from Russia as a boy of ten and by his keen intelligence and energy had worked his way up to the top of the tree in one of the largest radio companies. In his tastefully furnished private house in New York he gave a most delightful dinner party at which some twelve to fourteen men were present — all Jews with the exception of Owen D. Young and Alfred Smith (the Catholic candidate for the Presidency) and the General Secretary of the Young Men's Christian Association. The Jewish guests were known to me either personally or by name. That evening I met the well-known Rabbi Wise for the first time.

After dinner I spoke, as was my habit, as decently and tactfully, but also as honestly, as possible. But the fact that there was no discussion showed me that, as was to be expected, I had convinced no one. Nevertheless my host shook hands warmly as he saw me to the door and said, "Dr. Schacht, you have been a very good sport."

A few weeks later the World Economic Conference met in London to which Hitler's Government sent a deputation under the leadership of the Foreign Minister, Baron von Neurath, and in which Hugenberg and I among others were included. The National Socialist Party element was represented by Herr Keppler and Herr Krogmann, Mayor of Hamburg.

The meetings of the Conference split up into innumerable commissions and committees. The all-important subject was the return to stable currency conditions. Along with it, as happened so often before and equally often since, we discussed what measures could be taken from the point of view of commercial policy in order to set world trade going again. Despite extensive bureaucratic preparation the Conference lacked real leadership. And to expect unanimous decisions from a gathering of delegates from sixty countries was also perhaps not a very happy notion. I remember that some small, entirely insignificant resolution was nearly lost because the representative of Afghanistan refused to agree to it.

The opening of the Conference — as was only to be expected in London — was as impressive as could be. At a Royal Garden Party we were able to shake hands with King George V and Queen Mary, and at the opening of the Conference we listened to an address by the King.

During the Conference an unfortunate incident occurred within the German Delegation. Hugenberg felt justified in handing to the Conference Office a memorandum on colonial policy which he had not discussed beforehand either with Baron von Neurath our chairman, or with us his colleagues. The memorandum aroused unwelcome attention as it was really out of place in this World Economic Conference. It led to unpleasant results for Hugenberg himself: called to account by Hitler he resigned his offices of Minister of Economic Affairs and of Agriculture, thereby leaving a serious gap in the non-National-Socialist ranks in the cabinet. He was succeeded in the Ministry of Agriculture by the National Socialist romantic writer Walter Darré, and in the Ministry for Economic Affairs by Kurt Schmitt, hitherto Managing Director of the Alliance Assurance Company, who felt impelled to don the S.S. uniform very quickly and thereby take his place in the ranks of National Socialist bosses, although, according to his business and economic outlook, he was a Liberal.

The entire World Economic Conference broke up without having achieved any practical result. It fell to me to make the valedictory speech for the German Delegation culminating in the following words:

"With the failure to come to an international agreement it now becomes necessary for each country first of all to put its own economy in order. Once this has been done a new World Economic Conference will perhaps stand a better chance of success."

# XLI

## CONVERSION FUND AND "MEFO" BILLS

IN MAY, after my return from America and before my departure for London, I called a meeting of the banking representatives of our creditors in other countries. They came from France, Britain, the United States, Belgium, Holland, Switzerland and Sweden, each with the intention of keeping a watchful eye on the interests of his creditor compatriots. It is true that they came without legal mandate — it would have been impossible to execute such a mandate in view of the large number of creditors — nevertheless they were invested with authority by virtue of the very confidence which the creditors of their respective countries reposed in them.

At this Berlin Conference I submitted all financial and economic data which proved Germany's incapacity to continue paying interest on her foreign loans. Since it had gradually become clear that Germany could pay her debts only if she achieved correspondingly large exports I dwelt above all on the obstacles that other countries placed in the way of our export trade.

In a survey of the year at the end of 1931 the *Frankfurter Zeitung* confirmed that fantastically high tariff walls had been erected around those countries which had hitherto absorbed four fifths of German exports. In France tariffs had not only been raised, but for the first time tariff quotas had been fixed restricting the quantity of imported goods. Poland had increased her industrial duties by one hundred per cent. Many other countries were not content with increasing tariffs but followed the example set by France and restricted the quantity of imported goods by the imposition of quotas. Then followed the creation of import monopolies, special import duties, compulsion as to the expenditure on home-produced goods and similar measures; added to which Britain and several other countries had devalued their currency, thereby attaining considerable advantage over Germany in world markets.

Under no circumstances was I going to take the necessary steps on my own authority while, on the other hand, the creditors' representatives were unable to grant me legal power of attorney. We therefore agreed that, after joint consultation, the Reichsbank would have to set matters in train. The books of the Reichsbank were inspected and in spite of the painfulness of having to take certain resolutions, it was recognized that I had put all my cards on the table. The principles to be followed in future were determined jointly by the creditor representatives and myself:

(a) It was agreed that the Reichsbank's remaining reserves of gold and foreign exchange had reached such a low level that any further decline must imperil the Reichsbank's full function as a central banking institution and that it was desirable that these reserves be gradually increased.

(b) Further, it was acknowledged that the adverse balance of payments situation demanded the protection of the German foreign currency reserves.

(c) It was generally acknowledged that it was necessary to promote German exports by all possible means since only in this way would a resumption of payments be possible, for in the long run international debts can only be repaid by the free import and export of goods and services.

(d) In regard to the restrictions on transfers which had become necessary, it was recognized that these should *not* be extended to the Dawes and Young Loans, at least not for the interest on this latter.

(e) On the other hand, in regard to the remaining loans and debts, none should have priority over the others. At the same time a wish was expressed that the Reichsbank might consider the proposal to set aside a certain amount of foreign exchange to cover these liabilities for, say, the next six months.

In addition to these principles it was agreed that, first of all, from July 1, 1933, onward the interest and amortization of the Dawes Loan of 1924 should be transferred in full. Of the Young Loan, on the other hand, only the interest was to be transferred. The transfer of amortization payments on the Young and all other loans was to be postponed. The transfer of all other interest and dividends was to be cut by half.

These negotiations — which for a time were repeated every half year with changes in transfer percentages — bear witness to the fact that the restrictions on transfers and the promotion of German export trade were entirely in accordance with the creditors' ideas.

That I was later charged over and over again for these very measures betrays crass ignorance of the real circumstances.

But even if the transfer of payments on loans had been abolished I had no intention of allowing the German debtors to escape their liabilities. With this object in view, I created a so-called Conversion Fund, into which the German borrowers of foreign loans were to pay the amounts of interest and amortization in German Reichsmarks as they fell due. From time to time the Reichsbank undertook the transfer of these sums into foreign currency.

The stopping of interest payments meant, of course, that the foreign creditors suffered considerable loss. It is true that the amounts were credited to them in marks with the Conversion Fund but they were unable to change these into their own currency. In order that the creditors might not be left completely unsatisfied the Reichsbank authorized the Golddiskontbank to purchase these credits at half of their nominal value. Dealings in these vouchers for mark credits, known as Scrips, soon became very lively. The profit accruing from the fifty per cent saving went to the promotion of export. Germany's use of the Scrips to pay for additional exports gave the creditor countries an interest in buying as many goods as possible from Germany in order to preserve or increase Germany's ability to transfer payments.

In course of time the more German marks piled up in the Conversion Fund the more urgently did other countries seek opportunities to spend those marks. Many such opportunities were created in the interests of the creditor countries, such as travel in Germany, relief work in Germany, investments in Germany, the purchase of certain goods in Germany. This system of different mark categories — travel marks, register marks (*Registermark*), Aski marks (special foreign account marks) has been much criticized and ridiculed. The fact is that it reacted to the advantage of the foreign creditor, the losses he had originally envisaged being greatly mitigated thereby. Many other countries adopted a similar principle after World War II. Britain, for example, has greater varieties of pounds sterling today than Germany then had in marks.

In addition to the immense and difficult task of regulating the foreign loans the question of financing the Work Creation projects had to be dealt with. That first billion which I had sanctioned was insufficient, as we knew from the first that it would be. I reflected that if there were unused factories, unused machinery and unused stocks there must also be unused capital lying fallow in business concerns. To capture this capital by the issue of state loans would have been a hopeless undertaking. Public confidence in the state's ability to pay had been undermined by previous governments. I had therefore to find a way of extracting this fallow capital from the safe deposits and pockets where it now lay, without expecting it to remain absent for long or to lose its value.

From this train of thought there arose the scheme which later became known as *Mefo-Wechsel* (Mefo bills). The name Mefo derives from *Metall-Forschungs* A.G. (Metal Research Company Limited), a limited company founded, at the instigation of the government, by the four big firms Siemens, Gutehoffnungshütte, Krupp and Rheinstahl. The state assumed direct liability and security for all debts incurred by this small company. From now on all suppliers of state orders tendered bills on Mefo against their requirements. The Reichsbank declared its willingness to exchange these bills at any time for ready cash over the counter. That is the quite simple and plain idea behind the Mefo-bill system.

Where the working of the system was concerned, the state could use the Mefo bills to pay for its orders to business firms, orders which, as time went on, were extended especially to cover armaments. The suppliers could immediately exchange their bills for cash at the Reichsbank.

The question remained to what extent the Reichsbank might be compelled to accept Mefo bills against cash in its portfolio. In this connection what I had expected came to pass; namely that the money lying idle in the safes and cashboxes of business firms, not intended or able to be used for long-term investments, was immediately used to get possession of these short-term investments. Since the bills carried four per cent interest and could be exchanged for ready money at the Reichsbank at any time, they took the place of ready cash, so to speak, and earned interest in the bargain. In four years the total amount of Mefo bills had risen to twelve billion marks, and the above arrangement made it possible for a good six billion of these to be taken up by the market, which meant that they were never presented at the Reichsbank, thus avoiding any inflationary development in providing funds for Work Creation projects, and any decline in the value of money.

Once production had been set on its feet again — thanks to the accumulation of Mefo bills — and the money market was improving, the Mefo bills became a specially favored security for the short-term investment of bank funds. Any Mefo bills not absorbed by the market could immediately be included in the Reichsbank portfolio. When one considers that in 1930 the Reichsbank's holding in bills and secured loans had sunk to less than two billion marks, it is easy to realize how greatly the turnover of goods had declined in German business and how much scope the Reichsbank could offer for the intake of Mefo bills without thereby endangering the currency.

It may perhaps be necessary to explain a few technicalities to the layman, for many readers are not acquainted with technical expressions. The use of bills of exchange for trade purposes has arisen because the purchaser of a commodity has usually to wait for about three months before he can resell it and get his purchase price back. In order to be able to purchase his commodity and satisfy the seller he gives the latter a bond, called a bill of exchange, which is payable after three months have elapsed. The solvency of such bills is governed by a very strict law which makes this method a favorite one for trading purposes. On receipt of a bill three months' interest is deducted; that is, the bill is discounted. The rate at which the deduction is reckoned is the rate of discount. A bill of exchange can be used, or misused, as a form of payment for debts which are not backed by any purchase of goods. They are then known as accommodation bills. The Reichsbank is under obligation to accept only commercial bills bearing a certain number of signatures.

From 1934 up to the outbreak of World War II this system of Mefo bills was recognized throughout the entire international banking world as an ingenious and well-adapted method of providing funds. It was only after the collapse of 1945 that the denazification fanatics tried to set a trap for me by representing the system as unfair and illegal. The cabinet makers, commercial clerks, registrars, actuaries who constituted the judicature in the denazification tribunals knew nothing of the economic needs of the thirties, nor could they understand the relevancy of the Mefo-bills system.

In spite of being informed to the contrary both by the Administrative Court and the Supreme Administrative Court in Hamburg, Max Brauer, President of the Hamburg Senate, that is, the highest official of this commercial city-state, was not ashamed, despite these two verdicts, and under the cloak of his state immunity, to describe the Mefo system as a swindle. I quote a few sentences from the verdict of the Supreme Administrative Court of Hamburg:

The Directorate of the Reichsbank was acting within the framework of reasonable monetary objectives when, in considering methods of providing funds in advance, they took into account the fact that to increase the volume of money would also lead to an increase in production. In conjunction with State measures for creating employment the system of Mefo bills was well adapted for this purpose. It constituted a workable foundation for the overcoming of the economic depression. By abandoning its obstinate adherence to the cover principle, for which the former management of the Reichsbank has been blamed, and by endeavoring to carry out the functions of a modern business bank by providing funds for state investments, the Reichsbank acted according to the dictates of sound judgment.

In the meantime Herr Schmitt, Federal Minister for Economic Affairs, was tackling his job with considerable zeal but was forever encountering opposition from party groups in his endeavors to maintain a common-sense economic policy in face of the party's unseemly and absurd demands. He soon tired of the struggle, the more so as he was unable to do anything to remedy the conditions which tended constantly to decrease Germany's foreign exchange receipts. Being overcome by a temporary indisposition while making a speech he seized the opportunity to request Hitler to release him from his post.

Hitler had spoken to me now and again about the foreign exchange situation. On one occasion I attended a joint discussion at his office together with von Krosigk, the Minister of Finance. He turned first to von Krosigk with the enquiry as to how one could improve the foreign exchange position. When Krosigk failed to give a definite answer Hitler turned to me:

"What would you do, Herr Schacht, if you were Minister of Economic Affairs?"

My reply came pat and plain: "I would never buy any more than I could pay for, and I would buy as much as possible from those countries who bought from me."

We separated on that day without having come to any further decision. On July 26, 1934, I received a sudden phone call summoning me to a discussion with Hitler at Bayreuth where he was staying for the Festival. There I unexpectedly met Herr von Papen who, like myself, had been suddenly summoned by telephone.

Hitler first had a talk with von Papen on the morning of July 27.

After some little while von Papen came out and told me that he had signified his willingness to go as Ambassador to Vienna.

Then I was bidden to Hitler who informed me that he had been turning over our recent conversation in his mind.

"Owing to his illness the Federal Minister, Herr Schmitt, will not return to his duties. I must find someone else for the post and would like to ask you, Herr Schacht, whether you would be prepared, in addition to your office of president of the Reichsbank, to take over the Ministry of Economic Affairs?"

Once again I saw myself confronted with a weighty decision. The lines along which the party had developed, the way their bosses interfered in every phase of government; their efforts to get as much power as possible into their own hands; their outrages against the Jews; the way they held the churches up to ridicule; all this had meanwhile become as patent to me as to the rest of the world and I condemned it as scathingly. Worse than anything had been the events connected with the Röhm *Putsch* barely four weeks previously. Where, I asked myself at the time, could one begin to curb or prevent the abuse of governmental power and party rule? There remained the one and only possibility of working from within outward, of making use of those very governmental activities in an attempt to combat the excesses of the system and direct its policy along decent lines. As Minister for Economic Affairs I should have a much greater opportunity to put these ideas into practice than was the case in my capacity as president of the Reichsbank.

I signified my acceptance in principle but there was one matter I wished to have cleared up.

"Before I take office I should like to know how you wish me to deal with the Jewish question?"

"In economic matters the Jews can carry on exactly as they have done up to now."

I took note of this answer and quoted it later whenever I had occasion to discuss the question of the oppression of the Jews with Hitler. As long as I remained head of the Ministry for Economic Affairs I protected every Jew against illegal economic injury at the hands of the party.

# XLII

## A STRONGHOLD OF JUSTICE

I took over the Ministry of Economic Affairs barely four weeks after the Röhm rebellion. At that time I was far too deeply immersed in my duties to pay particular attention to revolutionary tendencies in any special section of the party. In this way I remained unaware of all the details concerning the preparation of the plot: in fact the press reports of the actual coup took me by surprise.

On the previous evening I had expected Dr. Goebbels and his wife to dine with us. My secretary had repeatedly telephoned Goebbels' home to ask what had happened but had received no reply.

The little doctor who, through his Ministry of Propaganda, exercised such a baleful influence not only on the German people but also on Adolf Hitler was my enemy by instinct. He hated me. In his opinion economics was a necessary evil. He was certainly in no mind to allow his position as "First Intellectual" to be filched from him by the government's economist.

Since I don't like being involved in unnecessary intrigues and enmities I had invited him to dinner, but, as already mentioned, he did not come and the next morning I learned the reason for his discourtesy. In Munich and neighborhood, under Hitler's direction, a *Putsch* on the part of S.A. "higher-ups" had been suppressed and many people shot, among them several who had nothing to do with the S.A.

Looking back, we know now that at the time an action was involved in the course of which one group of interests within the party, headed by Hitler and including Goering, Heydrich, Himmler and Goebbels, rendered the other group harmless. The fact that individual satraps took advantage of the event to settle their private feuds and add them to the general account, puts a very black complexion on the whole affair.

When I learned of the first details I shuddered. During periods of consolidation following a latent civil war such happenings may be unavoidable. What frightened me was the mendaciousness and slipperiness with which the facts were distorted or hushed up.

Although several hundred people had lost their lives — among them a man in Munich, a victim of mistaken identity — Hitler, in his Reichstag speech of July 3, 1934, gave the number of those shot as only seventy-seven. Even among those seventy-seven there were names which obviously had nothing to do with the Röhm revolt.

In a history book which appeared a year later the event was summarily dismissed with the statement that Hitler, as "the Supreme Justiciary of the German People," had delivered the conspirators to their well-deserved punishment. If this statement — that Hitler was the Supreme Justiciary — was intended to include absolute power over the life and death of individual citizens without trial, it was indeed a monstrous assertion. I could not refrain from saying to Hitler when I saw him after this event:

"How could you ever take upon yourself the responsibility of determining the fate of human beings without any judicial proceedings? No matter what the circumstances you should have allowed the trials to take place, even if they had only been summary trials."

Curiously enough Hitler took it quietly, replying with a few unconvincing excuses.

I was still more indignant that a man such as Gürtner, the Minister of Justice whom I had known as a fair-minded man, should submit to the cabinet a draft bill according to which the shootings of June 30 were "lawful." These executions and murders could never have been lawful. Not a single legal prescription existed which would have supported such action. It might be possible to decree indemnity but not to define wrong as right.

These latest experiences showed me more clearly than ever the path I must follow. I must endeavor by every means, both within the cabinet and in my own department, to uphold right and justice whenever and wherever occasion offered.

I began to look about for allies — but where were they? The military had meekly accepted the fact that General Schleicher, one of their most prominent members, had been murdered. The civil ministers had pronounced the shootings of June 30 to be lawful. The political parties of the Center had jointly and severally dissolved of their own accord. Von Papen had made a courageous speech in Marburg in May 1934 in which he had openly warned his hearers against the deriding of Christian principles as practiced by Hitler's

adherents within the party; but after he too had been threatened on
June 30 he had resigned his membership of the cabinet and his post
of Vice-Chancellor and a few weeks later had been appointed Ambassador in Vienna.

Could help still come from S.D.P. circles? At the opening of the
new German Bundestag in 1948 the former Social-Democratic Minister Paul Löbe, in his capacity of Honorary President, began his
opening speech by recalling the memory of the Social Democrats'
heroic resistance during the "last session of the Reichstag" on
March 23, 1933. On that day the Social-Democratic Party did indeed
vote solidly against the Enabling Law. But Herr Löbe deliberately
misled the public when he described that session as the "last session
of the Reichstag." The last session of the Reichstag took place on
May 17, 1933, when something very curious happened.

Herr Severing, a witness at the Nuremberg Trial, and Herr Rossmann, the Social-Democratic deputy who was a witness at my denazification trial, both stated that from the very first they had recognized Hitler as a War Chancellor. The whole electoral contest for
March 5, 1933 — so Rossmann declared — had been conducted by
the Social Democrats with the watchword that Hitler's election would
mean the road to war. In May 17, 1933, those same Social Democrats
fell completely into line with Hitler. At this session Hitler obtained
a special vote of confidence on the subject of his foreign policy. In
this connection not only did the Social Democrats *not* vote against
Hitler nor did they merely abstain, they voted with all the other
Reichstag parties *in favor* of confidence in Hitler's foreign policy.
They had obviously in the meanwhile come to the conclusion that
Hitler was *not* a War Chancellor. What support could I still expect
from the Social Democrats?

And what about the Church? Had not the Catholic Church made
its peace with Hitler through the Concordat? Had not the Conference of Bishops at Fulda on August 20, 1935, wired to Hitler: "The
Bishops assembled in Fulda for the forthcoming Conference send
to the Leader and Chancellor of the German Reich their loyal and
respectful greetings which, according to Divine Command, we owe
to the holder of the state's Supreme office and authority."

The crime of Potempa, the hundredfold murders of June 30, 1934,
and all other misdeeds did not prevent the Conference of Bishops
from expressing their loyalty and respect to the instigator of these
actions.

Was the Evangelical Church any different? On July 27, 1934,

after a talk with Hitler, the Evangelical Bishops published the following declaration:

> Impressed by the great occasion when the leaders of the German Evangelical Church met together in the company of the Chancellor of the Reich, they unanimously reaffirm their unconditional loyalty to the Third Reich and to its Führer. The leaders of the Church condemn in the strongest possible terms all machinations on the part of critics of the state, the nation and the movement calculated to imperil the Third Reich.

There remained finally only Business and Science. But the leaders of the business world saw only that under the new government their anxieties concerning the employment of their factories and their workpeople had been removed. And the scientists were absorbed in their studies and their research.

By far the most hopeless from the point of view of any resistance were those men who had emigrated and who, while persisting in their convictions, were not prepared to make sacrifices on that account.

I very soon realized that I could expect little help from any third party in my fight for justice and decency. Nevertheless I did not intend to follow any other path save that of justice and decency. And I do not believe that I have ever, for one moment, strayed from that path.

On August 2, 1934, I took office as head of the Ministry of Economic Affairs. My first action was to summon the senior officials and urge them to arbitrate justly and impartially and to tolerate no party interference. I would support any official who upheld that standard. My ministry should be a tower of justice.

Again and again I was constrained to make good my word in the Reichsbank as well as in the ministry. When my Reichsbank colleague Hülse was attacked in the *Stürmer* on account of his Jewish connections I compelled Hitler to print a public withdrawal of and apology for this insult. When the manager of the Arnswalde branch of the Reichsbank was publicly pilloried for having bought goods from Jewish tradesmen, and I was unable to obtain a public apology, I closed the Arnswalde branch until, on the eleventh day, the *Gauleiter* consented to apologize in public and to vindicate the official in question. When Sperrl, the head of a department, and Schniewind, a Permanent Secretary in the Ministry of Economic Affairs, were brought before the Public Prosecutor for contravening the so-called Treason Law I threatened to resign if the two men were not released forthwith and the charge withdrawn. When a member of the Reichsbank staff, a householder, was caricatured in the press because of a rent dispute I did not rest until he had emerged from the affair with flying colors. These are only a few instances that remain in my memory.

Nor did I confine myself to the defense of my own departments: I also had recourse to attack. Immediately after my opening address at the Ministry of Economic Affairs I sent for Herr Gottfried Feder, whom Hitler had previously appointed Secretary of State in the ministry. I told him that his connection with the ministry ceased on the day I took office.

"But, sir, I am prepared to co-operate loyally with you."

"That may be, Herr Feder, but I am not."

So Herr Feder departed. He will be remembered as the inventor of the "featherweight currency"

A few days after I took over the ministry Himmler sent over his Adjutant, Kranefuss, who announced: "My chief, sir, the head of the S.S., has instructed me to inform you that he does not approve of your taking over the Federal Ministry for Economic Affairs. The S.S. leader's views on economic affairs differ completely from those which you intend to carry out. You will meet with considerable opposition and unpleasantness from the S.S. Herr Himmler therefore urges you voluntarily to relinquish your post and place your resignation in the Führer's hands, in which case Herr Himmler is prepared to leave you unmolested in your position as president of the Reichsbank."

"My dear Herr Kranefuss," I replied, "that is really most interesting. Unfortunately I am not in a position to comply with Herr Himmler's wishes since the Chancellor himself has appointed me to this office. Please tell Herr Himmler that there are two ways of removing me from my post. The first, that he induces the Chancellor to revoke my appointment. I should immediately obey such an order. The second is that he shoots me from the front, for I don't allow myself to be taken in the rear."

"I greatly regret having to deliver such a message from you to the leader of the S.S. You will most certainly incur the enmity of the S.S. thereby."

"I should naturally regret that very much, Herr Kranefuss. But even so perhaps Herr Himmler would do me a favor?"

"And what might that be?"

"I see there are always two S.S. men in uniform outside the door of my study. I take it they are the guard provided for my predecessor, Herr Schmitt, in his capacity of S.S. Group Leader. Please ask Herr Himmler to withdraw these guards."

By the following day the guard had disappeared.

A similar incident occurred about two years later. Herr Keppler, whom I have already mentioned several times, had the effrontery to tell one of my reporters that he needn't bother to follow my instructions as I should very soon be "axed" by the Führer. My reply took the form of a circular order to all my staff in which I forbade them to have any official dealings with Herr Keppler, and instructions to the porters that Herr Keppler was no longer to be admitted. Since Herr Keppler was Hitler's personal adviser on economic questions and his office adjoined that of the Führer this step was not without its dangers. Years afterwards Keppler succeeded in doing me a dirty turn in the matter of the Austrian schillings.

Then I had to cope with a bit of general unpleasantness on the part of Herr Frick, the Minister of the Interior. He sent over an order one day according to which no employee who had been a Freemason was to be promoted or appointed to any position of trust. My reply, as always, was brief and to the point. I informed Herr Frick that I was not in a position to apply this order to my subordinate staff so long as a Freemason was head of the Reichsbank. (I myself was a Freemason.) My refusal created no repercussions. Henceforth too I graded and used all Freemasons on my staff according to their qualifications and character.

Once again, on another occasion, I informed the Minister of the Interior of my fundamental attitude to the subject of staff, for I was constantly having to note how persistently the party chiefs tried to extend their mischievous influence to the activities of the staff. I wrote Frick:

> The position of an employee is untenable in a state where, on principle, no employee can get anywhere against the will of the party authorities. It is dangerous for the state to appoint persons with no special qualifications to official posts and duties, solely on the ground of their party membership. Such action tends to bring into official employment persons who, for lack of knowledge and capacity, are unable to invest such employment with any authority.

The signature which the President of the Reich affixed to the document appointing me to the office of Federal Minister for Economic Affairs was Hindenburg's last official signature. It still displays the thick heavy strokes but the second half is very shaky. On August 2 the President departed this life. On August 1 Hitler had already compelled his cabinet to pass a resolution combining in his own person the offices of Federal Chancellor and President of the Reich, a resolution which was confirmed by public election on August 19. According to the American Prosecutor in Nuremberg, that day saw the real beginning of absolute despotism.

# XLIII

## THE NEW PLAN

My two offices kept me well and truly occupied. I began the morning at the Reichsbank and changed over to the Ministry, Unter den Linden, about midday. My secretary, Fräulein Steffeck, came with me. During my three years' absence from the Reichsbank she had held a job in the Statistical Department and had waited for me to come back. Her fellow workers had sometimes chaffed her a bit but she had taken it in good part.

Her nickname "S.S." often upset her in those days since it recalled Himmler's *Schutzstaffeln*. But it had originated in something quite different. When she had accompanied me to a conference in London in 1924 a society paper had commented on the important part played by the women secretaries of the German delegation, the "Smiling Slaves," as they described them, who discharged their arduous duties with unfailing pleasantness. The initials had caught my fancy and the nickname had stuck to her.

Like myself she took a decisive and somewhat frank stand against all party encroachments. One day when I was again in London a party pundit telephoned, obviously anxious to go to London, and demanding forthwith a sum in English pounds.

"What for?" enquired Fräulein Steffeck.

"We have to fly to London with a very important communication for Dr. Schacht."

"A telegram to London costs five marks. You can pay that at a German post office in German money."

"The information is much too confidential to be telegraphed."

"Then use a code," said Steffeck imperturbably. "Send it in cipher to the German Embassy. That's even quicker and cheaper than a plane."

The "brass hat" tried again several times. But S.S. was not to be persuaded.

In my activities as Minister of Economic Affairs Hitler accorded me the same freedom and independence that I already enjoyed as president of the Reichsbank. He understood nothing whatever about economics. So long as I maintained the balance of trade and kept him supplied with foreign exchange he didn't bother about how I managed it. Until the autumn of 1936 Hitler tolerated no measures that interfered with my activities. Then, however, we had the so-called Second Four-Year Plan which very soon led to my departure from the Ministry of Economic Affairs.

A large proportion of my foreign exchange was utilized by the Minister of Agriculture, Darré, a decent-minded fellow but more of a philosopher than a practical administrator. Many of his ideas — such as the hereditary farm holding, the control of markets, the canceling of farm debts, the stability of prices, the fight against waste, and so on — were sensible and successful. What Darré could not do was to meet the demand for foodstuffs from home production. Germany was too small and insufficiently equipped by nature for such a task. A considerable part of our food requirements had perforce to be met by imports from abroad, for which I had to furnish the foreign exchange. There was a good deal of wordy warfare carried on by correspondence; on one occasion, when turning down his request for foreign exchange, I ended with the words: "I can't conjure money out of a hat!"

The world economic crisis had seriously reduced German exports. Every country, both overseas and in Europe, was trying to cut down imports, whether by increasing tariffs, limiting quotas, or import bans. The fact that Germany was in arrears with her payments of interest on foreign loans induced certain individual countries to requisition their own payments on imported German goods although the matter concerned not national but purely private monies. This too contributed to the continuous reduction in Germany's foreign exchange receipts.

I had as soon as possible to find some outlet in foreign trade which would ensure that Germany would receive raw materials and foodstuffs sufficient to meet her requirements. In September 1934 my Foreign Trade Program came into force and was henceforth known as the New Plan. This New Plan represented a centralization of trade whereby imports were compulsorily regulated according to the means of payment available. Twenty-five supervisory centers were set up entrusted with the control of all turnover in foreign trade. Foreign exchange bills payable in cash or for settlement account were allocated for sanctioned import transactions.

Unfortunately this order involved the creation of an extensive control machinery and a whole lot of officials, for which I expressed my deep regret when the order was made known but which I described as unavoidable. I expressed the hope that it might soon be possible to restore normal trading conditions. Trade agreements were concluded with several foreign countries, in the course of which German purchases in the countries concerned were credited for offset account, and these countries were urged to utilize these credits for purchases in the German markets. This system was developed especially in the Balkan and South American countries. In the spring of 1938 such offset account agreements operated in no fewer than twenty-five countries, so that more than half Germany's foreign trade was carried on through these channels. By means of this bilateral trading system Germany was able to satisfy her requirements for raw materials and foodstuffs.

This policy laid me open to vigorous attacks from abroad. It certainly was in direct contradiction to previous conceptions of multilateral trading and to the most-favored-nation treatment. Scientists in every country stigmatized this system as a repudiation of every well-known economic theory. What mattered to me however was not the classical tradition of my economic theory but that the German people should be provided with the necessities of life. Today when the whole world thinks and acts in terms of bilateral treaties the reader will scarcely be able to imagine the turmoil created by Germany's trade policy in the thirties.

By destroying the conception of private ownership, by levying a war tribute which was economically intolerable, by discriminating against Germany's political economy in countless ways all over the world, by denying to German businessmen freedom to travel and live abroad, the dictated peace had shattered the very foundations on which traditional economic doctrine had been built up. I experienced great satisfaction when, at the opening of the Economic Conference of the British Commonwealth on October 4, 1946 — a few days after my acquittal at Nuremberg — Sir Stafford Cripps, president of the British Board of Trade, declared: "Schacht will take no part in any of the discussions arising at this conference. But Schacht's spirit will be present with us all. The question arises whether world trade, and particularly that of Great Britain, can be increased to the necessary extent without putting some of Schacht's ideas into practice."

In 1936 National-Socialist Germany was at the height of her international prestige. All limitations imposed by Versailles had been done away with. In spite of all difficulties Germany now had a balanced economy. The Olympic Games, which were held that year in Berlin, attracted an immense number of foreign visitors and were the occasion of an uninterrupted sequence of brilliant festivities, arranged not only with unusual splendor but with excellent taste and consummate organization. One had to hand it to Dr. Goebbels that in this instance he knew his job. No matter whether it was a question of big events in the actual stadiums, whether those taking part were invited to attend a theatrical performance, or whether plans had been made for excursions or sightseeing, everything bore the stamp of unusual though never obtrusive brilliance. Besides the sporting events, the highlight of the whole affair was the open-air evening fête on Peacock Island, situated in the river Havel between Wannsee and Potsdam. The Island was linked with the riverbank by a bridge of boats. As the guests stepped onto the bridge they were greeted on either side by girls dressed as pages, all in white and wearing knee breeches. The great park belonging to the island castle was illuminated and countless little tables had been set up with room for more than a thousand guests served by white-clad pages. Specially selected music and a truly fantastic firework display constituted the entertainment. By way of memento each guest received an artistic gift from the Berlin Porcelain Factory.

Hitler's public appearances during these days were likewise exemplary. What speeches there were, were moderate, pacific and friendly toward other nations.

The New Plan worked satisfactorily not only for Germany; all those countries with whom bilateral agreements had been concluded experienced business revivals inasmuch as they found in Germany an increased market for their goods. This was especially the case with farm produce and raw materials from the Balkans, which led to improved conditions in those countries.

In 1936, in order to consolidate the reciprocal trade position, I made a trip to the Balkans.

The thing that impressed me most during this trip was the far-reaching cultural influence on the Balkans of German character and customs. Just as in 1930 I had seen how, in Rumania, all the educated classes understood German, so in Yugoslavia the Croat section of the population continued to manifest its old tendency to turn to Vienna in all matters of language, art, literature and science.

In Belgrade the German Ambassador, von Heeren, invited the Minister and principal business representatives to an evening reception at which I explained the new German trade policy. I stressed the fact that it was not Germany's purpose to tie countries such as Yugoslavia permanently down to the level of an agrarian state. It would be quite wrong for the industrial states to set themselves against the gradual industrialization of the agrarian countries. The need of the agrarian states to develop on industrial lines was entirely natural and entirely comprehensible. Of course they would have to make a start with the technically simpler industries such as iron foundries and tinworks — not with automobile and watch and clock factories. Such development would not be detrimental to the industrial states: only the nature of the agrarian exports would gradually change. The higher the standard of living in the agrarian states owing to industrial development the greater and more important would be their requirements; their increased purchasing power would benefit the industrial countries.

It gave me real pleasure to see the enthusiasm with which this speech was received by the audience, which included the Prime Minister.

In the late autumn of that year I undertook a second trip, this time to Ankara and Teheran. This second journey, similar in essence to the previous one, turned out to be a particularly interesting experience, for it took me to two countries which were finding their way to democracy via dictatorship.

Kemal Atatürk, the Head of the State, was unable to see me immediately on my arrival in Ankara as he was in bed with influenza. The two following days were taken up with economic discussions and social events. On the second evening the Ministry of Foreign Affairs gave a dinner at which ladies were present. The Prime Minister, Mr. Inönü, came for an hour or two, and there was much eating, drinking and conversation. It was already late when the talk turned to the subject of national dances and a high official of the Turkish Government took the floor in the center of the hall and gave us a solo performance of those (to us) strange Eastern dances which consist solely of a succession of rhythmic poses. They told me that this was one of the Turkish national dances and asked me for one from Germany. I instanced the waltz but they would have none of it, for the waltz had long since become international. On the spur of the moment I asked the orchestra to play a Tyrolienne, and with one of the German ladies as my partner, I gave them a few turns of this

Tyrolese dance, which was accepted as a German example amid
great enthusiasm.

On the third and last day of our visit the President received me at
his Palace in spite of his influenza, of which he still showed distinct
traces. I was rather uneasy about this visit for a very mundane
reason. I had been told that Atatürk was much addicted to strong
drink and liked to offer it to his guests. Since my student days, however, I had all but given up alcoholic liquor. I hardly ever drink and
avoid strong drink whenever possible, for I find it difficult to keep a
clear head when taking liquor and it was essential that I should do
so on this occasion. So I was glad when coffee and cakes were handed
round to start with. This, however, was followed by a somewhat
milky-looking liquid in rather large glasses, in appearance exactly
like the well-known arrack.

There are times when the sudden materialization of something one
dislikes and fears has a curious effect. Anyway I was irritated but
determined to hold my own. Summoning my courage I seized the
glass, tasted and drank — a delicious lemonade for which I obviously
had to thank my host's influenza. My inner equilibrium was restored.

The interview was a lengthy one on the economic problems confronting Germany and Turkey, during which I gained the impression
that here was a dictator who fully recognized his limitations and
refused to entertain any unpractical or utopian proposals. Instead of
pursuing the idea of a Khalifate he had concentrated all his efforts
on the solution of the minor Turkish and purely Turkish problem,
and had achieved it.

Next morning my pilot, von Gössel, flew us to Adana through the
narrow gorges of the Taurus. After an intermediate landing at Aleppo
we continued nonstop via Palmyra to Baghdad and on to Teheran.

The Shah of Persia was not in Teheran at the time but was making
a tour of inspection in the North. As he had expressed a wish to see
me we drove to Resht.

Reza Shah had ruled Persia since 1925. His family belonged to the
lesser nobility and he himself had been a colonel in the Russian Army
when he deposed the last member of the Qajar Dynasty and seized
the throne. He tried to infuse the Fascist spirit into the Persian people and to found organizations for that purpose. We were treated to
examples of these in the shape of parades of boys and girls in
uniform.

Reza Shah must have achieved and maintained power by means

of extreme ruthlessness, for his ministers betrayed an almost physical terror before the Audience. A few months after my visit the Minister of Finance, with whom I had become particularly friendly, fell into disfavor and, as a result, took his own life.

The Foreign Minister reminded our Ambassador: "You know, of course, and I hope Herr Schacht knows too — one bow outside the door, one in the doorway and one inside the door."

Our Ambassador reassured him: "Don't worry — this isn't the first potentate to whom Herr Schacht has paid a visit."

The Shah came forward to meet me with outstretched hand and left me no time for bows. Within a very few minutes we had found a point of contact. The conversation proceeded in French, translated by the Foreign Minister, and turned chiefly on the economic situation of the country. The eighteen-year-old Crown Prince, just returned from boarding school in Switzerland, was present at the interview; but in reply to my question — in German — as to whether he had learned German there, he achieved only a distinct "No." As I took my leave the Shah raised his hand in the Fascist salute. Once again the three bows — inside the room, in the doorway and outside the door — never came off.

Late that same afternoon we drove eastward along the Caspian Sea to a hotel at Ramshar belonging to the Shah and managed in masterly fashion by a Swiss. The Shah's idea was to create a fashionable spa and watering place which should be the center of a Caspian Riviera. And indeed there already existed possibilities for such a center which should be to the whole of the Middle East what Nice is to the French Riviera. Climate and scenery have a beauty all their own. Systematic and vigorous steps, however, would have to be taken to counteract the plague of mosquitoes and I had already, in response to his request, given the Shah some important hints on this point.

For the present the Second World War has put an end to these plans for a Middle East Riviera. Our morning baths in the Caspian Sea provided us with a foretaste of what might be achieved.

At that time however the eighteen-year-old Crown Prince, who had replied in the negative to my enquiry as to his knowledge of German, did not know that, as his father's successor on the Peacock Throne, he would marry a Persian Princess who had spent her childhood in Berlin and was the daughter of a German mother. When I visited Teheran in 1952 I was able to ascertain that the Queen spoke German as fluently as my wife and myself.

# XLIV

## MAINLY ABOUT PICTURES

IN MATTERS of art, Hitler laid claim to infallible judgment, which may have been traceable to his original intention of becoming either a painter or an architect. His taste inclined more to the subject of the picture than to sound craftsmanship. He took a lasting interest in the House of German Art in Munich, which he had built to replace the Glass Palace, destroyed by fire. My present wife, who for five years was First Assistant at the House of German Art, was more frequently able to discern signs of this interest than was possible for his expert Ministers.

Hitler's scant knowledge of the history of art was clearly demonstrated with reference to a picture which he sent me on my sixtieth birthday. The gift was a painting by Spitzweg entitled "Only Thoughts are Duty-Free" featuring a stagecoach drawn up at a frontier customs house, with passengers and customs officials bustling around. It was framed in gold and fastened to the frame was a small plate with Hitler's signature by way of greeting.

No sooner had I taken one look at the picture, gleaming and smooth under the varnish, than I said to my wife: "That painting is quite definitely not genuine."

I knew, from having seen a good many examples of Spitzweg's work, that in the course of years tiny cracks, no larger than a hair, appeared on the canvas. Hitler's gift showed none of these tiny cracks — it was smooth as satin.

I learned that Heinrich Hoffmann had obtained the picture for Hitler. Hoffmann was Hitler's personal and official photographer.

The first thing I did was to have it confirmed by connoisseurs that the picture was undoubtedly a forgery. Then Herr Zinckgraf, a distinguished art dealer in Munich, helped me to trace the owner of the original. I went to see him and established various surprising facts. The original, which I now beheld, was painted on canvas, the forgery was on wood. Later I was able to obtain incontestable proof that the wood in question was an exotic variety which had never been imported into Germany prior to 1900, whereas the picture dated from the 1870's. Then, too, the dimensions of the forgery were entirely different from those of the original.

In our opinion, however, the most curious feature was that the colors in the original painting were in no way similar to the colors in the forgery. Then, with the aid of my adviser in Munich, we were able to ascertain that many years previously the firm of Hanfstaengl had published art prints of Spitzweg's pictures, including the one in my possession. But they had not been able to trace the original of my picture and had depended on a black-and-white reproduction, which the artist entrusted with the work had deliberately colored unbeknown to the publishers. When Hanfstaengl's learned of it they immediately withdrew the reproduction from circulation. A specimen print with the incorrect colors must, however, have been preserved somewhere or other, for my forgery had been executed from it.

So there we were, dealing with the forgery of a forgery. The remarkable feature of the whole thing was that it led one to not very flattering conclusions as to the knowledge of art displayed by Adolf Hitler and his adviser and agent, Hoffmann.

In the meantime I had not been able to resist telling Hitler that his present was a forgery. Hitler was considerably upset and made me return the picture, but I received the frame back with Hitler's signature. After a few months Hitler informed me that the picture was, after all, genuine: he had obtained a written expert opinion to that effect. I asked him to send me the certificate but I never received it.

The whole affair would probably have died a natural death if a forgery case had not been launched in which no fewer than forty-three Spitzweg forgeries were involved, including my picture. The trial revealed that a little copyist had executed the picture in all good faith to the order of some profiteer, and that two Munich painters had added a forgery of Spitzweg's signature. It also transpired during the proceedings that the certificate mentioned by Hitler was the work of one of the two forgers and had been obtained from him by Herr Hoffmann.

Herr Hoffmann informed me in a letter that Hitler intended to send me another picture to replace the first one. I never received it. Amusingly enough, Herr Hoffmann added that he had made nothing on the deal. As a matter of fact I never supposed he had. I stuck his letter in Hitler's gold frame and hung it in my room instead of the Spitzweg.

Yet another still funnier picture story. When Field Marshal von Blomberg celebrated his fortieth year in the Army I read in the paper that the National Socialist Party had presented him with an oil portrait of Blücher to mark the occasion.

A few days later some Freemason friends sent me three photographs. An accompanying letter contained the information that the presentation work was a contemporary copy of a Blücher portrait, the original of which had been in the possession of the "Three Rafters" Lodge at Münster, Westphalia.

In this picture "Marshal Vorwärts" was represented as Master of the Münster Lodge. Behind an altar table, on which was an open Bible surmounted by a sword, stood the figure of Blücher in full Masonic regalia, apron round the waist, blue ribbon with carpenter's rule around neck and chest, hand outstretched, grasping the Master's hammer, the hammer itself resting on the table; next to it the circle and other Masonic emblems.

The antique dealer who had obtained this copy had probably realized that, in its present guise, the picture was unsalable. So he had simply had the Masonic accessories painted out. Apron, ribbon, hammer, had disappeared. The one disturbing feature was that the worthy Blücher now pointed his finger downward at the empty air, for which there seemed no real justification.

While the first photograph showed the picture in its original form, the second reproduced it in the condition described above. But oh dear! there was the circle still on the table, which might look suspicious. The Bible need not be interfered with — it might be taken for any other book; and the sword resting across it actually gave the picture a desired military touch. But the circle must come out! So that too was painted over and now — as the third photograph showed — the painting was void of offense, and salable.

I thought it would amuse Blomberg to see how his picture had been transmogrified, so I sent him the whole story including the photos. But Blomberg obviously took it dead seriously. He handed the lot over to Rudolf Hess, the Führer's deputy, who had made the presentation. The reply was a two-page letter from Hess to Blomberg which said in part:

The fact that this picture was originally in the possession of Freemasons, and the original Masonic insignia have been painted over, is as great a surprise to me as it is to you . . . It is obvious that the gift cannot be said to have any symbolic connection with the attitude of the Wehrmacht or the party toward Freemasonry.

The fact that Blücher was a Freemason is equally without significance, since at that time, so far as we know, Freemasonry pursued no objectives that might be dangerous to our nation, nor in all probability had it become involved in international alliances to the extent that prevails today . . .

I must confess that it gives me even greater pleasure than it did hitherto, to know that the portrait of the great Prussian military leader is no longer in the hands of Freemasons, but with the Wehrmacht where it belongs. And I am especially delighted that the N.S.D.A.P. was the means — albeit unconsciously — of removing it from the possession of one who was obviously putting it to wrongful use, and transferring it to its most worthy owner.

There is, however, another side to the question — namely, how did the N.S.D.A.P. come to pay a price for this picture commensurate with the value of an old, historical work, whereas it should have been taken from its original owner — the Lodge — without compensation. I have ordered an enquiry into the matter. It is possible that when the Lodge was dissolved those concerned sold the contents for the benefit of public objects. Should anyone have made a profit on such a deal, I shall see to it that he is punished and that the purchase price is handed over to the Winter Distress Fund.

I should be grateful if you would ensure that these statements of mine are made known to all those who have written or will be writing to you on this subject — particularly former Freemasons.

But even Rudolf Hess could not do away with the fact that Blücher, the hero of Prussian history and the most determined opponent of Napoleon's dictatorship, should have been a "damned Freemason."

Whether Hitler knew more about music than he did about the other arts I never discovered, as I myself am not musically well informed. I have never known Hitler to be a Bach or Beethoven "fan," whereas I should say that he had probably heard Wagner's *Meistersinger* a hundred times. During a dinner, at which I sat next to Funk, the Minister for Economic Affairs, the orchestra played a melody of Franz Lehár. Funk remarked:

"The Führer is particularly fond of Lehár's music."

Coming as it did from Funk who was himself extraordinarily musical this remark did not seem to me to point to a very exalted taste in music on Hitler's part. I took advantage of the occasion and said jokingly:

"It's a pity that Lehár is married to a Jewess." To which Funk immediately replied:

"That's something the Führer mustn't know on any account."

"On the contrary, Herr Funk, you must tell the Führer."

"No, no, it's quite out of the question."

"But, Herr Funk, whatever happens you must tell the Führer, otherwise he'll develop an entirely wrong artistic taste."

# XLV

## AT ODDS WITH THE PARTY

FROM THE VERY BEGINNING I was on bad terms with the party. Prior to working with the Hitler Government I had met only very few party members. I studiously avoided social gatherings of the party and attended official assemblies only when unable to get out of doing so. When I occasionally came across an honest, decent character among party members I was glad to cultivate his acquaintance. Unfortunately these responsible and industrious elements were much less conspicuous than the braggarts, bullies and profiteers whom I often irritated with my sarcastic remarks, though without achieving much; a large percentage among them being quite unequal to the intellectual demands of their official positions.

My refusal to be daunted and my blunt speech were certainly effective against open interference and demands by party officials, but I was not always able to counter the intrigues engineered behind my back. It is true that Hitler backed me up vis-à-vis his adherents, but always in such a way as to suggest that they must put up with me, never in a manner which insisted that they should co-operate.

In the spring of 1937 I took the opportunity of attending a ceremony of the Berlin Chamber of Handicrafts at which a large number of apprentices were to be promoted to journeymen. Thanks to successful scheming on the part of Dr. Ley, leader of the Workers' Front, Hitler issued an order on the previous evening banning the event at which I was going to speak. Next morning I had to threaten Hitler with my resignation to ensure that the ceremony took place. News of Ley's plot had spread abroad and the great hall was packed with thousands of people.

I took advantage of my speech to state some arguments against the "philosophy" with which the party menaced our young people. Among other things I said:

"No community, and above all no state, can prosper which is not founded on lawfulness, order and discipline. No order can exist where injustice rules. There is an old Latin proverb which says: *Justitia fundamentum regnorum* (Justice is the foundation of kingdoms). The Bible expresses it in the words: Righteousness exalteth a nation. Righteousness, justice is also the most implacable enemy of all class differences. Therefore you must not only respect justice and law, but you must also stand out against injustice and lawlessness wherever you find them. Be upright and honest and do not be afraid of truth. Another wonderful line says: Strive for the truth unto death, and the Lord shall fight for thee (Ecclesiasticus, 4:28). That means, he who stands up for justice, decency and truth will feel himself imbued with Divine strength."

I never missed a single chance of protecting all inside and outside officials under my jurisdiction. If a president of a Chamber of Commerce, or a *Syndikus*, were attacked by the party he could rest assured that I should retain him in his post. If state banks and other financial institutions under my control were threatened by the party it was a foregone conclusion that the party would come off worst. I saw to it that numerous Freemasons either remained in employment or were appointed to various positions. The greatest problem was the Jewish question, of which I shall have more to say.

In a speech at the Stewards' Dinner at Bremen on February 14, 1936, I voiced some sarcastic remarks about the disruptive methods by which the party sought to reshape the world. I bade them take comfort in the thought that a philosophy which fails to conquer the world in the space of three years may even yet be worth something, adding that one should not label every man a scoundrel who, in the space of those three years, has not adopted this new philosophy. Having regard to Germany's thousand years of past history, I spoke in praise of the power of tradition:

"It gives me particular pleasure to see youth paying respect to age, as is happening at this banquet. I say this, not entirely without regard to the present day, when it sometimes appears as though the young were bringing up their elders, instead of the other way about."

The result of this speech was that Himmler, who was present, immediately issued an order banning its reproduction in the newspapers. To contradict me by word of mouth on the spur of the moment was something he did not dare attempt.

Not all the hostility of the party, however, could prevent me from continuing my efforts to lead Hitler in the way he should go. On May 3, 1935, I took part in the trial trip of the Norddeutscher Lloyd vessel *Scharnhorst*, with Hitler and a whole crowd of Ministers and others of his entourage on board. Knowing that I should meet Hitler I had prepared a brief memorandum on questions of special importance to me, and I handed it to him in person. I had, of course, worded the memorandum to suit his mentality. If I wanted to achieve results with him I had to start out as much as possible on his own level.

Hitler read through my document and at once sent for me to explain that there was no need to take my complaints so tragically — everything would turn out all right as matters developed.

This memorandum of May 3, 1935, said in part:

## 1. The Church

Officially the Third Reich takes its stand on Christianity, for which reason the churches are financially supported by the state. Further, one should recognize the government's desire to unite the churches of Germany as much as possible on national German lines. So far no legislative steps have been taken to achieve this end, but a Reichsbischof (State Bishop) has been appointed who has recourse to measures outside the law which serve only to provoke resistance on the part of the leaders of the various religious denominations. Clergymen are arrested, treated like jailbirds, with consequent detriment both to their prestige and their health, and all without the slightest legal foundation. Overzealous partisans are allowed to insult and injure members of the most varying denominations without the state according them the protection which it is in duty bound to extend. These conditions have aroused the strongest indignation, particularly in Anglo-Saxon and Scandinavian countries, and also, in so far as Catholic susceptibilities have been wounded, in the countries concerned; they have engendered a far-reaching resentment against Germany which in many cases has expressed itself in a refusal to have any business dealings with our country.

## 2. The Jewish Question

. . . What has revived and intensified the Jewish question is, once again, the unbridled antagonism vented upon individual Jews, not merely illegally but against the explicit government decree which guarantees to the Jew the opportunity of engaging in business. The agonizing persecution of Jewish individuals under the direction or with the connivance of party groups, and the failure of state machinery to take any effective countermeasures causes an ever repeated tightening of the Jewish boycott of German exports; for each incident, even the smallest, is magnified and spread abroad . . .

### 3. The Gestapo

No serious politician would wish to do away with the work of the Gestapo as a defense against Communism and other forces hostile to the state. The Gestapo's activities, however, extend far beyond this scope: numerous arrests, transfers to concentration camps, etc., occur often without the person concerned even knowing why he has been arrested; and often, unfortunately, where there is absolutely no question of guilt, but only of the merest suspicion. It is true that the Minister for Internal Affairs issues orders according to which such arrests are not allowed, but he only succeeds in exposing himself to ridicule, for the Gestapo pays no heed to such orders. Seven hundred years ago Magna Charta guaranteed individual freedom to the English citizen, and three hundred years ago the Habeas Corpus Act decreed that no English citizen might be arrested without being informed of the charge against him and without the right of recourse to legal proceedings. Since then the right to individual freedom and the claim to proper judicial hearing is reckoned the highest possession of civilized man. By contrast, the behavior of the Gestapo earns us the contempt of the whole world, and this contempt can develop into active enmity if — as has already happened — the arm of the Gestapo is extended, in defiance of International Law, against other countries.

I don't think anyone else in Hitler's entourage ever pointed out to him so plainly the errors and blunders of his system. And this occurred as early as 1935; that is, two years after his rise to power.

His vague expressions of reassurance after going through my memorandum did not satisfy me. I went a step further, and at the opening of the *Ostmesse* — the Eastern Fair — at Königsberg, East Prussia, on August 18, 1935, I made a speech which attracted the widest notice under the title of "The Königsberg Speech."

I was fully alive to the fact that with the enmity of the party I was exposed to the utmost personal danger. The American Ambassador, Mr. Dodd, has recorded in his *Memoirs* that I entered his room one day with the words: "I'm still alive."

That same ambassador came to see me in December 1937, immediately prior to his departure for New York, and begged me, with all the urgency at his command, to go with him to America. When I asked him, somewhat astonished, how he came by such a notion, he replied: "Dr. Schacht, I know for certain that the S.S. has orders to make away with you."

"Mr. Dodd," I returned, "I am most grateful to you for your concern about me; but I can't bring myself to emigrate. I shall do my best to protect myself against the S.S. If I don't succeed — well — I shall die — that's all."

# XLVI

## THE KÖNIGSBERG SPEECH

My first *public* criticism of the party's policy occurred at the opening of the Fair at Königsberg. To all appearances the speech started innocently enough. The occasion was the so-called *Ostmesse* in Königsberg at which several other neighboring countries, notably from eastern Europe, were represented. It was the custom to open this fair with a speech by a member of the Ministry for Economic Affairs. This time I decided to go myself, but told no one what I intended to say, although every word of the speech had been most carefully prepared beforehand. Since nearly all my speeches were printed in the Reichsbank's own printing works, I already had a printed copy ready for Königsberg.

It was no surprise to me that the opening speech should be picked up and broadcast by the German radio. That was the rule at such events. No one expected anything sensational.

I spoke clearly and distinctly, and had already begun to express disapproval of the party's attacks on Freemasons and Jews when Chief Group Leader Bach-Zelewski and two companions in full uniform arose from their seats in the audience and clattered toward the exit. I glanced up and was just about to say "Corridor, please, second door on the right" when I remembered I was speaking into the microphone. So I held my peace while the gentlemen walked out, and finished my speech without any alteration. As I left the platform to return to my seat my neighbor, *Gauleiter* Erich Koch, remarked:

"Brother, brother, you've a hard road ahead of you." (*Mönchlein, Mönchlein, du gehst einen schweren Gang.*)

I shrugged my shoulders and consoled myself with the thought that with Martin Luther I was in good company. But at the same moment I realized that from now on I was identified as an open adversary of the party.

Immediately after the opening ceremony I dictated a letter to Himmler, National Head of the S.S., protesting in the strongest possible terms against the behavior of his chief group leader in the presence of an officiating Minister of the Reich, and demanding that he be dismissed. Many weeks later I had the satisfaction of knowing that Herr Bach-Zelewski, though not actually punished, had been transferred to Silesia.

Goebbels now appeared on the scene, the contents of my speech having, of course, been promptly communicated to him. Its dissemination by radio was a *fait accompli*, but it was still possible to prevent its reproduction in the newspapers. My speech appeared in the press, with all the offensive passages left out.

I was in no mind to accept this mutilated version and had ten thousand copies printed by the Reichsbank and displayed on the counters of all our branches throughout the country. The demand was amazing. One edition after another had to be printed — each consisting of ten thousand copies — and found its way among the public, eventually reaching a total of two hundred and fifty thousand.

Almost every foreign newspaper noticed the speech. The London *Economist* wrote: "No one can doubt Dr. Schacht's courage . . . The arrows aimed at him by the Nazi Party leaders flew unpleasantly near their target. The Königsberg speech last Sunday represented his flaming counterattack on the party."

And the Danish poet Kaj Munk wrote: " 'Give us a law for the Jewish element in our nation' was Schacht's cry in our time all over Germany, a direct challenge to Goebbels. Schacht or Goebbels, the choice lies between these two. Who and what Hitler is depends on this choice."

As everyone knows, von Papen's Marburg speech had led directly to his temporary arrest during the Röhm *Putsch* in 1934, though he had nothing whatever to do with it. I wondered what personal consequences would be in store for me from my Königsberg speech. I had attacked party ideas and individuals. Would they take it lying down?

With an eye to the economic policy represented by the *Völkischer Beobachter*, the authoritative party organ, I had criticized its lack of appreciation of the difficulties of our financial problems:

"What financial and economic efforts are required for the performance of this task — that is something of which these unthinking amateurs have not the faintest conception. A big newspaper, for instance, mentions the new intention to give technical science priority over business, and according to which business is to be compelled to keep pace with the development of technical science, even to the extent of becoming breathless in the attempt. The author appears to assume that asthma is a particular incentive to increased production. What heart would not be thrilled on reading sentences such as: 'The flag is more than a bank account' or 'The nation, not the national economy, is of primary importance.' Such sentences are disarmingly correct, but what use are they to the economist in his practical work? When I recently drew attention to the fact that German economy must be kept free of embarrassment I read that the question as to whether a measure was calculated to embarrass the national economy was a sign of liberalism. My suggestion that to render our nation capable of self-defense presupposed the concentration of all — and I mean all — our economic and financial efforts, was dismissed with the remark that nowadays only old grannies got the jitters and asked, who was going to pay for all that? At the risk of being labeled an old granny I wish to state with all possible emphasis that the question of how materially to carry out the task entrusted to us causes me considerable anxiety. To gloss over the gravity of Germany's task with a few cheap phrases is not merely senseless, it's damned dangerous."

In the realm of foreign politics also I uttered serious warnings to the party chauvinists:

"We would emphasize that self-respect demands respect for others, that to maintain one's own manners and customs does not imply contempt for the manners and customs of others; that to appreciate other people's accomplishments only serves to enhance our own, and that the only way to victory in economic competition is by first-rate production, not by recourse to violence or cunning."

Curiously enough there was no official party reaction to my Königsberg speech. No attempt was made to prevent the distribution of the two hundred and fifty thousand printed copies; no refutatory articles were published anywhere.

About a week after Königsberg I had to see Hitler on another matter. He studiously avoided any critical remark on my speech from which he quoted only one sentence: "Herr Schacht, you were quite right when you said at Königsberg that we were 'all in the same boat.'"

This strengthened my conviction that I should continue my propaganda in favor of a moderate and decent policy, and I got Hitler to give me a chance of speaking about our financial and foreign-exchange situation to the highest party officials at the forthcoming party Assembly. I hoped for some of the effect that I had achieved with several speeches in the presence of military visitors to the Military Academy, in which I had emphatically stated that there was a natural limit to German armament imposed by the restricted economic possibilities to which Germany was subjected.

On September 17, 1935, according to my agreement with Hitler, I spoke on this subject at the Nuremberg Party Convention in the presence of all *Gauleiter, Reichsleiter,* and other top-ranking party officials. I pointed out that financial assistance to the Reich by the Reichsbank must decrease and that further armaments must be financed out of taxes or loans. In the matter of raw materials I emphasized that eighty-three per cent of our foreign trade was achieved by means of barter, that is, goods against goods, and that we received free foreign exchange for only seventeen per cent of our exports. This percentage I designated as totally inadequate. I pointed out that other countries had already provided us with goods in advance to the value of five hundred million marks which it remained for us to repay in manufactured exports. Finally I demonstrated once again the damage done to our export trade by party excesses.

"The resumption of violent methods in our cultural and racial conflict has caused widespread and definite deterioration of the atmosphere abroad during recent months. It is not merely a question of the Jews, who control a great part of the international trade in raw materials; it applies also to those who draw conclusions detrimental to the government as a result of our differences with Protestants, Catholics, Jews and Freemasons."

And I ended with the words: "It is therefore of vital importance that the methods employed in the racial and cultural conflict shall be put on a legal basis and brought into harmony with political and economic requirements."

When I had finished, Hitler asked me to leave him alone with his party henchmen. What his comments were on the subject of my speech I am unable to say. At any rate I gathered, from one or two statements that were made to me, that he had issued strict orders to those present that they were not to attack me. Later I assumed that this injunction represented to him nothing more than a strategic opportunistic move.

Still, I was glad to have had this chance of expressing my views direct to topmost party officials. I had come to Nuremberg expressly for this purpose for one day only, and took no part in any of the other functions of the Convention.

# XLVII

## THE JEWISH QUESTION AND THE
## CHURCH QUESTION

Prior to 1930 there was scarcely any sign of an anti-Semitic political movement in Germany. Inasmuch as it did exist to a very small extent, it could be attributed to economic motives rather than racial enmity among the lower middle class. Mixed marriages were frequent. In good middle-class society the Jew was a welcome guest.

The fact that Hitler made use of anti-Semitism for propaganda purposes can be traced back to his Vienna period. In Germany he was helped by the fact that, at the time of the Weimar Republic, an unusually large number of eastern Jews from Poland, Rumania and Russia poured into Germany, consisting to a great extent of suspicious or even desperate elements. They took advantage of the disturbed political conditions, not only to profit by inflation, but to play a particularly active part in the corrupting of officials who put them in the way of a good deal of black-market business. Nevertheless anti-Semitism never became popular with the masses of the German people even in Hitler's time. Every action launched by the party against the Jews had perforce to be carried out by specially detailed party members. The great mass of the population took no part in these excesses.

In the field of business, when the party proceeded against individual Jews I intervened in every case that was brought to my notice and successfully stood up for the Jews so long as I held the post of Minister for Economic Affairs. In November 1935 I issued a ministerial communication to the head of the National Chamber of Industry which was passed on to all affiliated organizations:

On October 14 I requested you to inform industrial groups that, pending the forthcoming re-assessment of the position of the Jews in industrial life, no steps are to be taken by affiliated organizations against Jewish firms. Your communication, as well as other incidents, impel me to instruct the National Chamber of Industry to see to it that all industrial authorities, whether of regional or special character, are to refrain from any measures which conflict with the laws at present in force, or which seek to anticipate constitutional regulations which are the express prerogative of the government. This applies particularly to the question of the participation of Jews in the domain of industry. Individual action in this connection has been repeatedly forbidden by the government and the leaders of the N.S.D.A.P., and I myself will not tolerate it. This applies particularly to measures which seek to restrict the scope of free industrial enterprise enjoyed by business undertakings on the ground of some special characteristic or other, or member of some organization, thereby causing a change in the conditions of industrial competition.

I would request you to ensure that any contravention in this direction is reported to me immediately.

Even if I did not succeed in maintaining the Jewish brokers in their Stock Exchange employment the right of attendance at the Berlin Bourse remained available to Jews throughout my term of office. I also managed to carry my point and ensure that, up to 1937 inclusive, the prospectuses for government loans offered for public subscription among the many other Banks, should also be underwritten by the Jewish banking firms of Mendelssohn, Bleichröder, Arnhold, Dreyfuss, Straus, Warburg, Aufhäuser and Behrens. These announcements appeared in all the big newspapers.

My attitude brought me into conflict with a whole crowd of *Gauleiter*. As an example of the mentality of these people, here is a letter which I received from Gauleiter Mutschmann when I acted on behalf of a Jewish firm in Chemnitz which was being harried and pestered by the Party.

I acknowledge receipt of your communication of November 30, 1936, and am very surprised at the attitude adopted by you in regard to the non-Ayran firm of Königsfeld & Co. in Chemnitz. This attitude is contrary to the National Socialist outlook and in my opinion amounts to a sabotaging of the Führer's instructions.

I would ask you, therefore, not to effect any change in the present situation, as I should otherwise be compelled to resort to countermeasures which might not be altogether pleasant. I shall also take the opportunity to make your attitude to this case very clear to the Führer. Anyway I do not intend to inform the authorities under my control of your instructions. On the contrary I am of the opinion that your attitude shows you to be completely the wrong man in the wrong place.

The tone of this letter is not exactly well bred. It ranges from the forthright "is contrary to the National Socialist outlook," which in Mutschmann's eyes is sufficient to deprive my intervention of any moral justification, to "countermeasures which might not be altogether pleasant"; that is, to a blunt threat of violence. The letter ends in a characteristically vulgar manner.

It was the more amusing that, when I went to Chemnitz to settle the case, Herr Gauleiter Mutschmann preferred not to be present.

Another instance may serve to illustrate the legal confusion created by the party in internal administration. The authorities of the district of Giessen canceled the trade permit of a Jewish business. To my instructions not to obstruct the firm I received a reply from Gauleiter Sprenger, no less churlish than that of his colleage Mutschmann. In collaboration with Frick, the Minister for Internal Affairs, I succeeded in inducing even the Secret Police to carry out my instructions, whereupon Gauleiter Sprenger retorted by setting up his own police force in opposition to the Secret Police.

In order to arrive at a thoroughly clear understanding with the party in view of the increasing number of actions against Jewish firms, I invited those Ministers interested in the subject, as well as the party, to a discussion. This took place in the great council chamber of the Ministry for Economic Affairs in the presence of several government Ministers and of Gauleiter Adolf Wagner (Munich) representing the party, together with many other representatives of the party and of official departments. The place was packed to capacity. I was only reminded of the details of this session when one of my staff described it under oath at my Ludwigsburg trial, in the following terms:

"In the course of his persistent and exceedingly contentious statements Dr. Schacht repeatedly used the expression 'barbarous' with reference to the party, so much so that Herr Frick, the Minister for Home Affairs, protested against Dr. Schacht's overtrenchant method of speech. The session had lasted nearly two hours; Dr. Schacht's attitude had been so aggressive that — apart from a few cautious provisos on the part of Frick — no one was bold enough to voice an actual contradiction. It finally led to an incident of which I still retain a particularly vivid recollection and which once again shed a glaring light on Dr. Schacht's attitude to the party. One of the younger officials, who introduced himself as representing the Ministry of Propaganda, undertook to challenge Dr. Schacht direct. He led up to a case in which Schacht had publicly defended one of his staff who had been attacked by a party newspaper because his wife had dealt with Jewish tradesmen. He described Dr. Schacht's method of procedure as uncalled for. Any differences of opinion on the Jewish question between the government and the party should be straightened out among themselves instead of being dragged before the public in this fashion. Dr. Schacht had let him have his say, and then had gone for him tooth and nail. He, Schacht, had publicly intervened on behalf of one of his subordinates who had been publicly attacked by the party, and he would continue to do so in future. He would protect his employees against the party. The party's action in the above-mentioned case was — to quote his own words — blackguardly, barbarous, infamous. Each vehemently uttered word re-echoed through the council chamber where deathly silence reigned."

A Jewish friend who had been baptized once told me that anti-Semitism was based on the fact that Christians could not forget that the Jews had crucified the Saviour. This view seemed to me extremely naïve. No Christian will ever entertain hatred of another religion. As I see it there is one single factor which gives rise to the widespread unpopularity of the Jews. It is not the religious antithesis; rather is it the fact that owing to his ability, and whenever he resides in a non-Jewish community, the Jew endeavors to insinuate himself into the intellectual and cultural leadership of that community. Even in Germany the proportion of Jews who had established themselves as laborers or artisans was of the very smallest. No one grudged the Jews a free hand in commerce and industry. But when the legal and medical professions showed an unusually high percentage of Jews; when most of the theaters, the press, the concerts, were under Jewish management, then this constitutes the incursion of a foreign element into the spirit of the hostess nation. All the above-mentioned professions exercise a civilizing influence. And civilization, in the long run, is rooted in religion. With the exception of the newly created state of Israel there is no state which is founded on the Jewish religion. A nation whose civilization is rooted in Christianity will therefore always be at pains to preserve Christianity as the basis of its civilization and to discourage foreign elements in its cultural life.

So long as the Jews fail to appreciate this fact they will come up against difficulties, as the history of many nations has shown.

I have been rooted and grounded in Christianity from my youth up, never narrow-mindedly but always on tolerant lines. My religious conviction has never altered from my seventeenth year onward, when I arrived at my own conclusions on the subject. For some years I had held to the idea that religion could get along without the Church. When I married, therefore, I thought I could dispense with the Church ceremony. It is thanks to my honored teacher Hans Delbrück that I realized my mistake.

If morality, right, justice and civilization spring from religion, it is impossible to envisage a state which does not manifest its religious character in some form or other. The Church may have many faults, she may from time to time amend or change her outward usages, but as the strength and stay of the state she is indispensable.

A common religious profession is essential for any community of life. One of the most insidiously disruptive statements ever made is that religion is a private matter. Religion cannot be a private matter. As exemplified in the Church it is the foundation of every state and of every national community.

For the European nations the well-being of the state is bound up in the Christian principle, in the Person of Christ, in the gospel of the Christian love of one's neighbor. This love of neighbor extends also to those adherents of other religious beliefs — to Mohammedans, Jews, Buddhists, Confucians, heathens. The state will grant them complete tolerance and protection. But it will not permit them to attain to those positions, nor can it allow them to exercise an influence which would admit of their directing the spiritual and moral life of the community along other than Christian lines. Religion is no private affair: it is the foundation stone of the state.

This realization led me, of my own accord, to have the Church wedding ceremony a few years after our civil marriage, and I have never wavered in my conviction.

I had ample opportunity of demonstrating this conviction during the Hitler regime. The party's attack on the Church showed me plainly the brutalization that would result if such an attack were to succeed. I had more than one occasion to discuss these matters with Hitler and can recall the following statements he made:

"I have always told Rosenberg one doesn't attack petticoats or cassocks . . ."

Another time Hitler mentioned having told Rosenberg: "Keep

your fingers out of that pie, Rosenberg. You're neither a prophet nor the founder of a religion."

I doubt whether Hitler himself had any real religious affiliations in spite of his many appeals to Providence. Probably he considered such matters solely from the point of view of his struggle for power. That was why he let his followers have free rein in their attacks on the Church — he did not want to lose them.

A few weeks before Christmas 1938 I was invited to tea with a family who had helped Hitler a lot in the days when he was still striving for power. According to the custom of the house I had to write something in the Visitors' Book. I wrote:

"No strength is worth anything, save moral strength."

Some weeks later Hitler visited the lady of the house and wrote in the Visitors' Book that this was the loveliest Christmas of his life. That was after the *Anschluss* of Austria and Sudeten Germany. Then he riffled through a few back pages, came upon my entry, stopped short, shut the book with a bang and (as my hostess afterwards told me) threw it angrily on the table.

It was of course a sore point with the party pundits that I openly proclaimed my church membership and frequently drove to church at Dahlem in my official car to attend Pastor Niemöller's services. Although the church was only five minutes away it gave me great satisfaction to know that the car, with its official flag, would be parked for over an hour in front of the church.

On a certain day in December 1936, the National Committee on the Churches sent me a questionnaire regarding my attitude to the Church and had forwarded my reply in pamphlet form to the Confessional Church for Church Election purposes. My reply was couched in the following terms:

"I consider the propaganda launched by certain circles against Church denominations is one of the factors most damaging to German national unity and to German activity in the rest of the world, for we are, and shall continue to remain, dependent on the rest of the world in our economic, intellectual and spiritual existence."

Some time later I received an official communication from Kerrl, one of the party Ministers and a humane man of sterling character. Kerrl was Minister of Church Affairs and also Minister of Space Planning, for which reason he was generally known as Minister of Space and Eternity. His official communication ran:

Enclosed I send you copy of a pamphlet from the Confessional Front with a statement by yourself. I would ask you to observe therefrom how statements of this kind by leading personalities of the government are made use of by opponents of the government for propaganda purposes in the Church conflict. Experience shows that not only is the Church policy of the state obstructed thereby, but the enemies of the state are incited and encouraged in their obstinate attitude.

From other information too it has repeatedly been brought to my notice that you exercise considerable influence on the aspirations of Church groups. I would therefore be greatly obliged if in future you would exercise restraint in matters relating to Church policy.

I knew very well that Kerrl, a humane and kindly man, had only written this letter at the instigation of certain party circles. The communication, however, afforded me a welcome chance of making my viewpoint clear. The following is taken from my reply:

The quotation from the pamphlet sent me is from a communication which, by request, I addressed to the National Committee on Churches as the official representative of the Evangelical Church, on December 5, 1936.

If I am given the opportunity to express my views on Church questions within the German Government I shall refer with all the emphasis at my command to the disastrous effects likely to be produced by the policy of certain party groups in this connection.

Notwithstanding my positive attitude to the Church I have never been interested in differences in Church matters. I am a convinced Protestant, but have always looked upon the common profession of the two denominations in regard to the Christian doctrine of salvation as the great essential and have always advocated every *rapprochement* between the two Churches. When we used to discuss the question of *Una Sancta* in Ludwigsburg Internment Camp I always took an active part from the constructive angle. And during my four years as political prisoner I was very conscious of the predominance of pastoral work over the sermon. I have always been glad that the dignitaries of the Catholic Church who knew me did not withhold their sympathy in the very worst periods of outward tribulation.

When that splendid character Bishop von Galen of Münster preached his sermons against National Socialism which have since become famous, I was not slow in openly voicing my appreciation.

When His Holiness Pope Pius XII sent me his greeting by one of his Bishops, I took advantage of a visit to Rome in December 1952 to beg an audience which His Holiness immediately granted. I experienced the great joy of meeting him again in a private audience in which I simply expressed my respect and reverence for this Prince of the Church without touching on any one of the burning questions of the day. It was just a meeting between two human beings which left me with a feeling of deep thankfulness and admiration.

# XLVIII

## REARMAMENT

REARMAMENT played a not inconsiderable part in the creation of employment, though it is entirely untrue to say that the creation of employment consisted solely of armaments. The first program provided only for repairs and restoration to houses, factories and machinery. This was followed by the great *Autobahnen* Program. Further, in all provincial districts, road improvements, new buildings, hydraulic works, embankments and so on were begun.

But the reason that armaments were very soon given priority was not merely their political objective but the fact that orders could be distributed among the large number of existing factories spread over the whole country, and could therefore be executed in equal proportions in every part of the Reich. For road construction, *Autobahnen*, embankments and the like the workmen had to be transferred from their homes to their places of employment, necessitating unwelcome family separations and considerable expense for accommodation. Orders for armaments which were dispatched to factories throughout the country gave employment to the working man in his own neighborhood and enabled him to remain with his family.

Among the ineradicable idiocies spread abroad is the one which persists in affirming that I financed the war deliberately engineered by Hitler, and the armaments necessary thereto. The entire armaments program, in so far as I helped to finance it, was in accordance with the political desire of all parties in the Reichstag. After his rise to power, Hitler repeatedly demanded the limitation of armaments in all countries and agreed to it for Germany also if the others would do the same. Again and again he pointed out that the Versailles Treaty had agreed to the disarmament of the victorious Powers after Germany — as actually happened — had disarmed. At the League of Nations sessions in Geneva the question of disarmament of all those taking part came up time after time, and time after time prominent foreign statesmen pointed to the need for disarmament on the part of the Allies. At no period of its history did the Social-Democratic Party ever deny the necessity of military preparations for purposes of defense.

From the very first I never contemplated any armament save that which would serve to defend Germany's neutrality or to repudiate a possible attack. At the Nuremberg Trial Keitel, Blomberg's successor at the War Office, submitted under oath the following table of annual expenditure on armaments:

| | | | |
|---|---|---|---|
| In the budget year 1935/36 | . . . . | 5 | billion Reichsmarks |
| 1936/37 | . . . . | 7 | |
| 1937/38 | . . . . | 9 | |
| 1938/39 | . . . . | 11 | |
| 1939/40 | . . . . | 20.5 | |

Of these totals, the following amounts were provided from Budget resources; that is, without any additional sums from the Reichsbank:

| | | | |
|---|---|---|---|
| In the budget year 1935/36 | . . . . | 1¾ | billion Reichsmarks |
| 1936/37 | . . . . | 3¾ | |
| 1937/38 | . . . . | 5¾ | |
| 1938/39 | . . . . | 11 | |
| 1939/40 | . . . . | 20.5 | |

From the end of the budget year 1937/38, therefore, the Reichsbank never paid or loaned another penny to the Reich.

At the Nuremberg Trial the American Chief Prosecutor expressly stated that no objection could be raised against armaments not intended or destined for a war of aggression.

From the middle of 1935 onward I strove consistently for a limitation of armaments. The uncertain and ever inadequate amounts received from foreign exchange made my task easier. On December 24, 1935 I addressed a detailed letter to von Blomberg, the Minister for War. The opening sentence ran:

"You expect me to furnish sufficient foreign exchange to meet your requirements. In reply I beg to state that under prevailing circumstances I see no possibility of doing so."

Subsequently, in the course of many ministerial discussions, I repeatedly endeavored to slow down and restrict armaments.

My four-year period as President of the Reichsbank was due to expire in mid-March 1937. Since Hitler intended to appoint me for another four years I began to consider whether I should accept office again. I was determined to do so only if loans to the Reich on the part of the Reichsbank were discontinued once and for all. Negotiations with the Minister of Finance and the Minister for War led to an agreement on March 6, 1937, which was arrived at only because on two occasions I sent Herr Lammers (Secretary of State at the Chancellery) home after a fruitless errand. Herr Lammers had brought me the new document extending my period of office. Twice I sent him back with the information that I would accept reappointment only if the Mefo bills of exchange were to stop. The agreement went so far as to stipulate that the Reichsbank would furnish the sum of three billion Reichsmarks in addition to the nine billions already in circulation. After that, however, the Mefo bills were to cease.

I had had ample opportunity in the meantime of experiencing Hitler's unreliability and lack of straightforwardness. I told Herr Lammers therefore that I was prepared to implement this agreement up to a total limited to twelve billion Reichsmarks, but that I would accept an extension of office for one year only. Should Hitler, for his part, fail to abide by the agreement I would resign my office at the end of one year. In this way I succeeded in putting an end to the Mefo bills. I hoped I had also put an end to further armament.

Hitler fulfilled the agreement to the letter and in the following year endeavored to raise money by the negotiation of fairly large loans. In 1938 the Minister of Finance did issue two big loans which were taken up by the public. The Reichsbank considered still further how armaments might be restricted and recommended the issue of yet a third loan, which was accepted for sale by the usual banking syndicate, of one and a half billion Reichsmarks. Now, however, it became evident that the capital market was exhausted. The banks were left with half a billion on their hands, clear proof that with the loan market fully engaged no money would be available for further armaments.

On January 2, 1939, I went to see Hitler at Obersalzberg to report on my London discussions of December 1938. On this occasion Hitler himself referred to the financial situation and told me he had now found a way of raising funds to meet government expenditure. I pointed out that the last loan had demonstrated the complete exhaustion of the capital market, and furthermore, that of the so-called Jewish indemnity of one billion Reichsmarks decreed in November — of which the first quarter had been extorted — only one hundred and seventy million Reichsmarks had been paid in cash; for the remaining eight millions of the first quarter the Minister of Finance had had to accept real estate lots, securities and so forth as payment. Whereupon Hitler remarked:

"But surely we can issue notes against these securities."

Now the cat was out of the bag! I had once said to Hitler on a previous occasion: "There are only two things, Chancellor, which could bring about the downfall of the National Socialist regime — a war, and inflation."

Now I could see inflation in the offing. At that time I still thought that one might envisage the possibility of preventing inflation from being followed by war.

I remained silent, and Hitler continued: "After I get back to Berlin I will ask you and the Minister of Finance to come and talk matters over and will go into the details of my financial plans."

"Then, Chancellor, before this discussion takes place perhaps you will allow me to hand you a statement by the Reichsbank on the subject."

This statement, signed by all eight members of the board of directors, was handed to Hitler on January 7. It contained the following sentences:

The currency is threatened to a critical extent by the reckless policy of expenditure on the part of public authorities. The unlimited increase in government expenditure defeats every attempt to balance the Budget, brings the national finances to the verge of bankruptcy despite an immense tightening of the taxation screw, and as a result is ruining the Central Bank and the currency. There exists no recipe, no system of financial or money technique — be they never so ingenious or well thought-out — there is no organization or measure of control sufficiently powerful to check the devastating effects on currency of a policy of unrestricted spending. No central bank is capable of maintaining the currency against an inflationist spending policy on the part of the state. During the two extensive actions connected with foreign policy in the East and in Sudetenland a rise in public expenditure was inevitable; it is a fact, however, that since the conclusion of these activities there is no sign of a reduction of this spending policy; on the contrary: everything points to a deliberately planned rise in expenditure, and it therefore becomes an overriding duty to draw attention to the effect of this policy on the currency of the country. The undersigned members of the board of directors have, consciously and gladly, staked all they possessed to help in achieving the great objectives set before us; but a limit has now been reached and they must now call a halt.

Nothing further came of Hitler's proposed discussion with the Minister of Finance and myself.

On January 20, 1939, I was relieved of my office as president of the Reichsbank.

Since, in Nuremberg, I was charged only in connection with preparations for war — no charge referring to war crimes or inhuman conduct was ever preferred against me — the Nuremberg verdict on my participation in the financing of armaments is particularly valuable. The final paragraph in my acquittal by the International Military Court reads:

"As early as 1936 Schacht began, for financial reasons, to advocate a limitation of the armaments program. Had the policy advocated by him actually been put into practice, Germany would not have been prepared for a general European war. His insistence on his policy eventually led to his dismissal from all positions of economic importance in Germany."

# XLIX

## HERMANN GOERING

HERMANN GOERING was the first National Socialist with whom I became personally acquainted. He came of a middle-class family, was brought up in decent surroundings and educated at the Military Academy. He was an officer in the First World War and ended up as a captain in the Luftwaffe. He was possessed of personal courage, not particularly cultured, but with an intelligence well above the normal. So long as he was obliged to live modestly his good qualities predominated.

Goering's unfortunate characteristics began to develop when, owing to his position in the party, he realized the great opportunities that presented themselves to acquire wealth and influence. His greed manifested itself in an astonishingly short space of time. I remember how, soon after the party assumed the reins of government, some business acquaintance cheerfully and cunningly summed him up as "a grabber." Goering openly flaunted his greed as only a man can do when he knows he has the power, and at the same time is sufficiently unscrupulous to set himself above law and justice.

Since I was on good terms with him before I realized his dangerous qualities, I attended his birthday party in January 1934 at which my wife and I gave him a very fine picture of a bison by a well-known Berlin woman artist who specialized in animals. At dinner the seat on Goering's right — the place of honor — was occupied by a man unknown to me, who afterwards turned out to be a successful publisher; throughout the entire period of National Socialist rule he did extensive business with Goering to his decided advantage. He owed his position at this dinner party to the fact that he had presented his host with a shooting-brake and four horses.

The Reichsbank's wedding gift to Goering was a dinner service in the famous Breslau porcelain from the Royal China Factory. After enquiring beforehand whether anyone else had thought of it, Goering's office replied in the negative, and at the same time asked that a list of the individual pieces comprising the dinner service might be forwarded. We sent the list. It was returned with the comment that the service was incomplete without two matching many-branched porcelain chandeliers and the request that these be added.

At a later birthday gathering I noticed a brilliantly gilded cocktail cabinet, a present from the German Workers' Front — I presume the workers themselves knew nothing about it.

Besides his greed, Goering developed an ostentatiousness which frequently verged on the ridiculous. Not only did he collect precious stones, gold and platinum jewelry in vast quantities, he wore them. He seized every opportunity to appear in a new uniform or new suit. Once, when I visited Karinhall with some friends from abroad to see the bison enclosure, Goering received us wearing high leather boots, a leather jerkin, white shirtsleeves, a huntsman's broad-brimmed hat on his head and a six-foot hunting spear in his hand. In contrast to the simplicity of Hitler's personal life, Goering enjoyed to the full the advantages of wealth afforded him by his position, indifferent to, even contemptuous of any legal or moral considerations.

Curiously enough, Goering's overbearing manner did not detract from his popularity. Wherever he appeared at gatherings or on other occasions where the populace were assembled he impressed everybody by his pompous ways and his deliberately assumed jollity and typical German bluntness.

At first Goering tried to establish himself to a certain extent independently, but on a level with Hitler. He looked upon himself as cast in a superior mold and liked to be described as a Renaissance type. I remember how on one occasion, after an argument with Hitler, he spoke of him to me as "that bounder" (*diesen Schlawiner*). But the more unethical Goering's conduct, the greater his dependence upon Hitler. Only a few years later, when my discussions with Hitler had already acquired a certain acerbity, I once asked Goering to back me up in my contentions.

"Please, Herr Goering, the next time you see Hitler, do make him see that matters can't go on like this."

"I promise you faithfully, Herr Schacht, that I will."

When a few days afterwards I enquired as to the result of his conversation with Hitler, Goering admitted: "You know, Herr Schacht, I always intend to tell Hitler exactly what I think but when I enter his room my heart invariably sinks to my boots."

The only people whose hearts don't sink to their boots are those whose conscience is clear and whose conduct is irreproachable — neither of which could be ascribed to Goering.

It was, unfortunately, owing to me in the first instance that Goering obtained a decisive influence in economic matters. I had still failed to realize that even the leading and most responsible brains in the government were not prepared to obey the laws of the land. I still believed that I could induce men like Hitler and Goering to uphold the fundamental principles of good citizenship.

At the beginning of 1936 the Reichsbank ascertained that central banks abroad were offering us large parcels of Reichsbank notes to be converted into foreign currency. Although everyone in Germany was legally bound to hand over to the Reichsbank all foreign bills received, the party had so far never obeyed these instructions, notwithstanding the receipt of considerable sums from its organizations abroad. For good or ill the Reichsbank had overlooked it. Now however we were faced with an open abuse which might have dangerous effects on our currency. The flood of German banknotes now flowing back into the country from abroad could only mean that party officials had sent these notes abroad unmolested by the customs and Foreign Exchange control. We received confirmation of this when on one occasion a parcel of banknotes which we had sent to one of the party centers was returned to us by the Dutch Central Bank in exactly the same wrapping in which it had left the Reichsbank.

I laid the matter before Hitler and explained to him that I obviously lacked the authority to compel the party officials to observe the regulations. I therefore requested that Hitler would appoint a man who would lift the burden of exchange control from my shoulders, and in reply to his enquiry I suggested Hermann Goering. At the end of April 1936 I was relieved of the exchange control. Goering immediately accepted the new task at Hitler's hands with the feeling that here was a jumping-off place for a fresh rise to power.

The opportunity to use this stirrup to swing himself into the saddle presented itself to Goering at the Party Conference of 1936. My incessant struggle to ensure saving and careful use of raw materials and foreign exchange, and my steady insistence on a slowing down of armaments must have gradually got on Hitler's nerves. A few days prior to the opening of the Conference in September 1936 Hitler informed me that he intended, at the Conference, to announce a new economic program, but without giving me any idea of its contents. I immediately scented disaster and tried to get hold of von Blomberg, the Minister for War. He would have been the only one among all the ministers to whom Hitler might perhaps have listened. Blomberg let me down completely. After I had once again explained the economic situation in detail, Blomberg plucked up courage and admitted:

"I realize fully that you are right, Herr Schacht, but you know I am quite convinced that the Führer will find a way out of all our troubles."

What else could I do but take my leave with the words: "God grant that your faith be justified."

At the Conference Hitler announced the program of autarchy of the so-called Four-Year Plan and Hermann Goering was appointed to carry it out. In order to do so Goering built up an organization, which soon had a staff of several hundred, next to the Ministry of Economic Affairs.

The Four-Year Plan achieved comparatively little in the way of positive results, save that there was a great deal of unnecessary to-do over everything, which caused an extensive and rapid revival of defense preparations abroad, whereas I had always tried to work without fanfare. Whatever was successfully accomplished under the Four-Year Plan was nothing but the continuation of measures I had inaugurated as Minister for Economic Affairs. Now, however, everything was rushed and exaggerated. The extraction of benzine from coal had been organized by me. The equipment of a whaling fleet had been started by me. The wholesale cultivation of staple fibers had been set on foot thanks to the steps I had taken. The Four-Year Plan did not put forward any of these things as new ventures — it merely boosted them on a large scale.

The extension of mining operations too had been tackled by me. At the end of 1937 I had linked them up with the Four-Year Plan and with industry, when the founding of the Hermann Goering Works took me completely by surprise. Hermann Goering sank not millions but billions in the exploitation of the so-called Salzgitter ore in Brunswick. It was immediately apparent that this mine would never be a paying concern under the prevailing methods of treatment, so the Hermann Goering Works bought up every similar undertaking they could lay hands on which showed a profit and would serve, to some extent at least, to conceal the loss on the processing of the ore. The necessary funds had one and all to be raised by the Reich by means of loans or in-payment of shares.

At first I tried to continue to run my Ministry in conjunction with and alongside this Four-Year Plan organization, but very soon came up against measures which I neither could nor would countenance.

On December 17, 1936, Goering called a meeting of a large number of business leaders in order to acquaint them with his intentions. At this meeting he put forth one idea after another which were clearly contrary to any political system and any economic principle. If any person brought foreign bills of exchange into the country (whether by legal or illegal means) no one would stop him. The only people to be punished would be those who resorted to illegal methods without bringing in any foreign exchange. Goering demanded that industry should produce, no matter whether it made a profit or loss in so doing.

Some few weeks later on the occasion of my sixtieth birthday, there was a special meeting of the National Chamber of Industry at which I was due to speak. It was practically the same audience to whom Goering had spoken. When I referred to his statements — though without expressly mentioning him by name — everyone knew that my remarks were directed against Goering.

"Gentlemen," I said, "I want first of all, in all seriousness, to refer to the factor which is absolutely fundamental to the art of government: no economy can function and prosper in any State which is not founded upon firmly established principles of law and order. One of the purposes of legislation, among others, is to guarantee the working of the national economy. Therefore, gentlemen, if somebody says: Never mind circumventing the law and the regulations laid down by law — it doesn't matter in the least — I warn you that I shall take proceedings against every person whom I know to be evading the regulations decreed by law."

That was a hit at Goering's foreign exchange policy. The following sentences were directed against Goering's conception of business: "All work done on uneconomic lines is a loss. When someone says, Your job is production, whether or no you produce economically is not important: I tell you that when you produce uneconomically you squander the stuff of which the German people is made. If I sow a hundredweight of corn to the acre and harvest only three quarters of a hundredweight it is the sheerest idiocy imaginable. I cannot and dare not indulge in uneconomic methods just because I might happen to feel like it, for in so doing I should be consuming the very life substance of the German people."

I was fully aware of the pungency of my remarks and of the conflict with Goering that would result, and I began the concluding sentences with the words: "So, my friends, if it be given to me to continue working with you for any length of time . . ."

The end of my official economic activities was not long in coming.

Toward the end of July 1937 Goering issued an order to the mining industry without first submitting it to me for my opinion and verdict, although the care of the mining industry came within my province. Further, he suggested that I should also call in the last remaining foreign securities still in private hands and use them to obtain raw materials from abroad. I took advantage of both these actions to draw the fundamental dividing line between Hermann Goering's idea of economics and my own, in a letter dated August 5, 1937, from which I reproduce a few extracts:

Thanks to the new trade policy inaugurated by me, imports of raw and semi-processed materials have risen from twenty-six million tons to not less than forty-six million tons. In face of this it is already apparent that foreign trade afforded us a quicker and better chance of increasing our supplies of raw materials. I seized this chance by transferring our exports to those countries providing us with raw materials, and by a special application of the clearing system avoiding cash payment in foreign exchange.

Again and again I have referred to the need for an increased export trade and have done my utmost to achieve this. The excessive requisitioning of our industry for home orders naturally reacted adversely on industry's willingness to export. The excessive requisitioning of raw materials and labor for public buildings, armaments and the Four-Year Plan threatens to bring about a decline in our export trade. I wish to make it perfectly clear that if there is a decrease in the foreign exchange accruing to us through exports, it stands to reason that the supply of raw materials will also slow down and this will lead to further gaps in our provision for buildings, armaments, and the Four-Year Plan.

Therefore — in addition to increasing our home-produced raw materials — our chief aim must continue to be to increase our foreign exchange income by means of exports. Notwithstanding this, one of your first steps was to order the seizure of all foreign securities in German possession as well as the speeding-up of the collection of export debts and the realization — to the greatest possible extent — of German shares abroad. In so doing you have plundered part of our capital and deprived our current foreign exchange income of the regular payments in interest and dividends accruing therefrom. Your new project for increasing the home production of iron ore involves the expenditure of many hundreds of millions, for which up to now no cover is available. The provision of banknotes and money in account does not imply simultaneous provision of raw materials and foodstuffs. You can't bake bread or cast cannon from securities. To invest raw materials and labor in new undertakings to the extent you have planned must lead to further restrictions in the allocation of raw materials to those industries which manufacture goods for export and for consumption by the people at home. We are already experiencing a shortage of many consumer goods in our daily life.

I brought my technical comments to a close as follows:

You will remember that I declared to you months ago that uniformity is indispensable to economic policy, and that I urged you to arrange matters in such a way as to enable you to take over the Ministry for Economic Affairs yourself. I have previously stated that I consider your policy on matters of foreign exchange to be wrong and I am not able to share the responsibility for it.

I sent a copy of this letter to Hitler with the request that he would release me from my office as Minister for Economic Affairs.

This caused Hitler no little embarrassment. For me to leave at this particular juncture would be highly inconvenient for him. I knew that I should experience considerable difficulty in obtaining my release. In a totalitarian state it was not possible for a minister simply to resign his post, as this necessitated the consent not only of the Chancellor but also of the President of the Reich. Hitler combined both in his own person.

Hitler immediately summoned me to Obersalzberg where a long conversation took place between us on August 11. At that time I did not yet realize the extent to which Hitler, inwardly, had already ranged himself against me. In connection with the announcement of his program of autarchy at the Party Conference in September 1936, Hitler had prepared a secret memorandum from which Goering read some extracts to me and one or two others. I only came to know the full context of it when my fellow prisoner Speer (who had received a copy from Hitler when he took up his ministerial appointment) acquainted the court with it. The parts which Goering had *not* read to us on that former occasion, and which I then heard for the first time in Nuremberg, embodied a single protest against my economic policy. I quote only three sentences:

It is not the duty of national economic institutions to rack their brains over methods of production. That has nothing whatever to do with the Ministry for Economic Affairs.

Here I must take the strongest exception to the assumption that an increase in raw materials can be achieved by a limitation of national armament.

The contention that the whole of Germany's blast furnaces need to be rebuilt is not worth considering, and above all it has nothing to do with the Ministry for Economic Affairs.

Perhaps it was a good thing — for the sake of my discussion with Hitler — that I knew nothing of these remarks when I went to Obersalzberg. I could thus proceed on the assumption that Hitler would to some extent come to an unbiassed decision.

Outwardly our conversation was on the most friendly footing. I met Hitler on the sun-bathed terrace in front of the house, surrounded by his faithful henchmen, among whom was Speer. Hitler took me into his spacious study where the windows stood wide open on this warm summer's day — which meant that much of our talk must have been heard outside.

Hitler begged me urgently to withdraw my resignation, but he avoided all objective treatment of economic questions and only insisted that he could not part with me.

To which I replied: "It is absolutely essential, Chancellor, that the country's economic policy should be conducted on uniform lines. Since my ideas are diametrically opposed to Goering's I must ask you to decide whether you want to adopt his ideas or mine. I should not be personally offended in any way if you were to decide in favor of Goering."

Still Hitler evaded replying to my technical arguments; rather he continued to urge: "Dear Herr Schacht, you must come to an understanding with Goering. I do beg of you to make yet another effort to arrive at some uniform *modus operandi* with Goering. I don't want to lose your co-operation whatever happens."

While I assured him that there was not the slightest chance that two such widely differing conceptions could ever be reconciled, Hitler kept returning to the personal aspect and overwhelmed me with expressions of appreciation for everything I had hitherto achieved.

For my part I was fully aware that Hitler only wanted to gain time to find a way out of his temporary discomfiture. So I remained unmoved even when Hitler finally assured me, with real tears in his eyes: "But Schacht — I'm fond of you."

And when, nevertheless, I persisted in my attitude, he said: "But you surely won't refuse to have another talk with Goering. I will gladly give you ample time for it. If, at the end of two months, you will tell me again that you cannot come to a uniform outlook on German economic policy, and therefore abide by your wish to resign, I will do as you ask."

No one was more glad than I to hear these words. I immediately expressed my agreement and changed the subject, commenting on the beautiful summer weather and on the lovely house at Obersalzberg. Then I asked to be allowed to leave, whereupon Hitler accompanied me to my car.

Goering replied to my letter of August 5 with a communication dated August 22, considerably longer than mine. My answer was very brief:

"I conclude, from the statement in your letter of the 22nd inst., that in our respective conceptions of economic policy there are fundamental differences which — as I hope — will lead the Führer to decide to entrust the conduct of German economic policy to your hands."

This exchange of correspondence with Goering was followed by a further talk with Hitler at the beginning of October, after which I wrote the letter which I reproduce below:

Oct. 8, 1937

My dear Chancellor,

Following our conversation of the 6th inst., I beg to point out that a successful German economic policy can only be achieved under a central authority. In view of the immense importance of our economy in relation to the preparedness of our defense force it is impossible to tolerate the proximity of a heterogeneous crowd of business officials, the continual intervention by outside elements, or the permanent jamming of economic activities by the German Workers' Front.

There can have been only one reason for the appointment of a Special Commissioner for the Four-Year Plan; namely, to invest this particular post with the authority of a person of high standing alike in the state and the party, as well as to direct the trend of the movement to the attainment of the desired objective. In accordance with this conception Herr Goering, the Prime Minister, had always stated that he did not intend to set up any new administrative machinery, but in order to achieve the necessary results, would make use of existing Ministries while upholding their policies and responsibility.

In actual fact the exact opposite has happened. The Four-Year Plan established today comprises several hundred persons and the executives of individual Ministries are ignored and overridden at will.

There can however be only one head of Economic Affairs. Who that head is to be, you, *mein Führer*, must decide according to the measure of your confidence in the abilities and loyalty of the person appointed. Special Commissioners — including therefore the Special Commissioner for the Four-Year Plan — can deal only with planning, proposed measures and public propaganda, but not with the executive, who must proceed according to existing government machinery. Hitherto, if individual Ministries (Economic, Food, Labor, Trade) were at odds with one another, Goering, as Prime Minister and President of the so-called Cabinet Council, has always been able to settle matters. This procedure should continue to be followed in future. In an emergency arising from questions of principle the correct procedure is to approach you and leave the decision in your hands.

In case, *mein Führer*, you do not intend to vest the conduct of Economic Affairs — including the executive — in the central authority, that is, the Special Commissioner for the Four-Year Plan, but to allow the Ministry for Economic Affairs to continue as such, I have ventured to set forth on the enclosed sheet a few points without which I am firmly convinced one cannot expect to run the Ministry of Economic Affairs in a responsible fashion.

It may amuse you to note that popular opinion has its finger on the spot in these matters. Today I found these verses on my desk:

> *Said Goering, just give me four years, and you'll see*
> *From the shackles of money I'll set industry free;*
> *Here's Schacht as hostage in the interim,*
> *If I should bolt, you can strangle him.*

A prospect which — speaking personally — fails to attract me.

Being determined that my request to resign should stand, I departed on leave on September 5; nor did I return to the Ministry for

Economic Affairs. Since no decision was taken on my above-mentioned letter I gave notice to Hitler of my resignation, the two months having meanwhile elapsed. Needless to say a further discussion with Goering which, at Hitler's request, took place on November 1 brought no agreement. When Goering finally said: "But surely I must be able to give you instructions."

I took my leave with the words: "Not to me — to my successor."

That was my last encounter with Goering. Our next meeting was in prison at Nuremberg when we were taken to a cell with two bathtubs where — I in one and Goering in the other — we each proceeded to soap ourselves all over. *Sic transit gloria mundi!*

At last, on November 26, 1937, my request to resign was granted. Although more than three months had elapsed since our agreement as to my departure, Hitler had found no suitable successor for my office. There remained nothing for him but to entrust Hermann Goering with the Ministry of Economic Affairs. Not till the following spring was Walter Funk appointed to the position.

When Goering entered my study in the Ministry he exclaimed: "How can one indulge in great thoughts in such a small room?"

Then he sat down at my writing table, got on the telephone to me at the Reichsbank and bawled exultantly down the wire: "Herr Schacht, I am now sitting in your chair!"

Take care you don't come a bad crash! I thought, and replaced the receiver.

# L

## FOREIGN POLICY

I HAVE NEVER laid claim to being a politician. Quite obviously I am minus certain qualities necessary for such a career. It seems to me also that a politician's reputation does not always depend so much on his ability as on favorable current circumstances which contribute to his success. I don't believe Mussolini's saying, that men make history. The men who have gone down in history as great politicians were very often only the instruments of their era. When the time for a new perception was ripe it favored many a politician who, for all his good intentions and efforts, would otherwise have been doomed to oblivion.

Economic policy is a part of general politics. With the increasing importance that economic policy has assumed for Europe since the 1890's, it was unavoidable that I should be drawn into questions of foreign policy. I have described my endeavors in London and Paris during the early 1920's to awaken understanding of the idea that reparations *à la* Versailles are thoroughly mischievous. In the years that followed I pointed out again and again that to make it possible for Germany to obtain raw materials and foodstuffs from overseas territories by her own labor and with her own currency would provide the only secure basis for conditions in Germany to develop on peaceful lines.

On this subject, as on the subject of currency, I was obliged to refute the classic principles of the doctrine of free trade. My study of British mercantile authors had shown me clearly that there is nothing of the abstract science about political economy. It was on their trade requirements that the mercantile writers had based their theoretical claims with which they had been able to found and to protect their wool industry and their shipping.

After Britain had succeeded in establishing her great industrial advance and the superiority of her merchant fleet, British political economists began to raise freedom of trade, that is, unrestricted competition, to the level of a standard economic theory, culminating in the most-favored-nation principle which would have ensured Britain's economic supremacy for all time, had not other countries finally rebelled against it from sheer necessity. The so-called classic political economy owes its long reign to the brilliant propaganda with which British scientific economists bemused the brains of the Continent. And if an economist should occasionally seek to defend the interests of his nation he was misunderstood and derided by his own country-men — especially if he were a German, such as Friedrich List.

Economic freedom is like political freedom — an ideal toward which men may confidently strive, but impossible to realize so long as not everyone thinks along ideal lines. The saying, "Whatever benefits my country is right," I have always looked upon as criminal, for right is rooted in divine principle. On the other hand the aim of every economic policy must be to ensure the possibility of livelihood for its own people from an economic standpoint: that has always been the foremost principle in all my dealings.

As early as 1926 I gave a lecture to the German Colonial Association, at which I put forward the claim that one or other of Germany's former overseas territories might be transferred to her for purposes of economic development. Even at that time I described as immaterial the question of German sovereignty over such territory. I was concerned solely with the economic development which should be undertaken by German *entrepreneurs* with German currency, for only through the use of our own currency would the question of obtaining foreign exchange be reduced to negligible proportions.

Today the opening up of undeveloped territories is universally recognized in fine phrases and resolutions as an essential for world economic policy. In practice, however, it is not possible for any German *entrepreneur* to obtain free entry into former German territories and set up in business without the permission of the British or French mandatory authorities. No international law serves to protect him against the arbitrary actions of the mandatory governments to which he is subjected, should occasion arise.

Following the experience of two world wars the whole world knows today that the problem of Germany is the central problem of Europe. If we do not succeed in making it possible for Germany to procure her own raw materials and her own foodstuffs, Germany's social problem will remain a threatening and disrupting factor in world politics and world trade.

Hitler of course was aware of this vital problem. The more I had

cause to fear that he might be seeking other solutions the more I
redoubled my efforts to get him to fall in with my ideas for overseas
economic development. By the early summer of 1936 I had brought
him to the point of agreeing to a suggestion of mine. I explained to
him that it must likewise be to the advantage of the Allies to find a
solution to the German people's need for raw materials and foodstuffs. I asked him therefore to consent to my going to Paris, where
I proposed to discuss the subject with the Léon Blum Government
then in office. After prolonged arguments he gave his written consent
to my undertaking the journey, for which I made my preparations
with Monsieur François-Poncet, the French Ambassador in Berlin.
Monsieur François-Poncet informed his government of my intention and ascertained, to my great pleasure, that Léon Blum would
receive me and talk over the matter.

My subsequent stay in Paris and my conversations with Léon Blum
and his ministers — among them Auriol, Minister of Finance and
now President of the Republic — belong to some of my pleasant-
est recollections. I was received with kindliness and courtesy, and
instead of the rejection which Hitler had feared I encountered widespread appreciation of the fact that a solution of the question I had
broached would do a great deal to ensure peace.

It was only natural that Léon Blum, for his part, should entertain
doubts as to Hitler's sincerity, an attitude which I entirely understood. I remember one of our conversations, walking in the garden
of the Elysée, when he expressed his surprise that Hitler should have
consented to my making the attempt, particularly where it concerned
himself, a Social Democrat Prime Minister.

"Surely Hitler knows, Monsieur Schacht, that . . ."

"Certainly, Mr. Prime Minister," I cut in, "Hitler knows that you
are a Social Democrat, a Freemason, and a Jew. But he has nevertheless empowered me to put forward these proposals. Your Ambassador in Berlin is fully aware of this."

Léon Blum announced his readiness — without prejudice to the
question of sovereignty — to explore the possibility of transferring
to Germany the mandated territory of the Cameroons for purposes
of economic development, but stressed the fact that he would have
to contact the British cabinet on the matter, a necessity which I
could not but acknowledge. During the months that followed, Blum
went into the question thoroughly with the British Government and
I acquainted my friend Montagu Norman with the situation.

The attitude of the British Government was at first negative, then hesitant, and finally not at all averse to entering into a discussion of the circumstances. Unfortunately all this took more than six months. In the spring of 1937 matters had so far advanced that the subject was to be discussed, along with others, at a previously arranged visit to London by Baron von Neurath, the German Foreign Minister. Then, suddenly, there occurred the Spanish Almeria incident which sent Hitler off at a tangent. Neurath's visit to London was canceled; the opportunity was lost. A more ready acquiescence on the part of Britain might have given a different turn to many future events.

In April 1937, on the occasion of a visit to the King of the Belgians in Brussels, I was able to lay my views before him. He asked me to interpret the German conception of the political situation.

"You know, Herr Schacht, that Belgium is vitally interested in the return to normal conditions of world trade. Do please tell me how, as Germany sees it, the present unfortunate state of affairs can be altered."

"Your Majesty may be sure that Germany is quite ready to come to an international agreement on the limitation of armaments on the part of all concerned, as well as on the subject of co-operation in a new League of Nations, provided the latter were freed from Versailles and from sanctions. But a fundamental of any peaceful development is that Germany shall be able to feed and provide work for her own people."

"Where do you see a chance of that?"

"Neither politically nor economically can we be dependent on the charity or the whims of the other great Powers. The only peaceable means I can see of obtaining access to raw materials and foodstuffs is for an overseas field of action to be restored to us in which we can make use of our own resources without let or hindrance."

"I appreciate your line of thought. I know full well what the Congo means to the welfare of the Belgian people. Have you any hope that your proposal may be carried out?"

"Since I believe, Your Majesty, that the Allies will eventually recognize the justice of my idea, I do not give up hope. But the dilatory fashion in which this problem is being handled politically creates greater difficulties in Germany than in the well-fed countries. This naturally tends to aggravate the sense of insecurity."

"Have you any specific suggestions?"

As I did not feel justified in recounting my discussions in Paris I replied: "Since I am no politician I would prefer not to make any specific suggestions. But since, too, the Belgian Government enjoys the esteem of its friends and can be sure of their attention in the course of its present activity, I should like to hope that Belgium would co-operate in solving this problem."

The King asked me about our relations with Russia.

"I would ask Your Majesty to consider here also that I am no politician and have no mandate from my government. I can only express my personal opinion."

"Please do so."

"So long as the Russian Government continues its propaganda of World Revolution we are obviously bound to look upon this as a menace to Germany. A highly industrialized country such as Germany cannot tolerate bolshevism under any circumstances. Should developments in Russia lead to an abandonment of the principle of World Revolution, Germany would gladly resume her former economic relations with that country."

During the whole of our lengthy conversation the King of the Belgians was very forthcoming, not only in the sense that he was courteous, but in his genuine interest and desire to help in any way possible.

After my talk with the King I visited Monsieur de Man, the Minister of Finance, whom I had known from earlier days and with whom I had been brought into closer contact through my daughter, who had studied with him. In view of the important influence of de Man during and since that time I append the account which I wrote down immediately after my visit.

In theory he is a Socialist, but with a great appreciation of practical essentials. The conversation turned, as indeed it does everywhere here, on the subject: what can one do to improve the economic situation, and in particular to reincorporate Germany in the international economic scheme of things. I put forward our ideas. De Man expressed his full appreciation and stressed his own keen desire to improve relations with Germany. On the question of colonies he agreed with me.

He voiced only one new viewpoint: namely, that in the event of a general international settlement from a monetary angle we should have to assimilate our currency to those of other countries. I replied that however much I was against any kind of inflation, I had always made it plain that I was prepared to discuss the assimilation of German currency to others, but always with the proviso that a final system of currency parities should be established which could once again serve as a firm basis for international trade.

As regards the general feeling in Belgium, de Man emphasized that this had completely changed during the last two years, especially where Germany was concerned. Nevertheless one must not underestimate the part played by the strong Left-wing antagonism to all Fascist ideas. The older Liberal groups of former days had lost their significance.

Co-operation in the cabinet, particularly between de Man and van Zeeland, was on uniform lines. It constituted, so to speak, a single force, at the head of which stood the King himself.

I have reproduced this report, firstly because it throws a light on the international relations prevailing at that time, and secondly because it is typical of the direction in which I sought to make use of my foreign contacts. By bringing about economic agreement I hoped to assist in laying the foundation for a lasting, peaceful coexistence between the nations.

There was a special problem connected with my visit to London in December 1938; it was my last visit abroad in an official capacity. It had been preceded by the disgraceful destruction of the Jewish synagogues on November 9, 1938, and the fine imposed on the Jews of one billion Reichsmarks. I had made no attempt to conceal from Hitler my opinion of this latest barbarism staged by Goebbels, and had told him frankly that this kind of thing could not go on.

"If you won't formulate some legal basis for the Jews in Germany by which they can live their lives in decent conditions, you must at least allow them facilities for emigration."

Hitler himself seemed ill at ease in face of the world-wide repercussions aroused by the bestiality of November 9. He gave me an enquiring look.

"Have you any suggestions?"

I unfolded my plan: "The whole of the property of Jews in Germany shall be brought into a trust company who will administer it according to law. This trust company shall be governed by an international committee, on which the Jews are also represented. On the basis of this property held in trust by way of security the committee will issue a loan in the international market amounting to, say, one to one and a half billion Reichsmarks. This loan carries an interest of about five per cent and is repayable by annual instalments over a period of twenty to twenty-five years. The German Government guarantees the transfer of interests and repayment instalments in dollars so that the loan can be issued as a dollar loan. Jews all over the world will be urged to subscribe."

"And what is to be done with the dollars?"

"Out of the dollar proceeds of this loan every Jew wishing to emigrate will receive a certain sum which will facilitate his reception in another country and serve as a foundation on which to build a new life."

I was well aware that this was not an ideal proposition. But I feared that any chance of economic existence for the Jews would be completely destroyed by the party unless something was done to prevent it. My suggestion would mean that Jewish property in Germany would be preserved intact over a period of years. In the meantime many new developments could occur.

To my great astonishment Hitler declared he had no objection to my attempt to put this idea into practice. At my suggestion he authorized me to convene a political discussion in London. The negotiations took place there from December 14 to 17, 1938. I contacted Lord Bearsted of the firm of Samuel & Samuel, who reacted sympathetically to the proposal, while other firms, as he informed me, turned it down. There followed a discussion with Mr. Rublee, the American and British chairman of the so-called Evian Committee, and Lord Winterton, the British Minister, both of whom as well as Lord Bearsted were interested in following up my plan and in getting to work on those lines.

But this attempt to relieve the international situation failed also when I was dismissed from my office of president of the Reichsbank by Hitler on January 20, 1939. My official connection with London was broken.

# LI

## I BREAK WITH HITLER

FROM THE MIDDLE of 1936 onward my relations with Hitler had slowly but steadily deteriorated. My influence on his policy had been considerable during the first years — especially in the economic field — but after the middle of 1936 it speedily declined. My announcement in March 1937, that he could expect no more money from me; the impossibility of extending his plans for autarchy to include foodstuffs; the complete exhaustion of the capital market demonstrated by the Reichsbank, and my condemnation of his anti-Semitic party policy; all these factors had obviously convinced him that he could no longer count on me in the pursuance of his warlike intentions, which he had so far managed to conceal.

Not until the Nuremberg Trial did I learn that, as far back as the beginning of November 1937, he had confided his military plans in strictest secrecy to the chief leaders of the Wehrmacht and to the Foreign Minister. As yet, therefore, I suspected nothing; I could not and would not give up hope of a peaceful outcome. The realization that things were otherwise dated from the beginning of January 1938. There is no need for me to recapitulate the events which have so often been described. Blomberg contracted marriage with a lady who obviously did not answer to that description. He resigned his position as Minister for War. General von Fritsch, Commander-in-Chief of the Army, was maliciously confronted with a groundless charge of homosexual practices.

Count Helldorf, Head of the Berlin Police, told me of the despicable part played in both instances by the Gestapo under the direction of Himmler and Heydrich. At the beginning of the National Socialist movement Helldorf had taken part in many brutalities and excesses; but in the course of years and owing to his experience with the party he had changed his views and endeavored to rehabilitate himself by joining decent groups. So my friends and I were put wise to all the details concerning the *affaires* Blomberg and Fritsch.

The manner in which Hitler dealt with both cases, without the slightest regard for justice, decency and morality; the fact that he assumed command of the Army; dismissed von Neurath from his post as Foreign Minister; sacked several generals of merit and decent outlook and removed several diplomats whom he disliked; everything pointed to the conclusion that Hitler was obviously bent on war.

The events connected with Blomberg and Fritsch created a bad impression both at home and abroad and resulted in Hitler and Goering's intensifying and speeding up the measures leading to the Austrian *Anschluss*. The unprecedented rejoicing over the *Anschluss* in Austria as well as in the old Reich raised Hitler's popularity to a hitherto unattained level and caused the Blomberg and Fritsch business to be forgotten.

After the march into Vienna the Reichsbank was faced with the task of taking over the Austrian Bank, thereby incorporating the Austrian economy in the German monetary policy. While all the other National Socialist functionaries from Germany were at pains to represent the former Austrian economic and administrative policy as a glorified hodgepodge of inefficiency, I paid tribute to the outstanding work of the Austrian National Bank and to the world-wide reputation it had achieved and maintained through the decades. Some hotheads among the personnel of the Austrian National Bank attempted to carry out a political "cleansing," but from the very first I categorically refused to countenance their efforts. Not a single member of the staff was dismissed after I took over the bank. Herr Kienböck, the president of the bank, was a former Minister of Finance, a clever lawyer and financier. It is true that I had to let him go, for it was not possible to offer him a position of equal rank; but I saw to it that he was able to retire on full pension and with flying colors though he was known to be of partly Jewish extraction.

During a discussion which took place a few days after the march into Austria, Hitler announced his intention of raising the market value of the Austrian schilling — hitherto reckoned at 50 German pfennigs — to 66⅔ German pfennigs. Secretary of State Keppler had managed to persuade Hitler that this increase in the value of the schilling would increase the value of the money in the working man's pockets. He overlooked the fact, however, that the working man didn't have much money in his pockets. He overlooked, too, what every student of political economy learns in his first term, that an automatic rise in prices is bound immediately to cancel out any artificial overvaluation of money. Apart from the fact that such a measure only served completely to upset the balance of the Austrian economy, the only people who profited by the higher valuation of the schilling were those with fixed-interest-bearing securities, that is, bonds and mortgages, who now received larger amounts in interest and amortization. That the capitalistic circles would be the very ones to profit by this measure was something Messrs Keppler and Hitler had not thought of.

In vain I put forward my views, which were diametrically opposed to this policy. Being unable to make any impression I ended by telling Hitler: "You have among your colleagues an expert on currency matters, considered by the whole world to be an authority on the subject — and you succeed in completely ignoring this man's advice."

The reply was: "I do so for political reasons."

If, nowadays, party-political bias seeks to gloss over or to minimize the historical fact of the Austrians' overwhelming unanimous rejoicing over the *Anchluss* with the Reich, I want, by way of refutation, to bear witness to what I saw with my own eyes and experienced through personal contact. Not only was I in Vienna for days on end: I traveled all over the Austria of that time and talked with people in all walks of life in the capitals of Austrian federated provinces. Nowhere did I come across any other reaction save that of relief, and the hope that they had at last emerged from all economic and national straits.

I shared in this rejoicing with all my heart, but it was not sufficient to allay misgivings arising from the Blomberg-Fritsch events. As the result of serious and anxious consideration I was forced to the conclusion that a continuation of the Hitler regime must imperil to the last degree the relations of our country and our people with other nations.

Together with my friends I began to deliberate how best to overthrow the Hitler regime. Following the Fritsch affair I had approached von Brauchitsch, the new Commander-in-Chief of the Army. I had sought out von Rundstedt, the head of the Wehrmacht detachment in Berlin. I had a long talk with Admiral Raeder. Finally I went to Gürtner, the Minister of Justice. With all of them I discussed the danger that threatened and implored them to take countermeasures against Hitler from the vantage point of their military and official positions. Everywhere I encountered deaf ears. Not one of these high dignitaries was prepared to take a stand on behalf of right and justice.

Every month I went to Basel for the meeting of the Bank for

International Settlements, and there I had the opportunity of regular contact with my colleagues on the board of directors and other bankers from the Western countries. Despite the reserve arising from the national ties of each one of us, we nevertheless exchanged a good many comments during these conversations, which left no doubt as to the reaction to the political atmosphere.

The more conditions in Germany approached a climax the greater my desire to make use of my connections in Basel as a means of preserving peace. In the course of the summer, therefore, I asked my British colleague Montagu Norman whether it would not be possible to bring British policy more into line with my efforts to maintain peace. Hitherto, Britain's policy had appeared to be to leave Hitler a free hand in foreign affairs.

When I met Norman again four weeks later he said: "I discussed your suggestion with Neville Chamberlain, the British Prime Minister."

"And what was his reply?"

"His reply was: 'Who is Schacht? I have to deal with Hitler.'"

This answer caused me considerable astonishment. It seemed to me incomprehensible that the British Prime Minister should set so little store by maintaining a certain contact with those circles which were ranged on the side of peace.

Slowly the conviction grew in me that only a bold stroke could put an end to the Hitler regime, since the attempt to guide it in the right direction by means of open resistance on the part of responsible generals and ministers had proved fruitless. Then a chance remark brought me into touch with General von Witzleben. In him I found a determined opponent of the regime. I succeeded in convincing him that an international military conflict was unavoidable with Hitler at the helm, that only by violent action could the regime be brought to an end.

The following months were taken up with our preparations for a *coup d'état*. The division commanded by the Potsdam General Brockdorf-Ahlefeld had been initiated into our plot. With their aid and that of Panzer forces promised by General Halder — who had succeeded General Beck, Chief of Staff, on the latter's retirement — Hitler and his immediate assistants were to be seized and brought before a state tribunal during the last days of September 1938.

First and foremost we discussed our plans with General Beck who, because of his suspicions of Hitler's warlike intentions, had tendered his resignation as Chief of the General Staff in the summer of 1938. Beck was a man of absolutely sterling character, highly cultured and possessing a great store of knowledge, not only of his own subject but over a very wide field. As Chief of the General Staff he enjoyed the complete confidence of the Army and was the acknowledged moral leader of the Staff. Nevertheless Beck was more of a scholar than a man of action. His retirement accelerated the moral disintegration of the General Staff. His departure deprived the higher military ranks of their only strong counterelement against Hitler.

It proved impossible to carry out the proposed *coup d'état* owing to the Munich Conference which led to the temporary solution of the burning Czech question.

I have recounted the events of this month in so far as I took any part in them in my book *Settlement with Hitler* (Rowohlt-Verlag, Hamburg, 1948). I will content myself therefore with the following summing up:

Although from now on I went in constant peril of my life I could not bring myself entirely to conceal my antagonistic attitude. It is true that I resorted to camouflage when necessary, as I had already done on previous occasions. Later, during the denazification proceedings, I was blamed for this camouflage. The American Chief Prosecutor went so far as to expostulate that there was nothing in my actions which had given them a clue as to my intention to remove Hitler. I replied that I couldn't possibly have advertised it in the newspapers beforehand. Anyone who did not understand the art of camouflage encompassed his own death and that of others as well. I had no wish to perish on Hitler's account: rather I desired to live for the sake of my people. That I set no store on living for my own sake I proved by the fact that for seven years I rendered myself liable to the charge of high treason.

It would have been easy for me not to return to Germany after my Indian visit. When I went for my honeymoon to Switzerland in 1941 I could have remained there without any further trouble. On both occasions I went back to Germany, for I did not wish to escape the fate that threatened my people. With the connivance of more than half a dozen persons I had played a leading part in preparations for a military revolt against Hitler. The slightest indiscretion, whether accidental or deliberate, would cost me my head. For seven long years I lived under the shadow of this perpetual menace without for one moment relinquishing my intention — to prevent the war, to stop the war, to eliminate Hitler.

Every Christmas the Reichsbank gave a party for the office boys which the president of the bank regularly attended and at which he gave an address. For years past the National Socialists had done their best — not, of course, without success — to snaffle the Reichsbank office boys for the party and instruct them in the so-called National Socialist philosophy. Once before I had urged these young lads not to keep Christmas only in secular fashion but to remember that for us the Christmas celebrations were the offspring of the thousand-year-old happy union of Christian faith and German character on which our entire civilization was founded. In my address to these young fellows at this Christmas party of 1938 I referred to the events of November 9:

"The deliberate burning of Jewish synagogues, the destruction and looting of Jewish businesses and the ill-treatment of Jewish citizens was such a wanton and outrageous undertaking as to make every decent German blush for shame. I hope none among you had any share in these goings on. If any one of you did take part I advise him to get out of the Reichsbank as quickly as possible. We have no room in the Reichsbank for people who do not respect the life, the property and the convictions of others. The Reichsbank is founded on good will and good faith."

Several party pundits were present during this speech.

The last meeting of the cabinet had been held on February 4, 1938, and there had never been another. Its sole feature had consisted of the information that General von Fritsch had been charged with criminal offenses of which Hitler could give no details at that time. There was no debate.

The Reichsbank Memorandum, in which we had demanded the stoppage of excessive expenditure on armaments, was handed to Hitler on January 7, 1939, without our having subsequently heard anything as to the result. The one piece of information conveyed to us by some minor officials was that, when he saw the eight signatures, Hitler had exclaimed: "That is mutiny!"

Hitler had always tried to prevent his ministers or other colleagues getting together in groups to discuss public events. Later he issued a written notice in which he expressly stated that under no circumstances were his ministers to meet together for mutual discussion. He was afraid — if not of conspiracies, at any rate of general opposition. The eight signatures to the Reichsbank Memorandum only served to irritate him still further.

On January 19, 1939, I returned home very late and found a whole heap of telephone and telegraphic messages bidding me come to the Chancellery punctually at nine o'clock the following morning. Next day the appointment was postponed by telephone till nine-fifteen. Scarcely had I entered the big drawing room looking out on the garden of the old Chancellery when the Führer came in and the following conversation took place:

"I sent for you, Herr Schacht, to hand you the written notice of dismissal from the office of President of the Reichsbank."

He handed me the document. I held it in my hand in silence without looking at it.

"You don't fit into the general National Socialist scheme of things."

I remained silent. There was a brief pause.

"You have refused to allow your staff to submit to political scrutiny by the party."

I remained silent. Another brief pause. Increasing irritation on Hitler's part.

"You have criticized and condemned the events of the ninth of November to your employees."

I had not replied to Hitler's earlier words, since I entirely agreed with his remark that I did not fit into the party scheme of things. As a result I had repeatedly informed Hitler — and had supported my contention — that I would not allow my staff to submit to criticism by the party. If I were entrusted with a job, I explained, I would have to choose my own colleagues for that job.

I did not consider it necessary to go over the same ground again. But after Hitler's reference to my office boys' Christmas party I replied, with all the sarcasm I could muster: "Had I known that you approved of those events, I should have said nothing."

Hitler was obviously at a loss. With an effort he said: "I am too upset to continue this conversation."

"I can always come back when you have grown calmer."

"And what you think will happen, Herr Schacht, *won't* happen. There will be no inflation."

"That would be a very good thing, *mein Führer.*"

Without another word he accompanied me through two other rooms to the front door, and I took my leave.

During the course of the day Hitler must have thought over how to explain my departure from the Reichsbank to the public. As I learned from the Chancellery, a farewell communication, couched in very stiff terms, was considerably modified and even expressed the hope that Hitler might continue to avail himself of my counsel. As a result of these second thoughts I did not receive a notice of dismissal from the post of Minister without Portfolio.

In the days immediately following I moved from my official residence in the Reichsbank to a house for one family only which was my own property in Charlottenburg, and gave this as my official address in connection with the duties of a Minister without Portfolio. This meant that I waived all claim to official "appearance," nor was I ever again called upon to act in my ministerial capacity.

Simultaneously with myself, Hitler also dismissed two of my colleagues who had been conspicuous in previous negotiations with the Ministry of Finance. Of the other five members, three tendered their resignations, which were accepted after some considerable unpleasantness. Puhl and Kretzschmann, the last two, remained in office. Unlike the rest of us they had long since succumbed to party pressure. We six had never sided with the party.

# LII

## FROM AN ATTEMPTED *COUP D'ETAT*
## TO AN ATTEMPTED ASSASSINATION

MY ATTEMPT at a *coup d'état* in September 1938, my refusal to grant further loans to Hitler and my dismissal on January 20, 1939, made me want to withdraw for a time from the searchlight of public life. More than half a dozen people knew of my attempted *coup d'état*, which intensified the risk of an unforeseen indiscretion. My definite repudiation of further armaments could only lead to increased tension between Hitler and myself. A prolonged absence from Germany would enable the events of the past months to be to some extent forgotten so far as I personally was concerned.

I therefore wrote to Hitler that I wanted to embark on a long spell of foreign travel. Hitler agreed. It must have been a relief to him to know that I should be absent from the political scene.

In accordance with correct procedure I called on Herr von Ribbentrop, the Foreign Minister, to acquaint him of my proposed journey. Ribbentrop greeted me with the words: "You want to make a trip round the world?"

"Not a trip round the world, Herr von Ribbentrop; I only want to go to East Asia and visit China and Japan."

"But surely you know, Herr Schacht, that we have a close alliance with Japan, whereas our relations with China have become very shaky. For political reasons I cannot possibly approve of your traveling to East Asia."

"But, Herr Ribbentrop, we haven't broken off diplomatic relations with China; I can see no reason why I shouldn't visit both countries. After all, I'm going as an ordinary tourist and not on any political mission."

"That has nothing to do with this particular case. I regret that I am unable to approve your journey."

"If that is so I will go only as far as the Dutch East Indies."

"Unfortunately that too is impossible. The Dutch East Indies are much too close to East Asia and you might not be able to avoid contact of some sort with East Asian politicians."

I was beginning to lose patience, but didn't want matters to develop into a heated agrument, and replied: "Very well, then. I will restrict my journey to British India."

"That won't do either. If you go to British India the public will assume that you will be extending your trip as far as East Asia."

That was too much of a good thing. "Well, Herr Ribbentrop, I expect it'll boil down to a short trip to the Harz Mountains," I said as I left the room.

Naturally I refused to be put off by this line of reasoning, and finally managed matters in such a way that no further objections to my journey to India were raised by the Foreign Office.

For the first time in my life I kept a diary of my travels. On my return to Germany I left it in the care of friends in Switzerland, as it contained so many disparaging remarks on the Hitler regime that I had to make quite sure it was safe from any possible interception. For this very reason, however, I find it particularly valuable in writing these recollections. I am only sorry that I was unable to produce it at the Nuremberg Trial. I did not receive the manuscript back until 1951.

The following is an extract from this diary:

Once again I have cut loose. I have done so because by no other means could I have broken free from the fetters which the loss of the war had forged for us. There was no filing through these fetters save by sacrificing one's strength; the only way was to burst them, and I deliberately and frankly helped to do so. But the main thing afterwards was to take our place once more and work on positive lines within the international framework.

The world has grown too small for us to elevate war to the level of a principle. Nations will have to learn how to get on with one another. The earth is still big enough to allow all nations room to live.

The difference in our fundamental outlook separates me from those elements which believe that by the destruction and oppression of other European nations they will be able to achieve freedom to expand. Brutality as a principle, mendacity as a tenet, perfidy as a permanent institution can never succeed because, in the history of nations as in the lives of individuals, there is a moral law which cannot be broken with impunity. If the dictated Treaty of Versailles failed to endure, it was because of its unethical foundation. Neither will our present unethical conditions endure.

Ephemeral success has no power to fool me. And I would rather keep my character than go down to history as a kind of demi-god. So for the time being I retire from the game. Perhaps there will be another chance for me one day. If so it will be an act of grace; if not I shall take comfort from Goethe's words: "We can lose everything if we remain true to ourselves."

My Indian journey gave me a very impressive picture of the material strength of the British Empire. The iron industry had a considerable manufacturing potential. The cotton industry was at its zenith. In many other industries production was increasing steadily. I did not feel justified in withholding my observations from the German Government and therefore I notified Hitler of my return home as well as Goering and Ribbentrop. From the first two I received no reply whatever. Ribbentrop did at any rate acknowledge the receipt of my letter.

The confidential reports I received almost immediately on my return to Berlin were disquieting. My long absence — from the beginning of March to the beginning of August 1939 — meant that I had missed much of what had been happening at home in the meantime. The quarrel with Poland, deliberately fanned by Hitler and finally brought to a climax in mid-August according to plan, was bound to lead to armed conflict.

On August 25 I was informed through the agency of Admiral Canaris, Head of the Abwehr, that the attack on Poland was due to be launched at once. Through the good offices of General Oster I immediately sought to push on to Zossen, where the headquarters of the Wehrmacht was stationed. I wanted to give General von Brauchitsch a last-minute warning and try to rouse him to counter-action. I had been working for a considerable period with General Thomas, in an endeavor to prevent a war. Through Admiral Canaris he now notified Zossen by phone of my intended visit. The reply came back that Brauchitsch declined to see me and, if I persisted, would arrest me forthwith.

We experienced a temporary relief on learning almost at once that the order to attack had been rescinded. We were the more astounded when, eight days later, the command went forth to march into Poland. In Hitler's challenge to the British and French ultimatums which expired on September 3 I saw the downfall of my last hopes of stemming the tide of war. Not a German-Polish conflict but the Second World War had begun.

The attitude of the military leaders seemed to me incomprehensible. In all the conversations I had had with generals of my acquaintance it happened again and again that Hitler had invariably reassured them on the subject of possible intervention by the Western Powers in the event of a war with Poland. When the ultimatums expired the leaders of the Army, Luftwaffe and Navy were obliged to state frankly either that Hitler had been mistaken or that he had deliberately misled them. They should have made it clear to Hitler that Germany was not equipped for a second world war and would never come through such a war. Nothing of the sort happened. The evil ran its course.

The military leaders are to blame, however, not merely because they failed in their moral and political duty but because of their military inadequacy. At the Nuremberg Trial Field Marshal Milch declared that at the beginning of the war the British Air Force alone was stronger than the German. Admiral Dönitz stated in court that at the outbreak of war Germany possessed a total of fifteen submarines fit for Atlantic use. And General Jodl gave the Army strength as only seventy-five divisions, some of which were not even fully armed. How could the High Command venture to embark on a world war with such disastrously inadequate preparation?

From postwar literature the world has learned of the various attempts to take Hitler prisoner and thereby prevent him from continuing the war. I knew about nearly all of these attempts, and encouraged and backed them. In these pages, however, I want only to describe my own experiences during this period.

At the turn of the year 1939–40 I was living as a private individual, partly in Berlin, partly in my country house. I was approached one day by one of the big American magazines with the request that I would acquaint the American public with the German situation, German frame of mind and German aims. In accordance with official etiquette I reported the matter to Ribbentrop, who agreed but asked me to send him the manuscript before despatching it, which I declined to do.

A few weeks later I received another similar offer from America. I wrote Hitler:

I feel it my duty to apprise you of the following:

On December 20, 1939, I received a telegraphic offer from *Foreign Affairs*, the highly esteemed American periodical devoted to foreign politics. They ask me to write an article on Germany's attitude to the present conflict and add that my name commands such respect over there that whatever I write would be certain to receive the greatest attention. I have informed the Minister of Foreign Affairs of this offer and, in case he should be interested, have placed myself at his disposal for the purposes of discussion. The Foreign Minister thereupon suggested that I should write the article and submit it to him for censorship. Since I could not possibly agree to such conditions, either for the sake of the Americans or for my own sake, I put the matter aside.

Now I have received a similar offer from the editor of the *Christian Science Monitor*, the well-known American daily. I do not wish to approach the Foreign Minister again, neither do I wish to let this second offer slip without at least drawing your attention to the fact that here at home the possibilities afforded us for bringing German influences to bear on American opinion are obviously inadequate.

On receipt of this letter Hitler sent for me. I pointed out that an occasional article in American periodicals was not sufficient to influence the growing anti-German tendency in the United States in our favor. I suggested that we should send over someone who would maintain steady contact with the public and particularly with the press. To the question whether I would be prepared to do this I replied in the affirmative. Hitler received the suggestion favorably and said he would discuss the matter with Ribbentrop. I never heard anything further on the subject.

Instead, Ribbentrop not long afterwards sent over a Berlin lawyer who was a member of the party . . . The gentleman did not stay long. On his return he told me how badly he had been treated over there. He had been exposed to constant threats by telephone against his personal safety; he had been expelled from no fewer than four hotels after only a short time in each, and had been unable to gain admission to a single club.

It might still, perhaps, have been possible to effect an improvement in our relations with America when Sumner Welles, the American Under-Secretary of State, made a tour of the European governments at the beginning of March 1940, in the course of which he also visited Berlin. Although the American Government had been informed of my dismissal it had stated that Mr. Sumner Welles wished to have speech with four persons: Adolf Hitler, Hermann Goering, Ribbentrop and Dr. Schacht. I was informed of this by the Foreign Office with audibly expressed surprise at Welles's intention to call upon me.

Ribbentrop quite obviously wanted to prevent a *tête à-tête* between Sumner Welles and myself. First he invited me to a luncheon to be given in honor of Mr. Welles; I could have a talk with him then. Curiously enough this luncheon was canceled. In any case Mr. Welles's express desire to talk to me could not be simply ignored. When the American Chargé d'Affaires invited me to a tea party for the purpose of a discussion with Mr. Welles the head of the Records Department of the Foreign Office sent for me and urged me to take an interpreter along.

Somewhat maliciously I replied: "I don't think that will be necessary, and I beg to dispense with an interpreter since I assume that Mr. Sumner Welles will speak at least one of the three European languages."

On Sunday March 3, 1940, at five o'clock in the afternoon I arrived at the house of the American Chargé d'Affaires, Mr. Kirk, where I met guests from the Diplomatic Corps — the enchanting wife of Signor Attolico, the Italian Ambassador; the Belgian Ambassador and the Netherlands Minister with their wives. Our host himself was not present. At midday he had gone with Sumner Welles to Karinhall to see Hermann Goering. Since they had left between twelve and one they had reckoned to lunch with Goering. When they returned to Grunewald shortly before six we learned that not only had they had no lunch but that no refreshment of any kind had been offered them all the time they had been at Karinhall. Their immediate need was to get something to eat.

From my private conversation with Sumner Welles I gathered that Hitler had not impressed him unfavorably. Why Welles should have been so badly treated from a social standpoint remains a puzzle. Ribbentrop, whose perfect mastery of the English language was known to everyone, actually went so far as to receive Mr. Welles in the presence of an interpreter and to have the American's speech translated.

During my talk with Welles it came out that he had discussed with Hitler the possibility of concluding a peace through American mediation. Hitler had stipulated that in the event of such a peace Germany must remain an ethnological entity; that is, with the frontiers of 1914, the inclusion of Austria and the Sudetenland, but excluding Alsace-Lorraine. To me his economic expositions were particularly interesting.

"We cannot know whether it will be possible to conclude peace any more than we can foresee the outcome of the war. But one thing is certain: whichever way the war goes the economic problems will remain the same as before. The war will not solve any of them. These problems extend far beyond the framework of the belligerent countries. That is the reason why America is already busy preparing for these problems."

"I find these statements extraordinarily comforting, Mr. Welles," I replied. "In my opinion the economic problems that the end of the war will bring are more far-reaching than the political ones."

"It is precisely on account of this view that I was commissioned to seek you out, Herr Schacht, and have a talk with you during my visit to Berlin. You know of course that in America you are very highly thought of as an economist."

After a lengthy exchange of views on matters economic I made no secret of the fact that I was diametrically opposed to the war, that the American Embassy knew this since Donald Heath, the American Councilor to the Embassy, occasionally came to see me. I should rejoice greatly therefore if the American Government were to embark on the work of mediation.

I saw Hitler on one more official occasion, when he returned from his successful campaign against France. All ministers and party leaders were bidden to come to the Anhalter Railway Station to welcome Hitler. My absence from this ceremony would have created a very bad impression: there remained nothing for it but to obey the summons. On the way there my car picked up the Minister Alfred Rosenberg. Rosenberg was an invariably reserved and silent man. I always had the impression that he was afraid to expose his intellectual insignificance if he took too great a part in the conversation. On this drive too it was almost impossible to get a word out of him.

On the platform all the officials and party pundits were assembled in uniform, all in gold braid. As the one and only civilian I must have created a strange impression in my lounge suit. But they were used to that where I was concerned. I have never worn uniform. Once, when I told Hitler that no one could hope to succeed with the party unless he held some rank and wore uniform Hitler immediately replied:

"You can have all the uniforms you want from me."

I raised both hands deprecatingly and exclaimed: "Oh, please! I would rather not!"

When the train steamed in Hitler alighted and walked down the line of ministers, shook hands and nodded and beamed on everyone. He was obviously in high good humor and spoke a few words to this or that individual. When he came to me he looked at me triumphantly and exclaimed: "Well, Herr Schacht, what do you say now?"

For a moment I did not know how to reply in such a way as to express neither praise nor censure. I simply took his hand and said: "May God protect you."

He walked away, completely unresponsive.

The welcome over, the whole procession drove to the Chancellery through the cheering, seething crowd. So far as I know this is the last occasion on which Hitler — full of pride at his victory over France — stood upright in his car to show himself to the multitude.

My car drew up at the Chancellery. I let Rosenberg get out — he was attending the reception which followed the station ceremony. He looked round at me enquiringly as I remained seated. I said: "Not my line," and drove home.

I made no secret of my opposition to the war, even to members of the government. In December 1940 Herr von Weizsäcker, Secretary of State in the Foreign Office, sent for me and warned me, on behalf of the Foreign Minister, to refrain from defeatist statements. I asked who it was to whom I was supposed to have made such statements, and was told Funk, the Minister for Economic Affairs. Whereupon I sent him the following letter:

My dear Colleague:

Today, on behalf of Herr von Ribbentrop, the Secretary of State in the Foreign Office, Herr von Weizsäcker, surprised me by pointing out that I had expressed pessimistic opinions in regard to the present situation. In reply to my enquiry as to how he came by such knowledge, your name was given as the source of information. I recollect very well having had one or two discussions with you on the subject of our economic situation, in which you frankly desired to know my views. These I made known to you on the lines I have taken for years; namely, that from an economic standpoint we are not equipped for a war of long duration. And that a war with Britain would be one of long duration was obvious to anyone with a knowledge of Anglo-Saxon mentality.

Herr von Ribbentrop's object in referring to this matter was, I regret to say, not made clear to me. If he desired me to alter my opinion he should have furnished convincing and material reasons why I should so so. Such was not the case. On the other hand I cannot imagine that Herr von Ribbentrop would wish me, in professional discussions with the Führer's councilors, to conceal or misrepresent my views. That would be to misconstrue my loyalty to the Führer.

I have asked Herr von Weizsäcker to reply to Herr von Ribbentrop that, so long as the Führer wishes me to remain a Minister of the Reich, it is my right and my duty to reply to any enquiry by a fellow Minister in a manner commensurate with my convictions and with the truth.

In view of Herr von Ribbentrop having referred to you in this connection I cannot refrain from bringing the above matter to your notice.

I sent a copy of this letter to Herr von Weizsäcker with the request that he would submit it to his chief.

On January 30, 1941, the eighth anniversary of the "thousand-year Reich," the *Völkischer Beobachter* devoted several large complete pages to a chronicle of National Socialist achievements during those eight years. Every tiniest detail was mentioned: the names of persons in leading positions, the decreeing of laws and ordinances; festivities and ceremonies, parades and exhibitions; in short everything that could be described as worth mentioning, if only for a brief period.

In this detailed chronicle there was no mention, not a single word, of anything I had accomplished. My existence was completely ignored, my name never appeared once in the whole long record.

In the hands of a totalitarian tyrant such dead silence is a terrible political weapon. It shows clearly how it was possible to keep the German people in blindness and ignorance. The path to publicity was barred to anyone not willing to kowtow to the system. No artist who went his own way, unapproved by Hitler, could get into any exhibition, any display, or obtain any kind of publicity. No bookshop would sell, no theater would perform, books or plays by anyone whose work was not "approved."

There were many martyrs to the Hitler regime but they disappeared noiselessly in the cells and graves of the concentration camps, without anything being heard of them. But of what use is martyrdom in the struggle against power if it is not made known and thereby given the chance to stir up others? Crimes committed by party members — and such crimes were legion — were never allowed to be made public, even when the verdicts were those of the regular courts of justice. When in January 1943 I finally managed to obtain my release from the nominal post of Minister without Portfolio no mention of it — not so much as a word — was made public.

The complete control of the means of publication and their misuse by evil rulers is a political danger of the worst kind, whether these rulers be the state, or party groups, or individual capitalists. In any reasonable press legislation, even dead silence should be taken into account. The right to publish and the duty to publish go hand in hand.

In February 1941 I visited Hitler once again, as I thought it my duty to acquaint him with my forthcoming second marriage. As I was on the point of leaving the room he called me back.

"A year ago you suggested that you should go to America. Do you consider it would still be possible to carry out such an intention?"

"I do not consider that such a journey would be possible today. Since the Lend-Lease law came into force I consider there is no chance whatever of achieving any positive results for Germany."

This was the last occasion on which I saw Hitler.

Early in March 1941 my wife and I were married. For our honeymoon we went to Switzerland where we met and had many interviews, not only with Germans living there and with members of the Embassy, but also with Swiss friends.

Coming as it did in the midst of the heartrending events of that time our wedding trip was like an oasis. It enabled me to forget the risk that my remarriage involved for my young wife; namely, that at any moment I was liable to be unmasked as a traitor. But my wife was equal to any emergency.

Of a serene, cheerful nature, receptive to all manner of beauty and to the things of the spirit, her main interest and study was devoted to painting, the plastic arts, and architecture. In addition she was fond of analytical and philosophic literature. As a grown-up woman she started to learn Latin. Her critical faculties in the realm of art and her knowledge of the history of art stood her in very good stead when the new Munich House of Art was opened. There she was a member of the staff, having been transferred from the National Lindenmuseum at Altenburg (Thuringia) where she had worked as an assistant.

I had come to know her in Munich when we had met as members of a jolly party at the Bonbonnière. Like so many others who do not know me personally she had pictured me as a stiff-and-starched, chilly sobersides, and was surprised to see me laughing heartily and unrestrainedly at the cabaret show.

What attracted me was not merely the slender figure or the well-cut features, curly fair hair and blue eyes which might have served as a model for the Epple angels in Bogenhausen Church; it was even more her brilliant wit, her aspiring soul, her uninhibited comradeship and sympathy. Nevertheless it was some little time before we finally understood one another. She had many other admirers; she was thirty years younger than I and had a satisfying career. Dare I tie her to myself, standing as I did politically in constant peril? Fate and love decided for us; neither of us has regretted it. But together with my gratitude to this woman for all the happiness she has given me, let me here express some of our undying gratitude to the women of Germany for all that they have been to their menfolk during the war and postwar years of tribulation. Courage in the face of the enemy we rightly prize as heroism, but even greater and more blessed was the heroism displayed by our women in their struggle against poverty and distress, humiliation and captivity.

For a brief three years I was able to safeguard my wife from care and anxiety. Then her sufferings began. I was arrested under Hitler with the prospect of being hanged for high treason; grave charges were preferred against me at the International Military Tribunal at Nuremberg; I was imprisoned for years by the German denazification tribunals; temporarily condemned to eight years in a labor camp; outlawed by the people of Germany at the instigation of those who had failed to make good under the Weimar Republic and had now been washed up again on the crest of the wave. I was subjected to palpable threats on the part of Communists and Social Democrats; my professional honor was impugned by the Social Democratic authorities of the Hanseatic city of Hamburg. Such were the blows that rained down upon my young wife. She met and overcame them all with exemplary steadfastness, dignity, fearlessness and energy.

No forebodings, however, came to trouble our Swiss wedding journey. We gave ourselves up to the happiness of the hour. Laughingly we welcomed the spring at Lugano, and strolled along mountain pathways at Gandria.

The Swiss papers were friendly and featured our visit in letterpress and pictures. I had friendly talks with representatives of the Swiss Government. That was in 1941 when I had already severed my connection with the Hitler regime. I little dreamed that ten years later Switzerland would refuse to grant me a visa to enter the country on the ground that I was an undesirable alien. What change had taken place in my outlook since 1941? I had been suspected by Hitler of high treason, imprisoned and threatened with death, while in Nuremberg the Allies, for completely opposite reasons, had wanted to hang me for conspiring with Hitler. Throughout this entire decade I had remained the same: it was the Swiss Government that had changed.

During this wedding trip I had an interesting discussion with one of the leading Swiss bankers over a question of which the pros and cons were being hotly debated by the Swiss Government. During the course of the war and down to the time of which I write, Switzerland had been actively concerned in the delivery of large quantities of goods to Germany, including of course much war material; thereby — as in the First World War — reaping unusually large profits. Hitherto the German Government had paid for these deliveries mainly in cash; now, however, the Reich had approached Switzerland with a request for a big credit. The question was whether to grant this credit or to restrict deliveries to those payable in cash. What did I think about it?

I replied that I would endeavor to answer this question entirely from the standpoint of the Swiss economy. Viewed from this angle it would be far better for Switzerland to continue to make deliveries against a partial credit than to have to give up the deliveries altogether. If a great part of the deliveries were to stop it would mean, among other upsets, considerable unemployment in Switzerland which would have to be met out of state funds. Social unrest might very likely follow, which could have an unpleasant effect on the domestic policy of the country, particularly in wartime, to say nothing of considerations of foreign policy being involved. Furthermore, the sum total of the credit would not amount to anything very excessive, since Germany made many counterdeliveries to Switzerland which not only covered part of the credit but which also, according to their nature, constituted important factors for the pursuance of Swiss economic policy. I referred especially to coal.

During this conversation I reminded my companion that I had once given his country a piece of good advice on a vital economic matter, which the Swiss Government of the day had unfortunately omitted to follow. It was at the beginning of Hitler's rule, not long after we had stopped paying interest on our foreign loans. I had suggested to the Swiss Government that they might obtain from

Germany a sufficient quantity of coal to enable them to stock up a full year's requirements. I pointed out that Switzerland was very dependent on coal deliveries from Germany and that it would be a great safeguard in any possible economic or political crisis if a stock of coal were available at all times for transport and industrial purposes. I would be prepared to send sufficient stocks of coal to Switzerland to set off the servicing of these loans. Despite this favorable offer the proposal was not accepted by the Swiss Government, the reason given being that it would be impossible to persuade the Swiss coal merchants to agree unanimously to such a step.

Early in April 1941 we returned from our honeymoon to our country place at Gühlen. In the course of the next few days I learned through my political and military indirect connections of Hitler's intention to attack Russia.

Relations between Germany and Russia — which had seemed to be on a friendly footing after the mutual agreement at the end of August 1939 — had not improved with the passage of time. The atmosphere during Molotov's visit to Berlin had been decidedly cool. An event which attracted little attention indicated the party obstructions to which Hitler had exposed himself when he signed the pact with Russia. This pact had never been approved by many party circles. For years a war of ideas had been waged against bolshevism through intensive propaganda — and now this was to be replaced by friendship. There is no room in ideological warfare for such tactical *volte-face*, reshuffling or regrouping.

When Molotov was expected in Berlin, Foreign Minister Ribbentrop sent a request to Lutze, the S.A. Chief of Staff, to provide the necessary complement of men to line the streets through which Molotov would drive on his arrival in the capital. Lutze turned down this request on the express grounds that he could not expect his anti-Bolshevist men to take part in a reception in honor of one of the chief representatives of bolshevism. I do not know if Ribbentrop reported this refusal to Hitler. At any rate, when Molotov arrived the cordons lining the streets consisted solely of S.S. men in their black uniform.

My friends and I were convinced that to attack Russia was sheer madness. If we had hoped, till now, that it might still be possible to end the war by recourse to any reasonable means, that hope was shattered by the inclusion of Russia in the ranks of our enemies.

Individual party leaders who suspected or knew of Hitler's intention to make war on Russia must have been equally aghast. The best proof of this is Rudolf Hess's flight to England, undertaken without Hitler's knowledge. But if Hess thought that by his flight he could avert destiny, it testifies only to the complete ignorance of foreign affairs that characterized nearly all the party leaders.

The first military encounters with the entirely inadequately prepared Russians were those great valley engagements which were among Hitler's successes and in which some millions of Russians were taken prisoner.

I took advantage of these initial victories to compose a letter to Hitler in September 1941. In this letter I explained that a turning point had been reached. Hitler was at the zenith of his military successes. The Allies, to a great extent, still overestimated Germany's strength. The moment had come for Hitler to seize the initiative for a vigorous peace policy. I concluded:

In the case of such initiative the method of procedure is of paramount importance.

(1) Public speeches should be excluded from the start.

(2) Equally, contact should not be sought on political grounds as that would be regarded as a sign of weakness. Rather, it should begin from an economic angle.

(3) It can only originate in America, with whom we are still not officially at war.

(4) I still think it stands a chance in that country, even now, in spite of everything.

Hitler's reaction to this communication was in the negative. Secretary of State Lammers wrote me: "The Führer has personally read your letter and instructed me to convey his thanks to you."

I heard indirectly that Hitler had told his generals of my letter and remarked: "Schacht still doesn't understand me." It was one of his few true statements.

Hitler's attempt to include Spain in his military calculations was a failure. The war was carried over into Africa. The conquest of Moscow, for which Guderian had reckoned three months at the beginning of the Russian campaign, failed to come off. The Russians pulled themselves together. Thanks to extensive material aid from the Allies their resistance grew continually stronger. German industry certainly did everything possible to ensure the supply of war material, but the dispatch of reinforcements from Germany became increasingly difficult.

In February 1942 a general fiat went forth to all Ministers of the Reich forbidding them to listen to foreign radio transmitters. Despite my protest the ban continued to hold good in my case also, but Lammers, the Secretary of State, wrote me:

"To enable you to obtain information *re* foreign radio propaganda on matters touching your professional field of action, I have arranged with the Minister of Public Enlightenment and Propaganda that a brief summary of foreign news items shall be delivered to you on request, in so far as it concerns your professional activities."

My protest had been rejected by Hitler on the ground that it did not affect my prestige in any way. My reply to Hitler was as follows:

The ban on listening to foreign broadcasts represents lack of confidence in my loyalty and my powers of discrimination. There are no grounds whatever for either. My prestige will not be affected. Prestige is not bestowed, it must be earned.

But if the result of your decision is to deprive me *professionally* of opportunities for obtaining information, and *personally* of your trust in me, then I would hereby request you to release me from my office as a Minister of the Reich.

In reply to Lammers' suggestion that Goebbels should furnish me with information I wrote: "I regret that I am unable to avail myself of the offer by the Minister for Public Enlightenment and Propaganda as this minister is not competent to pronounce an opinion on the material in which I am interested."

My release from office was not granted. But this correspondence shows how the tension between Hitler and myself had increased.

In November 1942 — obviously owing to an oversight in the Chancellery — there came into my hands the draft of a decree providing for the calling up of pupils from the upper forms in secondary schools for the protection of airfields and the prevention of air raids. This oversight gave me a welcome opportunity once again to state my views on the political situation. It was when furious battles were raging round Stalingrad which had not yet, however, achieved for Hitler the disastrous results that followed a few weeks later. I sent the following letter to Hermann Goering who had issued the draft order:

My dear Field Marshal,

By way of the Chancellery I am apprised of your draft order concerning the calling up of fifteen-year-old schoolboys for war service. Since the end of 1937, as you know, I have been a Minister in name only, without any official sphere of action. No cabinet councils have been held since 1938. I have never been called upon to attend any ministerial discussions. I live in the country in complete retirement. For some months past I have been expressly forbidden to listen to foreign broadcasts, so that my only source of information on the military, economic and political situation is that available to every discriminating German, whose numbers among the so-called masses should not be underestimated. Since I am not a member of the National Defense Council I have nothing to do with the passing of the draft order. Although I can therefore exonerate myself from any share of responsibility, my conscience and the desire to leave no stone unturned prompt me to send you these lines.

By way of preliminaries I may state that from the very first my attitude towards those in responsible positions has been that from the economic standpoint we were not adequately equipped for a *long* war. But that the war would be a long one must have been obvious to anyone with a knowledge of Anglo-Saxon mentality after Britain had given notice of her resolve to look upon a German attack on Poland in the light of a *casus belli*. Early in 1940 I suggested to the Führer that I should go to the United States in an attempt to slow down America's armed support of Britain, and if possible to prevent America becoming more deeply involved in the war. The Minister for Foreign Affairs declined this offer, which the Führer viewed sympathetically. I brought the matter to the Führer's notice again in the autumn of 1941 when we were then at the height of our successes, but to no purpose.

It may be necessary, from a military point of view, to call up the fifteen-year-olds but it will put a heavy strain on the German nation's confidence in victory. The facts, as the German people see them, are as follows:

(1) The original prospects of a short war have not been fulfilled.

(2) The promised rapid subjugation of Britain by the Luftwaffe has not materialized.

(3) The prognostication that Germany would be kept safeguarded from enemy air attacks has not been fulfilled.

(4) The repeated assurance that Russia's powers of resistance had been definitely broken has not been substantiated.

(5) On the contrary, the delivery to Russia of Allied war material and Russia's reserves of manpower have led to severe counterattacks on our Eastern Front.

(6) Despite repeated attempts the originally victorious advance against Egypt has so far proved a failure.

(7) The landing of the Allies in West and North Africa, described as impossible, has nevertheless taken place.

(8) The extraordinary large amount of shipping essential for this landing has shown that our U-boats, in spite of their considerable successes, have not sufficed to stop this means of transport.

Add to this retrenchments which are obvious to every member of the population — in the Civil Service, in transport, in war material, in employment of labor. The calling up of fifteen-year-olds will most assuredly strengthen misgivings as to how this war will actually end.

This letter was read aloud to the Bench by the American Chief Prosecutor at Nuremberg. From the manner in which he did so I was forced to conclude that the Prosecutor had previously failed either to read this letter right through or to read it carefully enough, for it exonerated me completely. At the end he could not refrain from remarking: "That's a very good letter."

It certainly was a good letter. But it was also a very dangerous one for me. Seven weeks elapsed before the reaction of those in authority followed. On January 21, 1943, Lammers sent one of his departmental heads who handed me my discharge by Hitler from the office of Minister without Portfolio. It was accompanied by a letter from the Secretary of State:

"In view of your general attitude in the German nation's present fearful struggle, the Führer has decided first of all to dismiss you from your post as Minister of the Reich."

That further action would soon follow this dismissal I gathered from the words "first of all." I did not have long to wait. The next step took the form of a letter from Goering:

"By way of reply to your defeatist letter, calculated to undermine the German people's powers of resistance, I hereby expel you from the Prussian State Council. Goering, Marshal of the Greater German Reich."

I could not help smiling over this letter. The Prussian State Council had never had any significance. It had not been summoned for at least half a dozen years. To be expelled from this assembly did not, therefore, constitute a very heavy punishment. It struck me as even funnier however that I was supposed to have undermined the German people's powers of resistance by means of a private and confidential letter to Goering.

Yet a further repercussion was that I received a letter, signed by Martin Bormann, instructing me on behalf of the Führer to return the party's gold badge of honor which had been awarded to all ministers — including myself — on January 30, 1937, to commemorate the Hitler Government's fourth year of existence. It gave me peculiar satisfaction to comply with this request.

But I would have to reckon with further measures and I endeavored to elude them as swiftly and as completely as possible. I had spent my birthday, January 22, at my country home. The next day I drove at once to my Berlin residence and noticed that the street was being watched by some of the Gestapo who, according to their easily recognized custom, were strolling up and down near my home after the manner of innocent pedestrians.

From there I drove to the home of my son-in-law at Schlachtensee and on the way realized that I was being trailed by a car full of Gestapo men.

I returned to Berlin, still followed by the Gestapo car, packed a couple of suitcases with necessities as quickly as possible and drove via Spandau to my country house. Shortly before we got to Spandau the Gestapo seemed to realize my intention and gave up any further attempt at shadowing me. The fact that for the next few months I remained exclusively on my estate probably induced the Gestapo to refrain from visibly molesting me further. All my mail was read, of course, and all telephone calls tapped.

The events following my dismissal had impressed upon me the need to let any connections with people of my way of thinking be as inconspicuous as possible. From the first I had been in close touch with Goerdeler; now, however, I quietly severed all contact with him, for his behavior seemed to me far too lacking in caution. On the other hand old friends came to see me from time to time in my country retreat. Particularly frequent visitors were Captain Strünck of the Reserves and his wife; he was working with Canaris and always brought valuable information. Being a keen hunstman his visits were always camouflaged as invitations to hunt. Directly or indirectly I remained in communication with — among others — Gisevius, Dr. Franz Reuter, Popitz, the Prussian Minister of Finance; Police Superintendent Nebe, Count Helldorf, Chief Commissioner of Police in Berlin; Herbert Goering, Reporter-in-Chief at the Ministry of Economic Affairs, cousin and confirmed opponent of Hermann Goering; von Bismarck, Governor of a Prussian province and a brother of Prince Bismarck, and others.

Great-grandfather
Christian von Eggers

Schacht's paternal
grandfather

His father,
William Schacht

His mother, Constanze
Baroness von Eggers

Schacht as a student
in 1895

At the turn
of the century: Ph.D.,
journalist, economist

With his eldest daughter,
born in 1903

With his first wife Luise
and their son Jens,
born in 1910

In front of the Reichsbank, whose president he was. Behind him
Chauffeur Riesel, who drove him for many years

**Schacht s'amuse**

Schacht amüsiert sich

La bataille autour des haricots
Der Kampf um die Bohnen

A famous cartoon
in *Aux Ecoutes*
on May 18, 1929

A cartoon published by the
*Muenchner Illustrierte Presse*
depicting Schacht's
daily routine at the
Young Conference

**Im Pariser Hauptquartier der deutschen Sachverständigen**

Ein Tag des Reichsbank-Präsidenten Dr. Schacht

Soeben aufgestanden ...

... schon unterwegs

... den ganzen Tag in der Konferenz

... und abends im Frack zum Empfang

„Münchener Illustrierte Presse" Nr. 16 (München) vom 21. April 1929

Gemäß den Vorschriften des Bankgesetzes vom 30. August 1924 in der Fassung des Gesetzes vom 13. März 1930 wird

Herr Dr. Hjalmar  S c h a c h t

auf Grund der heute erfolgten Wahl hiermit vom 17. März 1933 ab auf die Dauer von vier Jahren zum Präsidenten des Reichsbank-Direktoriums ernannt.

Berlin, den 17. März 1933.

Berlin, den 16. März 1933.

Die Mitglieder des Generalrates

Der Reichspräsident:

Der Reichskanzler:

Under the letter appointing Schacht President of the Reichsbank, Hitler's signature is next to those of three Jewish bankers: von Mendelssohn, Wassermann, and Warburg.

Schacht with Hitler in 1934 at
the laying of the foundation stone for
the new Reichsbank building

In prison, after his arrest
by the Gestapo in 1944

In the dock at the Nuremberg Trial

During a further two years'
detention by the government
of Wuerttemberg-Bavaria

Schacht with his
younger daughters

In front of his Munich house with his wife and former prime
minister Mirza Ismael of Hyderabad

General Neguib asks Dr. Schacht's advice on a matter of economy

Writing his memoirs

After the atmosphere in my neighborhood had quieted down a little I took another short trip to Berlin in order to attend various discussions.

In the summer of 1943 I made yet another attempt to intervene in the course of events. I wrote to Lammers:

"The fate of Germany, of National Socialism and of Hitler are so closely interwoven that even the treatment meted out to me cannot influence my loyalty and sense of duty. I should therefore be grateful if you would inform me whether the Führer would be prepared once again to accept from me a short written statement on the political situation."

Lammers replied on August 19, 1943:

"I have informed the Führer of your wish to send him a brief written statement on the political situation. The Führer requests that you will refrain from doing so."

I kept away from the fateful meetings centering around Goerdeler and Popitz, the Minister of Finance. Goerdeler's doings in particular were too apt to attract attention. Dr. Joseph Müller (later Bavarian Minister of Justice) stated at one of my denazification proceedings: "Goerdeler was like a motor engine that runs too noisily." That was also my impression.

I never took any part in Goerdeler's many discussions about the program of a future government and the formation of a future cabinet. Together with Witzleben I had already made up my mind in 1938 that, if we succeeded in eliminating Hitler, a military government must be set up first of all so as to ensure the formation of a subsequent government by means of general elections. Among other things we had provided for the appointment of an auxiliary council consisting of well-known representatives of the workers, who would act in an advisory capacity to the provisional military government. The working out of proclamations to the German people, and program manifestos for a future government — a favorite occupation with Goerdeler — seemed to me idiotic. Time enough for such things when the event had actually occurred, when they could be completed in twenty-four hours.

One of our adherents who was also a member of Canaris' Abwehr was Reichsgerichtsrat (member of the bar) Dr. von Dohnanyi. As early as 1942 he wanted to read me a proclamanation he had drawn up beginning with the words: "Hitler is dead!" I interrupted him at once with the request that he would let me hear the rest when Hitler really was dead.

To compile lists of ministers and commit them to paper seemed to me even more crazy than composing proclamations. There were none too many competent people to choose from. One could make a mental note of the few who were worth considering without setting them down in writing.

I continued studiously to avoid meeting Goerdeler. Shortly before the attempted attack on Hitler's life, therefore, the former Ambassador von Hassel came to sound me as to whether I would be prepared to join a Goerdeler cabinet. I told him that such an enquiry was much too premature. Apparently, however, he wanted to tie me down somehow or other, whereupon I declared that at this stage I wasn't going to let myself be tied down by Goerdeler in any way, since I was not at all certain what policy Goerdeler intended to pursue. In the event of a new government I should in any case consider that my duty lay in making use of my foreign connections in an endeavor to bring about an immediate understanding with the Allied governments. Our conversation had taken place in the park at Sansouci, Potsdam. Von Hassel left in an obviously dissatisfied frame of mind; he seemed to be afraid that I should obstruct his desire to become Foreign Minister.

Another important link was established through Lieutenant Colonel Gronau, an older friend of my son Jens and Administrative Officer of the Berlin Defense District. His reports were of great value. In the first months of 1944 Gronau enabled me to meet General Lindemann of the Artillery, one of the few senior officers whose dislike of the regime had reached the point where he determined to take definite action. Shortly afterwards Lindemann was appointed Master-General of the Ordnance and entrusted with the procuring of artillery equipment for the whole of the Armies of the East. In this capacity he was able to keep in closest touch with headquarters and soon made contact with the few other high-ranking officers who, like himself, were prepared to bring the Hitler regime to a violent end.

Here at last I had found a man who had direct access to Hitler, a facility I no longer enjoyed. Lindemann was stationed in the East, but whenever he came to Berlin we discussed the preparations for the attempt on Hitler and I used every opportunity to urge that it should be speeded up.

The final preparations dragged on for several weeks. Various dates that we had had in view had to be postponed because Hitler's movements meant that some obstacle or other was always cropping up.

But it became more and more clear that action, as planned, might be expected about mid-July.

On July 17, in order not to be held up in my local arrangements, I took my two small children by my second marriage to my daughter in Upper Bavaria. On July 20 I was in the Hotel Regina in Munich when I heard that the plot had failed.

The morning after the attempt on Hitler the hotel porter drew my attention to the fact that I was being watched by some of the Gestapo officials who were stationed in the hotel. I thought it would be wise to leave and on July 22 was back again at my country home near Berlin.

I spent the whole day alone with my wife listening to the radio reports of the arrests and shootings. It was not until much later that I learned of the events that had taken place at the Ministry for War in the Bendlerstrasse.

On July 23 at seven o'clock in the morning I was awakened by our cook knocking on my bedroom door with the news that the Gestapo wished to speak to me. Still in pajamas I opened the door.

I was informed that I was under arrest.

Quite calmly I dressed and told my wife, who immediately did likewise. I was able to hand over the most important keys to my wife in the presence of the police.

Then I was taken downstairs to the front door where several cars were standing. I bade farewell to my wife and called out that I should be back again in a few days. Her face was deadly pale and I could see that she did not place much faith in my prophecy.

# LIII

## CONCENTRATION CAMPS

THE PROCESSION of cars took me to Ravensbrück Concentration Camp in Mecklenburg. When I was conducted to my cell the guards, by way of a joke, mentioned that this was the same cell that my son-in-law had occupied before he had to undergo a sentence of two years' imprisonment.

From the moment I set foot in the cell at Ravensbrück until my final release on September 2, 1948 — more than four years — I had changed my prison no fewer than thirty-two times.

I spent over two years in solitary confinement. The cells were very much alike, measuring sometimes twelve square yards, sometimes less or rather more. Sometimes the W.C. was in the cell, sometimes not. If not you had to summon the guard to accompany you on every occasion. Sometimes the cells contained washing facilities, sometimes not. If not you had to wash under supervision. Treatment by the guards was sometimes decent, sometimes brutal, according to the character of the individual. Very scant provision was made for intellectual reading.

During this captivity of more than four years' duration I had for the most part to evolve my occupations out of my own head. The food was always sufficient but differed greatly in quality and was very often wretchedly poor. This was especially so in Ravensbrück where I frequently had nothing but cabbage soup or something similar for three days on end. On the whole, however, the treatment at Ravensbrück was not too bad at first. My chief warder could sometimes be persuaded to perform small favors in return for an occasional cigar from my scanty store.

So long as I remained in solitary confinement the separation from the other prisoners or camp inmates was strictly enforced. Only occasionally did I manage to get a glimpse of another cell, either in passing or through the shutter in the door which was opened when food was handed in. The building in which we were housed was only a small part of the very large camp and was obviously reserved for "politicals."

When we were taken across the courtyard for questioning I realized that there was a huge camp for women. Occasionally up to fifteen thousand women would be herded together in this place. From the window of the bathroom, which we were allowed to use once a week, I could see into a separate courtyard in which those mothers were crowded whose children had been born while they were in camp. Gradually, too, I was able to identify "prominent" fellow prisoners, among them General Halder.

My examination began a few days after I was arrested. From the first questions I realized at once that there was no really positive material evidence against me and that the method differed not at all from the customary formalities of the most elementary police procedure.

For my first examination I was taken by car from Ravensbrück to Drögen. It was here for instance, as I learned later, that Noske, the Social-Democratic Minister of Defense, and General von Falkenhausen were interned. On one occasion during a break in the proceedings I was allowed to take a short walk about the camp and noticed a column of men in military formation, consisting for the most part of "looted Germans" who had been commandeered in and transported from the occupied eastern provinces.

The first examination opened with the establishment of particulars as to my person by a certain Police Lieutenant John. Next to him sat a lady typist. To my surprise the first question, or rather the first order, was: "Give this lady particulars of your career."

After some humming and hawing as to range and content I proceeded to dictate to the typist the story of my career, in so far as I considered it safe for the Gestapo to know. It took several hours and the substance of these recollections differed considerably from the transcription.

At the next hearing, the following day, the order went forth: "Give the names of your acquaintances and friends."

I thought for a moment and replied: "No, I will not."

There ensued threatening gestures and some heated altercations before I succeeded in explaining myself: "I will not do so, in spite of your order, and for the following reason: If I start by mentioning any one name you will immediately assume that the person concerned might be of particular interest to you. If, however, I were accidentally to omit any name you would at once suspect me of having deliberately intended to conceal it. But I will make you another proposal. At my home, where my friends have frequently been to see me, we kept a visitors' book. Go over there and ask my wife to give you the visitors' book. You will find all the names you want in that."

I knew that this book contained only the names of guests who had spent the night at our house. Those who came for the day were not entered in the visitors' book. Among the latter, of course, were the many political visitors of recent times, so that I was safe not, accidentally, to give any name away.

The Police Lieutenant accepted this suggestion and the hearing was postponed for a few days. In the meanwhile Herr John himself had been to my wife to fetch the visitors' book, and it lay open in front of him when the hearing was resumed.

During the whole of my four years' imprisonment my wife, by her complete understanding of all the dangers and all the circumstances, was my greatest support. On this occasion she immediately entertained Herr John to tea and cakes, and as a result of her conversation his attitude toward me visibly improved.

In the intervening days I had managed, through my good warder Moschkus, to obtain the *Völkischer Beobachter* daily. One day, however, the newspaper was missing, and Moschkus declared it had not come. The next day he said it had been mislaid. As persuasively as I could I said to him:

"Moschkus, I still have one of my good cigars — the last. You shall have this cigar if you will bring me the *Völkischer Beobachter* of the day before yesterday."

The exchange worked perfectly — and then I saw why he had not given me that particular number. It contained the names of some twenty-eight officers and others who were implicated in the plot against Hitler, together with information as to which of them had been shot and which of them were still being sought for. Among the latter was my General Lindemann who had managed to escape.

At the thought of Lindemann I experienced a tremendous relief. I realized that in my association with Lindemann lay my greatest danger and I hoped too that he was safe. I resolved therefore that if I were questioned I would deny all connection with him.

Curiously enough at the ensuing hearing the question was never once put as to which of those twenty-eight men had been known to me, though any half-baked student of criminology would have asked it first of all. All subsequent questions were completely irrelevant. They dealt with my attitude to National Socialism and similar matters, which of course I was able to answer perfectly.

On August 28 the situation suddenly became critical. Early in the morning I was ordered to take off my clothes and put on the blue-and-white prison garb. On my feet I had great wooden shoes which could not be fastened, and in spite of all my efforts I could not persuade the camp superintendent — a real dyed-in-the-wool Gestapo man named Commissioner Lange — to let me keep my civilian clothes. I had never in all my life worn uniform; now I had to don convict's garb although I was only a so-called "security" prisoner; that is, at the worst liable to be questioned, and in no sense a convict.

The reaction of my inner self to the convict uniform was curious in the extreme. I did not dwell so much on the degradation inherent in the order, but I immediately experienced a kind of inferiority complex that I had not been strong enough to prevent these people from shoving me into convict uniform against my will. To such depths had I sunk that no right or justice, no resistance, no rebellion against such abuse of authority was of any avail. This feeling was intensified inasmuch as the entire personnel, warders and escorts, began at once to treat me as a criminal.

My next thought was, how many others were in a similar plight. I was filled with a sense of solidarity with the other blue-and-white stripes. I nearly had to give myself a shake in order to make the overseer understand that I did not belong with the convicts. How hard it was to separate one's own individuality from the uniform.

Hardly had I donned the convicts' uniform than I was handcuffed and hustled into a car like a bale of goods. Commissioner Lange himself occupied the front seat next the driver. I was being transferred to the underground prison at No. 9 Prinz-Albrecht-Strasse, the principal Berlin headquarters of the National Security Service.

At first I had to wait for hours in an empty anteroom without being given anything to eat or drink. Finally it transpired that in all the underground vaults there was not a single cell vacant. Whereupon I was driven to the Moabit Prison in the Lehrter-Strasse. My captors forgot to bring my suitcase containing my toilet things, and as I had no idea what they meant to do with me I did not at first notice that it was missing.

The change to the shabby cell in the Moabit was sheer torment. The cells remained lit up so that the warder could keep a check on the prisoner at any time through the spyhole in the door. For that reason I slept facing the wall on my plank bed; even so I awoke at intervals.

Once, when I opened my eyes, I saw a reddish-brown dot moving along the wall, barely a hand's breadth away. The electric light shone directly on it: a moment later it had fallen victim to my finger nail — a bug. An anxious search followed. That first night I managed to bag five. By day I combed all four walls of my cell. Big bugs, little bugs got what was coming to them. But curiously enough the wall was painted in such a way that hunting for the creatures was not easy. A yellowish ground color was thickly bespattered with brown spots, stripes and blobs, so that one hardly knew which was paint and which were bugs, especially as the dead bugs remained stuck to the walls.

It was not until the fourth day when I returned to Prinz-Albrecht-Strasse, where in the meantime a cell had become vacant, that my things were handed to me. My cell was in one of the vaults. A small window with a grating, high up near the ceiling, gave on to the open air. The room itself, however, was well below ground level. I spent four months in that cell without once getting a breath of fresh air. I was sixty-seven years old.

My captivity was lightened by the fact that I was now permitted to wear my civilian clothes again, and also that my wife was allowed to send me books and clean linen as well as some food to supplement my ordinary diet. During the first few days I was able to buy two small cigars a day which were passed through the spyhole.

In this prison the hearings were very soon resumed under a Commissioner named Stavitzki. His questions were no less idiotic than those put to me at Ravensbrück, but I gathered from the documents in front of him, on which he depended, that my transfer from Ravensbrück to the stricter discipline of the Prinz-Albrecht-Strasse must have resulted from statements that Goerdeler had made about me. This assumption was confirmed later by my friend Schniewind. In his case a page from Goerdeler's examination had found its way into his own deposition by mistake. When he came to read his deposition prior to signing it he saw Goerdeler's statements.

The following will give you some idea of the nature of these examinations:

"You attended meetings of a committee at which the political situation was regularly discussed?"

"Which committee do you mean?"

"The chairman of the committee was Reusch; those present were Messrs Voegler, Bücher, Wentzel, and others."

"I can't help laughing if you really think that this committee discussed politics. It was a gathering of about twelve persons, half of them industrialists, the other half farmers, who met at regular intervals to talk over the problems connected with the industrialization of agriculture."

"That is not correct. Herr Goerdeler has told us that this committee also discussed politics."

"I presume that if you have arrested me because I was a member of this committee you have taken all the others into custody as well. When you come to question these gentlemen you will find that my statements are correct. If by chance someone did let drop a political word or so it will have been during a personal conversation, but not as a matter of committee business."

"On the thirteenth of July you had a discussion with Gisevius in Berlin."

"That is quite untrue."

"We have proofs that you did."

"They cannot be correct. Please let me see these proofs."

"We will not let you see them. But we know that at that date you saw and spoke with Gisevius."

"I don't know how you came by your information, but if Gisevius was in Berlin at that time you must surely have arrested him meanwhile. Kindly allow me to meet him face to face."

"You also discussed a plan of escape with Goerdeler."

"I would urge you to let me confront Herr Goerdeler and you shall learn what it was that we discussed."

I had never heard that, shortly before the attempt on Hitler, Gisevius had left Switzerland, where he usually lived, and come to Berlin. I assumed that he was still in Switzerland. In his book Gisevius himself has described his activities during those days, and I was able, much to my satisfaction, to ascertain that within that inner circle of conspirators to which Gisevius and Strünck belonged every item of information which might have exposed them to danger was withheld, even from his intimates. I did likewise.

It was not possible to confront us with one another for the simple reason that Gisevius had succeeded in remaining in hiding from the Gestapo. My oft-repeated request — not only at the above-mentioned hearing but also at later ones — that Goerdeler and I might be brought face to face was never granted.

The complete failure of all these examinations to produce any results only served to increase the Gestapo commissioner's fury against me. While in the Prinz-Albrecht-Strasse, however, he was unable to vent his anger upon me, and it was only when we met again later in Flossenbürg Camp that I experienced it in full force.

On December 6th, the day my wife had had permission to visit me for the first time, I was sent for again to the office and received the information that I was to be taken back to Ravensbrück. I managed to whisper encouragingly to my wife, whom I met in the Commissioner's room, that the criminal hearing was over. There could only remain the political examination. When my wife said goodbye and shook hands she left a little packet of aspirin tablets in my hand. She knew that I occasionally took aspirin for sick headaches.

The accommodation at Ravensbrück was the same as before. A few days after my retransfer I was informed that there was a visitor for me. I was taken to Drögen to the same room in which I had been questioned. There, to my great surprise, I found my son Jens, now a lieutenant, who was in Berlin on leave from the front and had managed to get permission to come and see me.

This meeting with my son turned out to be vitally important for me. Before I was retransferred to Ravensbrück my wife had sent me a food parcel containing among other things an egg wrapped in a torn piece of newspaper, in which I read that the "deserter" General Lindemann of the Artillery had been arrested, that in the course of arrest he had received shots in the abdomen from the police and was now in the hospital. This information had revived all my former anxiety, since it implied the possibility of my being brought face to face with Lindemann.

Besides the official told off to keep an eye on us during my son's visit, there was also a typist in the room. There came a moment when the official began to exchange jokes with the girl, and I seized the opportunity to whisper softly to my son: "Is Lindemann alive?"

"Lindemann is dead."

"Have you seen Gronau?"

"Yesterday morning."

"Listen, Jens: go to Gronau and tell him — in the event of his being questioned — I have never set eyes on Lindemann in my life."

My son nodded silently.

He managed to carry out my desperate request and thus saved my life. He lost his own at the end of the war.

My dealings with General Lindemann had constituted the one supremely dangerous element: they were so unmistakably incriminating that I could not have escaped the death sentence. The fact that I knew Lindemann might have come out at any time if Gronau, or Lindemann himself, had been questioned, since neither was in a position to know what statements the other would make, or had already made. Now, with Lindemann dead and Gronau forewarned, I felt that danger was past.

A few days later Commissioner Lange entered my cell and said: "When questioned about your friends you made certain statements about Gronau, but they were very inadequate. We know a lot more about Gronau. You are to be questioned again immediately — come with me."

Gronau had indeed been arrested some few days previously. I felt certain, however, that my son had been able to warn him.

I realized from the first question that the authorities didn't know any more than I had told them and I stuck to my earlier entirely noncommittal replies. The proceedings culminated in the enquiry as to whether Gronau had not repeatedly voiced critical opinions in my house.

That roused my sense of humor. "Certainly," I replied, "we both voiced exceedingly critical opinions — on the miserably inadequate supply of fighter aircraft, the only kind that would have been any use against bombing attacks on German towns."

"Were there not occasions, in your house, and in conversation with you, when Gronau spoke of the National-Socialist system in very derogatory terms?"

"In my house? What are you thinking of? If he had dared anything of the kind I should have kicked him out then and there!"

I was taken back to my cell and was left in peace for two months.

In the Prinz-Albrecht-Strasse the only time we left our cells was when we dressed in the morning. Two men at a time were taken to the washhouse, while in a recess two more went under the cold shower. In spite of the icy water we never missed it, for it was our only chance of exchanging a few whispered words. The W.C. with its row of four or five seats offered far less opportunity as there were no doors and a warder patrolled up and down the whole time.

The only other occasions on which we left our cells was when we were questioned, and when there was an air-raid warning and we made for the shelter. When that happened we stood close together in a narrow passage, drawn up in two rows along both walls, and were absolutely forbidden to whisper or speak to one another. Sometimes we might pass a fellow prisoner on the way to the toilet or to a hearing; otherwise these gatherings in the shelter were our only opportunities for catching sight of the other inmates of the prison. Among them were many faces I knew in connection with previously mentioned events, and others who were unknown to me — General Thomas, Dr. Joseph Müller, Herbert Goering, General Fromm, Wenzel-Teutschental, Admiral Canaris, Dr. Goerdeler, von Schlabrendorf, Strünck, von Hofacker, and others.

In the shelter it was not easy to glean anything from the blank expressions of one's fellows, since each endeavored to present merely a stony mask. Most of them displayed only an iron determination to hold their own in the mental and psychological conflict with the commissioners.

Of all the faces I saw there none impressed me so painfully as those of Canaris and Goerdeler. The last, and comparatively recent, time I had seen Goerdeler he was still at liberty, alert and full of confidence; now he was in a state of complete collapse. His face expressed his whole inner disillusion and despair. Canaris was at bottom a great patriot; his face too revealed how the man's divided outlook, driven by necessity, had convulsed his whole inner nature and shattered his balance.

I had come to know Goerdeler fairly intimately in 1926 when I opened the new Reichsbank building in Königsberg where Goerdeler was Lord Mayor and delivered the speech of welcome in my honor. He had taken the opportunity of drawing attention to the very straitened financial circumstances in Königsberg, and the miserable housing conditions of the many refugees. After the ceremony Goerdeler had driven me to some of these overcrowded districts and had also introduced me to a big municipal gymnasium where the "dwellings" for individual families were separated only by sacks hung between each. I experienced a sense of shame at sight of this unhygienic, indecent, immoral accommodation.

The town of Königsberg was under an obligation to contribute one hundred and seventy-five thousand marks toward the cost of the new Reichsbank building. On my return to Berlin I suggested to my board that we should cancel this debt in order that the town might be in a position to provide accommodation for the badly housed inhabitants. Since then Goerdeler and I had been on friendly terms. When he was *Preiskommissar* (Price Controller), first under Brüning and later under Hitler, our professional activities also brought us into closer touch.

Goerdeler was entirely opposed to the National-Socialist outlook and as *Preiskommissar* and Lord Mayor of Leipzig he felt it incumbent upon him to carry out his duties to the best of his ability in accordance with his own economic conception, which was deeply rooted in liberalism. When the Nazi bigwigs took advantage of Goerdeler's absence on leave to remove the Mendelssohn Memorial from its site in front of the Gewandhaus, Goerdeler resigned his office as Lord Mayor by way of protest.

The firm of Krupp in Essen then wanted Goerdeler to join their board. Herr Krupp von Bohlen felt it his duty to notify Hitler of his intention and obtain the Führer's consent. Hitler refused and the negotiations with Goerdeler were broken off. In order to make up for the disappointment to some extent Krupp sent him on a tour abroad with instructions to send home reports on economic and business matters. At Goerdeler's request I gave him a number of letters of introduction in which I recommended him to my friends as a reliable partner in a discussion.

One morning soon after his return from abroad, Goerdeler turned up at my office in the Reichsbank in a state of great perturbation with the news that the Gestapo were after him. Something had obviously leaked out from his discussions with my London friends and had found its way to the Gestapo as material against him. He implored me to help him. After obtaining detailed information as to the subject matter and the partners in the London conversations I immediately dispatched a carefully worded letter to London, which would nevertheless enlighten those in the know as to the danger that might possibly threaten Goerdeler.

The London banking firm in question responded with admirable promptitude and equally admirable understanding. People abroad had no doubt learned by that time to read between the lines of that sort of letter from the Third Reich. The bank protested emphatically against the implication that their firm could possibly indulge in political activities directed against National Socialism, and declared that they would not tolerate any such imputation. The reply was so cleverly constructed that I was able to hand it to Goerdeler who was able, with its help, to prevent any further investigation by the Gestapo.

Now, however, fate had overtaken this honest patriot and blameless man who was much too decent, too scrupulous and too conscientious to start Putsches or revolutions. He leaned against the opposite wall in the air-raid shelter, pale and shattered, and we could do nothing but stare at one another in silence.

Christmas 1944 and January 1945 passed off quietly apart from the constant bombing raids on Berlin which we occasionally heard in the distance. Most of the prisoners had received Christmas parcels from members of their families, and we had called "happy" Christmas to each other through the shutters in the doors of our cells. To my great joy and surprise the warders, who were officially supposed to observe the Yule festival, had put up a little decorated Christmas tree in the passage and in our cells we heard their rather harsh voices singing "Silent Night, Holy Night."

My wife had permission to visit me again on February 3. She had walked several miles carrying a heavy parcel of books, food and clean linen. We had had barely twenty minutes together — always in the presence of a warder — when I was ordered to return to my cell immediately. There I learned that we were to be transferred from Ravensbrück that same day. The Russian forces had advanced so close to our camp that it seemed advisable to remove the political internees.

My wife waited another hour or so, when she was informed of the move and was forbidden to see me again, even for a brief moment.

Toward midday we were removed in one of the usual prison vans which the Berliner has christened "Green Minna." * We stopped at Drögen where we picked up General von Falkenhausen, Gottfried von Bismarck and one or two other internees, and drove toward Berlin.

That was the day on which Berlin suffered what was perhaps her most severe air raid. Scarcely had we reached the edge of the city when we saw burning and smoldering ruins everywhere. It is true that since the prison van had only some small barred windows in the roof we could see nothing but flames and smoke, no streets or houses. We drove, literally, through a continuous sea of flame. Every minute the van had to make a detour down side streets and it was a long while before we drew up at the well-known building at No. 9 Prinz-Albrecht-Strasse.

The cellar in the Prinz-Albrecht-Strasse looked bleak and hopeless in the extreme. Those parts of the building above ground had nearly collapsed under the bombing. Light and water no longer functioned. We undressed by the flickering light of a candle end, in spite of which each of us was once again confined in a separate cell. For nature's needs a pit had been dug in the yard with a bar nailed across it. It was here, sitting next to him on the bar, that I had my last talk with Dietrich Bonhöfer. Our glance fell on the barred window

---

* The German equivalent of Black Maria.

of a cellar, behind which a woman wrung her hands in despair and implored us, by signs, to help her.

The next morning we were awakened betimes and after a scanty cold breakfast were packed into a motor bus, through the windows of which we could at least see in what direction we were going. There were eight internees in all in the bus, and about twelve uniformed guards. Among the internees were General Oster, General Thomas, the Federal Austrian Chancellor Schuschnigg with his wife and little four-year-old daughter; Strünck, General Halder and myself.

The road led southward along the *Autobahn*. In the neighborhood of Bayreuth we turned eastward off the *Autobahn*, but in the gathering dusk were no longer able to tell for certain where we were going. Toward eleven o'clock we drew up before a camp surrounded with barbed wire, were told to get out, and once again locked into separate cells.

I had no idea what kind of camp this was, but the whole creepy atmosphere and the darkness gave me an inkling as to its character. Before we were allotted our cells and while we were still standing about in the passage I whispered to my neighbor: "No one will come out of this camp alive."

We were in Flossenbürg Extermination Camp near Weiden in the Upper Palatinate.

All of us were now resigned to the end which we knew awaited us in this place; we could see no hope of rescue.

The camp lay, completely isolated, between rocks and woodland; even by day it was gray and desolate. It appeared to be full. The building in which we were housed, and which was obviously reserved for important prisoners, did not enable us to learn the actual size of the camp. Its character was made clear to us by its mere outward appearance and by the screams and shots which we heard every night.

Every day we were allowed to exercise in the yard for twenty minutes, each one of us separately. Whenever my turn came in the morning I would see, regularly, a procession of stretcher bearers moving away from the camp, along the end of the cliff toward the wood. They carried wooden stretchers on which the bodies of those who had died or been murdered during the night could be clearly distinguished under the coverings that hid them. I have often counted as many as thirty stretchers in a single morning.

One morning an officer, accompanied by two others, burst into my cell shouting at me: "I don't suppose you recognize me?"

I did recognize him then: it was Stavitski, my Gestapo Commissioner from Berlin. He had been appointed Commandant of Flossenbürg Camp. I felt all the more certain of the fate that awaited me. A witness at my denazification proceedings at Stuttgart stated that Stavitski had told him that he had orders to shoot me as soon as the American Army approached Flossenbürg Camp.

It is extraordinarily difficult to put into words the inner sensation that sustained me and probably also my fellow prisoners throughout those two months in Flossenbürg, during every hour of which we had to reckon with death. Many persons as a result of scientific observation, feel they have no need to bother overmuch about the phenomenon of life. The problem of death leads even the most materialistic of men in the direction of the supersensual, the supernatural.

So I too reviewed my whole life in retrospect. Many were the sins of omission and commission that came into my mind. Against these I could only set the desire I had always felt, and had tried to put into practice, to do and to promote good wherever I had the opportunity. A few verses in which I summarized my impressions in the extermination camp at Flossenbürg may express this better than mere prose:

*When daytime's shadows in dusk are merging*
*And dusk in turn has been put to flight,*
*The long dark hours on thy soul converging*
*Haunt and mock thee throughout the night.*

*Every oppressive thought and sensation*
*Weighs on thee, soul, with burdensome themes;*
*Doubts, misgivings, in nightmare rotation*
*Harass thee still, half-awake, half in dreams.*

*"Yesterday — this day — did I do rightly*
*Such-and-such action or course to pursue?"*
*As a beast of prey hunts his quarry nightly,*
*Self-reproaches torment thee anew.*

*Rest thee, quiet thee, my soul; the terror*
*Will fade with the dawning of each new day;*
*No man is free from sin and from error*
*As he battles along life's way.*

*'Tis not thus the Eternal surveys thee —*
*By distance achieved and unclimbed ascent:*
*By these alone will His mercy appraise thee —*
*What thine endeavor, and what thine intent.*

For the rest my thoughts were first and foremost with my wife and children; my death would cause them profound grief and leave them in direst poverty. My children hardly realized my existence — they were two and a half and one and a quarter years old when I had been forced to leave them. So I made up my mind to set down some recollections which would emphasize the kindly and pleasant aspects of my life: I wanted to make them happy, even in the midst of their sorrow.

On the evening of April 8, to my intense astonishment, I was ordered to get ready for a journey the very first thing the following morning. I learned that some others too were to be moved. None of us knew, of course, where the "journey" would take us and whether it would lead to the expected end. Nevertheless the order gave me back the first glimmer of hope.

Before daybreak General Thomas, General Halder, Dr. Schuschnigg, his wife and child and I were pushed inside the Green Minna. The behavior of the guard led us to assume that the military situation must have deteriorated to an extraordinary degree. The foreign armies must have advanced considerably. Our guards were very uneasy.

We stopped first near Straubing where we fed and where several internees from a local camp were added to our number. The van was by now chock full with persons and luggage.

Among the newcomers was General von Falkenhausen, the two Britishers Best and Stevens who had been kidnaped by the Gestapo on the Dutch-German frontier, and a nephew of Molotov.

Late that evening we arrived in the courtyard of Dachau Camp. We had to wait several hours in the prison van as the Camp Commandant had obviously received no instructions and it was very difficult to find accommodation for us. When at last we were unloaded from the van the Lieutenant Colonel in command — a master craftsman from Munich — received us with the utmost courtesy. He apologized for being unable to find us suitable accommodation; unfortunately we would have to make do with whatever room was available.

This attitude did much to raise our hopes. We were housed in cells, either alone or in pairs; the doors stood open on to the corridor by day and night, so that we could visit one another at any time. By day we were allowed to stroll about the yard unhindered. We had the impression that this was indeed a camp for important prisoners, and we saw that our building was entirely separate from the others.

Here I met Niemöller, my old Pastor from Dahlem; I met Neuhäusler, the future Suffragan Bishop; Fritz Thyssen and his wife, Léon Blum and his wife, and a whole crowd of Britishers, Frenchmen, Greeks, Slovaks, Swedes, Dutchmen, Austrians, many of whom I knew personally.

The treatment and the food were good. The Schuschnigg family installed their radio and we listened to the news regularly every afternoon over coffee, which Frau Schuschnigg made in the fairly large cell that had been prepared for them. In this way we were soon *au fait* with the military situation and discovered the reason for the accommodating behavior of the guards.

These guards consisted for the most part of regular old soldiers, only a small proportion being Gestapo men; and they were obviously keen to provide themselves with some "good references" and make their escape when the final collapse should come — which not even the biggest fool could by now fail to foresee.

But we were particularly depressed on account of the uncertainty as to the fate of our comrades in Flossenbürg. Not until much later did we learn that, on the same morning on which we four were transferred the four others ended their lives on the gallows, among them my close friends Strünck and Oster. When the news reached me I recalled with a shudder the courtyard at Flossenbürg, at the end of which I had seen the gallows set up in a shanty which had been temporarily left open.

We were in Dachau for about a fortnight; then our way led further south to the hut camp at Reichenau near Innsbruck. Here, in addition to ourselves, other vehicles with internees arrived with several women and some children, the so-called *Sippenhäftlinge*, wives, children and distant relations of persons who had already been put to death or were awaiting prosecution. In this place we *Prominenten* (important prisoners) increased our total strength to one hundred and thirty. After three days we were dispatched in motor buses to Niederndorf in the Pustertal.

Here we waited for the Americans.

# LIV

## IN AMERICAN HANDS

OUR FINAL RELEASE from the Gestapo in the Puster valley enabled us once again to breathe freely. Up to the last moment there was always the chance of a shot in the neck. Now, however, we were that much further on toward our return to civilian life. At least so we imagined.

We had been moved to the Hotel Pragser Wildsee; there an American general assured us that he brought us liberty. The American front-line soldiers who now took charge of us were kindness itself. They provided us with food, smokes and supplemented our meager luggage with clothing.

In the evening we sat in the hotel lounge — it was almost unbelievable after our periods of captivity — where Isa Vermehren delighted us with her singing. On Sundays we attended Catholic or Evangelical Divine Service. In the daytime we reveled in the spring sunshine and went for walks in the wonderful woods above the Wildsee. In spite of the distressing news of the collapse at home we began to revive. The landlady of the Pragser Wildsee prepared our favorite dishes and her cellars produced many a delicious drink.

This marvelous state of things lasted but a few days. All of a sudden we were again "transhipped" and driven to Verona in a column of about forty cars. We were told that we were being taken from the front to the base where we were to be set at liberty. At Verona we were given rooms in the Golden Dove Hotel and treated just like any other visitors. When I arrived at the same hotel in 1951 they recognized me immediately and remembered the compulsory but none the less very pleasant visit.

The General realized that in releasing us he had released a group of determined opponents of Hitler and the N.S. regime who were to be treated to a certain extent as guests of honor.

Next morning we were driven to the airfield, embarked in three planes and flown nonstop toward Naples. As we drew near Rome our pilots made a wide swoop over the city and we had an over-whelmingly beautiful view in most marvelous weather — a unique experience for us who, only recently, had been awaiting death in Flossenbürg Camp, our only view the muddy courtyard and the gallows in the tumbledown shanty.

In Naples the scene underwent a distinct change. We were re-ceived by American base officers who did not impress us as being at all up to front-line standard, taken to the Hotel Terminus, and in-formed that we were no longer to consider ourselves as guests and were not to leave either our rooms or the hotel. Our personal treat-ment was brusque, not to say churlish.

We had defied Hitler at the risk of our lives. Now, without further ado, we were lumped together with the guilty ones of the Hitler regime.

Many of my companions in the camp at Naples were generals of the defeated German armies. Some of my more intimate friends and I asked the camp authorities for Divine Service on Sunday and observed how most of the generals ostentatiously absented them-selves. Those were the men who, for six long years, had swallowed every one of Hitler's crazy military suggestions and carried them out — often against their better knowledge — without thought for the millions of human lives sacrificed to such madness. Later, the in-mates of Kransberg Camp in the Taunus were for the most part scientists and armaments technicians, and it was contemptible to see how the victors took advantage of the prisoners' position to pick their brains for information on military and industrial matters. It was a scientific plundering of the helpless, an intellectual torture-chamber.

Humanity learned nothing from the First World War. How about the lesson of the Second War? No one seems to realize that both these wars represent a colossal moral defeat for Western Christendom. I certainly consider that a great share of the blame rests on the German nation, but the root cause of the evil lay else-where. The dictated Treaty of Versailles did not bring peace. Its determining factor was not the seizure of land and property: it was the policy of moral obloquy — harking back to the period of the worst religious wars — by which the enemy was branded as a criminal to be exterminated at all costs.

Victors and vanquished alike were lacking in moral depth. They had become worshipers at the shrine of mechanical power, of intel-lectual cleverness, contemptuous and ignorant of that spiritual force which will one day triumph over them. For I am firmly con-

vinced that out of all the misery of these two wars there will emerge
a new moral orientation for humanity which will be stronger than
any technical skill.

At the end of about four weeks some of us — including Halder,
Thomas and myself — were once again loaded into a plane like so
many unaddressed parcels. With us were other internees, among
whom we encountered Fritz Thyssen. We realized at last that the
Allies had some political objective in view, which made them anxious
to brand us as "criminals of the Hitler regime." The Trial of War
Criminals had already been planned and it was obviously essential
for the purposes of that trial that prominent economists and businessmen should be numbered among the accused. So far as I was
concerned I knew that from the beginning of the war the American
Government had been kept minutely informed as to my anti-Hitler
attitude. I looked forward fearlessly to further developments, glad,
if anything, that matters were moving.

After a wonderful flight from Naples over the Gulf of Liguria and
its islands toward the French coast, through a terrific storm in the
south of France, we landed finally at Orly airfield near Paris, about
twenty internees in all. This was the first leg of a journey that
finally led to Kransberg Castle in the Taunus Mountains. During
the war the castle had been chosen by Hermann Goering as a kind
of western headquarters for the Luftwaffe and done up for the purpose by Speer, who had added a large new part containing several
rooms and a great hall with a wonderful open hearth.

Now the castle was evidently being used as a so-called *Prominent-
enlager* or camp for the V.I.P.'s, particularly technicians and scientists. At times it may have housed a total of forty or fifty internees.
In short, there was a continually changing sequence of encounters
with important men, nearly all of whom I knew as part of the
economic or scientific life of Germany.

From the outward point of view the time I spent in this camp
from the beginning of July to the end of September was not unpleasant. The rooms were clean. The meals were excellent, we were
given chocolate, fruit, oranges, tobacco and other amenities as much
as we wanted; we spent our time playing cards, attending lectures,
talks and discussions which we arranged in the big hall. In the daytime we went for walks in the small, but well-planned garden belonging to the castle. But we were still prisoners.

Nor could the comforts of Kransberg allay the profound anxiety about my family which I had experienced ever since Flossenbürg. It was there that, after prolonged delay, I had received the last news of my wife, which was still written from our country home near Berlin. Since then, that is, since March 1945, I had had no news of any kind. I had no idea if my family were still alive, where they were, what might have happened to them after the Russians had taken Berlin. Reports received via the radio or in secret, indirect ways were in the highest degree disquieting.

Immediately on arriving at Kransberg I endeavored to get into touch with my wife. The British Lieutenant Colonel promised to forward my letter. Donald Heath, my old acquaintance from the American Embassy in Berlin, promised me most solemnly that he would use his diplomatic connections to send news of me to my wife. Neither of them kept their promise.

At last, toward the middle of August, I received news through a channel which we are accustomed to describe by the one word "underground." The housework at Kransberg was done by a number of charwomen who also washed our underclothes and came up to the castle from the village every morning. One day one of these women managed to get word to me on the quiet to come to the lavatory. There she handed me a box of cigars and a letter, both of which had been brought to the village of Kransberg by a friend and delivered to the woman. Since the collapse of Germany this friend had been living in my married daughter's little homestead in Bavaria. My daughter had learned that I was in Kransberg Castle and in the letter which accompanied the cigars she told me that the two small children of my second marriage were staying with our nurse's mother on Lüneburg Heath. Of my wife herself my daughter could tell me nothing.

On the last occasion we had seen each other I had advised my wife to remain in our country home at Gühlen and endeavor to preserve it for us against the time when the war should be over. My mind was still full of the out-of-date ideas of World War I when we still entertained respect for other people's property. In any case I could not do otherwise than assume, after reading my daughter's letter, that my wife had remained at Gühlen. In the meantime enough reports had reached us about the behavior of the Russians toward German women to arouse the greatest anxiety as to my wife's fate.

Then, toward the end of August, Dr. Brandt, one of Hitler's personal physicians, arrived at Kransberg. Shortly before he was arrested by the Americans he had had speech with my wife and was at least able to reassure me that she was alive. My first direct news from my wife did not reach me until much later when I was already in prison in Nuremberg. For nearly nine months I remained in ignorance of all she had endured.

# LV

## NUREMBERG PRISON

IN KRANSBERG, at the end of August, we heard over the radio which Germans were to appear before the International Military Tribunal at the forthcoming war criminal trials. To my great surprise I heard my name included among others. Besides Speer and myself none of the accused were in Kransberg. Up to now we had both assumed that no charge would be preferred against us.

By way of a foretaste of Nuremberg I was taken for three weeks to a camp near Oberursel, generally and appropriately known as The Cage. The cells were in fact just cages. The benches were simply wooden boards covered with a blanket. We had two meals a day — one in the morning, the other at four in the afternoon, consisting for the most part of half-cooked peas which were very indigestible. Exercise in the open air was limited to ten minutes a day. There was no reading matter of any kind. These conditions were the worst I had experienced in any of my prisons.

At the end of three weeks I was bundled into a car with General Warlimont beside me and Schwartz, the Treasurer of the N.S.D.A.P., in front. Once again we were not told the name of our destination. Only from the signposts did we gather any indication as to our direction, and in the afternoon we drew up at the Justice Prison at Nuremberg.

Even on my admittance to the Nuremberg prison I was treated most discourteously by the American Prison Governor, Colonel Andrus. I stated that I was neither a criminal nor a convict but a prisoner awaiting examination, and furthermore that I was not guilty. He replied that he couldn't care less.

The prison regulations which were drummed into us went so far as to forbid standing on the chair in case we wanted to look out of the barred window set just under the ceiling. This was intended to prevent any signal being given to anyone outside. The cells were originally furnished with solid, firm tables at which one could write.

But such tables could have been used to reach up to the window-panes. So one day the solid, firm tables were taken away and replaced by unsteady wooden erections of thin lathe with a thin sheet of cardboard nailed on top. Writing at this table was sheer torment for it wobbled continually; yet in the eleven months that the trial lasted we had a lot of writing to do, if only to supply regular information for the defense.

There was a W.C. in the cell. We were taken outside to wash and once a week for a bath. Books could be obtained from the prison library, but as there was almost nothing but National-Socialist literature which those responsible had evidently forgotten to throw away, I usually went without. After my acquittal I was described in an English newspaper as the most refractory of all the Nuremberg prisoners and I am rather proud of it.

One day Colonel Andrus came into my cell, his breath smelling of liquor, and announced that I was to be deprived of my daily exercise in the courtyard for a week, by way of punishment. On my asking the reason he replied: "For un-co-operativeness."

To which I immediately answered: "I have no desire to co-operate with you, Colonel."

On another occasion I withstood repeated attempts by journalists to photograph me. The first time I did not realize that I had been snapped at dinner in the very act of conveying a spoonful of food from the tin bowl to my wide-open mouth. This picture was reproduced many times in the international press, and as none of us wore collars and we all appeared somewhat unkempt it was not very flattering.

One day the journalists renewed their efforts and I told the American reporter that I preferred not to be photographed while eating. He went away, but notwithstanding my request returned to the charge in a minute or so. I called out to him to shut up: if he tried it again he'd get what was coming to him. After a few moments he made a third attempt: without more ado I seized my mug which was full of coffee and flung the contents at his head.

The effect was astounding. The American guards stationed behind each one of us burst into roars of laughter at this successful attack on the "freedom of the press," and the photographer beat a hasty retreat.

When, a week later, I was brought up for disciplinary action on account of my conduct the proceedings were short and sharp.

"You have insulted an American military uniform."

"The photographer was not in American military uniform: he was wearing a suit like yours, Colonel, but without any badges of rank."

There was nothing more to be said. Nevertheless I did not go unpunished. My coffee ration was withdrawn. I have never had so many offers of coffee as in the days immediately following. Nearly every orderly, whether German or American, who passed the open shutter of my door asked if I would like some coffee.

By the time I landed in the Nuremberg prison for the trial by the International Military Tribunal I had completed a total of sixteen months' captivity and been in more than a dozen prisons.

In such conditions one's chief need is for spiritual comfort and encouragement. It is true that there was a German-speaking American minister who looked after the prisoners, but I longed for a German pastor. It was not so much a question of services and sermon as of the opportunity to unburden the mind in spiritual matters. Our request for a German pastor was turned down, although the American clergyman himself gave it his express support. He himself felt that he needed the assistance of a German *confrère*. He was obliged to read his sermon, since his knowledge of German was not sufficient to enable him to speak *extempore*, and it was therefore all the more difficult for him to carry on a pastoral conversation with any of us.

Nevertheless there was a most moving quality in Pastor Gericke's zeal and devotion to his task. He was a dear, good, thoroughly well-intentioned man possessed of great personal tact and I hope if ever he reads these lines that he will rest assured of the gratitude of us all.

# LVI

## THE PRISONERS

ON THE TWENTIETH of October, 1945, the Bill of Indictment was handed to me by an American major. From it I ascertained that the indictment was divided into four headings; the first being "Taking Part in the Conspiracy to bring about the War," the second "Taking Part in Measures Preparatory to the Said War," the third "Perpetration of Crimes During the War," and the fourth "Crimes Against Humanity."

From this indictment I learned for the first time of the monstrous crimes committed against humanity, above all against the Jews, by Hitler himself and by his orders.

The indictment was not merely a general one: it was also drawn up in detail for each of the accused, informing him on which of the four counts he was charged. Most of them were arraigned on all four counts. Numbers Three and Four — "War Crimes" and "Crimes against Humanity" — did not apply in my case. I was charged only with "War Conspiracy" and "Preparations for War."

To both charges I could reply with a clear conscience. I knew that innumerable proofs existed that I had neither planned nor prepared for war but, on the contrary, had striven to prevent it. From that moment I knew that, provided judgment were given according to law and justice and not according to hatred and passion, the whole of the Nuremberg proceedings must result in my being acquitted. Fortunately, my faith was justified.

Among the accused were several whom I knew to be my avowed enemies. But there were also others of whom I knew that, though they had been weak, they were inwardly opposed to the Hitler regime and could be regarded as thoroughly decent people in ordinary life.

So far as I was concerned Goering's case presented the greatest difficulty. For a long while many had hoped that Goering would find and pursue the path of political moderation. At the beginning of the Hitler regime I too had shared that hope. Goering had more than once manifested a tendency in that direction. His criticism of Hitler *prior* to the latter's seizure of power was in striking contrast to his subsequent ostentatious display of Paladinesque fealty. When he realized that only through Hitler could he satisfy his own lust for power and wealth did he surpass himself in protestations of loyalty.

At the Nuremberg Trial Goering displayed great courage, both in his behavior and his half-audible exclamations. In the witness box he manifested such superior intelligence and quickness at repartee, together with an outward appearance of such surpassing dignity, that even the prosecution could not fail to be impressed.

Not even this outward appearance, however, could disguise the fact that Goering had committed blackmail, murder, robbery, theft and numbers of similar crimes. Personally I have always looked upon Goering as the *worst* among the accused on account of his decent origin and comfortable circumstances. In contrast to Goering, Streicher appeared to me to be a pathological monomaniac and Kaltenbrunner a callous fanatic.

From a human point of view Rudolf Hess always seemed to be a decent character motivated by the best intentions. He never knowingly took part in or consented to any crime. But that he was not fully responsible for his conduct was confirmed throughout the whole course of the trial. Eventually the great question turned on whether Hess could be regarded as a case of forty-nine or fifty-one per cent retarded intelligence. In prison his attitude was one of complete apathy and isolation.

For Ribbentrop there was only one excuse, even according to the most charitable estimation — his extraordinary stupidity. Every quality essential in a diplomatist — intelligence, tact, faultless manners, general affability — he lacked them all.

The general opinion of Keitel, was, so to speak, unanimous: he was his master's unthinking and irresponsible yes-man.

Number Four in the dock was Alfred Rosenberg who, with his usual reserve, kept himself to himself during the whole of the Nuremberg proceedings and clung to his philosophic fantasies right up to the moment of his execution.

A double cell on the first floor had been fitted up as a little chapel so that we might attend church. Neither Rosenberg, Streicher nor Hess ever came to a service. During the days I remained in prison after my acquittal I saw the American evangelical pastor talking earnestly to Rosenberg in the corridor, and being coldly and energetically repulsed.

Goering was one of the most zealous attendants at the services, though the rest of us were also glad of them: partly owing to religious conviction, partly owing to a warm feeling for the minister, partly because they afforded a good opportunity for mutual understanding.

From Catholic fellow captives I heard that their priest, Father Sixtus, spent himself most devotedly for the prisoners under his care and more than once managed to help them — by any ways not strictly forbidden — to get in touch with their families — which our good Pastor Gericke did not dare to attempt. But in our view Father Sixtus' greatest achievement was with Frank, the Governor of Poland, who, more deeply implicated than anyone in the Jewish murders, was reduced by this Catholic priest to a state of abject penitence.

Funk, my successor as president of the Reichsbank, cut a pretty poor figure. He was a decent enough fellow and not stupid, but he was lazy and lacking in understanding of the duties entrusted to him. I am convinced that there were many matters of which he had no knowledge whatever. He was a first-rate connoisseur of music and his preferences were decidedly for the artistic and literary. Unfortunately, like so many of the party leaders, he was strongly addicted to alcohol. In the witness box his defense was weak and lachrymose.

Dönitz and Raeder, as well as Jodl, referred to their military duties as the main reason for their conduct. I am quite certain that were they to be tried again today, the result would be different from what it was in that first period shortly after the end of the war.

Schirach too created a characteristic impression of immaturity and indetermination.

Papen, like myself, was arraigned only on the first and second counts. But in view of the fact that three of his closest colleagues had been murdered by Hitler while he had maintained a passive attitude, he could not escape severe moral censure.

Seyss-Inquart and Speer, neither of them real villains, conducted their defense very clumsily. Speer's final statements dealt with the problem that must have been exercising his mind for some time; namely, how had it been possible for the dictator to keep the German people in complete ignorance on the one hand, and on the other hand to ensure the execution of his plans and decisions by the issue of direct orders to the appropriate persons, even in the most subordinate posts? These observations by Speer on the influence of modern technique in communications and intelligence service are undoubtedly worthy of consideration.

"Hans Fritzsche Speaking" * was probably included among the important prisoners because — fortunately for him — the Russians had obviously desired to contribute to their number. As a result Fritzsche had been spared the fate that had confronted him during his imprisonment in the Lubianka.

Two of the chief accused never appeared in the dock at Nuremberg. Old Krupp von Bohlen lay unconscious on what was to prove his deathbed. And before the Trials had even started Robert Ley — after stopping up ears and nose and thrusting a gag into his mouth — had tried to hang himself by a twisted towel attached to the stopcock in his W.C. and had choked to death. Ley had been one of my bitterest enemies in the party although to my face he had always shown himself ostentatiously friendly. He was a notorious drunkard, given to every kind of erotic excess, and without the slightest sense of responsibility.

Ley's suicide led to our being more closely watched in our cells, more especially since Conti, the "Head of National Hygiene," had also made away with himself while in prison. Henceforth a guard was stationed day and night outside the open shutter in the door of each cell where he was relieved every two hours. There were, as I had reason to know, quite a few cads among them, but also many kindly souls who were not averse to carrying on a conversation now and then through the hole in the door. The behavior of the colored soldiers throughout was kindlier and more decent than those of our own race.

It was remarkable how nearly all the guards asked for our autographs. The demand increased to such an extent that in self-defense I acquired the habit of asking for a cigarette in return for each autograph. In this way I very soon collected a large stock of cigarettes which I was able later to hand over to my wife, thereby providing her with the only valid currency of the period.

In the United States an individual's capacity for employment is often determined by his Intelligence Quotient. The Intelligence Test has developed into a science which would, if it were possible, dispense good or bad luck to mankind in general, and for all one knows may even now do so in America.

Throughout the duration of the trials by the International Mili-

* The English translation of one of Fritzsche's books: *Hier Spricht Hans Fritzsche.*

tary Tribunal we were visited in prison by doctors and others who
had chosen to specialize and qualify in psychology. They engaged
in conversation with each prisoner in his own cell in order to ascertain his mental condition and from time to time to check up on
how he reacted to captivity and to the progress of the trial. A
dreary calling indeed.

Since I knew myself to be entirely innocent I was a comparatively
uncomplex, but probably therefore also a comparatively uninteresting subject. They could discover no abnormalities in me. On the
other hand I myself was all the more amused by the Intelligence
Test.

There were several versions of this test, the first being the figurative
interpretation of ink blots. I succeeded in "reading into" these blots
an astonishing number of pictures and shapes.

The second test consisted in the immediate repetition of figure
sequences. Finally we had to put together puzzle games ranging
from small plain-colored blocks to intricately cut-out shapes. Among
all the prisoners mine was the highest I.Q.

My wife had succeeded in persuading the former president of the
German Law Society, Dr. Julius Dix, to interest himself in my case.
I had previously approached Professor Kraus of Göttingen, who likewise expressed his willingness to undertake my defense. For several
years he had been a lecturer in American universities and was one
of the recognized experts on international law. When, however, Dix
consented to defend me I asked Kraus if he would take on the position of second counsel for the defense, since I knew Dix to be an
outstanding defendant's counsel in criminal cases.

I never had reason to regret this choice. I had been in communication with Dix over a number of years owing to our common political
outlook, which is perhaps best described as "conservative democracy." Dix was a man of exquisite tact and a gifted orator. His dislike of excessive formalistic work was offset by a high-quality and
quick-witted intelligence.

Like all other prisoners I was subjected to psychological observation by a young American, Professor Gilbert, of Austrian origin. Mr.
Gilbert's first duty was to note the effect on the prisoners of the
daily court proceedings and thereby to supplement the subject matter of the prosecution. My conversations with him were in part
exhilarating.

From the very first day my impression of the Bench was not unfavorable. The choice of British and French judges was undoubtedly good. It was evident at first glance that they were characteristic representatives of their profession. I was not so easily able to sum up the American judges; and the Russians, the only ones to appear in military uniform, were completely inscrutable.

The preliminary examination was exclusively in the hands of the prosecution, who not only ignored any extenuating data, no matter how clearly set forth, but unfortunately also had frequent recourse to distortion and misrepresentation of which I myself was able to identify one example. We were shown a film in which figured the gold articles taken from murdered Jews, among them the notorious gold teeth and spectacle frames. These articles were extracted from a sack on which the word Reichsbank was printed in large letters which the film reproduced with admirable clearness. Those sacks could never have been used to store articles of gold. The picture, too, turned out to have been taken at Frankfurt-am-Main. Later it was found to be a specially "posed," especially interpolated photograph.

Against such methods we prisoners were helpless. Further, owing to being completely cut off from all outside contacts, we were not in a position to furnish such documents and other evidence as would lead to our being exonerated. Counsels' opportunities for tracing such documents and witnesses were very restricted because, in that chaotic period, the only way to procure such documents and discover such witnesses was to go after them in person.

We were not allowed access to the ample material which the Allies had confiscated. The preliminary examination, so far as we were able to co-operate, was limited to frequent hearings by representatives of the prosecution, among whom were a large percentage of *émigrés*. One of my interrogators, to whom I once apologized for my English, replied — with an obvious indirect hit at these gentlemen:

"Oh, you speak very much better English than many of my colleagues."

# LVII

## THE NUREMBERG TRIBUNAL — I

On the morning of April 30, 1946, the Nuremberg Tribunal began its proceedings against me. Dr. Dix, my counsel, addressed the President in the particular style which the German lawyers were obliged to adopt in this remarkable court:

"I will commence my demonstration with a deposition by Dr. Schacht, and I would beg your Lordship to direct Dr. Schacht to take the stand."

On no other occasion was I so suddenly conscious of the unreality — I might even say the ghostly atmosphere — of this "International Court of Justice" as in those few moments needed to leave the dock and take my place on the witness stand. The great hall in which the proceedings took place was entirely without natural light. The windows of Nuremberg's former Court of Assizes had been hung with draperies so as to exclude the daylight. Artificial illumination shed a sickly unbroken glare over everything. Despite the fact that for the accused persons it was a matter of life and death the place vibrated with an unrest reminiscent of an ant heap. The prosecutors of the various nations were surrounded by their respective staffs. Messengers kept arriving with reports and papers. The sight of the American women secretaries at their clattering machines created a kind of optical confusion. To watch them incessantly chewing gum was to feel as though they were chewing on every word. On the press stand, immediately opposite the witness stand, it was not much quieter. Only the few German reporters — the only ones not in uniform and therefore immediately recognizable — remained unobtrusively in the background. The whole effect was something of a nightmare. Many of the accused suffered from overwrought nerves. In the building itself the shrill tones of American light music would frequently blare forth: curiously enough the song hit of that time was "Don't Fence Me In" and the guards played it over and over, day and night.

During the morning and also in the afternoon there would be a short break. Then we were able to go to the lavatories, passing between a cordon of American military police. Sometimes we were stopped in the passage. The military police would be drawn up on one side when the heavy silver trays of tea and shortcakes, doughnuts, etc. were taken into the courtroom for the Bench by German waiters, with American military police to see that they did not pinch so much as a doughnut on the way.

And now for an incident which struck me as typifying the whole atmosphere. There were about two hundred of the Allies in uniform standing about in the passage, who had business of one kind or another with the court. All of them were smoking cigarettes, and all of them carefully crushed the discarded cigarette ends underfoot, for the information had obviously been circulated that the Germans told off to sweep down the corridor were wont to gather up the cigarette ends. Long afterwards I was told by the solitary German journalist from the British Zone, who at the beginning of the trials was on the job in the press stand, that at sight of the place the officer in charge of him had exclaimed (in indifferent German): "Oh! but this isn't a court of law — it's a fair!"

In order to explain what follows, I must once again stress the methods of procedure in this court. They were based on the Anglo-Saxon legal usages. The prisoner could choose whether to appear in his own defense as witness under oath, or whether to refuse to give evidence. Naturally I did not refuse because I was conscious of my innocence.

I did not need the earphones through which were transmitted the French, Russian and German translations of the English speeches. Very often this apparatus failed to work. Then the President would exclaim somewhat plaintively: "I can hear nothing but Russian," which was a fact. Strangely enough the Russian language was in the habit of monopolizing the mechanism.

Sitting in the witness box I repeated the oath after the President, and in reply to my lawyer's enquiry — the questions had of course been agreed upon beforehand — I gave a brief account of my life up to the year 1930, when I resigned my post as president of the Reichsbank.

My lawyer questioned me again. I described how, in 1919, I had taken part in the founding of the German Democratic Party and then went on to tell them of my first contacts with the National Socialist Party and their ideas.

I told the court: "As regards *Mein Kampf*, my opinion today is the same as it has been from the beginning: it is written in execrable German, a bit of propaganda work by a half-educated man strongly, not to say fanatically interested in politics — the sort of man, in fact, that Hitler subsequently and invariably showed himself to be. There was one feature of the book, and to some extent also of the party program, which gave me much food for thought, and that was the complete lack of understanding of every kind of economic problem.

"From the point of view of foreign policy I considered *Mein Kampf* extraordinarily unsound, since it never ceased to toy with the idea that the extension of Germany's living space must take place *in Europe*. If these statements did not deter me from later working with a National-Socialist Chancellor, it was for the simple reason that in *Mein Kampf* Germany's expansion eastward was expressly pictured as contingent upon the British Government bestowing its blessing on the idea. I reckoned that I was very well acquainted with British policy; there was therefore not the slightest danger that I should take these fantastic theorizings of Hitler's any more seriously than I had hitherto done.

"In my own mind I was quite clear that for Germany to extend her territory in Europe by violence was an impossibility, and would not be tolerated by other nations. For the rest, while *Mein Kampf* contained a lot of idiotic, highfalutin statements, it also included several quite decent ideas. Two — and I should like to stress this — two of them gave me great satisfaction. The first was that if someone differs from the government on a political matter it is his duty to bring his views to the notice of the government; and the second was that while government by a leader must replace democratic government — or should we rather say parliamentary government — the leader himself could only function if he were certain of the support of the whole nation; in other words, even a leader depends upon general elections of a democratic type."

Then Dr. Dix, my counsel, raised the point that the American prosecution had charged me with being an opponent of the Treaty of Versailles. The American prosecution obviously considered that to be against the Treaty of Versailles was a crime in itself. It gave me immense satisfaction to be able to reply, which I did in the following words:

"I am somewhat surprised to hear this charge from the lips of a member of the American prosecution. The lieutenant who has just spoken is perhaps too young to have experienced it in person, but he could have learned it in school; at any rate it was, for all of us, one of the greatest events *we* had ever experienced, when the Versailles Treaty was rejected by America, and further — if I am not mistaken — that it should have been rejected with the overwhelming consent of the whole American people and, what is more, for the very reasons that I rejected it — because it was in direct contradiction to the Fourteen Points solemnly proclaimed by Wilson and because, where political economy was concerned, it contained a lot of preposterous suggestions that could not possibly be made to work in a world economic system. But I would not on that account accuse the American people of sharing in the Nazi ideology."

That was too much for the American judge.

Following the afternoon break (silver tea trays, tea service, doughnuts) my lawyer questioned me as to my attitude to the Nazi ideology of the "Master Race." I upset the Anglo-Saxons immediately by remarking: "I have always considered such expressions as 'Chosen People,' 'God's Own Country' and so on as examples of a very unpleasing mentality."

Then I went on: "As a convinced upholder of the Christian faith I take my stand on the basis of the Christian love of one's neighbor which I owe to all men irrespective of race or creed. I would add that all this blather about the Master Race, which some party leaders adopted, was the subject of violent ridicule on the part of the German public. Nor was it surprising, since most of the leaders in Hitler's party were not exactly ideal types of the Nordic race, and I know that among the populace whenever these topics were mentioned little Goebbels, for instance, went by the nickname of 'The German pygmy.' To do them justice there was only one thing most leaders of the party had in common with the old German tribes: they were always ready for just another glass. Excessive drinking was a great feature of Nazi ideology."

Dr. Dix passed to the Jewish question. The indictment contained no charge against me on this count, but it did include the charge of Nazi ideology, and my lawyer rightly inferred that "the practice of the strongest anti-Semitism was inextricably bound up with this ideology."

The result was exactly what we had expected. The American prosecutor, Jackson, sprang to his feet and interrupted the proceeding, exclaiming: "We concede that Dr. Schacht did give aid and support to individual Jews. But we maintain that he held the view that German Jews should be deprived of their rights as citizens, and we also maintain that Dr. Schacht supported and took part in the persecution of German Jews."

Dr. Dix immediately raised the question whether I was likewise charged with war crimes on land and sea, and demonstrated from the indictment that this was indeed the case. Jackson became very excited. The President intervened. My war crimes on land and sea were temporarily shelved and we returned to the Jewish question.

"The Jewish question," I said, "arose as early as 1930 when James Speyer the New York banker (who has since died) announced his visit. I went to Hitler and told him: 'Mr. James Speyer, one of the most respected of New York bankers and a great benefactor of his former country, is coming to see me and I intend to give a banquet in his honor. I take it that you have no objection.' Whereupon he replied, in very decided and striking fashion: 'Herr Schacht, you may do anything you like.' From this I gathered that he gave me full liberty to associate with my Jewish friends as hitherto, which I did. And the banquet took place. I mention this only because it was the first time the Jewish question came up between us. Two instances should suffice to illustrate the attitude I adopted on every occasion concerning the Jewish question — and I invariably sought a chance of doing so in public."

And then I described the Arnswalde case — already mentioned — and my address to the Reichsbank office boys at their Christmas party. I also described the conversation I had with Hitler in July 1934 about the unobstructed activities of Jews in business.

I found it almost painful to have to recount all that I had done for the Jews — painful because to champion such persecuted people is, at bottom, no more than the duty of any decent man.

My lawyer felt it would be a good thing to let the Tribunal know my opinion of Hitler. Scarcely had he expressed this view than Hermann Goering — so far as he could manage it — slewed round in the dock and partly turned his back on me. I told the court that I had always regarded Hitler as belonging to the dangerous, half-educated type, and still did so. In the dock Goering's attitude was the embodiment of ostentatious disapproval as I went on to elaborate:

"Hitler never had much schooling, but he made up for it later by an infinite amount of reading; he acquired a tremendous amount of book knowledge and showed off these accomplishments like a virtuoso in all debates and speeches. In some respects he was undoubtedly a genius. Ideas would strike him which never occurred to anyone else, the sort of ideas sometimes calculated to overcome great obstacles, whether by their staggering simplicity or frequently by their staggering brutality. He had a positively diabolical genius for mass psychology. General von Witzleben once confirmed that whereas I and one or two others never allowed ourselves to be entrapped in our personal conversations with Hitler, he contrived to exert a most amazing influence over other people; and in spite of his harsh, grating voice, and the way that voice would break and sometimes rise to a shriek, he managed to inspire huge crowds with the most hysterical enthusiasm. I believe that in the beginning he was motivated by impulses not wholly evil."

Goering turned so as partly to face me and stared expectantly at me as I went on: "There is no doubt that Hitler at first believed himself to be actuated by good intentions; but by degrees he succumbed to that very spell which he exercised on the masses. For whoever sets out to mislead the masses will himself end by being led — and misled — by those same masses. In my opinion it was this interplay — this leading and being led — that induced him to pursue the downward course of the herd instinct, which every political leader should avoid like the plague."

I conceded that I could not help admiring certain things about Hitler. "He was a man of indomitable energy, and a will that rode roughshod over every opposition. In my view it was due solely to these two factors — mass psychology and his own force of will — that Hitler was able to command the support of anything up to forty per cent and later nearly fifty per cent of the whole German nation."

Gisevius was then sworn as a witness by counsel. He had previously stated that I had displayed marked activity in my efforts to bring about Hitler's downfall. Dr. Dix wanted to know when I first realized the great extent of my own inner aversion to Hitler.

I said it was after the Röhm *Putsch*.

Dr. Dix pursued the subject and wanted to know the moment when I first became a "conspirator" against Hitler. I gave it as dating from the Fritsch affair.

In the course of the Fritsch affair — not suddenly, but over a period of weeks, even months — it became obvious to me that Hitler wanted war, or to say the least, that he was not prepared to do everything in his power to prevent war.

I said, literally: "Any possibility of political propaganda among the German people could be completely ruled out. There was no freedom of assembly, no freedom of speech, no freedom of authorship; it was not even possible to engage in conversation in small, intimate circles. The country was riddled with spies and snoopers and every word uttered in the presence of more than one other person was liable to endanger one's life. The only thing that remained was to proceed by force against this terror that admitted of no democratic emendation and no reasonable criticism. Eventually I reached the conclusion that the only way to end this Hitler terror was by an attempt at a *Putsch* and in the long run an attempt on Hitler's life."

"What was your feeling about Hitler at that time? Were you merely disappointed in him, or did you feel he had played you false?" enquired Dr. Dix. "What is your reply to that?"

"I was never disappointed in Hitler," I answered, "because I never expected more of him than was to be expected from a knowledge of his character. But I did feel that he had played me false, that he had lied to me and deceived me right and left, for everything that he had promised the German people at first — including myself — he afterwards failed to perform. He promised equal rights for every citizen, and to his followers — regardless of their qualifications — he gave many more rights than to all other citizens. He promised that the laws relating to foreigners should apply to the Jews; that is, that they should enjoy the same protection accorded to foreigners. He caused the Jews to be deprived of all rights and treated as outlaws.

"He promised to combat political lies, and his policy — aided by his Minister Goebbels — consisted of nothing but political lies and political trickery.

"He promised the German people to uphold practical Christianity and he tolerated and encouraged the profanation, vilification and condemnation of Church institutions. In regard to foreign policy he consistently repudiated the idea of a war on two fronts, and later allowed conditions to reach a point where such a war was unavoidable. He disregarded and disdained all the laws of the Weimar Republic which he had sworn faithfully to uphold when he became Chancellor.

"He mobilized the Gestapo against the freedom of the individual. He stifled all free interchange of news and views; he pardoned criminals and took them into his service. He did everything he could in order *not* to keep his promises. The whole world — Germany — me myself — he tricked and lied to us all."

Dr. Dix's next question annoyed the prosecution. He asked me why, as a member of the Reichstag, I had voted for Hitler's Enabling Law. He also wanted to know why I had immediately joined Hitler's cabinet.

I replied that I had never in my whole life been a member of the

Reichstag. A single glance at the *Reichstag Handbook* would confirm this. Furthermore, I did not join the cabinet immediately after the "upheaval."

Dr. Dix appeared astonished. "But the indictment affirms that you did both," he exclaimed.

"Unfortunately," I replied, "there is a great deal in the indictment which is not correct."

Members of the prosecution staffs put their heads together. The President announced: "It is now five o'clock. The court will adjourn for today."

Dr. Dix asked me to explain why I had joined the cabinet as Minister of Economic Affairs in 1934. I replied that, had I considered my own personal peace and comfort, I could have remained quietly at home in the country. But I should have asked myself how such action would have benefited the progress of German politics. So I joined Hitler's cabinet, not in a spirit of enthusiastic approval but because I realized that it was essential to go on working for the German people, and that the brake could be applied, and unsound measures rectified, only within the ranks of the government itself.

Judge and prosecution stared at me in astonishment when I declared that in my opinion the decent elements were numerically superior, even within the party itself. They were still more astonished when I said that in the beginning crowds of decent young fellows joined the ranks of the S.S. for the very reason that Himmler represented the S.S. as something that would stand for an ideal way of life.

I was keenly aware that the court listened with rapt attention as I explained how it was that Hitler understood how to attach his more intimate party associates to himself. He knew something about each one of them — some false step, some misdemeanor. He knew every detail of their lives and they all felt they were bound to him by the menace of possible disclosure.

To my great pleasure Dr. Dix put the question: "Did you ever receive information as to any secret understanding, any secret orders or secret allusions which had for their object an illegal breach of the peace?"

I could truthfully affirm that neither I, nor any of my ministerial colleagues, nor any other leading men who were not members of Hitler's inner circle, had ever been in a position to receive such information.

Counsel instructed me to explain the nature of my dealings with Hitler. I replied: "During the early years he repeatedly urged me to

lunch with him and a few intimate friends at the Chancellery. I tried
it at intervals on two occasions and I must admit that I was repelled,
not only by the level of conversation and the fawning attitude toward
Hitler's person, but the entire company was uncongenial. I never
went there again nor did I ever call upon Hitler in my private
capacity."

I then had to describe my dealings — frequent or otherwise —
with the other party bigwigs. When I had done so Dr. Dix read
from Mr. Jackson's indictment:

"Does anyone believe that Hjalmar Schacht — seated in the front
row at the Nazi Party Conference of 1935 and wearing the badge of
the party — does anyone believe that he was included in this Nazi
propaganda film solely for artistic reasons? In so far as this great
thinker lent his name to this shabby undertaking he invested it with
a certain respectability in the eyes of every laggard German."

First of all I expressed my thanks for the compliment. "Representative greatness, great thinker" were very pleasant. Then I caused
a fearful amount of embarrassment to Mr. Jackson and his large staff.
I possessed no party badge as early as 1935 — which was very tiresome
for the American prosecution. I described quite simply and straight-
forwardly that I had attended the functions in Nuremberg in 1933
and 1934. Then Dr. Dix brought up his heavy artillery. He asked
me whether the Diplomatic Corps had been present at these party
conferences in the person of the heads of their respective diplomatic
missions. I explained that, with the exception of the Soviet and the
American Ambassadors, all the other leading diplomats had been
present, "in considerable numbers, *en grande tenue*, and in the front
row."

This announcement immediately caused a great stir throughout
the court, not merely among the prosecution but also among the foreign journalists. Only the Russians stared proudly straight ahead. I
was well aware that it would not be long before the American prosecutor interrupted counsel and myself, for it was only too easy to see
what we were driving at. If the British and French Ambassadors —
not to mention any of the others — could attend the party conference as Hitler's guests, why not I? How to explain the presence of
foreign diplomats at the Nuremberg party conferences was what
my lawyer wanted to know.

"The Diplomatic Corps, as such, only attends state functions.
This, however, was purely a party affair. How can their presence be
accounted for?" he exclaimed.

Jackson was already on his feet. He objected to counsel's statement and to my own. Then, in a queer sort of sentence he declared that the whole business caused him no embarrassment whatever, "if indeed anything like embarrassment could arise." It struck me as being a bit muddled.

There was an uproar. Mr. Jackson's assistant pushed some papers at him. He held them together in his hand but did not read them: instead he waved them in the air and shouted:

"There is not the slightest value as evidence in anything this witness" (meaning myself) "may say concerning the conduct of ambassadors from other countries and his views thereon. The reasons for their presence at a party conference to which he lent his name seem to me to have not the slightest value as evidence. I do not demur to the fact of their being there, but I think that if he is just talking for the sake of talking, without producing any fact . . . I wish to make it clear that I have no desire to raise any objection to any fact known about the witness, nor have I raised any objection to most of the opinions on which he has expatiated at such length. But I consider that his attitude to the actions of foreign emissaries is outside the scope of important and essential evidence."

I tried to say something. So did Dr. Dix. The President interrupted us both. The Russians, full of conscious pride, continued to stare straight ahead, with an occasional sideways glance at the British and French judges. The President finally said Dr. Dix should proceed. But my lawyer had no mind to change the subject at present. He wanted to reply to Prosecutor Jackson and assured the court that he did so not from any desire to be obstinate but because it was important that they should realize how difficult it made matters for the German Opposition when representatives of foreign countries had made a point of attending the party conference.

The presiding judge was very fair. The gist of his reply was that if counsel wished to prove that these diplomats had been present at the party conference there was nothing to be said against it.

Mr. Jackson switched over to another equally important subject.

"You gave your support to rearmament through Reichsbank funds. Why?"

"The Allied Powers had promised a general disarmament," I said. "I considered that, politically speaking, Germany was entitled to the same rights as the other Powers. Since they did not keep their promise of general disarmament I felt that my own country would be obliged to re-arm within the usual limits." I described the function of the Mefo bills and told of the rearming of Czechoslovakia and

Poland at that time and of how, in 1935, Russia had announced her intention of bringing the total strength of her peacetime army up to a million men; and I regaled the Americans with a conversation I had with their then ambassador in Moscow — Mr. Davies — on the occasion of his journey through Berlin. I read out a sentence from the Ambassador's *Recollections,* in which he describes this conversation: "Schacht almost leaped out of his chair with enthusiasm when I expounded President Roosevelt's suggestion that rearmament should be restricted to such weapons of defense as a man could carry on his shoulder." I quoted another passage from Mr. Davies's book, according to which I pleaded earnestly for general disarmament. All this time I kept my eye on Jackson with the feeling that something would happen before long. Dr. Dix was of the opinion that I should tell the court how much money I had placed at the disposal of the Reich for purposes of rearmament.

Once again Mr. Jackson was on his feet. That, he asserted, was entirely beside the point. No one was interested in whether German rearmament had cost too much or too little.

Dr. Dix replied calmly that on the contrary, the court ought to be interested: for according to the vastness or paltriness of the amount it should be possible to establish without a doubt whether a war of aggression was being planned or whether rearmament was solely for purposes of defense. I must confess that I myself did not do much to facilitate the discussion, for I made a slip in quoting millions instead of billions. A faint smile of satisfaction went round the dock at this *contretemps.*

Dr. Dix reminded me that the indictment reckoned it a crime that during my period of office as president of the Reichsbank under the Third Reich, the national indebtedness had increased threefold.

To which I cheerfully and calmly replied: "The indictment might just as well have accused me because, during my period of office, the birth rate in Germany had risen considerably. I wish to state emphatically that I am guiltless of both."

The French judges smiled faintly; the others remained impassive.

Considerable argument ensued as to the sums spent on German rearmament for as long as I remained in control of the country's finances. This statement told greatly in my favor and the presiding judge allowed it.

In the afternoon the discussion centered round how much I had known of Hitler's immediate war aims.

This led to the disclosure of a remark by Speer. In the summer of 1937 Speer was at Hitler's mountain home. He was sitting on the terrace and heard, through the open window, how Hitler and I were quarreling. Speer saw me disappear. Hitler came out on to the terrace and said to him:

"I have just had a serious dispute with Schacht; I can't work with Schacht any longer, he upsets all my financial plans."

That was entirely correct; I did upset Hitler's financial plans, and for a vital reason. I did not wish him to prepare for a war of aggression and I had no intention of helping him to do so. In fact where Hitler was concerned I laid an embargo on Reichsbank funds. He was compelled to apply to the big banks, and it is easy to imagine what he thought of me. Easy, that is, for a German, but I had to make it quite clear to the others. In reply, therefore, to the question put by my lawyer, Dr. Dix, I elucidated:

"If I had said to Hitler: I'm not letting you have any more money because you mean to go to war, I should not be here and I should not be enjoying this stimulating conversation with you, *Herr Justizrat*. I should have had to consult a parson, and it would have been a one-sided affair for I should have been lying silent in my grave while the parson recited a monologue."

On Thursday, May 2, the subject came up of my dismissal as president of the Reichsbank. The indictment maintained that I had "wangled" my dismissal simply and solely in order to be relieved of my financial responsibilities. The prosecution contended that a memorandum which I had handed to Hitler, and as a result of which three of us were dismissed, contained no mention of our refusal to allow Hitler any funds for his war plans. Instead we had based our refusal of further credits on technical grounds, such as the excessive demands of the capital market, the impossibility of increasing taxation and such like. I explained to the court that under the Third Reich it just was not possible to tell Herr Hitler: I'm not giving you any money for your war. I told them also how, when he had received the memorandum, Hitler had shouted: "That's mutiny!"

I then went into details: "As early as 1937 I tried to ascertain which groups could be counted on for support in an attempt to overthrow the Hitler regime. I need only mention that scientists meekly sat and listened to the most absurd National-Socialist speeches without the slightest attempt at resistance. I remember how leading businessmen, when they saw that I no longer counted for anything in the business world, crowded into Goering's anterooms and disappeared from mine. In short, there was no relying on either of these groups. The only remaining dependables were the generals, the Army; the more so because one would have to reckon on armed resistance even in the Praetorian Guard of the S.S.

"As a result I first sought contact with generals, such as Kluge, if only to ascertain whether there were any men within the ranks of the Army with whom one could speak frankly. I have already related this here and don't want to go into it again. This first step brought me into touch with generals of the most varied types during the course of the war."

Dr. Dix asked what I had done following the outbreak of war.

"Throughout the whole war," I replied, "I approached every general who was in any way available."

A topic of discussion at the afternoon session was what Hitler said about me following the events of July 20, 1944. Speer knew exactly what he had said. On July 22 Hitler had personally made out the order for my arrest. While doing so he had been mad with rage and his remarks about me had been positively venomous. He had been seriously hampered by my "negative action." He would have done far better to have had me shot even before the war had started.

When I related how I had exhorted other countries again and again to pursue an economic policy which would afford the German people chances of livelihood, but that those countries had never paid any heed to my exhortations, the Russian General Rudenko lost his temper and exclaimed:

"Mr. President! For two days now we have listened to long-winded tedious statements by the prisoner Schacht, and I am of the opinion that the statement now furnished by the prisoner Schacht is in no sense an answer to concrete questions relating to the charge against him, but merely so much talk. It seems to me that it merely prolongs the trial."

The President, however, stated that the court did not desire to obstruct me in the conduct of my defense.

Dr. Dix put a very pertinent enquiry: "Why did you not emigrate?"

To which I replied: "If it had been a question only of my personal fortunes, nothing would have been easier. But my personal affairs didn't come into it. Having devoted myself since 1923 to the common weal the question for me was the very existence of my people, my country. In all history I have never known emigrants — I am speaking, of course, of voluntary emigrants, not of expellees — I have never known of emigrants to be of use to their country."

Dr. Dix now fired his parting shot. He returned to the subject of the foreign diplomats, the gist of his remarks being that for people like myself it was a matter of great significance when the whole international world was on the best terms with Hitler; whereas I had been against him — even officially — since 1938.

There followed of course a great argument as to which subject should or should not be discussed in court. Between the President and my lawyer the following was generally agreed upon: my lawyer would be permitted to ask: "How did recognition of the Nazi Government on the part of other countries react upon — how did it affect this group of conspirators with which the prisoner Schacht was connected?"

But the American prosecutor, Jackson, would have none of it. Of his own accord he said:

"We are gradually approaching a situation which in my opinion cannot be tolerated in this court, and I entirely fail to see how it constitutes an extenuating circumstance within the scope of Schacht's defense to point out that foreign governments maintained contact with the German Reich, even during the period of its degeneration."

He had summed up the situation correctly. He was really in an impossible position, as the outcome of the trial proved.

The President declared: "The court is of opinion that the question is one of importance."

So I substantiated my statement as to which foreign statesmen and missions were on friendly, even cordial, terms with Hitler, what time Hitler and I were already at loggerheads.

The court adjourned for ten minutes, and I knew that matters would soon take an interesting turn, for Mr. Jackson was to cross-examine me after the sitting was resumed. He was after my scalp. I had no mind to let him have it.

# LVIII

## THE NUREMBERG TRIBUNAL — II

IN ORDER even to begin to understand the methods employed by Mr. Jackson, the American chief prosecutor, when he started to deal with me after that ten-minute break, it is essential to bear in mind the international political situation in 1946. The Allies had won the war; they were very proud of it, and rightly so, for it had been a long and terrible struggle. Into this mighty fact of world history there intruded — now that it was all over — a lot of little human elements. Who had personally won this war? As always, world opinion on this question picked on the names of great statesmen and generals. But there were many small-part people and "extras" who wanted to snatch a leaf from the huge laurel wreath suspended above the heads of the great, that they too might go down into history. The Americans above all mistook temporary fame for historical immortality. The big American newspapers featured "The Nuremberg Trial" as front-page news. They made much of their compatriot, Mr. Jackson. For a time he embodied in his person the American Public who wanted to see the "war criminals" hang. Inspired by such considerations he proceeded to the attack.

The first question was very telling. He wanted to know whether, in 1938, I had or had not said to my neighbor at a dinner party: "My dear lady, we have fallen into the hands of criminals. How could I have foreseen that?"

Yes, I certainly had said so.

"I am sure," he went on with conspicuous concern, "I am sure you would wish to assist the court by telling us who these criminals were."

I saw at once what he was driving at and answered tersely: "Hitler and his associates."

Immediately he aimed his first shaft at me. He asserted that I myself had been one of Hitler's associates. "I want you to mention by name all those accused persons you consider to be criminals."

My answer was based on the premise that I had no idea who were the members of Hitler's inner circle. I had always counted Goering as one of them, I affirmed, and personally I would add Himmler, Bormann and Heydrich.

"Those last three men are all dead," replied Jackson angrily.

I couldn't help that. I conceded that von Ribbentrop, the Foreign Minister, must have been kept informed as to Hitler's plans; beyond that, I maintained, I was unable to answer that question.

He showed me some photographs in which I appeared with all the rest of the Third Reich outfit. That was the crowd I went around with, according to Jackson.

I protested: "Now, if you had snapped me with my other acquaintances as often as this, the pile would have been ten times bigger."

There was a faint murmur from the press stand. As quickly as possible he changed the subject; he blamed me for having done all I could to bring about a participation by the National Socialists in the government of Germany. I stuck to what I had already said with absolute truth, namely, that no government in a democratically governed country could afford to ignore the party with the largest number of adherents. That would lead — as indeed it had led — to disaster. Jackson instanced speeches that I had delivered on the occasion of Hitler's birthday, and I replied that it was the custom, the world over, to deliver speeches on the occasion of the birthday of the head of the state without having to weigh one's words.

I had never worn my gold party badge in everyday life. But, maintained Jackson, I had done so on official occasions.

I replied that wearing this badge had ensured many advantages in railway travel, care of one's car, booking of hotel accommodation, and so forth.

Finally he asked the most unbelievably foolish question. He wanted to know whether, when I entered the government, I told Hitler that I joined his cabinet "only to put the brake on his program."

Even today I shudder to think of what would have happened if I had done so. At Nuremberg at the time, I exclaimed: "Oh, no, I took good care not to tell him!"

Having hitherto fought a vanguard action, Mr. Jackson now suddenly attacked me from the rear. "I take it, anyway, that you admit to being partly responsible for Germany having lost the war?"

I said I considered that was a very strange question. I thought to myself, what is he driving at? Can he foresee that this "International Court" will acquit me? Has he so much personal animosity against me that he wants to discredit me in the eyes of my own countrymen?

"I am in no way responsible," I answered, "for the war ever having been started. So I cannot assume any responsibility for our having lost it. I never wanted a war."

Jackson changed the subject and embarked on the Jewish question. I managed to state my case coherently in spite of the fact that he made a point of cutting in after every few words.

"In regard to the predominating influence of the Jews in government, legal and cultural matters, I have always adhered to a certain principle. I do not consider that such predominating influence is good, either in the interests of Germany and the German people — a Christian state based on the Christian outlook — or in the interests of the Jews themselves because it arouses animosity against them. Consequently I have always declared myself in favor of limiting Jewish activity to a certain extent in all these fields — a numerical limitation, based not absolutely on population figures, but rather on a certain percentage."

Jackson blamed me for not standing out against the paragraph relating to Aryanism and state officials when it was passed into law. In addition, during my term of office as a Minister of the Reich, all Jewish lawyers had been forbidden to appear in court. And I myself, along with others, had put my name to a bill prohibiting Jews from dealing in foreign exchange and engaging in economic councils of investigation.

"And you also approved a law," he finally exclaimed, "providing for the death penalty for any German subjects who transferred German property abroad or allowed German property to remain abroad?"

"Certainly," I replied sharply.

"And you knew that this would hit those Jews who were going abroad, more severely than anyone else?"

I retorted: "I certainly do not hope that the Jews have proved worse cheats than the Christians."

Notwithstanding the fact that, at this stage in his examination, Jackson obviously sought to prevent my giving a detailed statement, I did succeed in explaining why I had taken part in all these activities. I did so because, while in my opinion they were all questionable, they were nevertheless not important enough to warrant my making a complete break with the Hitler Government. He wanted to know what my object had been in remaining in the government, what could have been sufficiently vital to induce me to put up with all these goings on. I told him that to me, the supremely important thing was to put Germany on an equal footing with the other Powers from the point of view both of economy and rearmament. And I added, in order to make it quite clear: "That was my opinion then, and I stand by it today."

I had the impression that Jackson was now anxious to come to the main point in the indictment, in which I was charged with having participated in preparations for a war of aggression since I had supplied the finances for it. He brought up the Mefo bills; he brought up everything he possibly could; he accused me of having encouraged export trade for the sole purpose of obtaining sufficient foreign exchange for the import of such raw materials as could be utilized for purposes of rearmament. Finally he charged me with having taken certain measures that would enable me to retain my hold on German finances.

He quoted from a memorandum which I had handed to Hitler: "The following contentions are based on the premise that the duty of German policy is to carry out the rearmament program in accordance with the prescribed schedule; that everything else must be subordinated to this end, so long as the one main objective is not jeopardized through neglect of other matters."

He asked me whether I had written that.

"I not only wrote it: I handed it to Hitler in person," I answered. "It was my business to control the party subscriptions and party monies which were extracted everywhere from the pockets of the German people. I could only get Hitler to agree, of course, by telling him: This is obviously being done in the interests of rearmament. Had I told him: It is being done, for instance . . ."

Mr. Jackson tried to interrupt. I asked him to let me finish. "If I had told him, This is being done in the interests of theater building or something similar it would not have had the slightest effect. But if I said to him, This or that must be done because otherwise we cannot rearm, *that* was where I could get hold of Hitler and that was why I put it that way."

Oddly enough Mr. Jackson considered that I had "misled" Hitler. I retorted: "I should not call it *mis*leading. I should call it leading, Mr. Jackson."

"But leading someone without telling him the real motives that prompted you?"

"If you want to lead anyone," I answered, "I believe you stand a far better chance if you don't tell him your real reasons than if you do."

He sprang to his feet in triumph. "Thank you for this frank exposition of your ideology, Dr. Schacht. I am indeed much obliged to you."

Mr. Jackson started going into technical financial details in connection with German rearmament and became quite simply dull. The journalists left. The court was frankly bored. That suited me very well, and I did nothing to relieve the general tedium.

So ended May 2.

May 3 began by the presiding judge, Sir Geoffrey Lawrence, informing Mr. Jackson and myself that the interpreters had complained that we spoke too fast. Mr. Jackson was very much the *grand seigneur*.

"I must ask the interpreters to forgive me. It is difficult to discard the habits of a lifetime."

The President agreed. "Yes, it is very difficult."

I said nothing: the interpreters were no affair of mine. I did not need them and I did not mind much whether they found their task easy or difficult.

Mr. Jackson broached the subject of my relations with Goering. According to him we had had differences of opinion of a private nature and up to the time of my retirement from all official posts we had not been on good terms.

"On the contrary," I retorted, "till then we were always very nice to each other."

"Really!" exclaimed Jackson in astonishment.

"Oh, yes."

Then he set a trap for me. "So your differences with Goering began with the contest as to which of you should be in charge of the military preparations?"

"No . . ." I countered, but Jackson cut in before I could say more. I protested against the interruption and declared: "The differences that led to my resignation arose from the fact that Goering wanted to direct the economic policy while I shouldered the responsibility."

Jackson was determined to prove that I had resigned from the government only because I was not allowed to prepare for a war of aggression on an even larger scale than — in the opinion of the prosecution — I had already managed to do up to 1938. He had all his data in a muddle and I told him he was not "correct."

He got no further ahead and finally gave in, remarking that at the moment he was not interested in the sequence of events.

Nevertheless I was on my guard. He went on to speak about the first years of the Hitler regime and proceeded to read aloud what I had once written about Goering:

> I have described Hitler as an amoral type, but I can only regard Goering as *im*moral and criminal. Gifted from the start with a certain *bonhomie*, which he knew well how to exploit in the interests of his own popularity, he was the most egocentric creature one could imagine. For him the attainment of political power was but a means to personal enrichment and personal luxury. He was consumed with jealousy over anyone else's success. His greed knew no bounds. His love of precious stones, gold and jewels was incredible. He was entirely lacking in *esprit de corps*. So long as anyone was useful to him — and only so long — he could be pleasant enough, and even so, it was merely put on.
>
> Goering's knowledge of all the subjects which a member of the government should master was precisely nil, especially in the field of political economy. He hadn't the faintest idea of any of the economic details Hitler entrusted to him in the autumn of 1936, although he built up an enormous staff and abused his power as economic leader according to all the rules of the game. His personal appearance was so theatrical that one could only compare him with Nero. One lady who went to tea with his second wife described how he came in dressed in a kind of Roman toga, sandals bestrewn with precious stones, innumerable rings on his fingers, and otherwise decked out with jewelry, his face and lips plastered with make-up.

He had scarcely begun to read when Goering flounced around indignantly. I could not quite see what had prompted Mr. Jackson to read my words about Goering aloud. Did he hope that Goering might possess some secret information to the effect that I did take part in preparations for a war of aggression? Whatever the reason I felt bound to protest at once:

"I beg of you not to mix up your dates again. It was not until later that I learned and experienced all the things you now mention, and not in 1936 as you make out."

Only then did Jackson stop juggling with dates, and proceed to his next question: Had I not drawn Hitler's attention to the question of colonies?

MYSELF: "Certainly."

JACKSON: "What colonies?"

MYSELF: "Our colonies."

JACKSON: "Where were these colonies?"

MYSELF: "I take it you know that as well as I do."

JACKSON: "*You* are the witness, Dr. Schacht. I want to know what you told Hitler, not what *I* know."

Until now he hadn't breathed a word about what I had said to Hitler. I answered: "Oh, what I told Hitler? I told Hitler we would try to get back some of our colonies, which we were no longer allowed to administer, so that we could work there."

JACKSON: "What colonies?"

MYSELF: "I was thinking especially of the African colonies."

JACKSON: "And you considered that these African colonies were indispensable to your future plans — for Germany?"

I told him that my colonial ambitions concerned only "our own property."

He thought he had caught me out. "And your property, as you call it, were the African colonies?"

"The term 'property'" I retorted, "was not my own: the Versailles Treaty describes these colonies as German Property."

His answer did not reveal any great presence of mind. "You can call it what you like," he said angrily.

That was just what I had done.

If — he asserted — I had wanted colonies, I must also have been in favor of naval rearmament in order to create a sea power which would safeguard our access to the colonies.

"It never occurred to me," I exclaimed. "How do you arrive at that idea?"

He repeated his question: "Did your colonial plan include such rearmament as would make of Germany a great naval power so that the route to these colonies would be safeguarded?"

MYSELF: "Not in the least."

Turning slightly toward the press stand he enquired very sarcastically: "Then your plan was to leave the trade routes unprotected."

"Oh, no," I said. "I had imagined that they would be sufficiently protected by international law."

There was a murmur in the press stand, but not for Mr. Jackson, and it seemed to me as if the Bench betrayed some impatience.

There was nothing left for the prosecutor but to change the subject. With much detail, and quotations from sundry speeches of mine, he accused me of having played my part as one of the crew that manned the Third Reich boat. The gist of my reply invariably was that I had never disputed the fact, but that I had emphasized my reasons for doing so. Then he suggested that I must surely deplore the use that Hitler had made of the Wehrmacht.

I agreed.

So I did regard the invasion of Poland as an unwarranted act of aggression?

My reply consisted of one word: "Absolutely."

JACKSON: "The same applies to the invasion of Luxembourg?"

MYSELF: "Absolutely."

JACKSON: "And to Holland?"

MYSELF: "Absolutely."

JACKSON: "And to Denmark?"

MYSELF: "Absolutely."

JACKSON: "And to Norway?"

MYSELF: "Absolutely."

JACKSON: "And to Yugoslavia?"

MYSELF: "Absolutely."

JACKSON: "And to Russia?"

MYSELF: "Absolutely, my dear sir; and you have forgotten Belgium."

He then went on to affirm that all these attacks had been carried out with that same Wehrmacht which I had helped to create in the early years of the Third Reich because I had furnished the necessary funds.

I could only reply: "Yes, unfortunately."

After the interval Jackson showed a film in which I appeared, together with several others, when we greeted Hitler on his return from France after the French capitulation. I had been bidden to attend on this occasion as Minister without Portfolio. It seemed to me that Jackson was out to prove that I nevertheless still exerted considerable influence.

When the film was over he asked me: "As Minister without Portfolio what did your Ministry consist of?"

MYSELF: "Nothing."

JACKSON: "How many had you on your staff?"

MYSELF: "One woman secretary."

JACKSON: "What was your office accommodation?"

MYSELF: "A couple of rooms in my private house."

After a few more questions of this sort which did not get him anywhere, he turned to my personal financial circumstances. But there was no information to be gleaned here, for I was paid by the Reichsbank, and my ministerial salary was included.

Then he wanted to know: "You are entitled to draw a salary and a pension, the one being offset against the other — that's the idea, isn't it? The agreement held good so long as you were a member of the regime?"

MYSELF: "That still holds good today — it has nothing whatever to do with the regime. And I hope I shall still receive my pension, otherwise what shall I have to live on?"

"Well," he said, not without a certain wit but with a note of malicious hope in his voice, "perhaps the cost of living won't be very great in your case, Doctor."

Toward the end of his examination he made a last, swift attempt to disprove that I had ever been in actual contact with the group of conspirators of July 20, 1944.

I no longer put myself out very much, for if indeed justice were to be found in this court that fact must already be deemed to have been proved by the evidence of the witnesses. And so it turned out. At the very last he raked up something I had once said, and gathered from it that I regarded those generals who had given Hitler their unqualified and unreserved support in his wars of aggression as equally guilty with Hitler himself. I *had* said that, and there was no getting away from it.

Scarcely had Mr. Jackson informed the presiding judge that he had no further questions to put to me than Dr. Hans Laterner jumped up and protested against my remarks about the generals. He was defending the General Staff and the Supreme Command, who were being arraigned *in corpore*.

Mr. Jackson stated that he would not make use of my answer against the General Staff and Supreme Command. Dr. Laterner withdrew his protest.

And now there appeared on the scene Major General A. G. Alexandrov, Assistant Prosecutor for the Soviet Union.

The General found himself immediately at odds with the President, for he began by asking the same questions to which I had already replied to Mr. Jackson. Several times I said to him: "I have repeatedly given my evidence on this question. Will you please refer to the same."

But Major General Alexandrov had a piece of paper in front of him on which were written the questions he wished or had been instructed to ask me, and he was obviously firmly resolved to carry out those instructions. Again and again he would say: "Will you kindly repeat that?"

The President however grew tired of this procedure and ordered: "If he has already given evidence on that subject, that is sufficient."

He consulted his list again and challenged me: "And what led you to collaborate with Hitler, since your outlook was opposed to his theory and to the theories of German fascism?"

But by now the President was really angry.

"General Alexandrov!" he exclaimed, "he has already told us why he collaborated with Hitler — you must have heard him."

Major General Alexandrov, however, actually wanted to hear once again what part I had played in Germany's financial affairs. I replied: "But I have already furnished detailed information on that point."

The President grew more and more irritated and protested: "General Alexandrov! The court has already listened to a long cross-examination and does not wish the same facts or points to be dealt with again. Will you kindly tell the court whether you desire to put forward any questions of special interest to the Soviet Union, which were not dealt with in the cross-examination."

But now the Russian General was angry too. He maintained that I had not given "sufficiently clear" answers to the American prosecutor's questions. The controversy between him and the presiding judge became critical; the latter was quite determined: "The court does not intend to listen to questions which have already been submitted."

The Russian was right off his stroke. His list had ceased to be of any use to him. It looked as though he wanted to seek further instructions, so he suggested that we should already adjourn for lunch, although it was still fairly early.

Once again the presiding judge was furious. There could be no question, he said, of an adjournment at this hour. The General could proceed. The General passed his handkerchief across his forehead and said: "But surely you were in supreme control of the economic conduct of the war?"

"That question has cropped up ten times already." I felt exactly the same as the presiding judge — sick and tired of hearing the same things again and again.

"I have not heard it from your own lips — not once," the Russian exclaimed in astonishment.

But the President had had enough. He told Major General Alexandrov: "The prisoner has always admitted it, and of course it is perfectly obvious that he was in supreme control of the economic conduct of the war. The question you put to him was whether, in that capacity, he had had any share in rearmament for a war of aggression, and he has declared over and over that such was never his object; that his object was the obtaining of equal rights for Germany. That is what he said, and we have to consider whether it is true. But that he did say it is quite certain."

Right up to the midday break the Russian General and I continued our heavy-footed skirmishing. I harked back continually to the fact that to all the questions he asked me I had already given my answers — to Mr. Jackson; and I persisted in this vein until the President announced that the court would adjourn for lunch. That was Friday, May 3, 1946.

After the adjournment General Alexandrov announced: "Mr. President! Out of respect for the wishes of the court and the fact that the prisoner Schacht has already been examined in detail by Mr. Jackson, I have been through the minutes of this morning's procedure and am now in a position to reduce considerably the number of questions addressed to the prisoner Schacht in the course of my cross-examination. I now have only two questions for the prisoner Schacht."

Both these questions took no account whatever of anything that had been previously said, and even today I often wonder what kind of problems the General had been mulling over in his mind, while proceedings against me had been taking place in his presence.

His first question was whether I admitted having taken an active part in Germany's economic preparations for wars of aggression.

I replied in the negative.

Secondly — and he quoted a statement of mine — he wanted to know whether up to 1938 my attitude had not been such as to give the impression that I agreed with Hitler and his methods of government.

My reply to that: "I was in complete agreement with him so long as his policy tallied with mine; afterwards, no, and then I left."

General Alexandrov retired and my place in the witness stand was taken by Wilhelm Vocke, a former director of the Reichsbank and member of the board. I had returned to my seat in the dock.

Vocke described my early period at the Reichsbank and then began to tell an interested audience about an event that occurred in 1936.

"In 1936," he said, "the board of the Reichsbank received a communication marked *Strictly Confidential* from either the High Command or the General Staff, with instructions to transfer the bank's stocks of gold, securities and notes from the German border territories to a more central zone. The reason given for these instructions was as follows: in the event of an attack on Germany on two fronts, the High Command is resolved to evacuate the border territories and concentrate on a more central zone which can be defended under any circumstances. From the map which accompanied this communication I can still recall that for purposes of defense the eastern frontier stretched from Hof right up to Stettin. Of the western frontier I have less clear recollection, but Baden and the Rhineland were both mentioned. On receipt of this information the Reichsbank in fact became extremely alarmed by the threat of an attack on Germany on two fronts involving the surrender of huge tracts of German territory, as well as by the monstrous suggestion that, in the event of foreign occupation, the bank should leave the population entirely without funds. On these grounds we turned down this last-named request, but consented to remove the gold and transferred it to such other centers as Berlin, Nuremberg, Munich. On one point there could now be no further doubt; namely, that our rearmament was of a purely defensive character."

For me this was an extraordinarily important piece of evidence. It proved to the court that in 1936 the military "high-ups" mentioned to the Reichsbank the possibility of such a desperate defense situation. Who now could still maintain that, as far back as 1936, I had any idea that Hitler was planning a war of aggression?

Vocke then went on to describe an incident dating from 1937.

"In that year, when the economic system was running on oiled wheels and fresh funds kept pouring in, Schacht invoked the aid of German professors and national economists, and invited them to a conference with the object of persuading them to adopt his policy of restraint. One of those present on that occasion suddenly asked Schacht: 'And supposing war were to break out?' Whereupon Schacht rose and said: 'Gentlemen, in that case we're finished — it would be all up with us. Please let us drop the subject — there's no point in racking our brains over it.' "

I noted with satisfaction how the court listened to Vocke's reliable and clearly spoken evidence; but I saw too that Jackson was growing restless.

Vocke proceeded to speak of the first days after the outbreak of war.

"Schacht had invited those directors who seemed to him reliable, to a discussion. The first thing he said was: 'Gentlemen, this is a betrayal such as the world has never before witnessed. The Poles never received the German offer. The newspapers are lying in order to hypnotize the German people into a sense of security. The Poles have been taken completely by surprise. Henderson never even received the offer, only a brief extract from the note by word of mouth. When a war breaks out, the question always arises as to who was responsible for it. This is a clear case of war guilt, if ever there was one. One cannot imagine a greater crime.' "

Vocke described how I had exclaimed: "Our rearmament is useless. We have been tricked by rogues and knaves. The money has simply been poured down the drain."

He spoke of my general conception of politics and of how I had once remarked: "A foreign policy without any sort of armament is impossible in the long run."

He continued: "Schacht also said that the neutrality he desired for Germany would have to be an armed neutrality if there were any question of a conflict between the Great Powers. Schacht was of the opinion that it was essential Germany should rearm if she were not to remain permanently defenseless among armed nations. He was not thinking of any particular attack, but he said that in every country there was a war party who might come into power today or tomorrow and, where her neighbors were concerned, a wholly defenseless Germany was an impossibility in the long run. More: she would constitute an actual danger to peace and a temptation to other nations to invade her sooner or later."

After Vocke had concluded his evidence, Mr. Jackson endeavored, but without success, to pull it to pieces. Vocke's evidence remained on record; it had obviously created an impression.

From May 3 to July 15 I was obliged to remain in the dock and listen to the sometimes grim proceedings against the other prisoners.

On July 15 Dr. Dix began his speech for the defense as follows: "The unique character of Schacht's case is evident at once from a glance at the dock, and from the story of his imprisonment and defense. As has been established here in this court, Schacht was sent to a concentration camp by Hitler's order. The charge against him was one of high treason against the Hitler regime. The People's Court would have sentenced him to death but for the turn of events which meant that from being Hitler's prisoner he became the prisoner of the victorious Allied Powers. In the summer of 1944 I had been instructed to defend Schacht in Adolf Hitler's People's Court; in the summer of 1945 I was asked to undertake his defense before the International Military Tribunal. This too is a self-contradictory state of affairs which, in so far as it concerns Schacht's person, likewise compels serious consideration on the part of all connected with the trial.

"Very few Germans living in Germany," he said, "were aware of the balance and allocation of power within those groups which were apparently or actually called upon to devote their best efforts to the molding of the political mind. Most Germans will be astonished at the revelation of this state of affairs. How much more impossible was it for a foreigner, at the time the charge was preferred, to gauge the sociological conditions in Hitler's Germany, particularly those relating to constitutional law and internal policy? But to gauge them correctly was essential to the proper preferment of any charge based on actual, valid premises. I am of the opinion that in this respect the prosecution is faced with an insoluble task."

The prosecution had mobilized one witness against all the prisoners in the dock, a man who had something to say — and that was the former Prussian Minister Severing whose death occurred recently. When, at the Nuremberg Trial, he had told the court how everything had started, the foreigners had been struck dumb with amazement, unable to take their eyes off him; his evidence was well-nigh incredible. On July 20, 1932, he said, two police officials had called at his house, stating that the President of the Reich had sent them and that he — the Prussian Minister of the Interior — was to resign his office at once. Such a demand, such procedure, were in no sense compatible with the constitution on which von Hindenburg had taken his oath. Severing had the right — one might say the duty — to resist. The Prussian Police, who came under his jurisdiction as Minister of the Interior, was still at that time completely disciplined and absolutely reliable inasmuch as each official did exactly what he was told.

But what had Herr Severing done? He had offered no opposition to this abrupt and unconstitutional dismissal. He had trotted meekly home, tendered his resignation and drawn his pension so long as the Third Reich had lasted. Hitler never looked upon him as his adversary, nor threw him into a concentration camp as he did me: he left him entirely in peace and — as history has proved — he was right.

But there is more to come. Severing was a prominent Social

Democrat and had played an important part as a labor leader of rank and title. It was to the German working classes, however, that the words of the poet applied:

> *All the wheels stand silent, stilled,*
> *Since thy mighty arm so willed.*

Once in the course of German history all the wheels did stand still because a mighty arm so willed it. That was during the Kapp *Putsch.* On that occasion the power of well-organized troops collapsed before the resistance of the trade unions which had called the General Strike. But neither in 1932 nor in 1933 did Severing call upon the unions to resist. He did nothing to prevent their silent and complete dissolution. He risked nothing, neither did he lay himself open to any unpleasant consequences.

Yet we know from the history of the European working classes that there was a time — a time of desperation and intense bitterness — when they struck against German troops; namely, in Holland during the Occupation. The Dutch labor leaders called a strike. But in Germany Herr Severing never got that far. In Nuremberg, to the great satisfaction of the prosecution, he described me as "not to be trusted" and said I had "betrayed the cause of democracy."

To my way of thinking, democracy in Germany — at any rate the Severing variety — threw in its own hand.

The court was all attention as Dr. Dix expounded this theme and contrasted Severing's complete passivity with the activity I had displayed.

"Schacht," he asserted, "has just proved himself an apostle of activity. All he lacked at the beginning was the intuition of true insight into the personality of Hitler and certain of his satellites. But this is no punishable act, nor is it any indication of criminal deception. This intuition was lacking in most people, both inside and outside Germany. Intuition is a matter of chance, an unaccountable gift of grace. Every man, even the wisest and cleverest, has his limitations. Schacht is undoubtedly very clever, but in his case cleverness has prevailed at the expense of intuition."

He then proceeded to assess all the facts that had come before the court and brought his speech to a close.

"After the Elections in July 1932 it was clear that Hitler would — that he was bound to — seize the reins. Schacht had previously warned the other countries of this contingency: he did not therefore do anything to bring it about. After Hitler had assumed power there remained for him, as indeed for every German, only two alternatives: either to hold himself aloof or to take an active part in the movement. The decision which he made at this parting of the ways was a purely political one, devoid of any criminal intent. We estimate and weigh the reasons that prompted other countries to co-operate with Hitler in far more intensive and pro-German fashion than they had done with Germany's previous democratic governments: in exactly the same way we must recognize the *bona fides* of all those Germans who believed that they could be of greater service to their country and to mankind by joining the movement — that is, either within the party or in some official capacity such as the Civil Service — rather than as a disgruntled outsider. To serve Hitler as a minister and as president of the Reichsbank was a political resolve, the political wisdom of which we may question now — *ex post facto* — but which was completely lacking in criminal character. Schacht has always remained staunch to the fundamental reason for his resolve; namely, to face up to every kind of radicalism and be in a position to combat it effectively. The world, though well aware of his attitude, gave him no sign, either to put him on his guard or support him in his resistance. He saw only that the world continued to put its trust in Adolf Hitler far longer than he himself did, and accorded him honors and successes in matters of foreign policy which made Schacht's work increasingly difficult when for a long time it had already been directed toward the overthrow of Adolf Hitler and his regime. The courage and consistency with which he pursued this fight must make it seem like a positive miracle that he is alive — that it was not until after July 20, 1944, that fate overtook him in the form of the concentration camp, and that he was in danger of losing his head, either at the hands of the People's Court or of some S.S. thug. Schacht is sufficiently clever and self-critical to know that, viewed from a purely political angle, his portrait will figure in history — at any rate in the immediate future — blurred by party favor and party hatred. In all humility he surrenders to the verdict of history, even though one historian or another may describe his political attitude as wrong. It is in all the pride of a good conscience, however, that he surrenders to the verdict of this high court. He faces his judges with clean hands. He surrenders to this tribunal in confidence, as he has already stated in a letter addressed to the court prior to the opening of proceedings. In this letter he states that he welcomes the chance to demonstrate to this court, and to the world at large, his conduct and his actions, and the reasons that motivated him. He surrenders to this court in confidence, for he knows that party favor and party hatred will carry no weight with them. While he himself recognizes the relativeness of all political action in such difficult times, he is nevertheless full of self-assurance and confidence in respect of the criminal charges preferred against him — and rightly so. For it does not matter who may be adjudged to be criminally responsible for this war, and for the cruelties and atrocities perpetrated during this war: to him — after the minutely accurate establishment of the actual facts in this court, Schacht can exclaim in the words addressed by William Tell to Parricida, the Emperor's murderer: 'Unto the Heavens I raise my stainless hands, my curse upon thee and upon thy deed!'

"I therefore move that Schacht be adjudged not guilty of the charges against him, and that he be acquitted."

It is a matter of history that the International Court at Nuremberg did acquit me. The world had testified to my innocence before what was probably the most severe court of justice that has ever existed. After this tribunal had acquitted me and pronounced me innocent of any crime, I fell into the hands of my fellow countrymen.

# LIX

## THE DENAZIFICATION TRIBUNALS

IMMEDIATELY after the conclusion of my trial at Nuremberg, as described in the two preceding chapters, the psychoanalyst Gilbert paid me his customary visit in order to check up on my mental condition. He could find precious little abnormal about me. Instead, we drifted into conversation in the course of which I asked:

"Why doesn't the American prosecutor withdraw the charge against me? After all, there was no question of a conviction; that was incontestably established at the trial."

Gilbert shrugged his shoulders, but did not answer.

"You might pass the suggestion on to Jackson, anyway," I insisted.

The psychoanalyst from Vienna with the American name promised to do so. Presumably he kept his word and mentioned my proposal to Jackson; but the American prosecutor declined.

Four weeks elapsed between the trial and the verdict, during which we waited and did nothing. A humane feature of this tribunal was that they allowed us to see our families.

Only someone who has been behind prison bars and in concentration camps will understand how I felt when I stood face to face with my wife and my two daughters, Konstanze and Cordula, for the first time in more than two years. Konstanze, very like her mother in appearance, was five years old and remembered me only vaguely. Cordula — always called "Bee" — was a year younger than her sister, a typical Schacht; she had no idea what her father was like, for she was exactly one and a half years old when the Gestapo arrested me.

Our meeting took place in the same room where we prisoners held consultations with our lawyers. That is to say, we were separated from our families by wire netting and glass partitions, with a stern-faced American military policeman seated in attendance, loaded pistol in hand.

It is easy to imagine how we felt. My wife, to whom I was bound by the closest of ties, was torn with anxiety lest I should be convicted. The children, who understood nothing, gazed blankly at me. Cordula saved the situation. So far as she knew this was the first time in her young life that she had seen her father. Suddenly she stood on tiptoe and whispered through the grille: "I like you very much."

It was like a message from another world.

Then the children receded into the background, for now, for the first time, I learned from my wife all she had gone through since my arrest.

Comparatively speaking she had not fared too badly under the National Socialists — if one excepts the constant anxiety resulting from the verdict of the People's Court against the conspirators of July 20, 1944. Later she told me that, to a certain extent, we owed it to Hitler that we were able to preserve some of our possessions. For, since the Gestapo confiscated part of the conspirators' property, she had sent off certain pictures and pieces of old furniture to friends in Munich, even before the end of the war. The large copies she had had to leave behind as by that time there was no packing material available for them.

In April 1945 my wife had remained at Gühlen, as we had agreed. Battles between Russians and Germans had been fought on our estate. In my park alone sixteen German soldiers lay buried. My wife had contrived to hold her own against the first Russian troops. As soon as a decent orderly body of soldiers had been installed on the estate she had sent a letter to the Russian Commander-in-Chief, General Zhukhov, on whose orders one of his adjutants had been sent to fetch her, and all my documents had gone with her. For six weeks she had been kept prisoner at Russian Headquarters, east of Berlin. Both accommodation and food were adequate. She was, so they informed her, treated in the same way as a captured general.

She had been told at the time of her arrest that there was a prospect of her being sent to Moscow. But finally, after going through all my papers and thoroughly cross-examining my wife, they obviously desisted from the idea. My wife, together with my papers, was escorted back to Gühlen and provided with a telephone connection with instructions to give the alarm immediately in the event of her being molested in any way by undisciplined troops.

What the Gestapo in its time had omitted to do the efficient Russians made up for; they went all around the house and in the vicinity with mine detectors and in so doing discovered a deedbox which I had buried there years ago. It contained a whole lot of anti-Hitler books which had been published abroad, and a manuscript of mine completed in 1942 in which I had systematically described — and rejected — National Socialism; all of them works which, prior to the capitulation, would have deeply incriminated me. Later, in Kransberg, I endeavored through my American interrogator to recover the deedbox and its contents from the Russians, for this manuscript was bound to be of the greatest use in securing my discharge. Unfortunately I have never seen or heard anything more of it. The Russians were obviously not interested in my exoneration.

My wife had stayed on in Gühlen for the next few months and carried on with the remaining available labor until the introduction of the so-called Land Reform in the Eastern Zone when the Communists took possession of the house and estate. In the autumn of 1945 she was informed that she must leave Gühlen within three days. She was allowed to take nothing but her personal possessions. She was given an address in Mecklenburg and advised to go there. But she smelled a rat and, suitcase in hand, made instead for Berlin — a two days' journey on foot. Later she learned that all the inmates of the Mecklenburg camp were deported to Russia.

As a next step my wife then sought permission to move into our Berlin home, but the German authorities refused. For several weeks she was obliged to spend the night with different friends and acquaintances until finally she succeeded, as one of the staff and under another name, in accompanying a party of children who were being sent to the Western Zone by a religious organization. And there, in the little village of Hollenstedt on Lüneburg Heath, she met again our children's nurse and her family.

That had happened about a year previously. A few days after her arrival a British soldier had driven up to the house and ordered my wife to go with him. Since he carried a written warrant she was obliged to obey and leave the children behind. The British took her to Winsen-on-the-Luhe where for five months she was "confined" in a country inn known as Dammans Gasthaus run by a dignified Lower-Saxon landlady named Mathilde Bruns. The British ordered her and her husband to keep watch on Frau Schacht by day and night.

"And what for?" enquired Mathilde in her quaint patois, a mixture of High German and *Plattdeutsch*.

"She might commit suicide," was the British reply.

"Did you ever think of committing suicide?" I interrupted.

"Not for a moment!" she answered. "But the British probably imagined that the one idea of a woman in my position would be death. In any case they wanted the Brunses to stand surety for me . . ."

The Brunses refused, for reasons easily understood. They said they were far too busy with farming and housekeeping to carry out an inspection of their confinee's room every two hours during the night. Eventually they compromised. My wife was given a room with a wooden partition. On the other side of the partition was the bed in which the Bruns daughter slept. This girl was instructed to report at once should anything unusual happen in my wife's room. "They meant, she was to report if she heard me in the death throes," said my wife.

At last, after five months, she received permission to return to her children at Hollenstedt. Owing to lack of space, however, she was unable to remain in the same house and she was therefore allotted a summerhouse. Water had to be fetched from another house over two hundred yards away. The closet was some hundred yards distant in the wood. "Romantic atmosphere of Lüneburg Heath," as my wife put it.

Here she stuck it for two winters and one summer. The purchase of the barest essentials meant a walk of at least two miles. In addition she possessed not a penny and in those first chaotic months it was extraordinarily difficult to establish contact with German and foreign friends who would have been able to help her with money or CARE * parcels.

Such was my wife's report. Now at last with tears in her eyes she sat opposite to me in the Nuremberg Prison, tortured by the possibility of my conviction and full of anxiety for her own future and that of the children. She had reached a pessimistic state of mind, thanks to the misleading Allied reports of the trial to the British press. Of all the reasons conducive to a favorable verdict not one appeared in the newspapers or was mentioned over the radio.

Naturally I had no idea of all this and expressed the greatest confidence without managing to convince her. She probably took my optimism for an illusion, so that, notwithstanding all our joy at seeing each other again, this first time together was not without a painful undercurrent. I saw my wife on other occasions during the following days until visits had to be suspended.

* Initials of the superb organization Committee for American Recovery in Europe.

At last October 1 arrived, the day of my acquittal.

Not until after that day could we embrace each other again for the first time in years.

The verdict *Guilty* or *Not Guilty* was announced in the presence of all the accused. One and all received their sentences with impassive countenance. One might have expected the first *Not Guilty* (my own case) to have released some display of emotion. On the contrary; I myself and all the other prisoners maintained their iron composure.

After the verdict we were escorted to lunch, the three of us who were acquitted — Fritzsche, von Papen and myself — in a separate room.

In the afternoon there followed the announcement of the penalty, when each prisoner was led up individually before the judges. I was not present.

In the meantime the three of us who had been acquitted were taken back to prison and told to present ourselves before a group of journalists. I protested at first against being put on exhibition but could not very well let my companions down.

A great hall was packed with pressmen. American soldiers offered us candies, drinks, cigarettes. The journalists asked a lot of unimportant questions to which we gave equally unimportant answers. The whole thing was a superfluous — and to me very unpleasant — spectacle.

The only remarkable thing about it was the atmosphere of the foreign press which immediately veered in favor of Hans Fritzsche. Interesting to me personally was the way Louis Lochner — whom I had always assumed to be fundamentally well disposed toward me — remained ostentatiously at the back of the crowd and took no notice of me.

All too soon I was to learn what was afoot. Fresh troubles, fresh beastliness awaited me.

Some of the Provincial Ministers then in office publicly voiced their indignation at my Nuremberg acquittal. At their head was Dr. Högner, the Bavarian Social-Democratic Minister who, as witness, attended the execution of those condemned to death.

In the press and on the radio the Bavarian Government announced that it would immediately arrest me as soon as I quitted the Nuremberg jail. I was now to be brought before the German denazification tribunal.

I had informed Colonel Andrus of my intention to go to the British Zone. Although the International Military Tribunal had decided that I was to be released at once, the Colonel demanded that I should first obtain an entry permit for that zone. I was urged to remain voluntarily in prison until I had received this permit. I agreed, since I should have been arrested by Dr. Högner the moment I set foot in Nuremberg. A request for an entry permit addressed to the Commander-in-Chief of the British Zone remained unanswered. In order to safeguard himself Andrus submitted a paper for my signature in which I declared that I remained in prison of my own free will. I signed it.

After three days however I had enough of this intrigue, and demanded my immediate release.

Finally at midnight I was put into a delivery van and driven to the house where my wife was billeted when she stayed in Nuremberg. As I was about to enter, two Bavarian Gestapo men standing at the door announced that I was under arrest and forbade me to leave the house. My liberty had been of short duration — from the American delivery van up to the front door.

About two o'clock in the morning Stahl, the Nuremberg Chief of Police, arrived and intimated that I was to accompany him at once to the nearest police station. There was nothing for me but to obey. There the Chief of Police gave orders that I was to be taken to prison. Now, however, I raised such hell and swore that all those concerned should answer for it that Herr Stahl was compelled to get in touch again with the Americans. One and a half hours later I was taken back to the house where my wife lived, though I remained under surveillance.

Then matters took a new turn. The next morning an official from the Bavarian Ministry told me, in the presence of my lawyer, Dr. Dix, that the Bavarian Government had agreed to allow me complete freedom of movement throughout Germany, on condition that I reported to the police from time to time and notified them of any change of address before undertaking a journey. A minute to this effect was drawn up.

Thanks to this gratifying document I was able the following morning to inform the American Commandant and the Nuremberg Chief of Police that I intended to leave their inhospitable Bavaria and betake myself to my wife's permanent home at Seppensen, stopping en route to pay a short visit to my friend Reusch in Württemberg.

To go through Württemberg was, as it turned out later, a great mistake on my part. The Württembergers, with whom I had nothing whatever to do, proved to be even more uncouth and inconsiderate than the Bavarians. In fact, anyone reading the following pages will have a vivid picture of Germany at the time of *le Roi Soleil* when every petty princeling did what he pleased in his own domain. In my own case Württemberg's petty princeling was one Reinhold Maier, the Prime Minister of the "petty state."

We sent our children and their nurse on ahead and set off in a borrowed car. We arrived at my friend's house and were actually having coffee with him and his daughter when some members of the Stuttgart Police suddenly burst in. Despite all protests, despite the Bavarian *laissez-passer*, they arrested me and that same evening handed me over to the Stuttgart jail to be detained on remand.

Next day too all protests were again unavailing. Notwithstanding the fact that denazification proceedings against me had already been started in Nuremberg and that, from the point of view of the denazification law, there was nothing whatever about me which could apply at Württemberg, I was kept in custody and new proceedings instituted against me. After a lengthy period of preparation these took place at the end of April 1947 and lasted some twenty days. Although my entire life history and my anti-Hitler activities were set forth in detail, this court actually contrived to sentence me, as an "arch-criminal," to eight years in a labor camp.

After sentence had been passed I was transferred to Ludwigsburg Internment Camp. There at least I was no longer in solitary confinement but in the general cells. My appeal led to new proceedings which opened before the Ludwigsburg Court of Appeal in August 1948. On this occasion the judges included an academically trained President and two fully qualified lawyers. The proceedings resulted in my being acquitted. On September 2, 1948, I was at last able to set out on the road to freedom. Another two and a half years had elapsed after my acquittal by an international tribunal before these German simpletons realized that one cannot deliberately tamper with the law. And even after this acquittal I was by no means a really free man; for I was subsequently "confined" for five months by the British Occupying Power, and it was two and a half years before I finally emerged from the jungle of German postwar jurisprudence.

# LX

## FREE ONCE MORE

WHEN I WAS RELEASED from Ludwigsburg Camp on September 2, 1948, I had exactly DM. 2.50 in my pocket. A kindly fellow prisoner had entered my name in the list of workers during the last few days in order to be able to hand me at least a small sum for traveling expenses. My wife and children had been living until now partly on assistance from friends, partly on charity.

I no longer possessed any bank balance or securities of any kind. My various accounts had been carried by the Reichsbank in Berlin, and, as I now learned to my sorrow, the Reichsbank had failed to transfer any photographic copies to a place of safety in the West. My entire fortune was lost: there were no means even of ascertaining what I had once possessed.

My Gühlen property was in Communist hands. Three small dwellings that I owned in West Berlin, each housing a single family, were partly bombed, partly requisitioned at the time the trials began. I was heavily in debt to my lawyers who had defended me at Nuremberg and in Württemberg.

I was so completely destitute that I gladly accepted the offer of a friendly British journalist to take my wife and myself to Seppensen in his car.

Naturally I had to look around at once for some means of earning in order to ensure our livelihood. My wife, in the meantime, had already made contact with the Hamburg publisher Rowohlt, who evinced great interest in the book *Settlement with Hitler* which I had written in the prison camp. Only three days after my arrival at Seppensen he came to see me; we fixed things up and I entrusted the manuscript to him for publication. Although written during the trials and still therefore in strongly defensive vein, the book ran into a quarter of a million copies. The first foundation was laid for the support of my family.

In the meantime the Württemberg order for the delivery of my person had been received in Hanover, where they showed a distinct inclination — contrary to all law and justice — to hand me over again to Herr Reinhold Maier as his special prerogative. Once again it was a policeman who saved me — this time the Chief of Police in Lüneburg. He told the Government of Lower Saxony that he had no legal authority to deprive me of my liberty and pack me off to Württemberg. So the order was ignored.

Then came the news that Württemberg did not recognize my acquittal.

By now I was sick and tired of the whole business and of my own accord asked that I be denazified. I was seventy-one years old; I had a family to support and needed that freedom to pursue my career to which every German is entitled in a federal democratic country.

As a non-denazified person I was debarred from following my profession — in a word I was condemned either to starve or to depend on the charity of my friends.

The British agreed that I should be billeted in Winsen-on-the-Luhe, which was obviously destined to be a permanent "place of confinement" for the Schacht family.

"What did you do with yourself all that time?" a journalist asked me afterwards. "Work?"

"I worked on my denazification case," I said. "And if you have ever done such a thing in your life you will realize that it's not just spare-time activity but a whole-time job!"

Finally the way was clear for a denazification hearing in Lüneburg. On November 9, 1950, I made my final speech before the Lüneburg denazification tribunal. I was finally acquitted by a German jury.

Seven years had elapsed, nearly one tenth of my whole life — during which I had lived under the most varied governments, a prisoner and an outlaw, in my own country.

Even according to German law of pre-Hitler times, my arrest under Hitler was legal and the suspicion of high treason justified. That it could not be proved was another story. But the denazification law had been formulated by the Occupying Powers and foisted upon the rulers appointed by those same Occupying Powers. From a legal viewpoint it was a monster of injustice and political hatred. The names of those ministers functioning in the German provinces, who accepted this law as a German law instead of leaving its administration to the Occupying Powers, will go down to history as an inglorious example of unworthiness.

Now, once again, I would be able to drive a car, follow my profession, go where I pleased, and possess a passport.

During the period of my "confinement" at Winsen-on-the-Luhe, the Hamburg publisher Otto Meissner came to see me and asked if I would not write something for his firm.

"With pleasure," I said, "on condition that you can get hold of a table for me to write at."

Meissner provided me not only with a table but with an entire home.

The firm of Meissner had rented from the Lower-Saxony Ministry of Justice an old building in Bleckede dating from the year 1650 and therefore under state protection as a "building of historic interest." It was an ancient rural castle, complete with moat, and a barn over the stables which Meissner had fitted up as a "residence for authors."

It had sloping walls, and to reach it one had to climb a step-ladder. The windows of the barn were very small, but state "protection" precluded any larger windows being let into the roof and the place was therefore somewhat gloomy by day. Also, the roof leaked in several places. For this reason the police had never requisitioned the building.

But it was homelike and comfortable in spite of the fact that we were living in an "unpermitted" building belonging to our adversaries the Ministry of Justice of Lower Saxony. I fear Meissner must have been the recipient of many an unkind remark concerning his subtenants. If that was so he never gave a sign. He was always the same kind, friendly fellow. For the first time in endless years I had a real study in which I wrote the book entitled in German *Mehr Geld, mehr Kapital, mehr Arbeit*. In Germany it ran into sixteen thousand copies and appeared under the title of *Gold for Europe* in English, French, Italian and Spanish.

Next to my study — where I also slept — we had a living room where my wife slept, and a room for the two children who attended the Bleckede elementary school. Once again we were a real family; I was able to repay some of the debts incurred during past years and could look forward to the future with somewhat greater optimism.

It was in this house at Bleckede too that for the first time I received a deputation from Indonesia led by the Minister for Economic Affairs of this Far Eastern country, who enquired whether I would care to go to Indonesia.

The time was not yet ripe for a trip abroad — we had not really given the matter sufficient consideration. Although I did not intend to work for an indefinite period in another country I was very keen to afford other nations the benefit of my experience. I therefore told the deputation that I was prepared, at the appointed time, to furnish the Indonesian Government with an expert opinion, free of charge, on economic and financial matters if the government would undertake to bear the cost of the journey and hospitality.

Shortly before we left I slipped and broke my arm. Examination disclosed a fracture of the upper arm just below the ball of the joint, as well as damage to the socket. For seven weeks I had to go about with my arm in a splint.

"Now you will have to have massage, radiant heat and hot-air baths," the doctor told me.

I did not have a single massage, radiant heat or hot-air bath, but on the day after my medical discharge my wife and I got into our Volkswagen and drove through Germany to Meran where we spent four restful weeks, and then on to Rome, where also we lingered. Finally we garaged the car in Rome, drove out to the airfield and boarded a K.L.M. plane for Cairo. Egypt was to be our first port of call on our way to the Far East.

# LXI

## OFF TO THE FAR EAST

WITH OUR DEPARTURE by air from Rome I began to pick up my former links with the East. It was exactly twelve years since I last left Europe. A few months prior to the outbreak of World War II I was on board ship bound for British India. What would the East be like today?

We slept the night in the plane. Early next morning the machine glided gently on to the airfield at Cairo. My wife pointed from the window to a group of civilians assembled on the airfield, obviously awaiting the arrival of our K.L.M. aircraft. "Evidently," said my wife, "there's a V.I.P. on board."

As we descended the steps from our plane some Egyptian gentlemen advanced to meet us. One of them came up to us, bowed, and informed us that he was there to welcome us on behalf of the Egyptian Government.

"My government, Dr. Schacht, begs that during your stay in Cairo you will consider yourself the guest of our country. We have ventured to reserve accommodations for you at the Hotel Semiramis. Our Minister for Economic Affairs and our Finance Minister will be delighted to meet you."

I have never looked upon myself as a Very Important Person and did not conceal my astonishment as I accepted this charming invitation. We remained for a week in the Land of the Pharaohs. The military *Putsch* which spelt *Finis* to King Farouk's monarchy had not yet taken place. Farouk at that time was absent on one of his many trips abroad.

After the agonizing years we had spent in Germany these seven days were like a dream out of the Arabian Nights. We were overwhelmed with the most touching hospitality. We were shown all the sights of the city; we went for excursions out into the country under the guidance of first-class experts. I discussed economic questions with members of the Ministries of Economic Affairs and Finance. We made many personal friendships.

We could hardly tear ourselves away from the Tut-ankh-Amen treasures which were displayed in the Museum in masterly and indescribably impressive fashion.

Dr. Sumitro Djodjohadikusumo, the Indonesian Minister, had flown with us from Rome but had immediately continued his journey to Indonesia in order to make ready for our arrival. During the months that followed Dr. Sumitro revealed himself as a supremely cultured, well-informed, active and intelligent statesman. He took charge of us in the most cordial manner throughout our stay in Indonesia and rendered me inestimable service in the preparation of my report on his country's financial and economic situation.

Our visit to Indonesia deserves a separate chapter, so I will describe our homeward journey in advance. We stayed three weeks in India during the return trip. Here I felt I was on more familiar ground and was reminded of many incidents of my prewar travels. It gave me special pleasure to show my wife all the places which had attracted me then: the famous banyan tree in the Botanical Gardens at Calcutta, the Burning Ghats of Benares, the Mogul Forts at Fatehpur Sikri and Delhi, and, not least, the Taj Mahal at Agra. Mr. Birla's hospitality enabled us to fly to Darjeeling at the foot of the Himalayas where, thanks to good weather, we had some marvelous views of Mount Everest and Kanchanjanga and came across temples and people, both already completely Tibetan in type. Darjeeling is the point of entry into India for the Tibetan traders who come here to buy and sell after trekking through the mountains.

From Delhi we flew to the Vale of Kashmir on a visit lasting several days, and enjoyed everything that had enchanted me twelve years previously. We stayed with the Prime Minister, Mr. Abdullah, and with my old friend Mehta who runs a big photographic business in Srinagar. Again and again we were surprised to come across Germans, even in these most distant places.

But ours was not entirely a pleasure trip. From Gulmarg, where we had a wonderful view of Nanga Parbat in all its radiant loveliness, we went back to Delhi where I discussed economic and financial questions with several Ministers. Most memorable was the visit of my wife and myself to Nehru and his charming daughter. Nehru confirmed the impression I had received from others — of a supremely humane, thoroughly wise and enlightened man. Mr. Bajpai, his right-hand in foreign politics, very frankly and clearly explained India's international attitude, which is unwilling to subscribe either to the Western materialistic outlook or to Russian communism.

It gave me deep satisfaction to hear this experienced foreign politician express his views on the need for the reunion of Germany's two sundered halves and at the same time emphasize how great was the Indian nation's faith in the moral qualities of the German people. After the many inflammatory accusations which, by reason of a criminal dictatorship, had in past years been poured out against the German people, this sign of humane understanding of our nation was a real blessing.

I could not forego the opportunity of a pilgrimage to Gandhi's shrine.

Nehru had asked me to arrange some discussions with the members of his Five-Year Plan Committee, of which the draft had just been published. On these occasions I was unable to veil my criticisms behind mere polite speeches. All these Four-Year Plans, Five-Year Plans and suchlike have invariably seemed to me pretty senseless. In this instance also I could not refrain from demonstrating that the vast program which had been envisaged for a period of five years could never be realized during that time. Still less would the means set down on paper suffice to carry it out. It would be necessary to count on double and treble the cost as well as double and treble the amount of time required.

Plans of this sort are above all useful for purposes of internal propaganda. They are intended to arouse hopes, to postpone events, to rely on future prospects for the alleviation of present economic anxieties. But they achieve their purpose in an ever lessening degree. The public will continue to enquire suspiciously how much of these marvelous plans had been carried out. Criticism and dissatisfaction will remain on the alert, ready to seize every opportunity of expression. It seems to me far better to tackle a certain job each year — even if a smaller one — and to see it through so that, when completed, one can point to it as an example of progress and growth.

On the return flight from Calcutta to Rome an incident occurred that might have developed into tragedy. We wanted to go by K.L.M. via Cairo, but all the seats were booked, so we accepted the offer to change over to S.A.S. But in so doing we had not noticed that we should be flying not via Cairo but via Tel-Aviv. We were aware of it only when we landed on Lydda airfield in the early hours of the morning. Officially Israel was still in a state of war with Germany. We were obliged to give up our passports and betake ourselves to the waiting room at the airport. My wife was worried to death and unable to swallow a mouthful. By contrast

I did my utmost to register complete calm. I ate not merely my own breakfast but my wife's also, and endeavored to make my presence as inconspicuous as possible.

When he came to clear away, the Jewish waiter enquired, in purest German: "Were you satisfied, *Herr Präsident?*"

I glanced up and replied in the affirmative. After a minute or two the waiter returned.

"Would you please give me your autograph, *Herr Präsident?*"

Once again he turned up after a couple of minutes and asked for an autograph for his colleague. I thought it was time I said a few kind words.

"Where were you before you came here?"

"In Frankfurt, *Herr Präsident.*"

"Nicer than this, eh?"

"Oh, *Herr Präsident,* if only I could go back!"

We went to the counter where they were just handing out the passports. Thank goodness! the last two were ours. We took them and hastened out to the airfield.

That same afternoon, when the news of our journey became known, Prime Minister Ben Gurion declared in reply to a deputy's reproachful question: "Had I known that Dr. Schacht was at the airfield I should have had him arrested at once."

Invitations subsequently reached me from various governments which resulted in a second visit to Egypt, and then on to Teheran and Syria. In the first half of September 1952, Prime Minister Mossadegh invited me to discuss the Persian situation. My wife went with me, as well as to Cairo and Damascus later on.

I had not been in Persia since 1937, and was amazed at the spectacle presented by the capital with its broad avenues and modern palaces — all of them the work of Reza Shah. The achievements of this ruler have left their permanent mark on the city and on the whole country.

In Mossadegh I met a statesman of highest intelligence, supremely well versed in the practices of diplomacy, and of iron determination. The main topic of our conversation was, of course, the petroleum question. I could not but recognize the moral claim involved, and upheld by Mossadegh, and even now I deeply deplore that Western diplomacy has not understood how — by exercising a certain flexibility — to bring about a solution of the Persian oil problem. Domination of the Persian oil industry by foreign Powers, is something which the Persian people will never again tolerate, no matter what may be Mossadegh's ultimate fate.

There is another point, however, which seemed to me even more important. In the chain of countries surrounding the Communist Russian center and stretching from Japan to Lisbon, Persia occupies a key position which may prove a blessing or a curse according to the political turn of events. Neglect of this viewpoint will not be compensated for by any conventional maxim or economic sacrifice which, in the event of an agreement, would not be very great in any case.

Besides these discussions I renewed my old links with the Milli-Bank and came away with increased faith in the future of this Near Eastern economic territory.

I had met the Shah in 1937, as an eighteen-year-old youth in his father's house. I now paid a visit to him, as well as to his wife, who is distinguished for her beauty and charm. I had the opportunity also of a talk with his younger brother Abdul Reza, who displayed an outstanding knowledge of economic conditions. My wife meanwhile spent a delightful hour with the Queen and her German mother.

My visit to Egypt as guest of the Egyptian Government followed in the second half of September. In the meantime the revolution had taken place. At the head of the government was now General Naguib, one of the finest embodiments of political knowledge and statesmanship in our topsy-turvy world. My wife and I agreed that we had never met any political leader who understood so well how to combine political moderation with the necessary energetic action. In addition, his personal charm and unassuming manner aroused in us a genuine liking for Naguib the man.

While my wife went sightseeing in Cairo I spent many hours with El Amari, the Minister of Finance, and his colleagues in discussing economic and financial matters. In addition I got in touch with private business circles, first and foremost the Chamber of Commerce and — by way of a particularly delightful meeting — the members of a gathering of academicians, all of whom had studied in Germany.

In December 1952 I accepted an invitation of the Syrian Government to visit Damascus. They wanted my professional opinion on the proposed draft bill for the founding of a state central bank, the license for a central bank for Syria and the Lebanon having hitherto been in the hands of a private bank. The government afforded me the opportunity to visit large parts of the country. We flew over Palmyra, those mighty ruins of the Graeco-Arab era, over the Plain of Ghab to Aleppo, and on another occasion to the northeast corner of Syria where the so-called Plain of Jazirah extends beyond the Euphrates. I realized the amazing, undreamed-of possibilities which would result for Syrian agriculture if artificial irrigation were introduced into this part of the country. Here is one of the vast granaries, hitherto unexploited, for the feeding of mankind.

On Christmas Eve 1952 we were at home again in Munich with our children.

# LXII

## UNDER THE GARUDA

THE OLD DUTCH COLONIAL Empire of Insulinde no longer flies the colors of the House of Orange. Everywhere we are greeted by the Garuda, the Indonesian Eagle of Liberty.

Our visit to Indonesia lasted three months during which we grew to love the land and the people. The country is one perpetually lush green garden in which it is difficult to find a single foot of earth without rioting, luxuriant vegetation. In the garden of our hotel, situated in the modern business quarter of the town, the trees were ablaze with red and blue blossoms and from our veranda we could almost grasp the orchids that grew on them.

We had been warned against the tropical climate, but there was hardly an occasion when we found the heat really oppressive. At weekends it took us one and a half hours at most by car to reach Bogor in the mountains where the government maintains a guest house at Tugu, more than two thousand feet up, and where it was often actually cold at night.

Tugu was halfway along the road to Bandoeng and already in a part of the territory where surprise attacks and fights with gangs of bandits were frequent. There was still a great deal of insecurity in the country, though mainly confined to West Java, and the road to Tugu was occasionally patrolled by sentries. But we never encountered any unpleasantness. The rural population was always friendly; kindliness is, in fact, a characteristic of the whole Indonesian people. During our stay we often drove through the countryside in Bali, northern and southern Sumatra, and also in central Java and never met with any mishap. We visited several plantations in northern Sumatra where the owners and managers all told us that they got on very well with the population. True, they had lost some of their land which had been seized by the workers, but on the whole the people were both willing and industrious.

In the towns people are showing a real desire for education. The secondary schools are very well attended. In the larger villages too elementary schools are springing up everywhere and illiteracy will soon have disappeared from Indonesia.

There is a very strong anti-Dutch feeling in Indonesia. Nevertheless not a single Dutch estate has been expropriated. Dutch plantations and Dutch-owned shipping lines still exercise a strong influence, but their importance will gradually diminish. Unfortunately the whole problem of foreigners in Indonesia is affected by this anti-Dutch feeling. In many instances this hostility to foreigners is elevated into a political catchword and many party circles thrive on it.

The Ministry of Finance had allotted me an Indonesian secretary who, in addition to Dutch and English, spoke excellent German. Mrs. Zulia Jahja was a slender, bronze-skinned woman of medium height, with four sons, the eldest of whom was twelve years old. She was the only woman of her generation to attend the secondary school, was highly intelligent, invariably industrious and willing and consistently kind and charming. She had kept her girlish figure and the marvelous colors of the sarongs that she wore were admirably suited to her whole appearance. My wife fell in love at once with these Indonesian materials, and whenever I could spare time from my work we spent long hours in the bazaars in the Old Town. Like every newcomer she allowed herself at first to be fascinated by the colors which, as it seemed to me, were just right for the dark-skinned Indonesians but not for a fair Northern woman. She very soon tired of these color blends and learned to distinguish and appreciate the genuine designs of the different islands and tribes. With Mrs. Jahja's help she learned also how to bargain with the Chinese traders

The government had asked me to prepare a report, not, however, in the sense of a general survey of existing conditions. What they wanted were recommendations and opinions as to the ways and means by which existing difficulties and the country's financial and economic problems in general could be overcome. I prepared this report, which was published by the government in the form of a booklet printed in German and Indonesian and presented to every government official. In it I emphasized very frankly and outspokenly what it was that the country lacked, and put forward several suggestions which, in my opinion, might be useful to so young a state which had still to be molded into shape. Some extracts from my report dealing with the general situation may not be out of place:

The difficulties confronting the young Republic of Indonesia arise from the fact that, through a sudden upheaval, a nation of seventy-five million souls, with the most widely differing languages, customs, ways of life and primitive social conditions, was violently wrested from a superimposed, foreign, but nevertheless smoothly functioning administration, and left to its own devices. Further, these events were influenced by such political catchwords as Democracy, Freedom, Self-government, which, even among the most highly developed and educated nations, have acquired a certain value only when qualified by corresponding limitations, but which can prove positively devastating when voiced by a completely ignorant, illiterate crowd. The highest praise is due to the very small educated native upper class which today bears the political responsibility for this heterogeneous mass of people. This tiny leading class should not consider it derogatory to their colleagues that the latter are inferior to the previous administration in knowledge and experience. It is not their fault that they are able only now to catch up on this knowledge and experience. The responsibility rests, not on the present Indonesian leading circles, but on their former rulers. . .

The fact that their republican liberty is such a young growth makes it easy to understand why the Indonesian nation today is extraordinarily jealous to safeguard its sovereignty. Nevertheless the nation should realize that, in pursuing its upward trend, foreign assistance is entirely compatible with the preservation of its sovereign rights — indeed it is indispensable. This applies first and foremost to the machinery of government . . .

Still less is it possible to dispense with foreign co-operation in economic matters. All undeveloped countries which have adopted European methods and European civilization have followed the same road that Indonesia must now tread, to their highest advantage . . .

Fear of possible misuse of foreign capital to the detriment of Indonesian interests has developed an inferiority complex among the Indonesians which is entirely unjustified. The formal restrictions imposed on the inflow of foreign capital should be done away with at once. It should not be forgotten that, during the colonial period, foreign capital operated under foreign law, whereas now foreign capital is subject to Indonesian jurisdiction. The one obligation attendant upon these changed conditions is that foreign capital shall be dealt with on the same principles as native capital, without any discrimination, as happens in the leading civilized Western States . . .

Without the aid of European capital not a single one of the extra-European countries has been in a position to develop on modern technical lines. Before the First World War — that is, prior to 1914 — the United States of America, which today leads in technical civilization, was a country in which between eight and ten billion gold dollars' worth of foreign capital was invested. In the United States today all former foreign undertakings are in American hands. The Argentine Railways were built from beginning to end with British capital. Today they are in Argentine hands. The industry of Rhineland-Westphalia in my own country, Germany, was started one hundred years ago, mainly with Belgian and British capital. It did not need more than a few decades before the Germans had earned enough to buy back all foreign property. Indonesia can look forward to just such a possibility. That is why she should open her doors wide to admit foreign capital in order that Indonesian production, industry and trade may develop as rapidly as possible on modern technical lines . . .

The standard of living among the Indonesian population is very low. The demand for the most elementary equipment for household, clothing and trade is enormous. It is true that, while the government can help to meet that demand and raise the standard of living, both must really accrue from the labor of the people themselves. From all well-informed reports and observation the fact emerges that the work accomplished by the population today lags considerably behind that achieved during the colonial period. The demand for higher wages on the part of working people, coupled with a decline in output, has resulted in many plantations becoming unprofitable. The population must be made to realize again and again that undertakings which fail to provide a surplus are compelled to close down and to dismiss staffs. Furthermore, the population must realize clearly that there is a fundamental connection between wages and output. Where no surplus is achieved, no surplus can be distributed. The man who produces more must receive a higher remuneration than the man who produces less. Liberty is not synonymous with laziness. Freedom is not given away: it must be earned daily, in war by force of arms, in peace by the work of brain and hand. Whoever desires better housing, clothing and food must work for it. That is God's law. But it is also the essential condition of all economic progress in a country. If prosperous America is to be regarded as a model of democratic freedom we must also regard American working output as a model which has achieved this prosperity and thereby assured her liberty. The East will attain equality of civilization with the West only when it assimilates those Western virtues which have hitherto enabled the West to enjoy its pre-eminent position in the world. For this the requirements are self-discipline, a sense of responsibility, and willingness to work. The Western world is not actuated merely by desire for gain. It has reached its present position by taking interest and pleasure in work and in the output connected with and resulting from that work. It knows that work is linked with a sense of responsibility to the community. The idler receives no "lucky breaks"; the good worker achieves liberty and life, both for himself and for his people . . .

The idea of a welfare state as a kind public benefactor under official leadership is an assumption leading directly to totalitarian communism, but which has nothing whatever in common with the sense of responsibility of the individual. When the first Englishmen emigrated to America they found no ready-made houses and gardens, no roads, streets or water supply, no hospitals or sports grounds. They had to provide all these for themselves. From the wilderness they and their descendants created the most powerful country in the world without any previously established social services, sanitary authorities and suchlike. The state does not exist to make its citizens happy — that is the citizens' own job. The state exists to protect its citizens. Gifts and acts of charity are bad educators: difficulties and hardship are the making of men . . .

It is of course essential to get the present railway system into working order again and increase its volume of traffic as much as possible. Furthermore, traffic policy should not be directed toward the extension of the railway system, but rather to the construction of big main roads for long-distance traffic. Since the unprecedented advance of the automobile, not merely as private transport but especially in the transport of goods, it is safe to say that the railway era is past. The countries now in process of development have this advantage over the old industrial states, that they are able, so to speak, to bypass costly railway construction and concentrate instead on the building of long-distance roads. Road construction and road transport are both cheaper than the railway with its complicated service. Apart from the import of some not-too-expensive machinery, road construction can be carried out with native material and native labor, whereas everything for the railway — from the actual track, and including locomotives and coaches, to the complicated signaling system — has to be imported from abroad against payment of expensive foreign exchange. There is no need for the government to worry about providing vehicles for road traffic. The provision of delivery vans, trucks and omnibuses can safely be left to private enterprise, which will gladly seize such new business opportunities. The construction of new roads is also the ideal basis for new settlements in hitherto unopened-up districts . . .

A young state which is in need of capital for everything is consequently always liable to find itself in the danger zone of inflation, because it has to resort to loans from the central bank. Such a state must, above all, insist on rigid economy in government spending. It may undertake only the most urgent tasks and must put everything aside if the necessary sources of income are not functioning. This necessity for economy is in contrast to the understandable desire of parliamentary representatives to meet the economic wishes of their electors as far as possible — wishes which nearly always involve state expenditure. If, for lack of income, a Finance Minister is debarred from acceding to these requests, the blame will fall primarily on him instead of on the deputies who put forward demands which are financially incapable of fulfilment. A really good Finance Minister is seldom popular. Not until a later epoch will justice be meted out to him. The government should resolve to discuss no items of expenditure in Parliament unless at the same time it can indicate how the cost is to be met. There is so much talk now all over the world of "deficit spending," so much support for this policy of exceeding the Budget in order to tide over economic needs. But every expense not provided for in the Budget will have somehow or other to be met out of cash. Indonesia does not possess a money market where this could be achieved by the issue of short-term treasury bills or similar measure. To have recourse to the central bank threatens the stability of the national currency. In her financial policy, therefore, Indonesia must endeavor in all circumstances to maintain the balance between income and expenditure. A small, well-paid staff of officials is better than an overlarge, badly paid staff. In particular, the remuneration attaching to the highest state appointments should be so calculated that their incumbents know themselves to be unhampered by material anxieties and can devote themselves entirely to their governmental duties. Payment of the remaining staff must also be reckoned in a manner calculated to ensure that they are proof against illicit material transactions. Every official must realize that he has the honor of his country in his keeping . . .

The people of Indonesia are intelligent, obliging, and, like all primitive races, possessed of a strong sense of justice. As a result of the long period of colonial rule they are lacking in self-control. But he who cannot rule himself is in danger of being ruled by others. The people of Indonesia are faced with a vital choice: whether to choose their rulers from among themselves or once again to succumb to foreign influence. There can be no doubt as to the answer. But if they wish to elect their own government they must confer sufficient power on that government to enable it to maintain discipline and insist on obedience to its laws. Democratic Parliaments do not exist for the purpose of discussing every tactical government measure beforehand. They should prescribe a certain standard of conduct and, subject to its limitations, should leave the government free to act. They can criticize serious mistakes and miscalculations afterwards and even remedy them when occasion demands. Mistakes and miscalculations can happen anywhere, but it is only by our mistakes that we learn anything. A government without full authority to act cannot act at all. Parliaments are not rhetorical training grounds, but mandators fully aware of their responsibility. With all the disorder, the insecurity, the insubordination rampant throughout the country, Indonesia needs a government capable of action, with the will, the strength, and the power to punish and eliminate every revolt against public order with the full weight of its authority.

The Indonesian has no desire to be a member of a colonial people. "East is East and West is West, and never the twain shall meet" is repugnant to him. He wants equal rights with other nations without giving up his individual characteristics. He refuses to have a foreign way of life foisted upon him. He appreciates wealth and possessions and Western comfort, but he values also certain things which are not for sale — human dignity, a sense of honor, national consciousness, good breeding, loyalty to God. Only someone who understands this philosophy can be of real help to him. He recognizes and respects the fellowship of the human race as expressed by Goethe:

> *East and West belong to God,*
> *Northward, Southward, all the lands*
> *Rest secure within His hands.*

Personal contact with Ministers and higher officials was always on a very friendly and confidential footing. We were particularly impressed by the *Merdeka* — the official Indonesian State Festival which took place on August 17 in a large field in front of the President's Palace, where stands and benches were arranged in a huge square. Every seat was taken, and a crowd of several thousand stood throughout the proceedings. The highlight of this Festival of Liberty was the hoisting of the flag, which was borne by a little group of gaily uniformed girls. They carried it to the President, who dedicated it, and it was then hoisted at the flagstaff in the center of the square.

In the evening there was a display of Indonesian national dances in the grounds of the President's Palace at which the entire diplomatic corps and all the higher officials were present, as they had been earlier in the day.

It was a real Indonesian party, with dances from the most widely different islands. *Gamelan* bands played. The dancers — men and women — swayed to and fro in the light of torches and candles, their fingers describing mysterious figures in the darkness and their arms writhing like serpents. Every movement, every step had its own esoteric, mystic significance. At intervals demons appeared wearing fierce-looking masks, brandishing swords and endeavoring to overcome the good spirits. The whole was accompanied by the muffled, soft, vibrating, sinuous music of the *gamelans*, the complete antithesis to the hard staccato rhythm of American jazz.

The dancing display was preceded by a review of troops who had prepared a most deeply moving surprise for us. We had come from a Germany which was in a state of chaos; we had lived for seven years as outlaws in a homeland where all tradition appeared to be forcibly destroyed and trodden underfoot. Now, suddenly, in distant Asia, there appeared before our very eyes a military detachment, led by an Indonesian band as precise and assured as only a Prussian military band could have achieved. And the airs they played were the old familiar Prussian military marches. When they started to beat a tattoo, which we had not heard for about fifteen years, flutes, kettledrums, band pieces followed one after the other, just as they did in peacetime in any German garrison parade ground. Amid the breathless silence of the spectators there rang out the mighty hymn, "I Pray unto the Power of Love," ten thousand miles from the country from which that music originally came.

After concluding my report I wanted to complete my impressions by visiting those parts of the country I had not yet seen. We traveled by car and plane to Bali where the beauties of scenery and people still hold the Western world entranced. We flew over the highest volcano in Sumatra, around which our pilot described a full circle because we had a marvelous view, such as he had seen only once before in all his five years' flying on Sumatra. We stopped at Padang and Palembang and walked along the Bukit-Tinggie Canyon and Lake Toba.

Wherever I went I found my observations confirmed. Indonesia is one of the richest countries in the world. With the exception of cotton, for which the climate is too tropical, and wool, for which the sheep cannot find the proper pasture, there is scarcely a raw material which is not present in this island country and only awaits development. What seventy-five million people will make of it only the future will reveal.

Many Western onlookers may be disappointed that the ideals of present-day Western democracy are not over highly esteemed. That applies not only to Indonesia but to almost all Mohammedan countries. Naturally, among all educated and cultured persons, the excesses and crimes of the Hitler regime continue to incur unqualified condemnation. But the social and economic achievements of the early years of the Hitler era have met with a most interested reception on the part of these peoples. Furthermore, they all realize that it is to the Second World War they owe their final deliverance from colonial rule. Obviously therefore the Hitler regime cannot here be regarded as a hundred per cent damned.

It stands to reason that all the peoples of southern Asia have adopted the parliamentary system of government. That, however, does not make them slavish imitators of the West. They fear that over-Westernization might lead to a decrease of their hereditary culture and religious outlook. It is not so much their political interests that differ from those of the West as their anxiety to preserve their own characteristic features in cultural, intellectual and religious matters. Anyone wishing to work alongside these nations must accustom himself not to treat them as downtrodden people, according to the old Anglo-Saxon manner, but must meet them halfway with a feeling that they are entitled to the same rights as other members of the human race.

While we were bathing with our Indonesian friends in the swimming pool at Tugu one of them let fall a remark that I shall not forget: "Three years ago it would have been impossible for white and colored people to have bathed together in this swimming pool."

Truly, we have much to atone for.

# LXIII

## FINALE

Now I AM BACK in Germany once more. On my desk are the proof sheets of these Memoirs. These seventy-six eventful years of my life comprise at the same time seventy-six years of German history. Of much that is noteworthy I have recounted only my own experiences — confused, checkered, contradictory enough in all conscience. My own life, with its ups and downs, has kept pace with the ups and downs of this historic epoch. Unlike so many others I did not seek to escape them. I always felt that my roots were those of my people, my destiny bound up with theirs. The easygoing *Ubi bene ibi patria* was never my line. I have never gone here-there-and-everywhere in pursuit of a life of luxury and pleasure, but have sought to create and promote the comforts of life among my own people.

No matter how deeply I may be rooted in the German people, I have never entertained chauvinistic ideas. Nationalism for me has invariably meant living and working in a manner that others will look up to and imitate. What holds good for the nation holds good also — in my view — for the family. I am convinced that only a family man can fully appreciate his responsibility toward the whole nation. The family is the germ-cell from which nations are born. It is from the family that the civilization and morals of the nation develop.

Twice in my life I have founded a family. Today, my daughter by my first marriage is the mother of four children with her own cares and responsibilities. It is a long time now since we climbed the summit of the Jungfrau together. It is even longer since that unhappy eleventh of November, 1918, when the signing of the Armistice at Compiègne spelled the ruin of Imperial Germany. On that day I wrote in my daughter's birthday book the verse which expresses my fundamental political outlook and which I have used as the motto at the beginning of these Recollections:

*Neither violence nor power of the purse*
*Fashion the universe.*
*Ethical action, spiritual force*
*May reshape the world's course.*

Violence I have always loathed. Money I have striven for only in so far as its possession has left me free to devote my energies to the promotion of the common good. The material wealth I was able to save after the breakdown following the First World War was still sufficient to enable me to enter public service. The total loss of my material possessions after the Second World War compelled me once again to resume my professional career.

My first marriage gave me Jens, my only son, who lost his life on the death-march of prisoners to the East in the last days of the war. He would have carried on my name. *Sans peur et sans reproche*, with his cleverness, his simplicity and his acquired knowledge he was a lad of great promise. He had no enemies — only friends — and knew how to get on with gentle and simple alike. He would have become one of those men whom Germany especially needs today, an economist of distinction. When he launched out for himself I presented him with a translation of a poem by Rudyard Kipling * which embodied my view of life as well as his own. The loss of Jens remains the greatest sorrow of my life.

My greatest happiness I owe to my second wife, whom I married when I was sixty-four years old and who presented me with two daughters, our joy and our hope. During those seven years of outlawry, political persecution and menaces the thought of my wife and children again and again comforted and encouraged me.

During those years of persecution, as indeed during my whole life, I was able to hold my own. If I had a job to do I got down to it, undeterred by favor or jealousy. True, I have made many mistakes; there is much that I have failed to understand; but I have never gone against my convictions or against my conscience.

There are two kinds of people for whom I have no use whatever: those who shirk their duties and those who are always wise after the event. They come under two headings, to which the following verses may apply:

### No. 1

*As a holy terror I'm always seen*
*By the shirker, the lukewarm, the not-so-keen.*

* TRANSLATOR'S NOTE: A masterly translation by Dr. Schacht of Kipling's "If."

*If they could they'd have eaten me whole, although*
*They know*
*They couldn't digest such a tough old bean.*

### No. 2

*Oh, how nice it is to know*
*(When we've played our inning)*
*What we really should have done*
*Right from the beginning.*
*If we would but hearken to*
*This or that adviser,*
*Always — after the event —*
*We'd be much the wiser.*

When confronted with any job, whether or not of my own choosing, I have tackled it without regard to party politics, in which I have never taken any pleasure. Where the welfare of my people was concerned, no party politics could keep me from seeing the job through.

Apart from many minor duties, I have been able on three occasions to take a hand with some success in the molding of economic and social conditions.

The first was when the Communist peril was averted by once again giving the German people a stable currency. This was not achieved by the mere theoretical institution of Rentenmark or Roggenmark. The decision to do so involved a struggle which lasted for months in order to maintain the stability of the Reichsmark, and a credit policy which for years kept the value of the said Reichsmark at the same level.

When at the beginning of the 1930's unemployment figures reached the seven-million limit, the question again was how to cut the ground from under the feet of communism. The introduction of common-sense, if daring, methods of finance enabled us to provide work for all the unemployed in a little under three years without endangering the currency. The country's financial position improved visibly each year.

The third success was the restoration of the balance of trade through the introduction of bilateral and offset agreements with those countries whose economy was complementary to the German; and by abandoning the hitherto prevailing multilateral "most-favored-nation" policy which had operated solely in the interests of those countries enjoying a strong economic position.

On all three occasions I was able to break new ground. I abandoned the central banks' so-called classic discount policy. I embarked on a program of productivity expansion not dependent on savings (that is, on a restriction of capital expenditure) but on the actual creation of new money. I rejected the trading methods which classic British economic theories had bequeathed to us.

These successes, however, were overshadowed by the tragedy of historical events. My monetary policy was undermined by the reckless piling up of debts on the part of the Weimar Government and by the extortionate reparations imposed by our enemies. My plans for creating employment and improving trade were set at naught by Hitler's war mania.

I was still able to do my bit in achieving the cancellation of reparations; but my efforts to prevent the outbreak of war were frustrated. The man under whom I succeeded in eliminating unemployment and adjusting the balance of payments ruined everything later on by his war policy. My critics seized on this as an excuse for stigmatizing my early work under Hitler as a crime. Well, let them! On this question history will pronounce judgment. History will also ask what my critics did to avert the disaster.

My readers may perhaps want to know what I think of Germany's future. I am full of confidence. The whole world is amazed at the way in which, after the cruelest ordeals, the German nation arises swiftly and purposefully from the ruins and proceeds to re-establish order and prosperity.

The reason for this "miracle" is to be found in the German people's love of work, of civilization, of their fellow men, their love of orderly and peaceful development. From this attitude I have again and again derived comfort and hope. The life of an individual is a patchwork, as mine has been. The life of a nation has often been described as eternal. It will be so only when the nation remains true to itself, as I have tried to be throughout my long life.

# INDEX

*

*

# INDEX